D0931115

SPIRITUAL INTIMACY

SPIRITUAL INTIMACY

A STUDY OF COUNSELING IN HASIDISM

Zalman Meshullam Schachter-Shalomi

JASON ARONSON INC.
Northvale, New Jersey
London

Production Editor: *Adelle Krauser*
Editorial Director: *Muriel Jorgensen*

This book was set in 10/12 Goudy Oldstyle
by Alpha Graphics of Pittsfield, New Hampshire.

It was printed and bound by Haddon Craftsmen
of Scranton, Pennsylvania.

Library of Congress Cataloging-in-Publication Data

Schachter-Shalomi, Zalman, 1924–
    Spiritual intimacy : a study of counseling in Hasidism / by Zalman
Meshullam Schachter-Shalomi.
        p. cm.
    Includes bibliographical references and index.
    ISBN 0-87668-772-9
    1. Hasidism.   2. Pastoral counseling (Judaism)   3. Rabbis—
Office.   I. Title.
BM198.S295   1991
296.6'1—dc 20   90-43138

Manufactured in the United States of America. Jason Aronson Inc. offers books and
cassettes. For information and catalog write to Jason Aronson Inc., 230 Livingston Street,
Northvale, New Jersey 07647.

Contents

v

Preface

The mystery of what transpires between two souls in high moments of spiritual intimacy had gotten hold of me before I yet had an inkling of what was involved in such encounters. In 1955, after having trained in hospital chaplaincy with a concentration on psychiatric wards, I first enrolled in Boston University's Graduate School to study for a Master's degree in pastoral psychology. The late Dr. Paul Johnson, a pioneer in the field of pastoral psychology, founder of the Danielsen Center for Pastoral Counseling at Boston University, was gracious in accepting me into his program. I wanted my learning and my experiences—particularly those with the Havurah in Antwerp, Belgium in 1938–1939, with Rabbi Shneur Zalman Schneersohn's Yeshivah in Marseilles, France in 1939–1941, and those at Lubavitch, Brooklyn beginning in 1941—to be connected with my growing awareness of the psychological disciplines. I believed in the mutual enhancement of both on contact with each other. My special mentor was the late Dr. John Copp, a person with rare courage and a warm heart as well as deep spiritual discernment. He encouraged and guided me.

Barukh Hashem, I also had the good fortune to be guided to study with the late Dr. Howard Thurman, dean of the Daniel Marsh Chapel of Boston University, who taught a course in Spiritual Disciplines and Resources. He used experiential labs just as my late *mashpiy'a* Rabbi Israel Jacobson had used farbrengens to give us "hands-on" experiential immediacy to the material we studied. Elsewhere I have described my meeting with Dr. Thurman which was without doubt a momentous yehidut. (For synonyms and a detailed discussion of the yehidut, see Chapter 5.)

After receiving my M.A. I was appointed director of the B'nai B'rith Hillel Foundation and invited to head the Department of Judaic Studies at the University of Manitoba. I accepted these positions with the blessings of the present Lubavitcher Rebbe Shlita, and went to Manitoba. I remained there for nearly twenty years.

At United College, now the University of Winnipeg, I began what is now the Department and Clinic of Pastoral Psychology. As I continued to work and read in the area of pastoral psychology and spiritual direction, Prof. Jakob J. Petuchowski, with whom I shared many a wonderful adventure teaching weekend seminars, kindly encouraged me to enroll in the Doctor of Hebrew Letters program of Hebrew Union College in Cincinnati, Ohio.

Dr. Robert Katz, author of *Empathy: Its Nature and Uses* (1963) and other studies in pastoral psychology, was an exacting and patient dissertation adviser, my *Doktorvater*. This study, my doctoral thesis, was guided, criticized, pruned, and encouraged by him.

This study was first published as a resource for students and others through the Department of Near Eastern and Judaic Studies at the University of Manitoba and later the Department of Religion at Temple University. Entitled *Sparks of Light, Counseling in the Hasidic Tradition* (Shambhala 1983), and co-authored with Dr. Edward Hoffman, it contained many valuable reformulations of the material in my original thesis. And now, eight years later, *Spiritual Intimacy*—based on the complete and original version of the material—contains more of my voice and my personal experience. I am grateful to M. L. Paterson, who in this work served as my friend and editor/typist, and who with an attuned heart and felicitous ear for connotation, helped to hone my words to precision.

To Mr. Arthur Kurzweil of Jason Aronson, Inc., who encouraged me to bring this work to the present publication, and to his helpful staff—especially Goldie Wachsman, who meticulously copy-edited the manuscript and made many helpful suggestions, and Adelle Krauser, the Production Editor—I want to express a warm "May you merit to do more Mitzvot!"

THE DISTANCE TRAVELED

From Hasidism, called ultra-Orthodoxy in the press, to the Reform bastion of Hebrew Union college was quite a stretch. I considered myself at that time to be a loyal Lubavitcher. Indeed, I had first tried to find an aegis other than H.U.C. for doing these studies. Institutions more to the center and right were, oddly enough, not so hospitable to Jewish mysticism as was H.U.C. I was amazed and delighted by the hospitality granted to me by its faculty, as well as the administration and the library staff. Some of the rabbinical students and I spent many a delightful hour in conversation in the "bumming room."

On the occasions when I traveled to Cincinnati I often visited the late Thomas Merton at the nearby Cistercian Monastery at Trappist, Kentucky. These were blessed encounters, generating dialogues that still reverberate within me. Trappist spirituality touched me deeply and I got to know spiritual directors, monks, and nuns in other convents and monasteries. Parts of this work were written in the scriptorium of St. Norbert's Abbey in the vicinity of Winnipeg.

I began to see the chain that reached back to the Sons of the Prophets, the Therapeutae of Philo, the Dead Sea Scrollers, and the Desert Fathers. I realized that these were the ancient sources of the empirical science of soul-guidance, and that the mashpiy'im and Masters of Novices and transpersonal therapists have been greatly inspired by these mentors across the centuries.

THE MEETINGS WITH THE LATE REBBE נשמתו עדן

From my first meeting in the spring of 1941 with the late Lubavitcher Rebbe, Rabbi Joseph Isaac Schneersohn, I felt a connection that defies verbal description. He read my life in sure swift glances, eliciting from me what I needed to see to be able to receive his guidance and blessing. There were many more meetings, each one of them pivotal, opening my life to new insight and rededication. My last yehidut with him was a few months before his passing. Only now, more than forty years later, does the importance of the details of that meeting begin to come into focus. I am reminded of the talmudic adage (*Avodah Zarah* 5b), *La qaim inesh adaatey drabbeyh ad arba'im shnin*, "Forty years may elapse before one truly grasps the intent of his master." At that time, however, a transmission took place that was a seed of empowerment.

When the present rebbe was affirmed I felt a deep loyalty to him. I had met him in Marseilles even before I met his late father-in-law. His total recall in Torah, Halakhah, and Habad, integrated with his studies at the Sorbonne; his spiritual–historic vision and his caring warmth; his burning concern for the continuation and expansion of

Jewish life in the post-Holocaust world—these were all an inspiration and a model for me.

There have been shifts in the conduct of hasidic courts. When Lubavitch first began on Eastern Parkway in Brooklyn there were far fewer students in the yeshivah and fewer hasidim in the neighborhood. There are so many more today that personal contact must be maintained in a different manner, one that is more appropriate to the present conditions. I write mainly from my own experience with the late rebbe in 1941 through 1950 and—to distinguish between life and the higher life—the present rebbe from 1950 through 1962.

I GRADUATE FROM LUBAVITCH

Lubavitch-Habad was for me a good community and a good school, from which I subsequently graduated. I learned basic spirituality and philosophy there. Its literature, which continues to inspire and sustain me, is for me the discloser of many useful reality maps. What I subsequently learned from followers of other paths, both inside and outside of Judaism, made sense to me because of the basic kabbalistic orientation I received at Lubavitch.

Habad served also to reassure me through the upheavals of religious and cosmological reorientation that I, among so many others, was experiencing. The Habad notion of seeing a *seder hishtal'sh'lut*, an evolution of consciousness, in history made it clear that our transition from one cosmology to another was not part of an accidental breakdown but the result of the birth pangs of the new post-Holocaust and thus messianic order. This opened me to dialogue with the ideas of Teilhard de Chardin, Ken Wilber, and Tom Berry. In other places I have written about the current paradigm shift.

Habad, because it stands for vital prayer and meditation, opened me to the immediacy of *davenen*. No longer was prayer something I would only know "about." When I met others who actually prayed, we talked an intimate "shop" regardless of the credos and languages of our differing liturgies. Habad helped me to hold my own in the dialogue of devoutness. And because Habad's scope is cosmic, the widest panoramic vista I could then find in Judaism, it opened a window to "worlds without number." Kabbalah and the Soul, ascending levels of consciousness, after-death states, and reincarnation are all viewed as reality in Habad thought. This has also helped me to make sense of out-of-body and near-death experiences.

Perhaps, rooted in the traditional perspective, Habad fostered too strong a connection to the realities it *de*scribed and *pre*scribed, so that as a result it was inevitable that I transfer my allegiance to the wider, global life. I graduated from exclusive loyalty to the traditional institutions and grew to other dimensions, following both the continued impulse of the seeding I received in Lubavitch and the call that drew me from the larger world-to-come.

At this point I hasten to urge the reader not to assume that the masculine pronouns that predominate in this work are a gender-political statement on my part. I believe that the hasidic establishment would to this day express itself in the language that we now experience as sexist, as it did when I translated the texts and conveyed the world-view expressed in them.

In *The Dream Assembly* (Gateways Press, 1989) I wrote about an imaginary meeting with Rebbe Hannah Rachel, the Maiden of Ludmir, from a position much closer to my own current egalitarian stand. But I did not want to alter the wording in this edition of this material, as it would have both misrepresented the past and been extremely clumsy to read. With this word for an egalitarian position I still stand by the work as it is.

I discovered that psychology too had its own PaRDeS of *Pshat* = behaviorism, *Remez* = psychoanalysis and Gestalt, *Drash* = humanistic and cognitive psychology, and the *Sod* = transpersonal psychology. That which in Habad is functional and empirical–experiential is also the generically spiritual and real. It is therefore gratifying to read how people trained as secular therapists are beginning to open up the spiritual dimension of their interaction with their clients/patients. The field of spiritual direction has in the meantime become prominent, organized and recognized to the point that secular therapists often dare to own the conviction that they do their best work because of their spiritual commitment.

There has also arisen an understanding that if the client cannot enter into the holy–cosmic dimension, she or he may not be able to get well. In the light of our study it is clear that the "Twelve Step" programs work because they are an empirical and powerful process of teshuvah in people's lives. In some circles spiritual intimacy has been the rule and many have experienced it. In Zen it is called *Mondo*, in Hinduism *Darshan*, and in Sufism *Sohbet*. Thus many a person who reads this book will, in their own *Aha*'s, experience *re*-cognitions and *in*-tuitions.

Therefore this work is even more timely now than when it was first written. It is my hope that the therapists who discover the *rebbe* within (it has been said that the therapist is a secular tzaddik) will be stimulated by the rebbes they read about in this and other works and will derive the courage to risk becoming helpers for the soul as well as the mind.

When I first wrote this work there were fewer hasidic texts available in the original and still fewer materials in translation. A current bibliography of Hasidica, and other books relating to the subject, have materials that bear on this study; it is beyond my scope. Thousands of photomechanical reproductions of pre-Holocaust editions are now in circulation, in addition to scholarly reprints of the hasidic classics. A large number of these works and hagiographies are currently available in English.

Whereas I perused all the volumes listed in the bibliography at the end of this work, I found that both Professor Martin Buber's and Rabbi Louis I. Newman's works contained a large number of the stories and sayings quoted. Nevertheless I often felt the need to go back to the originals, and to retranslate or retell what I had heard at farbrengens, since these sources underscored important emphases and nuances. Moreover in my personal witness as an apprenticed hasid-rebbe I have *experienced* the stories as more than mere bibliographical data. I absorbed the stories I heard, reexperiencing them with a fervent heart and an open mind at *farbrengens*. So too with the yehidot I experienced with my late Rebbe—and, to differentiate between Life and life, the present Rebbe, may he live—and other rebbes who allowed me to meet them in sacred space. Living and writing this work was also, to some extent, my own psychoanalysis of *my* place in the rebbe–hasid relationship. The labor and birth of this work was both painful and freeing.

The classical rebbe–hasid encounter took place in an hierarchical environment. Thus, the democratic rhetoric in which most psychological work takes place does not harmonize easily with the hasidic model. Both are in need of reexamination in view of an emerging holistic, organic model that allows for the gradations imposed by the system of hierarchy, as well as for the democratic values of the rebbe–hasid relationship.

In the hasidic setting there was also a basic presupposition: the rebbe is a complete zaddik. Even when he states with humility "Like I am a *beynoni!*" as Rabbi Shneur Zalman said, quoting Rabbah's comment, he witnesses that in actual behavior he and the tzaddik are indistinguishable. The heavy moral expectation does not allow a transfer of the rebbe modality to those of us who would not qualify for the loftier rungs. Does that mean that in a present-day encounter we cannot make any part of the rebbe function that is not part of the hasidic social setting our own? In our experience, a person who serves as rebbe is not *always* in the rebbe mode. As counseling is a function so too is rebbe-ing.

*Perhaps this obtains even in the classical hasidic setting. Once I came to
see the present Lubavitcher Rebbe shlita and was not admitted. A few days later
when I was admitted to see him, he said to me, "The other day when you wanted
to see me, that one whom you came to see was not here. Today he is."*

In the hasidic world-view, the rebbe was seen as a universal, general
oversoul, a *n'shamah k'lalit*, and the hasidim who came to him saw
themselves as particular souls clustering about him. The charismatic of
today is no less a general soul, but, and this is decisive in our context, one
is not a rebbe—rather one *acts*, one functions as a rebbe, is in an interac-
tive and reciprocal process with others and only for the time that one is
rebbe-ing. So in dealing with such a dynamic system and process it is
possible that different persons will each at times be rebbe-ing in a havurah, an affinity group. Thus in the end the ultimate function of rebbe is
one of attunement.

The rebbe is the one who at a given time functions as the attuned
mouthpiece of the group's God-presence. As Rabbi Shneur Zalman in a
tour de force in Chapter 42 of the *Tanya* states: "Each and every soul from
the house of Israel has within her [something] of the category of Moses,
our teacher, peace upon him, a rootedness . . . deriving from the root of
the soul of Moses. . . ."

The one function everyone can learn from a rebbe is that of giving
blessings. In the hasidic interpretation of Genesis 12:3 all the children of
Abraham are heirs to the divine promise: "I shall bless those whom you
will bless." The blessing still flows through those who allow it to flow
through them. The practice of praying for the counselee and of blessing
her or·him is also on the increase.

My blessing for you, the reader, is this: *May you be blessed in all ways
and on all levels. May you experience the awakening within you. May what you
read herein be a blessing for you and for those with whom you will be in contact.
May the great Rebbe, the spirit of guidance, come through us as S/He came
through the rebbes, whose lips, as we quote them, will move along with ours.
Amen.*

Written in Philadelphia, City of Brotherly Love (Luba-vitch means
the same in Russian) on Erev Rosh Hodesh MarHeshvan 5751, when we
read Genesis 9:13: "My rainbow I have set in the clouds. Let it be the sign
of intimacy between Me and Earth"; and when we observe the Yahrtzeits
of Reb Mendl Vizhnitzer and Reb Avraham David of Buczacz.

Chapter 1

The Scope of the Subject and of Our Work

Even the true teacher must remain a seeker until he finds his Self again in order to rediscover the holiness which he has received from his own master's holy spirit. Only then will he truly be able to guide, counsel and speak to the condition of the people coming to him. For it is extremely difficult to counsel and help anyone who is free to choose.

Only by the amazing graces of God which the tzaddik draws down from the upper worlds to this world, and the sincere stirring from below, is it possible to counsel.

In working with people to bring them to themselves, one must work at great depth, a depth scarcely imaginable.

R. Nahman of Bratzlav (Sihot Haran)

OUR TASK

Our task in the present study is to deal with the counsel offered by the rebbe, the hasidic master, to his disciple, the hasid. The rebbe acts as the helper and the hasid as the subject in need of help. While the relational field of rebbe and hasid is larger than that generally occupied by helper and client, both share in the broad field of human interaction.

There are many helping functions in which the rebbe engages; our central concern is that of counseling. In the rebbe's work, there are areas of overlap with other healers or helpers who employ suggestion or who rearrange the subject's environment. However, we are here mainly concerned with the definition that the rebbe and the hasid give to their interaction.

The Yehidut

In Habad[1] language, the interview between rebbe and hasid is called yehidut. The yehidut has several distinct phases. We will deal with the function of each phase contributing to the purposeful structure of the yehidut.

The yehidut is not identical with psychotherapy. If we define psychotherapy as

a psychological treatment, whereby a trained therapist develops a planned relationship with a patient or client with the expressed pur-

3

pose of relieving suffering, it will include therapy carried out by a
variety of individuals with differing background and training.

then this definition does *not* apply to the yehidut. Permitting ourselves to
use this form, however, we would define the yehidut as a spiritual treatment whereby a trained rebbe, who stands in a deliberate contractual
relationship with his hasid, listens to his problems and advises him to
engage in actions which are designed not only to relieve his suffering, but
also to align him with God's will for him.

The yehidut may include blessing, intercession, and the prescribing
of cameos,[2] and may at times involve other hasidim or specially trained
personnel such as *mashpiy'im* (influencers; sing., *mashpiy'a*). It may include referral to other rebbes or helpers. Problems raised in the yehidut
are as varied as life itself. The hasid, by the very act of seeking yehidut,
gives implicit consent to abide by the rebbe's counsel. The rebbe has no
obligation to motivate the hasid to follow his advice—this he takes for
granted. The rebbe's counsel is not subject to appeal or revision. There is
generally a provision for the hasid to reciprocate the rebbe's concern by
taking on some financial obligation toward him.

Of all the psychological helping methods, the yehidut is closest to
pastoral psychology and counseling; yet there are many distinctive features. In the process of this work, we will compare and contrast the
yehidut with pastoral psychology as well as with other kinds of spiritual
direction.

The Rebbe

A rebbe is one who undertakes the task of leading a congregation
that forms around him. He may or may not be a descendant or disciple of
other rebbes. The majority of rebbes, however, were both.

Hasidism

By Hasidism we mean the movement established by Israel Talismacher, the Ba'al Shem Tov[3] (Besht). A hasid is one who has accepted a
hasidic rebbe as his spiritual director and joined, whether by a greater or
lesser affiliation, a hasidic congregation. He is generally known as a ——er
hasid (the missing letters for the rebbe's domicile—the cities of Lubavitch, Satmar, Ger, etc.). The nonaffiliated Jew is also considered a hasid if
he seeks a particular hasidic rebbe's counsel.

SPECIFIC QUESTIONS TO BE EXPLORED

What Is the Relationship that Obtains between the Rebbe and the Hasid?

The rebbe and the hasid in the yehidut stand in a relationship not unlike that of the helper and the client. Each has certain expectations of the relationship, and hopes that they will be met by the other.

What gain does the hasid have in mind as he sets out to travel to his rebbe? How does he know to whom to travel? Who told him about the rebbe? What made the hasid think that the rebbe could help him? Presumably, the hasid does not begin his journey unprepared. What preparations does he make for his yehidut, and what obligations toward the rebbe does he undertake? In entering the rebbe's presence, what rituals does the hasid observe?

How Does One Become a Hasid?

What is the mode of belonging and how does the term *hasid* establish an identity for a person? What is the process by which a person becomes a hasid? What social sanctions does the hasid take upon himself as a result of his hasidic affiliation?

When a hasid arrives at the rebbe's court, how is he received? Who else besides the rebbe does he find there? What hierarchy of persons does he have to relate to?

How Does One Become a Rebbe?

Does being a rebbe demand a special ancestry, and if so, how did the first rebbe of the dynasty *become* a rebbe? How does a rebbe's disciple become a rebbe? What training did the rebbe undergo in order to become one? What are the ceremonials by which a rebbe-to-be assumes his full vocation?

How does the rebbe view himself in his function and person? What kinds of rebbes are there, and what determines a rebbe's choice of role?

What Happens to the Rebbe and the Hasid at the Yehidut?

How does the rebbe receive the hasid? What expectations does he have for the hasid and what goals does he set for him? How does he know how to deal with the hasid's problem—as he sees it and as the hasid sees it? How does he overcome the hasid's inertia? How does he conduct and terminate the interview?

What Are the Rebbe's Resources?

Who are the rebbe's helpers? What settings help the rebbe in his tasks? What rituals and ceremonials act as his resources? What are his theoretical resources? What is his view of humanity, of Jews, of ethics, of authority and responsibility? What are the categories of health and disease he employs? In short, what are the techniques and resources specific to his calling?

Finally, what relevance does this study have for the pastoral counseling work of the contemporary rabbi?

THE NATURE OF THE SOURCES AND THE WAY IN WHICH THEY ARE TREATED

This book is not based on interviews, questionnaires, or other instruments of social research. Though I met with several of the rebbes of our day who are actively engaged in counseling on the level of the yehidut, I did not question them in order to obtain data for this study. These meetings were invaluable in themselves, but for the purposes of this work I relied on anecdotes that came to me by word of mouth or that were found in the literature concerning the counselor (the rebbe) and his client (the hasid). These two basic sources are discussed in the following pages.

Word of Mouth

As mentioned, word of mouth was a primary source of information. In the hasidic setting, several occasions may involve the oral transmission of anecdotes. For example, during the yehidut, the rebbe makes a point with a story as part of the counseling process. At a larger hasidic gathering, such as the farbrengen, the rebbe may do likewise as part of the teaching process, or, if he is not present, one of the hasidim may illustrate a point anecdotally during the group discussion. In a study session, the *mashpiy'a* may relate a story for didactic purposes. Last, in a friendly discourse with a colleague, a hasid might stress a point by means of an anecdote.

Written Sources

The written sources from which we gleaned our information fall into the following categories:

Letters
Books, Recipes, and Anthologies of Recipes
Anecdotes recorded by rebbes and their hasidim
Anthologies

Letters

Even in the time of the Besht, a rebbe might write a letter to a hasid or a hasid might send a plea for help in a letter.[4] A number of these letters are from historically questionable sources. However, for our purposes, it is enough that R. Shalom Dovber of Lubavitch thought them genuine in content.[5] He was actively engaged in hasidic counseling, and as long as he considered them significant to his practice, they are germane for our purposes. A stronger index of their importance is the literature we find in books and recipes.

Books, Recipes, and Anthologies of Recipes

Before a hasidic book was printed, it usually circulated in the form of *quntresim*—short, hand-copied essays. A rebbe's Torah thoughts were written down by a disciple and sometimes corrected by the rebbe. Or, the rebbe himself might make notes for his public discourses and later write a detailed essay based on the discourse. The rebbe consented to printing only when it was found that in the process of repeated copying, the sense of the message was at times grossly distorted.

Most books followed the older model of the kabbalists who preceded them (Riccanati, Al-Sheikh, Qaro, and many others), in which material was organized in what seemed to them to be the natural order, that is, the weekly lectionary. Hasidic discourses were given orally in the same manner: the opening sentence of a rebbe's discourse was generally taken from the current lectionary. As R. Shneur Zalman of Liadi told his hasidim: "One ought to live with the times, the weekly portion."[6] The title of the book was generally patterned after an earlier custom: an allusion to the author's name was in some way contained in the title. *Toldot Ya'aqov Yosef* contained R. Jacob Joseph of Polnoye's name in unmistakable clarity. At times the name was suggested in an acrostic or in a numerological device: Menahem Mendl is the numerical equivalent of *Tzemah Tzedeq* (R. Mendl of Lubavitch) or *Tzemah Tzadiq* (R. Mendel of Vishnitz). At times, when a rebbe had earned a particular epithet, he gave this as the name of his book. If the book was published posthumously, his hasidim attached this epithet to it (*Ohev Yisrael* of the Apter Rav and *Buzina d'N'hora* of R. Barukh of Mezhibuzh).

The content and structure of these books are basically homiletic. Substantively, they deal with the rebbe's insight into the structure of the Bible verses, expanding their meaning to cosmic proportions. In his discourse, the rebbe shows that the text can serve the isegetic meaning, or inner reading, he gives it. The process discussed by Jakob Petuchowski as "The Bible of the Synagogue" continued in hasidic literature.

Without recourse to the homiletical works of rebbes, our understanding would be distorted. Rebbes delivered the hasidic equivalent of sermons and lessons to their hasidim. To read the *Shivhey HaBesht* without checking it against the *Toldot* is to misunderstand the Besht. The rebbe's conceptual framework and associative method were imparted to hasidim on many teaching occasions. Some of these were formal—"The rebbe says Torah"; some were informal—*sihot* or *shmussen* (conversations).

It is not easy to discover the true substance of these spiritual gems. Rebbes did not write in the Sephardi style. Unlike Maimonides, who stated his premises before he began his work, the Ashkenazi style began homiletically. With the exception of the *Tanya* (and even there the style, which begins with a homiletical problem, is preserved), most other hasidic works were published as *d'rushim* (sermons, sing., *d'rush*) and organized around the Torah lectionary.

Often a paragraph will begin with, "And the counsel for this condition is . . ." Hasidic literature prescribes etzot (counsels; sing., etzah) and it is here that we find much relevant material for our study. Not only are complete books written in this manner but hasidic anthologizers also gleaned their counsels out of such books. Thus we find compendia like the *Liqutey Etzot* of R. Nahman of Bratzlav and the *Tzava'at Harivash*. Smaller selections that did not even complete a pamphlet were called *zettlakh*, and here we have a number of prescriptions such as R. Elimelekh's *Zettel Qatan*.

The earliest text of hasidic material, *Toldot Ya'aqov Yosef*, was published in 1780. The first book of recipes was the *Tzava'at Harivash*. It was soon popular. In it we have the constellation of virtues that Samuel Dresner celebrated under the title *Prayer, Humility, and Compassion*. Psychologically, these three deal with the hasid's relationship with God—prayer; his relationship with himself—humility; and his relationship with others—compassion. The *Tanya* of R. Shneur Zalman of Liadi was another work of this genre. R. Elimelekh of Lizhensk wrote his *Zettel Qatan* and *Hanhagat Adam* as such recipes. We will deal with a number of these recipes and show their psychological method. They are important because, as R. Shneur Zalman in his Foreword to the *Tanya* says:

> All of these are answers to many questions which the faithful in our country have constantly asked, *seeking advice*, each according to his station so as to receive moral guidance in the service of God.

Anecdotes Recorded by Rebbes and Their Hasidim

The yehidut, the farbrengen, and the table talks were occasions in which hasidim were treated to *ma'asiyot* (stories, sing. *ma'aseh*) told by rebbes. Heschel defined the ma'aseh as "a story in which the soul surprises the mind." Its purpose is to celebrate the rebbe's wisdom and sanctity and to prepare the hasid to emulate them in his life. The rebbe would often tell a ma'aseh in order to highlight a point made earlier in his discourse. He would also use a ma'aseh as an effective way of introducing a new point.

Ma'asiyot were recorded by hasidim or even by rebbes themselves. In the Habad dynasty it was the custom of each master-to-be to record such ma'asiyot as part of his training. Often these anecdotes dealt with questions asked at the yehidut and with the answers received. No one can become a master unless he first serves as an apprentice. Thus, each one of the rebbes brings the hasid's point of view with him to his vocation. The *Shivhey HaBesht* was the first volume in which hasidim recorded ma'asiyot. The purpose of this literature is avowedly hagiographic; yet there is also the wish to edify the reader with

> stories that are penetrated with Hasidut, filled with *moral instruction* and the fear of God, good manners and *ways in the service* of His Blessed Name. They give fervor to the heart of the reader to strengthen himself in His blessed service and to achieve through them faith in God and *faith in the tzaddikim.*[7]

In these stories we observe the hasid in the act of retelling how he was helped by the rebbe. They tell us what brought a hasid to the rebbe and what his expectations were.

Anthologies

Were it not for anthologies, we might often be required to search endlessly for a passage. In anthologies various topics were arranged in thematic order and printed in small pocket format. These anthologies are popular among hasidim and have been part and parcel of hasidic literature since its inception. The earliest such work was the *Keter Shem Tov*, containing teachings of the Besht culled from other texts, particularly the *Toldot Ya'aqov Yosef*. The *Keter* was edited by Aaron Hakohen of Aptov. R. Nahman of Bratzlav, recognizing the need for his counsel to be available in anthologized form, asked his disciple, R. Nathan, to organize these into a manual. R. Nathan did so and the *Liqutey Etzot* was published during R. Nahman's lifetime. For our purposes, we have utilized the edition published in Jerusalem in 5716 (1950). Anthologizing the discourses of the present Lubavitcher Rebbe, Zeirey Agudat Habad published the *Liqutey Sihot* of R. Menahem Mendl Schneerson II of Lubavitch in Brooklyn in 5722 (1962). In English, Newman and Spitz issued the *Hasidic Anthology* in 1962.

Method of Dealing with Source Material

If our field were literary criticism, we would be under an obligation to trace the earliest source of a story. But since we wish only to show the rebbe–hasid relationship in operation, such research is not called for here. Moreover, each story can be used by the rebbe in different ways, depending on the application.[8]

We shall follow this same pattern. In translating and paraphrasing, I take responsibility for having translated the material into an idiom that is more consonant with our use. Anyone who reads Habad literature will find that Habad masters translate the most abstruse speculations of the Kabbalah into their own psychological terms. Rashbatz, one of the great *mashpiy'im* of Habad, the mentor of the late R. Joseph Isaac of Lubavitch, made this an explicit principle.

AN OVERVIEW OF THE HISTORY OF HELPING

Although the yehidut at times parallels psychotherapy, we could not arrive at a real understanding of it if we did not recognize its distinctiveness. On the other hand, it is necessary to briefly consider other helping systems so that we do not view the yehidut as an isolated, unrelated phenomenon.

On the applied and practical level, we are concerned with transferring some of the hasidic methods to the modern rabbi's study, where he counsels his client; to that end we will offer a few working hypotheses to be verified, we hope, in subsequent work by rabbinic–pastoral counselors. Even here we must sound a note of caution. The present situation in the Jewish world has radically shifted from the hasidic universe of discourse. The contemporary rabbi and client do not hold to the same suppositions as rebbe and hasid. On the other hand, neither do they hold to the same suppositions as do secular counselors. Rabbi and client have a commitment based on revelation, covenant, and God's concern with human actions and salvation.

The modern counselor is not the first one who, in a professional role, has answered the call, "Help me." As a father helps his child, so the head of the clan expected to be asked for help and responded either directly or by sending help. Since, for greater efficiency, labor had to be divided, specially gifted persons became the official helpers. The medicine man became the tribal helper and, because life had not yet become fragmented, he was asked to assist in almost all areas of life.

A History of Counseling in Judaism

Among Jews, the *kohen* or priest was the general helper. He helped the sinner in bringing his offering. He taught him the Law.[9] He diagnosed his disease[10] and healed him. In cases where the course of action was unclear, the priest advised.[11] While the prophet did not like to see the priest coerce God with ritual magic to comply with his wishes, the people still looked to the priest to influence heaven to grant their wishes. The priest had to help his flock make various transitions in life. He was the hierophant in charge of the "rites of passage." His counsel was concerned mainly with offering sympathetic, magical, agentic[12] means.

After the Babylonian exile, the elder, often a nonpriest, was both legislator and counselor. There is an inherent relation between the two functions. Laws are usually first promulgated as good advice.[13] Only later, when sanctions are needed to make the unwilling follow that advice, is counsel turned into law. The very word *Torah* underscores the function of directing the other and then making him aim and "cast out" (from the root *y.r.h.*) in this direction.

In Tannaitic times, the master was more than the teacher of the Law. Often he was seen as a supernatural mediator. From the scriptural Elijah and the talmudic Hony Hame'agel (Onias) on, a chain of precursors of the hasidic rebbe appeared who "implored mercy and he was healed."[14] One who studied the Torah for its own sake was granted the gifts of the spirit: of such a man it is said that "one can benefit from his counsel and be helped by him."[15] This role made the Torah student into a holy man. "The secrets of the Torah are made known to him."[16] Elijah would consort with him. He was the Jew par excellence, yet he was an accessible model.

If Rabbi Akiva, as an archetypal model, entered the Pardes (PaR-DiSe) and "left it in peace,"[17] he was also the one who, as an accessible model, pioneered in the field of late vocations to Torah. Rabbi Shim'on Bar Yohai, after having spent the additional year in the cave that made him a yea-sayer to life, became the paradigm for medieval kabbalists. Not only did he know where to go in the ascent to heaven, he also possessed the great redemptive capacity to atone for the sins of others.[18]

The great tzaddik (in medieval usage he was called hasid, a term denoting a generosity to God and humanity, exceeding that of the just man) operated on two levels. Rabbi Judah the Pious of Ratisbon was not only a popular model and helper to the simple Jew, but was also a master of disciples and revealer of arcana.

The great writer of responsa was more often the advisor to colleagues than a popular counselor. And since finding an answer also entailed influencing the heavenly spheres, the counselor who was rooted in secret lore was more popular. Reports of his marvels brought many people to him.

The charismatic saint was also a model to those who admired him and wished to follow in his footsteps. The higher the level of the student, the more penetrating his questions became. Whether he sought instruction in the "act of creation" or in the art of "ascent to heaven," he could not seek such instruction in books. It was forbidden to commit the sacred lore to writing. The postulant had to learn such things b'yahid,[19] by being alone with his master. This is perhaps one of the reasons why the hasidic interview with the rebbe is called a yehidut. Much counseling took place in the yehidut in a one-to-one relationship between the master and the disciple. The esoteric does not suffer the public eye and ear.

Non-Jewish Counseling

Yehidut was not unique to Judaism. The Catholic priest too listened to the confession of his penitent and counseled him on how to avoid occasions of sin. As moral theology became more sophisticated, the priest was charged with helping his penitent to gain insight into the causes of his sin. In modern times, Catholic writers of manuals of moral theology accept either one or another system of psychology, basing their method on the theories of Freud, Adler, Jung or others. At the same time, they integrate these insights with those of their great spiritual directors. Some Protestant writers have done the same. Others evolved systems of pastoral psychology based on their reading of the Gospels, modern psychology, and their own personal experience. Their personalist philosophy, Christian concern, and understanding of psychology made them review and study verbatim reports of counseling sessions in order to learn more about reflecting feeling with the patient and moving with him out of the problem. The interview of the pastoral counselor with his client is now an important and powerful adjunct to the church.[20]

Islam, Judaism's other spiritual child, had its own spiritual directors, and in India the rishis (seers) taught disciples in a similar manner. India has long held first place in spiritual direction and has exerted a considerable influence upon the Western world. In China and Japan, the master teaches his disciple at the mondo (yehidut). Thus, in all of the major religions we find a situation comparable to that of the yehidut, in which the master counsels and instructs the disciple.

Analysis

The helper is a qualified individual upon whom a projection of great value rests. He is either a paragon of religious virtue—a tzaddik, an illuminated one—or the bearer of an advanced degree in the helping profession. No matter how nondirective his approach, the fact that so great a person sees fit to accept the one in need and is not frightened by a client's lack of adjustment to the proper norms of behavior is of redemptive significance. In this relationship, it is implicit that the one in need can be helped and that the helper can assist him. Even in the most hierarchical systems, there is a temporary suspension of the distance between the helper's rank and that of his client. (The distance may have to be resumed after the interview.) Yet this distance is not altogether suspended: the "rigor" of the helper's position is turned into a "grace" with redeeming power.[21]

The differences between the approaches of various helpers can be plotted on many continua. One such continuum is defined by the poles, directive–nondirective: this one deals with method. Another is defined by the poles, adjustment to this-worldly–other-worldly norms. The salvational goal may be one of freer function or freer feeling, or greater insight into cosmic purposes or of adherence to divine laws. Or, it may be interpersonal, concerned with freer interaction with persons and the environment. Behind each method there are different assumptions as to the nature of reality and humanity, the purpose of life, and the good society.[22]

All these approaches are based on ad hoc relationships dedicated to the solution of the client's problems. Presumably, the result of this relationship will be more than the mere relief of symptoms. The client will have found an identity for himself. He will be under fewer illusions as to his expectations from the cosmos and from other persons. He will be able to see through more situations than before, arrive at action-directed conclusions, and act in a deliberate and firm manner. When this has happened, the client will be free to terminate the relationship, having completed the purpose for which the relationship was originally established. The client has now incorporated the insights that he gained by relating to the helper. Where the helper has organized a group dedicated to a common life, the completion of the postulancy and the novitiate usually entitles the client to become a more advanced member of the order.

To remove the client from a harmful environment is relatively simple. To change him enough so that he will be psychologically free is the more difficult task:

> To take Israel out of Egypt took only a short time. To take Egypt out
> of Israel took forty years. Many a time did Israel want to find a new
> head and return to Egypt.[23]

All helpers experience this crisis in their relationship with their clients.

Counseling and psychotherapy are dedicated to the task of liberating the client from his "Egypt." After the preliminary work of opening the client to insight and the working-through have been achieved in a dyad, group sessions are often a fruitful avenue for further growth. This externalizes and extends the healing process instead of limiting it to counselor and client in the privacy of the consultation room. Yet the privacy between client and helper, their interaction and the insight generated, are the typical forms of counseling and psychotherapy. In counseling, patients learn what they should want to do in order to solve their problem. In psychotherapy, they learn to remove the blocks that keep them from implementing the solution. Any process takes time, and the time it takes for the working out of the solution sought by the client is dependent upon the motivation of both helper and client, their openness to the process, and their sensitivity and insight.

Ours is not the first work dealing with an aspect of Jewish pastoral psychology. Abraham Franzblau, Robert Katz, Joshua Liebman, and Yeshaia Schnitzer, to name a few, have all made contributions to the field.

Chapter 2

The Hasidic Setting: Sociological, Historical, and Ideological

---

   . . . *Within a geographically small area and also within a surprisingly short period, the ghetto gave birth to a whole galaxy of saint-mystics, each of them a startling individuality. The incredible intensity of creative religious feeling, which manifested itself in Hasidism between 1750 and 1800, produced a wealth of truly original religious types which, as far as one can judge, surpassed even the harvest of the classical period of Safed.*

        Gershom Scholem (from S. H. Dresner's *The Zaddik*)

In order to understand the life cycle of the hasid and the various stages at which he seeks the rebbe's counsel, we must first examine the conceptual framework that underlies Hasidism, providing the social, historical, and ideological determinants of the rebbe–hasid relationship. The rebbe's role as counselor and his ability to discern his own and his hasid's life tasks are intrinsically related to these determinants.

JEWS IN FEUDAL VILLAGES

History[1] provides us with an understanding of the background in which Hasidism shaped its teachings.

Geographical Location

Geographically, Hasidism flourished in Eastern Europe. At the time of its greatest expansion (circa 1850), Hasidism was active east of Silesia, in western and eastern Galicia, Hungary, Czechoslovakia, Rumania, Poland, White Russia and the Ukraine. It already had some outposts in Vienna, Berlin, and St. Petersburg. Although the Holy Land had hasidic settlements from the time of R. Gershon Kittover, the Besht's brother-in-law, Eastern Europe was the true center of Hasidism.

Village Life: Social and Economic Conditions

After the Chmelnitzkian massacres in 1648 and the Sabbatian debacle in 1666, Jewish hope lay dashed on the rocks of despair. The reconstruction of life demanded that Jews settle in villages owned by the feudal gentry. The local peasants were treated as serfs, and although the Jews had some privileges, these were all too soon revoked when a Jew did not manage to pay his rent to the *poritz*[2] (the name the Jews gave to the non-Jewish lord of the manor, the "country squire"). Many hasidic stories hinge on the problems the Jewish lessee experienced in his efforts to pay the squire on time, and the consequences of nonpayment.

Yet village life had its own good side. There was a great deal of stability in the fact that several generations lived in one house. Values were transmitted in a transpersonal manner. It is important to point out that this is not so today. Parents are often rejected by their adolescent children; and since, with the new social mobility, grandparents seldom reside under the same roof as their children and grandchildren, their values are often rejected along with them. In the past this was not the case. Grandchildren accepted the values of their grandparents, who were generally well-accessible models. This factor managed to delay the influence of the Enlightenment on the Eastern European Jew.

Another element that contributed to holding back the Enlightenment was the Jew's lack of respect for the dominant culture surrounding him. Government officials affected a different language from the local dialect. There was little to entice the Jew to integrate with the non-Jew. Jewish family life served as a model for the Gentiles, not vice-versa. Unlike their neighbors, Jews were generally able to read and write. In this setting, it was more natural for Hasidism to regenerate Judaism from within than for any other force to do so from without.

Still another reason for the retardation of the Enlightenment was the fact that Torah learning had created its own aristocracy and class system. The *parnas* (alderman) and the *gevir* (wealthy man) were secular leaders of the shtetl by virtue of their affluence. The wealthy aristocracy strove to marry into the Torah elite. This brought about a blending of the two; yet it also widened the gulf between the learned rich and the untutored masses of the poor.

These social conditions had their economic counterpart. The average Jew lacked the basic capital for the accumulation of wealth. The circulation of money was extremely slow. Most people had to make their living from petty trade. Few were craftsmen, and almost none were farmers. As Jews could not reside wherever they wanted, they often missed out on the most lucrative earning opportunities.

Government officials were hated. A good official was "one who could be bought." "He is a good one; he takes," was the attitude. When the Czar began to forcibly induct Jews into the Imperial Army without giving them any opportunity to rise in the ranks, their weakened patriotism was further attenuated. When children were abducted from their parents in order to swell the ranks of Nikolai's armies, the hostility to *fonya ganev* (so Jews referred to the czarist regime) was reinforced.

Poverty became a chronic condition. Jews could not escape the fact that they were in exile. Some great souls, remembering the martyrdom of the holy kabbalist, R. Shimshon of Ostropol (d. 1648) and others like him, took to roaming the countryside incognito in order to gain more merit for the redemption of Israel and raise the morale of the masses. Others traveled as itinerant preachers, forecasting doom in order to move people to penance. The Besht lived and traveled with the first group of secret saints—*nistarim*—and often engaged in verbal battles with the spreaders of gloom.

> Never before in Jewish history was the sense of the power of evil so haunting and keen as in the seventeenth and eighteenth centuries in Eastern Europe. As a consequence of that consciousness and strongly convinced of man's ultimate superiority to the power of evil, the Jews mobilized their might, attempting to subdue the foe within the heart, the appeal of brute matter. They fasted every Monday and Thursday and underwent fierce mortifications to purify themselves. The evil urge, they believed, pursues every man, ready to make him stumble at any false step. This state of mind led both to rapture and to sadness: the Jews felt the infinite beauty of heaven, the holy mysteries of piety, and also the danger and gloom of this world. Man is so unworthy and disgraceful and the heavens are so lofty and remote—what must man do in order not to fall into the Nethermost Pit?
>
> . . . Then came Rabbi Israel Ba'al Shem, in the eighteenth century, and brought heaven down to earth.[3]

The New Hope of Hasidism

The Jewish masses, being neither wealthy nor learned, had few hopes to sustain them. Even the spiritual haven offered no refuge, and wild demons barred the way. Hasidism offered new hope, a new social integration—and, as it lowered social barriers, it created a new popular elite. Spirituality became again loving and benign.

With the new hope of Hasidism, the masses, now more ready to seek to improve their lot, were moved to consult their leaders for assistance and counsel. Heretofore, the institution of yehidut, in which a man learned in Torah concerns himself with the problems and life tasks of the unlettered person, would have been unthinkable. Yet rebbes allowed their social inferiors to consult them even on such mundane matters as business and health. The rebbe's hope was that, by counseling the hasid even in these matters, he could also help him to rise on the scale of Torah and observance.

The increasing influence of Hasidism did not go unchallenged by the opposition, which was dedicated to maintaining the status quo. Ugly suspicions of heresy were raised; but in the end, Hasidism was accepted as a parallel option to Rabbinism in normative Judaism.

> When Israel had fainted as a result of its exhaustion, God, in His mercy, took some of the radiance of the Messiah and gave it to Israel that it might revive. This was the Ba'al Shem Tov.[4]

Transition

By the close of the First World War, Hasidism had established its majority power; but this brought other problems in its train. Very few rebbes remained in the shtetl; the majority of rebbes operated out of larger urban centers. The city created new problems for hasidim and the rebbes tried to deal with them. Notable in this connection is the work of R. Arele Roth of Bergsas and R. Kalonymus Kalmish of Piasetzno.[5] Both opposed the habitual conformity of their hasidim to the dictates of a sensate majority culture. To some extent, the Piasetzner even began to grapple with the crisis of identity faced by young adults.[6] He not only dealt with issues related to the struggles of life in the ghetto of Warsaw, but also tried to make some theological and psychological sense of the terror of Nazi-oppressed existence during the Holocaust, in which he and his family and followers eventually perished. Lubavitch and Satmar had to overcome the trauma of resettlement in America, and Belz the problems of resettlement in Israel.

Hasidism's Psychological Milieu

It remains for us at this time to describe the type of psychological milieu to which Hasidism addressed itself. We must approach our task from a dynamic point of view. Only then can we see the shifting panorama in which the remedy to one pathological condition created the next.

The Jewish Personality Prior to the Besht

Political conditions created their own psychological atmosphere. A morose world faced the Jew after the Chmelnitzky massacres. Evil was the governing principle of the world, and the psychic atmosphere was thick with demonic invaders. The Jew was subject either to deep depression or to explosions of wild excess. The magical hope in the antinomian principles enunciated by the Sabbatians, which would, in one mighty heave, combine the polarities of good and evil, was disappointed. The Jew had no recourse but to repress spontaneity in himself. A compulsive–obsessive observance characterized the Eastern European Jew. Salvation was to be sought in ever more detailed prescriptions of acts to be engaged in or avoided.

A safe outlet was found in the most refined modes of pilpulistic cerebration. Nonscholars could seldom engage in such conceptual luxuries. The social structure was kept tight. Decision-making was left to aldermen and rabbis. Thus, the layman could avoid the responsibility of choosing and making the wrong choices. The tight hierarchical structure gave the *am ha'aretz*, the ignoramus, a moral holiday.

The effectiveness of repressive measures could not be maintained indefinitely. In the dissociation from responsibility, hysterical modes of psychopathology became a favorite malaise of those who could no longer stand the stress of repression. The dybbuk had to take responsibility, not the person.

One of the reasons this psychic atmosphere did not produce more dementia was the fact that in the shtetl culture, familial loyalty—*getreishaft*—was great. One could rely on family for basic support—for food and shelter as well as advocacy in conflict. Oral satisfactions were a basic means for the reduction of anxiety. The child who ate a spoonful for Daddy and one for Mommy was less apt to become a schizophrenic. The structure of the family was warm. Even hostilities were warm. The Industrial Revolution had not yet desolated the little shtetl.

The shtetl did not cause as much alienation as did urban anonymity. Identity in the shtetl was sharply defined. Each person had nicknames of various sorts. Some of these were terms of honor, others of disapproval. Isaac Bashevis Singer, in the opening of his famous *Gimpel the Fool*, captures the significance of the nickname and of the identity it creates. Gimpel says:

> I am Gimpel the fool. I don't think myself a fool. On the contrary.
> But that's what folks call me. They gave me the name while I was still
> in school. I had seven names in all: imbecile, donkey, flax-head, dope,
> glump, ninny, and fool. The last name stuck.[7]

Shunning and excommunication were the most effective social sanctions. A personality that could not slip into catatonia or psychopathic behavior had to conform sooner or later. There were few models of schizoid or lawless behavior, and those few that existed were empty of romantic, Promethean connotations. Thus, the psychopathological catalogue was limited to hysteria–possession syndromes for those who did not conform. The popular solution for dealing with the self tended to follow a compulsive-oppressive pattern.

The Psychopathology of Hasidism

Despite all the asceticism of Kabbalah, the hasidic rebbe and his followers accepted body libido, joy, and spontaneity. Instead of turning these potent energies against themselves and despising the body, both rebbe and hasid accepted them, transmuted them, and found action outlets for sublimated libido in song, dance, and fellowship. The hasid no longer saw joy as bringing with it loss of control over his bodily drives. Instead, he feared the constricting and depleting effects of ascetic practices, for "A small damage to the body causes a large damage to the soul."[8] The Joy of the Sabbath came into its own. Religion that had been pressed into the service of repression was now pressed into the service of life. Sadness, though not deemed a sin, was considered to inflict greater damage than any ordinary sin. Joy, on the other hand, was not a mitzvah, but it could bring man to a state that no mitzvah could.[9]

There was less threat from within the self, and even the landscape that had before produced in the frightened psyche a host of pursuing demons became friendly. Projections of unconscious shadow became more benign. Primary processes such as eating and drinking were made more accessible through ritual. This also meant that everyone—not only those who were trained to play the cerebral pilpulistic games—could take part in some form of enjoyable life play. Even the simple Jew now had emotive and ritual means to enhance his enjoyment of life. The arena of action moved away from the control of the forebrain, and the limbic system could do its share in the process of "regression."

There were some dangers inherent in this new behavioral syndrome. The person who in the past was overcontrolled was now capable of reaching high levels previously inaccessible to him. But along with peaks, deep depressions were also chanced. R. Levi Yitzhaq of Berditchev, the great ecstatic, experienced a period of such depression.

> For a period of two years he had lost all his [spiritually attained high] rungs and said his prayers from a small siddur. He was out of his

normal[ly higher] mind. Only later on did he regain his former rungs
of joyous light.[10]

Hasidic masters had to prescribe against the new manic–depressive syndrome. R. Nahman of Bratzlav conducted a vigorous campaign against
despair—*yi'ush*. All the material on despair was gathered by his disciples
into a booklet, the *Meshivat Nefesh*. Because despair appeared at times as
apathy, R. Shneur Zalman of Liadi had to deal with *accedia—timtum
hamo'ah vehalev*—the dulling of the brain and heart.[11] He counseled that
psychological mortification be utilized. This would at first aggravate the
condition, rendering it acute, and in its crisis would break the hold of
accedia. Then the hasid could once more practice joyous meditation with
new delight.

As each condition was cured, new diseases arose, often brought on
by the cure itself.

Tzaddik and Hasid

As early as R. Shlomoh of Karlin, the tzaddik, who could generally
manage his spiritual economy better than the simple hasid, took it upon
himself to act and to lift his hasidim with him. The hasid was counseled to
abstain from doing the great work himself.[12] This attitude gave rise to
Tzaddikism.

Tzaddikism operated on the belief that "The tzaddik by his faith
shall invigorate [the follower]."[13] In Tzaddikism, the gulf between rebbe
and hasid is well nigh unbridgeable. As one hasid said at a farbrengen:
"Sometimes I think that the rebbe looks at us like we look at a fish in a
bowl." The hasid might as well concede that the tzaddik is qualitatively
different, and avail himself (for a consideration) of the tzaddik's saving
work.[14] *Yesod Ha'Avodah* quotes the Magid of Mezhirech as saying:

> "Lord of the world, who ruled before all creation was made." The
> tzaddik is called the creation. God ruled before creation, but now the
> tzaddik is here. "Once [the tzaddik] is made," everything goes "accord-
> ing to his will," for God decrees and the tzaddik destroys the decree.[15]

Reaction against such paternalism resulted in the revolution of the
Polish school led by the Yehudi (in 1813, during the time of the Napo-
leonic War). Under the Polish school, each hasid was required to do his
own work. The rebbe's task was to make his hasid independent of him as

soon as possible. This could not be done by a rebbe who attracted masses of hasidim. Only a rebbe who wished to direct an elite of hasidim so that they might learn how to stand on their own could accomplish the task. The Kotsker (Menahem Mendl of Kotsk), the Yehudi's successor, wanted to take no more than 200 hasidim with him into the woods, and there, with this elite, bring about the Redemption. In this way, each one of the hasidim could become a rebbe himself.

The Polish school was not without its own opposition. R. Naftali Zvi Horwitz of Ropshitz (the Ropshitzer), a contemporary of the Yehudi, objected to the Polish school on the grounds that it invited nonholy energies by accelerating a process that normally occurred over a much longer period of time.[16] The Ropshitzer's attitude is characteristic of paternalistic solicitude, and it was in reaction to this paternalism that many hasidim became Polish-style rebbes. Yet, in spite of this fact, when dynasties consolidated their positions two generations later, Tzaddikism spread even in Poland.

The Polish school, which culminated in the individualism encouraged by the Kotsker, was a rebellion against Tzaddikism. But it was not a successful rebellion. For twenty years, the Kotsker retreated in order to search for his authentic self.[17] He disdained the Besht's warmth and compassion, both for himself and for his followers. According to Abraham J. Heschel's interpretation of Kotsker Hasidism, compassion is a lie, and all of its grace is deceitful. "As long as a person resides in falsehood, his kindness is a false illusion."[18] The Kotsker Rebbe relentlessly sought to define himself in his ascetical search for truth. He rejected the social field in which he existed. To him all comfort was repulsive; even the comfort of myth was to him out of bounds. To his hasidim he offered not solace but shock. However, what was good for highly motivated hasidim was not good for those who had not yet reached that level. The Kotsker's own disciples and successors took pity on their hasidim, and once more the door was open to paternalism.

Ger and other Polish successors of Kotsk moved either toward the normative or, like R. Mordecai Joseph of Izhbitz, toward the antinomian. Socioeconomic upheavals eventually interrupted this process. The Industrial Revolution and the advent of the railroad unleashed great changes, especially in the life of the shtetl. Mobility was increased, as was the frequency of visits to the rebbe. Business trips and visits to the rebbe were planned together. The inner preparation for the visit to the rebbe, and the sacrality of the visit, were now diminished to some degree.

In the feudal shtetl the rebbe was, to some extent, the Jewish *poritz* or "squire," a factor that abetted Tzaddikism. The rebbe wore the clothes of the Polish *schlachta* (aristocracy) and drove in a six-horse carriage. With the diminution of the *poritz's* influence, the larger city became more influential and the rebbe's image changed. After the First World War, many rebbes no longer lived in their ancestral villages; they moved instead to larger urban centers. (Their hasidim nevertheless continued to identify the rebbe and themselves by the name of the rebbe's ancestral village.) The crisis of identity became a problem in the cities as conformity beckoned the hasid to become a bourgeois citizen. Between the two wars, this problem was dealt with, but not solved. The Nazis' "final solution" interfered.

In review, then, the major factors with which Hasidism had to contend were the following:

(a) The relaxation of behavior from compulsive–obsessive forms.
   (1734–1766: The Besht's ministry)
(b) The resultant cyclothymic personality with its problems of despair.
   (1790–1810: R. Nahman of Bratzlav's ministry)
(c) The paternalism of Tzaddikism in attempting to manage this despair.
   (1773–1812: R. Barukh of Mezhibuzh's ministry
   1790–1837: R. Mordecai Chernobiler's ministry
   1827–1867: R. Israel Ruzhiner's ministry)
(d) The revolt against Tzaddikism, which brought about a Promethean ego defeat.
   (1820–1860: R. Mendel of Kotsk's ministry)
(e) Socioeconomic conditions that resulted in problems of identity in urban settings.
   (circa 1900–1914)
(f) The impact of the two World Wars in creating further upheavals.
(g) The Holocaust and its effect in undermining belief.
(h) The traumas experienced in the transplantation from Eastern Europe to America and Israel.

Though these factors are listed according to the historic periods in which they manifested themselves, the reader should understand no one period was exclusively occupied with one particular problem. The aforementioned problems overlap, and the transition from one period to the next is not clearly defined. Our chronology, therefore, is a generalization based on the characteristic preoccupations of a given period.

Summary

Hasidism appeared at a time when repressive means were being used to overcome inner tension; this tension caused hysteria, obsessive traits, and paranoia. In contrast, Hasidism encouraged its adherents to trust in primary processes and regressions in the service of the sacred. This alleviated some of the pressure and permitted sane acting out so that hysteria was no longer the only available way to deal with inner tension. Obsessive traits were mocked, and paranoia was given a "reality peg" in the battles with *mitnagdim* (opponents of Hasidism). This produced in some a cycloid personality: intense manic highs and depressive lows were newly threatening. The lure of Tzaddikism was great, since it reduced the emotional amplitude by means of rebbe-watching. This produced a "spectator" Hasidism. The Pshysskha group saw the dangers and placed Hasidism on the Promethean striving continuum. This in turn produced frightening isolation.

Subsequent social changes created a new setting for Hasidism, bringing much of urban psychopathology to adversely affect a group unprepared for cosmopolitan life. The Holocaust and its aftermath further uprooted the survivors who, in addition to their sociological problems, had to deal with the theodicy with an unprecedented urgency. In each of these stages, the solutions of Hasidism created new problems; the rebbe and the hasid worked together on these problems, often with great originality and creative insight.

DIMENSIONS IN A HASID'S LIFE

The life of the hasid is multidimensional, each dimension contributing toward a meaningful life pattern. The particular hasidic group to which a hasid belongs, his ethnic origin, his stage of life and the transitions he must make from one stage to another—all contribute toward shaping the hasid's life pattern, which in turn shapes his thoughts, emotive expressions, and actions.

In describing the various life stages through which a hasid will pass, our approach will be ahistorical: the atmosphere of the *bet midrash* (house of study, common room) is ahistorical. In his awareness in the experiential present, the student engages in a dialogue with God, prophet, and talmudist, as well as with rebbe and hasid of the past. We have adhered to this same anachronistic time-view, which fuses the significant past with the experiential present, in describing the hasid's life pattern. Our description has relevance to both past (anywhere from 1830 on) and present.

Hasidic Affiliation and Ethnopolitical Affiliation

The idea of relationship is implicit in the word *hasid*. The hasid's identity is shaped by his allegiance to his rebbe. When a hasid professes to be a Satmarer hasid, for example, we know that his attitude toward the state of Israel is negative, and that his political attitudes in general are activist and demonstrative. We also know something about the way in which he relates to his fellow Jews and to his fellow hasidim. Similarly, the name "Lubavitcher" or "habadnik" affords us a set from which to view these particular hasidim. We are thus predisposed to assume that a habadnik's attitude toward the state of Israel is ideologically negative, but politically positive. He considers his mental framework more philosophical and intellectual than that of hasidim of any other affiliation. In his attitude toward his fellow Jews and vis-à-vis other hasidim, the habadnik places himself at the top of the hierarchy; yet he employs a double standard in that he professes to be open to *klal Yisrael* (the totality of the Jewish people). The ethnic origin of a hasid today is more difficult to determine than it previously was. For example, very few present-day habadniks are actually rooted in the ethnic home of Habad—White Russia.

In his relationship with other Jews, the habadnik sets up the following descending hierarchy: fellow habadniks, hasidim of other rebbes (the order in which he will rank them shifts continually and depends greatly on the amount of political collaboration or enmity currently in force with them), militant non-hasidic Orthodox Jews, and nonmilitant observers of Sabbath and kashrut. Non-observers of Jewish Law are treated in the following manner: The groups to which they belong are summarily rejected; as individuals, however, they are judged according to their usefulness to the hasidic movement, either in terms of the monetary contributions they make or in terms of their openness to hasidic influence. Generally, the hasid's relationship with the middle class or with outsiders is not regulated by any overt group attitudes, but depends upon individual preferences.

Hasidim who frequent more than one rebbe's establishment are suspect by both. Group cohesion treats defection from one hasidic group to another as a minor apostasy. To a committed hasid, the change of fealty from his rebbe to another one has adulterous connotations. Yet he has to show honor and respect to another hasidic leader, though not on the same level as the honor and respect accorded his own rebbe. Hasidim relate a story of R. Shlomoh of Karlin, who came to visit R. Shneur Zalman of Liadi and wanted to entice R. Benjamin Kletzker away from R. Shneur Zalman. R. Benjamin refused, saying, "The lord is a lord, but not mine; the lad is only a lad, but not thine."[19] This phrase, often repeated by hasidim of other masters, became the classic response of the loyal hasid to the blandishments of other rebbes.

The Hasidic Hierarchy

Within his own hasidic group each hasid occupies a specific place on the hierarchy, as determined by his age bracket and the particular role he plays. Does he consider himself to be a *real hasid?* This would depend on whether or not he gives a monthly *ma'amad* (retainer fee) to the rebbe, and whether he is prepared to listen to the rebbe's counsel in all matters of his life; in fact, whether he is prepared to be sent by the rebbe for the furtherance of Judaism to the ends of the earth. Or, is he a *hasidisher Yid,* a hasidic Jew, an adjectival hasid. A true hasid, a *yoshev* (literally, one who sits; pl. *yoshvim*), sees himself as being completely in the rebbe's hands. In Lubavitch, however, the category of yoshev has not existed for the last three or four generations. Belz still had yoshvim up until the First World War. Jiri Langer, the author of *Nine Gates of the Chassidic Mysteries* (Kafka mentions that Langer introduced him to Hasidism), describes his experience as a yoshev in Belz in the following terms:

> We "who are really in earnest" do not board at the inn like those who "merely journey" to the saint of Belz. We belong to our own society, or *chevre,* the members of which are called *Yoshvim,* or *sitting ones,* because they live, or sit in Belz permanently. Our society lives on small contributions earned with difficulty from the more wealthy visitors to Belz. We cook for ourselves. The dining-room is small. Deep holes yawn in the unplaned boards of the dirty floor. We crowd together round the table on a narrow bench. There is a great shortage of crockery. We young people often eat two out of one dish, with our hands, of course. To use a fork would be an indecent innovation. [Langer 1961, Introduction]

The true yoshev looked askance at the intruder or at those who felt they merited to be called "hasidim" merely because they made periodic journeys to the rebbe. Jiri Langer, who was well trained in Western modes of thought and a convert to Belzer Hasidism, describes his own treatment among his fellow hasidim:

> I am still a foreigner. People are very polite and full of respect when they talk to me, but they are mistrustful. The mere fulfillment of religious injunctions, however precise and conscientious, is as little adequate to inspire confidence here as is the utmost zeal over one's study. Excessive religiosity is not welcomed. But now that my beard and side-whiskers are well grown, now that I am able to speak some Yiddish and have begun wearing a long *shipits* (an overcoat similar to a caftan) instead of a short coat, and ever since I have started wearing a black velvet hat on weekdays, as all the other Chassidim do, this ice-wall of mistrust has gradually begun to thaw. But why even now am I not completely like the others? For example, why am I not gay, all the time, as a true Chassid ought to be? . . .
>
> At last, when my face is pallid from undernourishment and illness, and my emaciated body has acquired a stoop, it is clear to nearly all of them that "I am really in earnest." No longer will the gates of Chassidism be closed in front of the youth from Prague.
>
> The Chassidim are becoming kinder to me every day. My lot is being improved in every possible way. Better bread, and milk. But my weakened stomach resolutely refuses all these extra comforts. Moreover, the insects are becoming crueller all the time. They have absolutely no pity on me. The mice nibble at my clothes. I sleep on the ground on a heap of old straw. My whole outward appearance testifies that I am gradually turning into a complete *chnyok* and *katcherak*. These two words are untranslatable nicknames used by the Chassidim to mock any of their fellows who are totally indifferent to their outward appearance. [Langer 1961, Introduction]

A hasid's position on the hasidic hierarchy is to a large extent determined by his age group. Each age group is generally associated with a particular role. Thus, the hasid's move from one life stage to the next is marked by an accompanying change in role. These transitions might prove disturbing and even traumatic for the hasid were it not for the fact that he has recourse to the rebbe's counsel. (Because this writer is most familiar with the hierarchy that operates among Lubavitcher hasidim, we will follow the Lubavitcher through his life cycle. However, a similar hierarchy is operative in each of the hasidic groups.)

Bocher

The *hasidisher bocher* is an unmarried hasid. Usually he is a yeshivah student. If he is a student at the Lubavitcher Yeshivah, Tomchei Tmimim, he will be called a *tamim*. This is a title of distinction and will appear on letters and invitations addressed to him. The *tamim* is higher on the hierarchy than the less closely affiliated hasid. The Lubavitcher bocher (pl. *bochrim*) can usually be distinguished by his physical appearance. Most bochrim have beards, and a beard is mandatory at Lubavitch. The Lubavitcher Rebbe, in one of his responsa, forbade shaving on the grounds of transvestism; and since the rebbe is the halakhic decisor, hasidim treat his diet as law. The bocher will also be identifiable by his long double-breasted *reckel* or jacket. (At prayers, the bocher will gird himself with a *gartel*, or prayer sash, and on the Sabbath he will wear a silken caftan and a black plush beaver hat.) A young hasid presuming to wear his identifying dress before his sincerity is generally accepted will incur *bitushim* (verbal barbs), as will the hasid who delays wearing distinctive garb when it has already been decided that he belongs to the Lubavitcher community. It is assumed that the contemporary *hasidisher bocher* will behave in a certain fashion: he will not see movies, he will not smoke until the age of twenty, he will visit the *miqveh* (ritual bath) regularly, especially after a nocturnal emission, and he will not talk socially with girls or take them out unless he is serious about marriage.

It is obvious that the life of the bocher requires a great deal of discipline, and that he will require the assistance of both rebbe and *mashpiy'a* in order to implement and maintain this discipline. Without the rebbe's guidance and counsel, and their implementation by the *mashpiy'a*, the bocher would be lost. The major areas of the bocher's concern, and those in which he will most often require the rebbe's counsel, are study, prayer, and vocation. The rebbe's task is to guide the bocher during these formative years. He counsels the bocher on how best to manage his own particular life tasks; but the actual supervision of the bocher is in the hands of the *mashpiy'a* or the *rosh yeshivah* (dean of the yeshivah).

During the time that he is a bocher, the hasid will have several occasions for seeing the rebbe. First, he will have a general yehidut at which he will submit his *kvittel* (note of petition) to the rebbe, and which will constitute his official initiation as a hasid. This yehidut is necessary even if the bocher does not have a specific question or problem to bring to the rebbe. The rebbe himself will raise questions concerning the young man's course of studies, his general background, and the salient features of his life. He will offer the bocher suggestions and guidance regarding any area of his life that may require redirection or strengthening of motivation. If the bocher has come with a specific problem, the rebbe will deal with the problem, although he may see that the hasid's manifest problem is merely symptomatic and that the true problem is much deeper. In this case he will deal with the problem as he sees it, and not necessarily as the hasid himself sees it. At a later interview, the rebbe will probably counsel the bocher on reparative work for the sins of his youth. Usually this is a euphemism for masturbation; but in the case of a bocher who is a convert from a non-observant Jewish home, it would also cover such things as the consumption of forbidden foods and the desecration of the Sabbath. Any other problem that the bocher might have, he is free to bring before the rebbe, although the rebbe will prefer to deal with his spiritual problems.

The Bocher Prepares for Marriage

The bocher does not have any real social intercourse with members of the opposite sex until he is ready to consider marriage seriously. Then he will probably ask a friend to introduce him to a suitable girl. The criterion for suitability is not that the young bocher be pleased by her appearance or personality, but that she be willing to lead a hasidic life together with him, over which the rebbe will be the sole and final arbiter. Once the hasid has been introduced to a girl, he will not dawdle, but will be expected to make up his mind after three or four meetings. If he finds the girl suitable, he might propose to her by saying: "Is it all right with you that we ask the rebbe whether we ought to get married?" The rebbe is the final judge regarding the suitability of the match, and the bocher will submit to his judgment. He knows that the rebbe does not merely see the girl in her physical self. He takes out the girl's file from heaven in order to see whether or not it has been decreed that this girl should marry this lad; for it is written that forty days before a child is conceived, a proclamation is issued in heaven deciding who is to be that child's mate.

Once the hasid has received the rebbe's approval of the match, rebbe and hasid will want to discuss an auspicious date for the wedding. Since the study of laws pertaining to the intimate aspects of marriage has been postponed until this time, the bocher will now want to discuss with the rebbe the Code and other books that he has been studying in preparation for marriage. On the eve of the wedding the hasid will come to the rebbe for a blessing. During this yehidut, the rebbe may give the hasid some counsel pertaining to the act of marital union, thus reinforcing the work that the *mashpiy'a* has already done, or he may want to raise for discussion items that the *mashpiy'a*, in preparing the hasid for his forthcoming marriage, may have omitted. Rebbe and *mashpiy'a* work together to help the hasid through this important transition in his life. Both will want to discuss with the hasid what constitutes understanding between husband and wife, explaining that what the husband calls understanding is not identical with what the wife calls understanding.

> One young *khosen* (groom) came to his *mashpiy'a* after his prenuptial yehidut with the rebbe. The rebbe had discussed with him the differ-ence between the understanding of the husband and the understand-ing of the wife. The *mashpiy'a*, in elaborating on the yehidut, ex-plained that if a Yiddish-speaking Ashkenazi were to marry a Ladino or Arabic-speaking Sephardi, this would constitute an intermarriage, and therefore would be fraught with many kinds of danger. Interpre-tation of differences and the need for great understanding between the two partners would be required in order for the marriage to be successful. Then the *mashpiy'a* added: "But the Ashkenazi and the Sephardi, they are both Jews; whereas with the husband and wife, he is male and she is female, and between them there is a distinction and a difference that goes much deeper than the distinction between Ashkenazi and Sephardi."[20]

The Wedding

The wedding itself is preceded by a prenuptial farbrengen, and together these constitute the hasid's rite of passage from bocher to *yungerman* (recently married young man). At the prenuptial farbrengen, the group of bochrim with whom the young groom has been associated meet with the *mashpiy'a*, who discusses with them the meaning of the home and its opportunities for holiness. He also discusses with them the "second descent of the soul," the second *yeridat han'shamah*.

> It was bad enough and a traumatic event for the soul to come down into a physical body; but at least there was one consolation—it came down into a physical body that had all the mitzvot to do, that studied Hasidut and Torah, that came to farbrengens and that *davened* at great length. But now there stands before you another descent into a soul which will need an equal amount of involvement, and of *birur*, of separating the wheat from the chaff, the good from the evil; and this time it is a descent into a body that did not study Hasidut, that has fewer mitzvot, and that is so difficult for a male to understand.[21]

The *mashpiy'a* will continue to talk about marriage, pointing out that now that one's sex life is permitted, it first needs to be sublimated and then directed in the service of God. Mournful melodies will be sung at the farbrengen, and allusion will usually be made to the fact that the farbrengen itself was held in heaven before the descent of the soul.

The rebbe himself seldom officiates at weddings, although he will send a letter to the young couple, When this letter is read at the wedding, the guests rise as if the rebbe were actually present. His role lies in preparing the hasid for his transition to yungerman and in counseling the hasid in his new role. On the eve of the marriage, the rebbe may allow the bocher to enter the room of the late rebbe and to recite his afternoon prayer, along with the Yom Kippur confessions, out of the late rebbe's siddur.

The wedding itself is arranged by the parents of the young couple, provided that the parents are themselves hasidim. If the parents are not hasidim, the children will be guided by the rebbe's instructions. The wedding is celebrated in defiance of regular conventions. The music is exclusively hasidic; the men and women have separate banquet halls and dance separately. The young couple does not leave for a honeymoon following the wedding, but during the first week celebrates what is called the *sheva brakhot*, the Seven Nuptial Blessings, recited at the homes of various friends.

At the wedding farbrengen, the young hasid, now a yungerman, is dressed in a *kapoteh* and wears a sash around his waist. He listens as an older hasid asks the question:

> Why is it that we celebrate the mating of a male and a female? If that is such a great *simhah*, why don't we celebrate it when a cow is being taken to a bull? Obviously, we don't celebrate the animal part. But since the two souls, who have been united and were one before they descended to earth, have, after such a long time of separation, found each other again, this *simhah* is of the unification of the *yihud* because it betokens and foreshadows the great *simhah* of the union between God and all of Israel, and the coming of the Messiah, which is likened to the consummation of the marriage.[22]

It is for this reason that the *sheva brakhot* are celebrated after the wedding. Thus, the occasion of the wedding is a great joy; but it is a joy tempered by the seriousness with which the young hasid has been taught to look at marriage, its duties and responsibilities, as well as its difficulties.

The Yungerman

With his marriage, the former *hasidisher bocher* now takes on a new social role, that of the *hasidisher yungerman*. As a young married man, his relationship with the rebbe will be strengthened and he will have attained a higher status on the hasidic hierarchy. At this time, he will usually turn to the rebbe for counsel regarding a vocational decision. However, if his father-in-law has pledged to support him, the hasid may continue full-time study and, by study and prayer, rise on the ladder of perfection in a contemplative manner. This happens rather seldom today. It is much more usual for young married hasidim to become involved in a career other than the contemplative. If the young hasid has capabilities in this direction, and if there are suitable positions open, the rebbe will expect him to pursue a vocation involving *harbatzat Torah*, the spreading of Torah. This was especially true from 1944 to 1950, when many hasidim came to America from Europe and the number of hasidim increased greatly. Today, vocational choices run the gamut from greengrocers to rabbis, with the majority of hasidim choosing "secular" careers, and the minority choosing sacerdotal vocations.

With his new role, the yungerman assumes new responsibilities. His garb differs somewhat from that of the bocher, in keeping with his new role. Since he is likely to be involved in a secular vocation, he will not wear his kapoteh on weekdays, but only on the Sabbath. If he does wear a kapoteh on weekdays, he will probably wear a silken one on the Sabbath. His beard will be worn loose, and sidelocks will be either absent or subdued. His wife will either wear a *shait'l* (wig), or will use some other type of head covering.

The specific counseling problems confronting the yungerman will be those dealing with marriage, home, vocation, and children. His spiritual problems will be those arising from his new condition—that is, involvement with family and business. Any psychopathological material that may be brought to the rebbe at this stage will usually involve such matters as guilt over the new accessibility of sex, doubts about marital or vocational choice, and any existential problems produced by the young hasid's withdrawal from the sheltered life of the bocher.

One of the problems the yungerman must face is the conflict between family and business interests and obligations and those obligations to prayer and study that he undertook as a bocher. Even though he may be involved in a business career, he is still expected to spend at least one hour per day in the study of Hasidut, in addition to the time he must devote to his other religious studies. It is assumed that he will pray each day with a slow *minyan* (quorum of at least ten men), and that on the Sabbath he will pray *b'arikhut*—that is, to set for himself a contemplative pace, which often can take his prayers long into the afternoon hours. At least once a month he will consider it his obligation to attend a farbrengen in order to resharpen his sensitivity toward the work of Hasidism—the service of God. As for the financial expenses of the yungerman, he is expected to support those enterprises that the rebbe endorses. All these demands often caused the yungerman to feel a conflict between his religious obligations and his commitment to family and business. The attitude of one rebbe, R. Shalom Dovber of Lubavitch, toward this conflict is illustrated in the following passage:

> And so it is in all things. He must renounce wife and children. The wife is screaming, let her scream. All right, so she'll have a headache. So what. She won't die from it. So she's excited and says: "Robber! What do you want from me? What do you make of me and my children?" So let her scream. She won't die from screaming. The child is screaming? Let him scream. He won't die from screaming. I must do what the Most High demands of me.[23]

Although this attitude is obviously the extreme, in general, the prevailing attitude in Hasidism is that religious duties take precedence over familial and business obligations. However, if a hasid finds himself involved in a serious conflict, he can bring his problem to the rebbe, and the rebbe will usually help him find a dual solution enabling him to fulfill his religious obligations while also maintaining *shalom bayit*, peace and harmony in the household.

The Ba'al Habayit

The next hasidic life stage is that of the *hasidisher ba'al habayit*, the hasidic head of the household. The transition from yungerman to ba'al habayit is less pronounced than that of bocher to yungerman. It is not an abrupt change, but a gradual process by which the yungerman becomes a ba'al habayit; and as such it is not marked by a specific ceremony. When the yungerman has been married for some time, and his vocation and family are well established, he is considered a ba'al habayit. When he seeks the rebbe's counsel, the rebbe sees him as a householder who is very much involved in the world: he may even be a wealthy man. The rebbe's task at this time is to remind him of the purpose for which any hasid becomes involved in worldly affairs: the service of the Most High. The rebbe seeks to strengthen the householder's ties to Hasidism. Yet he is also the person upon whom the rebbe relies for financial support. The rebbe depends on the ba'al habayit for large monetary contributions, for important missions, and occasionally for prestige work. Since the ba'al habayit's children are usually already married or are of marriageable age, he no longer has to be constantly concerned for their welfare, and thus is freer to serve the rebbe in this capacity.

Even though the rebbe has come to rely on the head of the household for financial support, he is nevertheless aware that it is part of his task to ensure that the ba'al habayit not become one of those lost souls who forgets his true vocation. For this reason, in counseling him, the rebbe will want to remind him of his life-task in order that he may continue to make spiritual as well as monetary gains. In fact, he will explain to the ba'al habayit that because of his very involvement in the world, he has more opportunity for spiritual advancement than the bocher or the yungerman. Owing to the great fervor of his *yetzer hara*, his evil inclination (a result of his worldly involvement), he is capable of experiencing much greater fervor in prayer. It is for this reason that R. Shneur Zalman suggests that it is the ba'al habayit who should lead the congregation in prayers on the Sabbath. Just as the bocher yields to the yungerman in the synagogue, so the yungerman must give his place to the ba'al habayit.

The Elterer Hasid

When the hasidic ba'al habayit has reached the stage when his children are ready to take his place, he is expected to spend the rest of his days as a renouncer of worldly involvement. He has now passed from ba'al habayit to *elterer hasid*, from a hasidic head of a household to an elder hasid.

The elder hasid is almost a rebbe himself. To the younger hasid, he is the model par excellence. "Hasidim who think that they can be hasidim, without having observed older hasidim, are wrong."[24] The elder hasid is the truly individualized man, and the younger hasid, who sees him as a model, molds himself by observing the older hasid. Yet the relationship and the benefits are reciprocal. The elder hasid, by extending himself toward the younger hasid who emulates him, gains fervor through his "choice children," who are more the fulfillment of his hopes than the children of flesh and blood. The elterer hasid himself, having discharged his familial and business obligations, can become a true *yoshev ohel*, one who sits and studies in the tent of Torah. The model for the elterer hasid is the *elterer mashpiy'a*.

The elder hasid may still require the rebbe's counsel, but generally the rebbe relaxes the formality of the yehidut in dealing with him. The rebbe himself respects the elder hasid as one who has attained a very high rung on the hasidic hierarchy. The elder hasid's problems are likely to be the problems of his children and grandchildren rather than his own.

It is clear that the hasidic identity cannot be easily assumed. The process by which this identity is molded demands a lifetime of dedication. The hasid is always in the process of "becoming," assuming the various roles necessary to his development as defined by the hasidic framework to which he is committed. The rebbe keeps in mind that at each stage of life the hasid needs to be helped over the basic hurdles. In counseling the hasid, the rebbe takes into consideration the life tasks that brought about the hasid's present incarnation. He helps shape the hasid, from bocher to elder hasid, so that he will best be able to fulfill his life tasks. As a bocher, the hasid needs to learn how to order his life in accordance with his physical, mental, and spiritual endowment. His ideals need to be aligned with his endowment, and then reinforced. The yungerman needs the rebbe's help in facing the realities of marriage, vocation, and family. The ba'al habayit needs to be given practical counsel that will help him deal with the exigencies of life in this world, as well as spiritual counsel in order to reinforce his hasidic vocation. The elder hasid, whose grip on life is waning, needs to be given a purpose for the remainder of his life, and to be helped into the next life by counsel that will prepare him for death. The rebbe's task is to meet the hasid on all of his life stages, and to help him make a creative adjustment to all the realities of his life situation and present incarnation.

THE PSYCHOLOGY AND COSMOLOGY OF HASIDISM[25]

The hasidic universe of discourse is like an iceberg. The world apparent to the eye is only a small fraction of the "real" world. The unseen is very real, since much real activity is transacted in it. In fact the rebbe, who has been called the geologist of the soul, does most of his work in these unseen regions.[26] The mere fact that these worlds are indiscernible to the average eye does not mean that they lack empirical reality for the hasid. In fact, the process of the yehidut would remain unintelligible (except on the level of simple advice) if we did not adjust our focus to encompass the psychology and cosmology of Hasidism. The conflicts and problems the hasid brings to the rebbe are usually related, either directly or indirectly, to his hasidic commitment and to the psychology and cosmology to which he adheres. This is the screen upon which the drama of the yehidut is projected.

Eschatology Equals Psychology

Many writers who compare the religious disciplines of East and West draw a contrast between what they call the "method" of the East and "dogma" of the West. However, in creating such a dichotomy, one must be careful not to advocate one path to the exclusion of the other, i.e., method over dogma or vice-versa. The dogma provides the necessary conceptual framework within which the method can be imparted; but the dogma without the method is an empty vessel. Habad Hasidism always turns the dogmatic statement into a methodological one: in other words, the dogmatic statement is usually translated into psychological terms. Thus, the functional requirements of the rebbe–hasid relationship—the working through of purgation, preparation, and finally, enlightenment— correspond to the eschatological teachings of Hasidism. The eschatological teachings provide the model for the laboratory work that the aspirant must do.

Death Equals Initiation

Hasidic eschatology taught the hasid the importance of dying in full possession of his consciousness. Many descriptions of deathbed scenes have been handed down in hasidic circles. Often a *nigun*—a Hasidic melody—and a deathbed scene are interwoven. The Ba'al Shem Tov had his disciples sing the melody of R. Yehiel Mikhael of Zlochov (the Zlotchover) and promised in future to come and join any who would sing it out of true repentance, adding that he would pray for their intentions. He explained to members of the holy brotherhood, *hevrah qadisha*, how the soul was leaving his body, bidding them to observe how life left the extremities when the small clock ceased to tick. When life had left his lower body, he busied himself with his own prayers. The last words he uttered were "Do not bring me to the foot of pride."

A story is told of a hasid who invited ten men to his deathbed and taught them a new melody. When they had learned the melody well enough to carry it by themselves, he leaned back, offering his soul to God, and expired.

The quality of life that inspired a serene death, not infrequently accompanied by radiant visions, was very often the subject of hasidic tales. Hasidim prepared themselves for death by asking the rebbe for advice about what "unification" to meditate on in the moments of their passing. R. Simhah Bunim of Pshysskha taught that sleep was a sixtieth of death: he who prepared himself properly for sleep, offering his soul up to God, would be able to pass on to the other life with ease. It is told that when he himself reached the time of passing, his wife moaned and wept, but he turned to her and said: "All my life I have been preparing myself for this moment. Stop weeping."

Viewed in eschatological terms, the moment of death becomes the event of initiation. Monastic orders and others who use initiation rites often use the death model. The old Adam is buried and the new one is resurrected as a different person. In the method that the master imparts to his disciple, the disciple has to become dead to the world. R. Shneur Zalman counseled that the disciple must not be attached, must not have his true heart in his worldly involvements.

Death can at times be very painful. The pangs of birth, the pangs of death, and the pangs of the Messiah are often described as constituting one and the same kind of separation pain. Yet, if the hasid has been truly prepared, death can be "like removing a hair from the milk,"[27] or like walking out one door and into another.[28] The freed self, the self that is capable of free-choosing and making decisions, has no problem with the death experience; but in order to free a hasid from the pangs and the pain and the attachments, a master may have to use severe techniques such as *bitush* and mortification. It was for this purpose that R. Barukh of Mezhibuzh once shamed a man in public. Later he was visited by another master who asked him: "R. Barukh, is it not written that he who shames his fellow in public, who causes him to blush or to blanch in public, it is as if he had actually killed him?" R. Barukh replied: "If this is what he needs at present in order to be helped, it is my duty to forgo my part in the world to come for the sake of my hasid."[29] R. Barukh had to transcend the social contract with his hasid in order to lead him to the freedom that he needed. In this experience, both rebbe and hasid experience a liberating death.

The third meal of the Sabbath was given special emphasis in hasidic life, as it was compared to a death experience. The rebbe and his hasidim practiced dying with the dying day. Kalonymus Kalmish of Piasetzno (the Piasetzner) compared the power of this third meal to that of *n'ilah* (the closing prayer) on Yom Kippur. The Besht, because of its significance, insisted on celebrating it at the House of Study, a custom that survives to this day. It was he who taught that, because the additional soul departs after the Sabbath, this meal is comparable to the death experience.

In short, death itself, preparation for death, and the death model assume great importance in the hasidic eschatology. A hasid's life, viewed from this perspective, is seen merely as a preparation for death. Thus, death is the goal orientation of life, but only if death means union with the *Eyn Sof* (the Infinite One). Hasidism teaches that yearning and longing for God are not enough.

> The truth is that when one comes before the Lord, one must be clear and pure. One must be able to realize this clarity and purity in disciplined action. The higher one is, the greater one can fall because longing and yearning, without the balance of a disciplined life, is called "death." Concerning this, "The Lord commanded Moses to tell Aaron" (who was the manifestation of the powers of the soul) that in order to attain holiness and sanctity—to attain what lies "*before* [beyond] the *kaporet*" [the covering of the Holy Ark, in this sense the sensible reality] which is the contraction of the *Eyn Sof*—one must know that over the Ark, which also stands for the manifestation of the mind, there is a "cover." The cover is intention and purpose, so that he who enters there "may come and not die." In other words, he ought not to remain merely with the longing and yearning, for "in the cloud shall I be made manifest, over the cover." The purpose of this first contraction and hiding is the subsequent manifestation [of the Light]. The entrance gate to this manifestation is the "No!"—the self-effacement that prompts one to do as Hasidism directs, and not as one's own reason directs. Only then can one come to realize that which is holy.[30]

After Death, the Identity Crisis

The identity of a soul as it stands before the Heavenly Court is significant. The hasid's life is so ordered that his soul identity may become intrinsic to him and will thus remain with him even after the shock of death. At times, either the rebbe or his *gabbai* (secretary) will give the hasid a nickname, and this adds to his awareness of his soul identity. When the hasid brings his kvittel to the rebbe, the kvittel will contain his name, his true identity vis-à-vis the rebbe and God.

The earthbound soul falls prey to an identity crisis if it is unable to separate itself from the body, even through the pain of death. It is in

danger of experiencing a decay of consciousness and turning into nothing-
ness. For this reason, there is an angel—*Dumah*—who is charged with the
duty of preventing this decay. In order to do this, he asks each person for
his Hebrew name. The Rabbis describe how some people suffer from
amnesia as a result of the shock of dying, and so are unable to remember
any identity beyond the corporeal. In order to avoid this, a mnemonic
device is counseled to dispel the amnesia in the following way: At the end
of each *Amidah* prayer (the Eighteen Benedictions, recited standing), the
worshiper is told to "sign off" with a Torah sentence that begins with the
same letter as his own name. Among Sephardic Jews, each boy at bar
mitzvah and each girl at bat mitzvah is initiated into his or her own
sentence. The worshiper thus reinforces the memory of his own Jewish
name and his own soul at the end of each prayer. Even if he is unable to
remember his name, he will be able to remember his Torah sentence,
because the Torah is eternal and cannot decay. Thus, he will be able to
remember who he was, and will be able to follow the angels who summon
him before the Heavenly Court.

Worms and Mortification

The next step in postmortem purgation, according to the dogmatic
teaching, is *hibut haqever*—the beating of the grave. "Like a needle in living
flesh, so does the corpse feel the worms."[31] For most people, the passing
from one life into another is fraught with danger. Most human beings are
unable to think of themselves apart from the body. We cannot visualize our
inner, real selves except in the features of our bodies, despite the fact that we
know that our real identity is something more abstract than the contours of
the flesh. This earthboundness must be cured before the soul can ascend.

Earthboundness is incurred by the seeking of sense pleasure for its
own sake. Anyone who indulges in such self-gratification as an end in
itself—even though the pleasure is a halakhically permissible one—will
suffer the pain and anguish of the grave—*hibut haqever*. The soul that—by
sensual indulgence—has become fully and completely identified with the
body, is unable to separate from it because it sees itself as body only and
not as something more and apart from it. For this reason, it is painful for
the soul to have to accompany the body to its final resting place and to
behold its putrefaction and decay. No writer is so dogmatic as to insist
that *hibut haqever* be taken in its literal interpretation. Rather, it is interpreted as meaning that the identification of the person with his body, his
implicit faith that the body is a true self, must be broken. He needs to
discover that beyond the flesh there is another self.

On the level of spiritual work, *hibut haqever* takes place in several ways when the hasid practices *itkafia*—self-denial. He is eaten by the worms of his wants. Each time the hasid says "No" to his physical wants, he separates himself from his bodily identity. He beats the horses, so they know they are horses, and he, the rider, is not identical with them. A hasid who once asked the Tzemah Tzedeq about *itkafia* was told not to scratch an itch. This attitude is close to that of Francis of Assisi, who spoke of his body as "Brother Ass." The soul is the real person, the body another sort of being.

A more positive means for the separation of the soul from the corporeal identity is prayer offered in great *kavanah* (sincerity, or intent). In such prayer, one becomes oblivious to the body and the environment.

Once the hasid has attained the separation of identities on a gross level, the content of his mind is refined in the next stage.

Stilling the Noise

In addition to the problem of maintaining his identity, another challenge faces the hasid. Since man is usually driven by his urges and desires, by all the syllables and words and sounds that he has heard during his life, these sounds vibrate like clanging coins in a gourd, and he is unable to achieve the subtle stillness necessary to receive angelic or heavenly voices. Even we, who are yet in the flesh, are disturbed by this sensual "static." Anyone who has attempted to sit in silence for a few moments with his eyes closed can easily testify to the inner disquiet he experiences when all the decaying images and desires, which were once forced into the unconscious, now attempt to invade his mind. In order to rid the soul of this "dust," the soul must be shaken in the *kaf haqela*—catapult. The Sages use the image of two angels, one at each end of the world, who toss the soul from one end of the world to the other. This, too, has great psychological significance. Often we find when we try to worship that we are being tossed "from one end of the universe to the other," from the most exalted heights to the lowliest of drives and desires. It is almost as if the angels try to rid the soul of its accumulated psychic "dust" by putting it through a cosmic centrifuge until only the soul remains. Were this treatment of *kaf haqela* not administered to the soul, it would be unable to silence all the sense images and noises and would have to wander in the world of *tohu* (chaos). In one hasidic tale, a dybbuk who has already roamed for hundreds of years in this void confesses: "Would that I had already reached Gehenna." In order to reach Gehenna the soul must be purified of the dust and the aberrant images of the past life.

In quiet meditation, the *kaf haqela* is experienced. All the market-place images return. To enter into yehidut and to be confronted by images from beyond the rebbe's sanctuary is of this level. For the constant battling with such thoughts, there is no easy palliative. As the Besht told his disciples: "This is man's constant work in this world."[32] Hasidism does not attempt to solve this problem, yet a technique the Besht used deserves to be mentioned. It is close to some of the Far Eastern methods of mindfulness. The hasid is instructed to follow the thought back to its source. This is close, also, to what Theodor Reik describes as constant self-analysis. The aim here is a reductionism of another sort. The hasid wants to know from what divine attribute the "evil" thought has issued. Once he has followed it back to its source, he can cause it to yield something special in the service of God, which he had hitherto been unable to attain. (R. Shneur Zalman, it should be noted, does not suggest this practice for the average man.) The person who has completed this level of reparation is ready to enter Gehenna.

Hot and Cool Alienation

No Jewish soul can remain in purgatory more than twelve months, because Abraham stands at the gate of purgatory and anyone who has entered into the Abrahamitic covenant by circumcision is freed before the twelve-month period expires. But Gehenna is incurred for the unatoned sin committed in the pursuit of pleasures gained illicitly, in a halakhically unacceptable, sensual way. These impurities so stain the soul that even the treatment of *kaf haqela* is unable to cleanse it. It then has to descend into Gehenna. Gehenna was often described in lurid physical details of fire and extreme cold; yet the rabbis warn again and again against the error of seeing Gehenna as a material entity. They point rather to the pains of anxiety due to the absence of background noise and to the depth of realization of the wrong done, and say that this constitutes Gehenna. Thus, every evil passion fulfilled must be seared out of the soul, and the soul, as if cauterized by this shock, is healed of the spiritual hemorrhage flowing from the self-inflicted psychic wound.

Gehenna is emptied on the Sabbath. Some contend that this respite is granted only to those who have kept the Sabbath in this life. Others disagree and say that Gehenna is emptied for all Jews. If not for this weekly bliss in which the soul is raised into the light of the Sabbath, the soul would be unable to bear the anguish of the week in Gehenna. The hasid who, in life, wishes for a Sabbath of bliss, will descend into the remorse of *Gehinnom* on Thursday night. On this night, he will recite the long Yom Kippur confession and seek to feel the remorse like fire, and his alienation from God like ice.

The Miqveh, River of Light

When a soul is ready to enter *Gan Eden* (Paradise), it must first be immersed in the River of Light that flows from the fervent perspiration of the Heavenly Hosts as they sing glory to the Highest. This immersion rids the soul of the remaining earth images (even those that were good in themselves) so that when the soul is finally emptied of them, it may, without further illusions, see heaven as it really is.

Both soul and body need to be purged in the River of Light. Almost every hasidic master imparted to his disciples the secrets of ritual ablution in the miqveh (ritual bath). The four walls of the miqveh represent the four letters of the Divine Name. In dipping four times, one intends, by this total submersion, to be included in God. It is told of one hasidic master that, when health or geography did not permit him access to a miqveh, he would gather ten hasidim about himself in order that they constitute a quorum of ten men, in which the Divine Presence resides; he then would bob up and down in their circle saying, "miqveh Yisrael HaShem." This was done in accordance with Rabbi Akiva's statement:

> Beatific is Israel. Before whom do you purify yourself and who purifies you? Your Father in heaven, He purifies you, as it is written, "The hope of Israel is God." Do not interpret "the hope of Israel," but "the *miqveh* of Israel, the immersion pool of Israel is God."[33]

The miqveh is often discussed and interpreted as the feminine element of the Divine: dipping in the miqveh therefore constitutes a return to the Divine Womb.

In hasidic literature, the pool of souls is called *guf*. The Sages declare that the Messiah, the son of David, will not come until all the souls have issued out of the *guf*, the body. Who is that body? According to the Zohar,[34] we are speaking of *gufa d'malka*, the body of the King, the very being of the King. The ultimate hope of prayer, of dipping in the miqveh, and of death is *lehishta'ava b'gufa d'malka*, to be drawn into the very body and being of the King. Thus, as the body dips itself into the miqveh, the soul dips itself in the higher spheres of miqveh, up to the level of the River of Light. The River of Light is the miqveh derived from the sweat of the

heavenly hosts, and immersion therein washes off the images of the soul.
The miqveh does the same for the body, and thereby begins its purification.

Paradise and Higher Levels

The rebbe often wishes that he could spend more time with hasidim
who desire help on the higher, more illuminative levels of the soul. Yet the
attitudes toward spiritual work of this calibre express a dichotomy. Those
rebbes who were proponents of Tzaddikism (notably R. Shlomoh of Karlin)
felt that hasidim need not work on these higher levels, and that their rebbe
would raise them through his own effort. On the other hand, great
masters such as R. Shneur Zalman taught that the hasid, though guided by
the rebbe, should do his own work. R. Shneur Zalman worked to render
such instructions into a system for the non-tzaddik, the *beynoni*. He led his
hasid to more exalted spheres of Love and Awe; yet he did not teach that a
person could raise himself any higher than his soul's origin permitted,
even though he demanded tremendous exertion of his hasidim in order
that they attain levels higher than they themselves thought possible.

R. Nahman of Bratzlav saw no barriers impeding the ascent of souls.
"Do not say that I arrived where I did because of an exalted soul: it was
work that raised me and can raise you also."[35] Yet, despite the attitude
expressed in this view, he also made statments reflecting a paternalistic
attitude. Perhaps he was advocating a double standard, one for disciples
and another for lesser hasidim.

Another dichotomy existed between the rebbe who insisted that his
central mission was to counsel on matters of spiritual work, and the rebbe
who counseled only on personal problems of a material nature. R. Shneur
Zalman insisted that hasidim come to see him only for spiritual counsel,[36]
and even this only after they had exhausted the obvious.[37] He wanted to
help only in cases of doubt concerning the course of service a hasid was to
take. In this way, he reserved for himself the function of spiritual helper.
Here he was willing to take a definite stand, imposing his reading of the
hasid's reincarnational record and its resultant direction in the hasid's
service of the Divine.

R. Ber of Radoshitz, on the other hand, quoting R. Jacob Joseph
Isaac Horowitz (the Lubliner), maintained the following:

> One cannot tell anyone which way to follow. There is a way of service
> in the study of Torah, and there is a way of prayer, and of psalm

recital. There are those who serve by eating, and those who serve by fasting. There are those who serve by charitable acts, and others who serve in other ways. *Each one must see to which way he is attracted, and in this way he is to serve with all his strength.*[38]

The Lubliner, in allowing his disciples greater individuality, also allowed them greater productivity, and thus had more disciples than, for example, R. Shneur Zalman, who had many great hasidim cut to his stamp, but very few disciples. The ideal rebbe was one who could "listen" to the disciple; discover and maximize his strengths; and help move him in the direction to which he was suited.

The Goal

How does a hasid know when he has received illumination? Even for this, he needs to have a model. The hasid must meet an illuminated model in order to know when he has graduated beyond the point of preparation and purgation and achieved illumination. There is a tendency to search for hysterical symptoms of the illuminated state. This false tendency arises from the expectation that the earmark of illumination is the experience of something not under conscious control. The truth is a complete contradiction of this expectation. The illuminated person has become capable of acting freely and is no longer driven by anything beyond his control.

It is very easy to simulate the behavior of the illuminated without having experienced illumination, and it is one of the problems of the hasidic situation that the rebbe's spontaneous outpouring becomes the hasid's deliberate imitation.

Hitpa'alut, the state of ecstasy (derived from the reflexive verb *hitpa'al*), comes neither from without nor from within (autosuggestion). *Hitpa'alut* is translated as: to be in ecstasy, in a state of emotional stirring. R. Dovber of Lubavitch, the Middle Rebbe, utilizes the reflexive verb, thus translated, in order to avoid the notion that ecstasy comes either from "without" or from "within." The true tzaddik, the one who has experienced illumination, is always completely aligned with the divine process. He is utterly at one with and inseparable from this process. The rebbe teaches his hasid the way to illumination, but he does not transform his hasid into a tzaddik. The way has to be undertaken by the hasid as a service to God. The concepts, the spiritual direction and growth, the rebbe's help and the hasid's work—all are for the sake of walking the way of *avodah* (divine service). The yehidut is the place where rebbe and hasid covenant and plan for divine service.

THE REBBE: HIS MOTIVATION

Hasidism sees itself as *p'nimiyut*—the interior of Torah. The hidden, rather than the manifest, is its special area of concern. Although the hasid learns to expect certain overt behavioral patterns on the part of the rebbe, his faith in the rebbe is founded in the rebbe's hidden qualities, and he is forever in search of his master's *ruah haqodesh*—spirit of holiness. In considering his master's motivation, the hasid is not satisfied to see him merely as a salesman of observance, although he may tell the mitnaged that this is what the rebbe is, because he does not want the mitnaged to know about the secret and esoteric part of Hasidism. Hasidim, in comparing themselves with mitnagdim state that mitnagdim fear the *Shulhan Arukh*—the Code of Law—while hasidim fear God. Because hasidim will seldom bother to explain the subtleties of Hasidism to the "unsubtle" mind of the mitnaged, Hasidism has been accused of being antinomian. But the initiated know better. For the hasid, the study of Hasidut and the act of prayer share a common purpose: "that the essentially undisclosed core and substance of the soul be made manifest."[39] The rebbe's task is therefore to disclose the undisclosed. This is the supreme illumination. It represents the unitive state where the soul and God are one.

If the rebbe himself has experienced this supreme unitive state, why does he concern himself with his hasidim? If he has had the great illumination, so that he now knows the nature and Oneness of the universe, why should he involve himself in the world when he knows that it represents but a fleeting moment in eternity? The answer hinges upon the covenant the rebbe makes before he enters the state of illumination. He enters, like Rabbi Akiva, in order to come out in peace. His commitment to the world as it is, the commitment to make the hidden reality manifest, is the anchor with which he enters the void of the self, the unmanifested part of the soul. He partakes of the unutterable bliss of being and the unbearable pain of death and disease, discovering "He [God] Who in their affliction [of the Jews] is afflicted."[40] But he does not do so merely out of the promptings of cosmic curiosity. He enters the void in obedience to the command to serve God. Having glimpsed both the joys and the agonies, he is committed to reduce the agonies of God and His people by taking some of them onto himself. He becomes the *moreh derekh* (guide) in serving God so that others may share in the beatific vision of the self and may know that soul's self and God's Self are one.

In seeing the true Self, the rebbe has also learned the reason why things are as they are. Such knowledge creates difficulties. A rebbe who has this knowledge knows that certain things must be, and this makes it difficult for him to pray for his hasid. Unless he forgets the burden of his vision, he cannot pray that things be different. If he cannot pray for his hasid, he must send him to one who does not know, and herein lies the paradox: the person who can better intercede on behalf of the hasid is the one who is less privy to this secret knowledge.[41] With all the insight the rebbe has gained in his illumination, he may still have to "play the fool" in order to help his hasid. In this way, he is committed to enter into the folly of his hasid. He cannot remain aloof and survey the problem objectively: he must become involved. From his position of involvement, the rebbe may remind God that His reputation as King, Helper, Savior and Shield is at stake. The hasid who has implicit faith in the miraculous powers of God, but who has not yet received the great illumination, needs, from time to time, to see the manifest workings of God in order to sustain his faith.

The Rebbe: Sanctifier of God's Name

God can be moved by petitions for the sake of bettering His reputation among men. The petition after the Amidah prayer contains the words: "Do it for the sake of thy Name, for the sake of thy right hand, do it so thy beloved ones will be well." The supreme sacrifice can be demanded of Man in the name of God's reputation. *Qidush HaShem*—the sanctifying of His Name—is paramount in the Jew's hierarchy of values. Where the opposite of *qidush HaShem* is concerned, one is not to honor even one's master. The hasid committed to giving his utmost for the sanctification of God's Name can approach God with the petition that He do something for the sake of His own Name.

The rebbe is, above all, concerned with the sanctification of God's Name; his entire life is devoted to this purpose. Before revealing himself as a rebbe, the Besht asked that his colleagues join him. Only then did he feel free to make himself known in order that "His (God's) Name will be magnified and sanctified."[42] The fact that the rebbe is always in the public eye must not hinder him from acting freely; but his intention must always be "for the sake of heaven." No task that will bring about the sanctification of heaven's name can be considered too menial.

The rebbe does not hesitate to use miracles if they further the sanctification of God's name. Whereas he will refuse to use them merely for his own repute, he will gladly do so to sanctify the Lord. Aaron Marcus relates how R. Menahem Mendel of Rymanov once prayed for the healing of a gentile lad. When the lad's mother approached him to intercede on her behalf, the rebbe asked: "Why do you come to me? Is it because I am a wizard?" Only when the woman protested that she had come to him because, by his service, he was so close to God, did he agree to pray for the child.[43] The rebbe prays for God to intercede in order that His own work be better accomplished.

God himself desires the prayer of his tzaddikim. Why does God "lust" for the prayers of the righteous? Why does he "lust" to dwell among man? Hasidism, in its wisdom, replies: "You don't ask questions where 'lust' is concerned. Instincts are their own justification."

The Rebbe: A General Soul

Another explanation for the rebbe's involvement with this world is his position as a general soul—*n'shamah k'lalit*. As such, he is really working instinctually for his own preservation. The fact that he is a "general soul" means that all his hasidim are like limbs of his own body. Hasidim often speak of the rebbe as feeling their pains and joys. Because he is a general soul, the rebbe is able to empathize with each particular soul.

> . . . Just as the child is derived from the father's brain, so, as it were, is the soul of each Israelite derived from God's thought and wisdom [*hokhmah*] . . . and He and His wisdom are One. . . . For through attachment to the wise [the rebbe], the *nefesh*, *ruah*, and *n'shamah* of even the ignorant are bound up and united with their origin and root in Him . . .[44]

Thus, the self-concern of the rebbe as a general soul ensures his involvement in the lives of his hasidim.

The Rebbe: A Sinner Making Reparations

Hasidism believes that its founder, the Besht, had in his previous incarnation attained the highest levels under the tutelage of Elijah the Prophet. However, since the Besht did not, at that time, share his attainment with others, he had to return to earth "so that the world would be filled with his fragrance." So too with the rebbe. He is a tzaddik, but being a tzaddik in private is, in a sense, a failure. In order to make good this failure, the rebbe must become reincarnated. Here, we see the syndrome of the Davidic Messiah. David, after his sin with Batshebah, pledges: "I shall teach the rebels Thy ways, and sinners will return unto Thee" (Psalm 51:15). The most desired epitaph for a rebbe is: "Many has he brought back from sin (*Malachi* 2:6). Disciples of the Great Magid of Mezhirech who became rebbes reported that those disciples who did not become rebbes had not sinned. Thus, a rebbe might have to be reincarnated in order to make reparations for a past sin, or in order to atone for his failure to share his illumination with others.

The same value syndrome obtains among hasidim. There is a saying that no one can be a hasid who has not previously been in hell. The esoteric is not accessible to the good soul because the good soul is simple and lives only in one dimension. Wherever a primal split has occurred (this is one of the many meanings of sin), the atonement must begin with the duality. Wherever there is more than one level, the esoteric, with its correspondences, appears. On the exoteric level, it is not good form to seek a leader who has been a sinner. On the esoteric level, none other will do. How can a soul seeking to repair its damages come to one who has never tasted sin? How could such a soul empathize with the sinner?

> A story is told of a poor man who came home very late on a Friday evening, coming very close to breaking the Sabbath. When the man desired to do *t'shuvah* [repent], R. Michel Zlotchover gave him a very severe penance. At a later time, the Besht involved R. Michel in the same situation and then rebuked him, saying "Now you see how heartbroken that poor man was. A slight penance would have been enough after such heartbreak."[45]

R. Arele Roth of Bergsas (and Jerusalem) tells of a tzaddik who did not wish to be reincarnated though heaven wished it so. Since no one can be forced to assume unwanted burdens, it was decided that he must go to hell for a few hours for a slight infraction, and then he could go to heaven. However, hell was heated to such a degree that even three-days' walk from hell, it was terribly hot. Upon discovering this, the tzaddik relented and consented to his reincarnation.[46] R. Arele also referred to himself as a "sinful rebbe."

The rebbe sees his life task as the sanctification of the Divine. Having known the great illumination, he knows the purpose of his present incarnation as well as of his past incarnations. He is also able to "read" his hasid's incarnations and prescribe according to the hasid's reincarnational needs. In helping his hasid, he is, in reality helping himself. In his service of the Divine, he is fulfilling the purpose of his reincarnation.

Chapter 3

Range and Variety
of Help Sought

When you find one who can take out your innards, wash them, and replace them, while you are still alive—that is a rebbe.

R. Yitzhaq Isaac Kalov (E. Steinman, *Rishonim Aharonim*)

He who counsels must not insist that his advice be followed. Nothing on earth is complete, and evil is included in everything. I am very firm—on not insisting.

R. Nahman of Bratzlav (*Nahal Nove'a*)

The whole Torah is nothing but 613 counsels on how to cleave to God in the world.

The Besht (*L'shon Hasidim*)

One is to ask counsel only of one who knows the secrets of Torah.

R. Nahman of Bratzlav (*Nahal Nove'a*)

I am not a learned man, but I know supernal counsels.

R. Zvi of Rymanov (E. Steinman, *Galicia*)

Three things one does not give unasked: a marital match, a loan, and counsel.

(Yiddish Proverb)

In every encounter between counselor and client, some problem is raised. We wish to survey the range and variety of problems for which a hasid sought help from his rebbe.

For the Jew, all problems can be divided under the headings: the sublime heavenly needs (*tzorkhey gavoah* or *heftzey shamayim*) and the needs of the body (*tzorkhey haguf*). There is, of course, a definite interrelation between the two, "for if you scrutinize all the prayers of Israel, you find only money; but if you scrutinize the money, you find only mitzvot."[1] As the Besht said, "God made the material world from the spiritual, and the Jews turn the material into the spiritual."[2]

Although it is not part of the hasidic way to sharpen the dichotomy between matter and spirit, rebbes did categorize their interest in counseling under the following general headings: (a) Physical—children, health, and sustenance; and (b) Spiritual and Religious—Torah, *t'shuvah* (repentance), prayer, and acts of benevolence.

SITUATIONS AND NEEDS PRESENTED

The hasid who comes to the rebbe has a reason for doing so. The rebbe has something he needs—an etzah (counsel), an exhortation, an opening for repentance, or an opportunity for learning Torah "as it is taught in the celestial academy." Or, it may be that the hasid looks upon the rebbe as a significant model for his behavior. The hasid may not even be aware of his reason for coming to the rebbe; but for the rebbe, there is always a reason. The rebbe lives in a state of constant significance: for him, no experience is insignificant. The hasid wants to learn how to give meaning to his life; and the rebbe employs the structure of the deep myth in order to translate experience into meaning for the hasid. The rebbe is the channel through whom all blessings flow to the hasid.

The rebbe is motivated to help his hasid by love and by his awareness of the cosmic import of his role on earth. The rebbe is aware of his hasid as a person in need. Even if the hasid does not see anything in particular lacking in his life, the rebbe utilizes all the means at his disposal to discover his latent needs and bring them to the hasid's awareness. The rebbe wishes to bring his hasid to *sh'lemut*, a state in which there is a wholeness to the totality of his life. According to the Talmud, one who has attained *sh'lemut* is "complete in his person, his body, and his money; complete in his Torah."[3] In Mussar literature, this completion refers to wholehearted and singleminded devotion to God's service.[4] In the Zohar, the complete man is the one who is "conjoined to his consort."[5] In Hasidism, completion becomes a combination of Torah and service in prayer and good works. The rebbe keeps this salvational model in mind when counseling his hasid.

The Human Agenda: Children, Health, and Sustenance

The rebbe's task is to help the hasid not only with his spiritual concerns but also with his more mundane problems. Yet the rebbe does not wish to deal only with worldly affairs. Knowing this, a hasid may play up to the rebbe's expectation by talking about pious matters instead of revealing his real concern. He hides his true concern by attempting to mask it with a more pious one. The skilled rebbe soon brings the hasid's hidden agenda to the fore.

Children

While it is not a matter of theological credal doctrine, to the folk mind a man lacks any real possibility of salvation if he is not blessed with male children who, after his demise, will recite the Kaddish. Ever since Elisha the Prophet promised a son to the Shunemite woman, the tradition of the holy man's blessing was kept alive in the popular imagination. Ever since Hannah brought her son Samuel to Eli the High Priest, the belief in the potency of presenting a child to a tzaddik for his blessing has remained alive. So great was the desire for male children that even if the rebbe warned the hasid that he might have to suffer or lose his life as a result of becoming a parent, the hasid agreed. The mother of the Hussyattiner Rebbe and the father of R. Isaac Safrin of Komarno lost their lives in order to have children.[6] Jewish family structure so strongly depended on surviving children that barrenness (after ten years of marriage) constituted halakhic ground for divorce. In spite of this fact, the rebbe had to be convinced of the parents' real desire to serve God in this manner; otherwise he refused the blessing.

Health

When a hasid came to the rebbe about a particular ill, it was generally hoped that the rebbe's blessing alone would provide the cure. The hasid would usually feel more reassured of the potency of the blessing, however, if he received an amulet, a *s'gulah*, from the rebbe. At times rebbes even prescribed medicinal cures. These ranged from the herb cures of the Besht to the highly sophisticated medicinal prescriptions of the Piotrikover Rebbe-Doctor (also known as the Zalushiner Rebbe) Dr. David Bernard,[7] and the pre-World War II Rebbe of Piasetzno.

Physical health was also a condition of *sh'lemut*. A sick person is exempt from observance of mitzvot,[8] yet man must perform the mitzvot in this life. On this basis, the hasid sought the rebbe's help. However, the rebbe did not always heal. At times he suggested that the hasid bear his ill health for greater salvational reasons. When R. Dovber, the Magid of Mezhirech, came to visit the Besht, the overt reason was his sickness. "If the Besht had wanted to cure him, he could have. Even the Magid himself could have performed the cure; but there was a reason for not doing so."[9]

The barren parent is "like one who is dead"; those who suffer from incurable disease, maimedness, or poverty are similarly compared to the dead.[10]

Sustenance

Poverty lay within the primary domain of the rebbe. The very word for livelihood, *hiyuna*, points to this fact. With blessing, counsel, and specific advice, the rebbe would help the hasid who lacked sustenance. Although some rebbes had a reputation for not wanting to help their hasidim escape poverty (some even prayed for their children to be forever destitute in order that they remain dependent upon God), generally rebbes showed great concern for the material welfare of their hasidim.

In all of these cases, whenever the rebbe was successful, stories would soon be told, bringing others to seek him out to receive help as well.

The Social Agenda

Interpersonal Conflict

In cases of interpersonal conflict, many sought the rebbe's help. Husbands and wives, parents and children, in-laws and partners, all came to seek an equitable settlement and a reconciliation before the rebbe. Personality conflicts and cases of abandonment were brought to his court. Sometimes hasidim frankly sought the rebbe because they wanted him to persuade their recalcitrant spouses, parents, children, or business partners to do their bidding.

Gentiles, as well as Jews, came to seek the rebbe's help in settling conflicts among themselves or between themselves and Jews. They also sought his blessings and help with regard to their children, health, and livelihood.

Social, Economic, and Other Problems

Rebbes were sought by hasidim to adjudicate in cases of social and economic problems. Instances of *hasagat g'vul*, when opportunistic Jews sought to take concessions away from those who had occupied them for a number of years, and who had established a *hazakah* (holding, or tenure) were arbitrated by the rebbe.

As noted earlier, economically the hasid depended largely on the country squire. The payment of rent and tax was a great burden. Often a rebbe was called on to help in a substantial way. Many rebbes engaged in the task of raising money for their destitute hasidim. When hasidim were incarcerated for nonpayment of rent, the rebbe had to seek their release by ransoming them.

Merchants needing a tip on buying or selling came to the rebbe, hoping to hear his advice. Partnerships were formed and dissolved at the rebbe's court and legal matters adjudicated. At times a rebbe would rule in a case and then help the defeated party by giving or lending him the money to fulfill his obligation.

The needs of the people were manifold. Financial problems were not confined to the loss of concessions or livelihood. Many a match was threatened by the inability of the bride's father to pay for the wedding and remit the dowry. Where else but to the rebbe did the hasid turn?

Problems such as forced conversion and the abduction of sons and daughters by the local gentry and clergy brought hasidim to their rebbes.[11] In each case, the rebbe sought to counsel and help.

Hasidim also came to the rebbe in the hope that his miraculous intervention might help them escape induction into the Imperial Army.[12] Even little children were threatened by Imperial decree. There were informers to the government who brought their own brethren to peril.[13] Hasidim sought the rebbe's protection from such informers.

Childless widows, bound by levirate law to their brothers-in-law, came to the rebbe for help in locating them. In cases where the brother-in-law had become legally incompetent,[14] they came to seek release by the rebbe's supernatural intervention. Lost articles and lost people were sought with the rebbe's help, just as Saul came to seek Samuel's counsel about the lost donkeys (Samuel 1:9). *Agunot* (forsaken wives unable to remarry owing to the absence of a Jewish divorce) came to the rebbe, hoping that he would help them locate their husbands so that they might obtain a divorce or bring them back home.

The Spiritual Agenda

The Realm of the Supernatural

In the supernatural realm, there were the ever-present forces of evil. Witchcraft was feared, and the rebbe was asked to render the demonic threats impotent. Incubus and succubus[15] oppressed the hasid, and they too had to be exorcised. Anti-Semitism was not only a natural phenomenon: the Jew was also attacked by hosts of demons. Hasidim came to their rebbes seeking protection from the witchcraft they attributed to the local clergy.[16]

The weather and its influence on economic conditions brought hasidim to the rebbe as well. They hoped that he would influence the upper spheres to give rain or snow as needed.

Matters Dealing with Spiritual Life

While a rebbe would address all the needs of his hasid with compassion, he wished most often to fill those arising from the hasid's spiritual life. After a whole day of accepting *kvittlekh* dealing with material needs, when the Apter Rebbe received a "Ba'al Shemske kvittel,"[17] one concerned with purely spiritual needs, he rejoiced. In responding to the hasid's material requests for help, the rebbe saw himself as freeing the hasid for the really essential task of divine service.

Hasidim came to the rebbe to learn how to generate religious feelings to God. All social and economic preoccupations were only secondary to the service of God. The spiritual life was the Jew's main occupation in this world. In order to justify his existence in the service of God, a Jew needed to know which acts are pleasing to God and which acts are not. He could not discover the answer in books.[18] Not all commandments deal with outer behavioral actions. Commandments requiring inner attunement and shifts of attitude and context—the ones Bahiya ibn Paquda called the "duties of the heart"—have no talmudic treatises discussing them in detail. The rebbe himself, according to the Berditchever, was to be the tractate of Love and Awe.

The manifest part of the Torah did not satisfy the hasid who yearned to be put in touch with the constantly issuing voice from Sinai. He wanted to receive a hidden word from God, via the rebbe, in the present. The tenets of Hasidut, as defined by hasidim, are the innermost part of the Torah—the *p'nimiyut hatorah* and the *nistar*. No one but the rebbe can reveal them. The hasid believes the rebbe has actually beheld, rather than heard, the hidden Torah, and he consequently trusts in the rebbe's teachings. He believes that the rebbe reports these to his follower at the time they are revealed in heaven. The rebbe is revered as the Moses of his generation, and the hasid comes to learn the innermost aspects of the Torah from his master. The framework of the rebbe's teaching, however, is always geared to service—*avodah*, and not to mere indoctrination.

SPIRITUAL HEALTH

Not only was the rebbe concerned with preventing spiritual malaise and retardation, he often acted as the spiritual healer as well. He diagnosed spiritual illnesses and wrote both prophylactic and curative prescriptions. Yet, in spiritual matters, some rebbes refused to cure one who had gone astray if the party reporting the case was not himself deeply involved and ready to endure all kinds of austerities for the sake of his wayward brother. If this was not the case, the rebbe considered the report about the backslider as a species of gossip. Once the afflicted person came to the rebbe on his own, no effort was spared by the rebbe to heal him. Rebbes considered the work of spiritual healing a sort of resurrection.

REPARATION

T'shuvah *in this life.*   Penitents seeking a prescription for atonement were a basic part of the rebbe's ministry. In such cases, rebbes would often refer hasidim to another rebbe, considering the other to be a kind of specialist in the matter at hand.[19] R. Dovber of Lubavitch wrote a special compendium on repentance for a hasid.[20] Each rebbe vied for the epitaph, "Many did he turn from sin." The implicit promise of many a rebbe to his hasidim was that anyone who had once touched his doorknob would not die unrepentant.[21] Whereas in the past, penitents were treated to a uniform prescription intended to repair the sin, Hasidism came to treat the sinner and not his symptoms.

Since *t'shuvah* comprises lower and higher aspects, it was not enough for the rebbe to assist his hasid through the preliminary levels of remorse and acceptance of future discipline. He also prescribed reparative acts according to the hasid's individual life style. The rebbe gloried in teaching the hasid ways of service beyond the reparative levels. How to achieve Love and Awe before God, how to meditate—these were among the questions R. Shneur Zalman answered in his *Tanya*. From his preface to the book, we learn that many hasidim raised the identical questions with him. A literature of recipes arose, paralleling such literatures in other cultures.

Tiqun (*reparation*) *after death*.   Even after death, a rebbe had obligations toward his hasidim. If a hasid died during the rebbe's lifetime, he could still hope for the rebbe's intervention on his behalf.[22]

A hasid who dreamed that his parents were suffering in the afterlife would entreat the rebbe to help them. A hasid dreaming that he was called to the other life would approach the rebbe to ask his help in avoiding the summons. Hasidim sought the rebbe's advice in choosing names for their newborn children in order to placate demands from the other world. No hasid dared act in relation to the deceased without the counsel and guidance of the rebbe. Often the survivor needed the rebbe's counsel on how to make reparations and amends to the deceased one. It was easier to expiate sins committed against God or against a living person; both were still accessible to reparations. But once the other was deceased, the hasid needed the rebbe.

The next section explores why hasidim brought all these needs to the rebbe, what they expected him to do to fill them, and what they thought of him and of themselves in relation to him.

IMAGES OF SPECIFIC HELPERS AND THEIR CLIENTS

In all of the helping professions, there is a correlation between the expectations of the patient and the specialization of the helper. In the early period of Hasidism, hasidim knew nothing of specialists. The word *rebbe* and the Rebbe who resided in their vicinity were synonymous. Even today, a rebbe is identified by the locality that produced him. However, when referring to their *own* rebbes, hasidim will omit the geographic identifier (Lubavitcher, Satmarer, etc.) and speak of "the Rebbe, may-he-be-well-and-healthy." It is the rebbe who shapes his image in the minds of his hasidim. Specific images are formed by the individual personality and professional traits of the rebbe. When Hasidism expanded and there were several rebbes in a given area, people came to see them in terms of the function in which they excelled. This amounted to specialization.

The Rav: The Community Rabbi

For all the revolutionary impetus of Hasidism, it was unable to dislodge the simple faith of the population in the masters of Torah and in the *rav* (ordained rabbi) of the community. Although some rebbes wanted to unseat this popular piety (*sheynfrumkeit*), R. Shneur Zalman objected to this. [23] He did not want to see the students of Torah degraded in the eyes of the simple folk. The Magid of Mezhirech wanted his great disciples to become communal rabbis. Rabbi Jacob Joseph of Polnoye served as the model rebbe-rabbi. Since the Besht, his master, maintained him in this position, he served also as the model for Rabbi Levi Yitzhaq of Berditchev,[24] and for Rabbi Shmuel Shmelke Halevi Horowitz of Nicholsburg, and his brother, Rabbi Pinhas of Frankfurt am Main. R. Shneur Zalman was called the Rav of the *Hevriyah*, the group of the Magid's disciples. R. Hayim of Chernowitz served as a communal rabbi in Galicia.

Many rebbes preferred the appellation *rav*. R. Shalom Roqeah of Belz was known as the Belzer Rav. R. Hayim Halberstamm of Zans was known as the Zanzer Rav, and his dynasty kept this title as well. The present-day descendants of the Halberstamm-Zans dynasty are know respectively as the Bobover, and Klausenburger Rav. Satmarer hasidim refer to their rebbe as "the Rav."

As a communal rabbi, the rebbe enjoyed the established authority predicated on the old Torah hierarchy. In the popular view, the ordained rabbi decided not only the law on earth, but also the law for heaven. Thus, people felt that they could come to him and summon even God to judgment. The ordained rabbi was sought more for his rabbinical decree than for his blessing. God and Man had to abide by his halakhic ruling.

The Good Jew and the Seer

The Good Jew (*Guter Yid*)

The popular expression *S'iz shver tzu zein a yid* describes the difficulty of being a Jew; but he who did manage to be a Good Jew was favored by God. The simple Jew, who came to the public lecture at the synagogue between the afternoon and evening prayers, learned about the Tannaitic and Amoraic heroes who were the prototypes of the Good Jew. If Hony Hame'agel could pray for rain, and if Rabbi Pinhas ben Yair and Rabbi Hanina ben Dosa could intercede for others, he was sure that their present-day successors could do likewise. Even if a man had once sinned and repented, he could intercede mightily, for "On the place where the penitent stood, not even the most righteous could abide."[25] Menashe Unger reports how multitudes came to seek counsel of R. Berishil of Krakow.[26] He was once a debauched student and had turned penitent as a result of hearing a hasidic melody.

Heroic virtue calls for emulation, and if not for emulation, then at least for adulation. In *Hassidus un Leben*, Unger writes of a number of such popular types as R. Nota of Chelm, R. Nahum of Grodna (the cobble-stone-layer of Piotrikov), and R. Berishil, the penitent of Krakow. The hagiographer relishes this type of helper over the others. He is much easier to draw and to celebrate than the esoteric savant.

Rebbes reinforced the popular image by relating stories to their hasidim that extolled the Good Jew as a model to be followed. Though unassuming, this type of tzaddik speaks most directly to the condition of people struggling to become Good Jews themselves. Stories of R. Leib Sures, who confronted the Austrian Emperor, were not too fantastic for the popular imagination. For such virtue, nothing was too marvelous a reward.

The Good Jew was a paragon of trust in God. He never allowed cash to remain in his house overnight. Each day God helped him anew. How could he keep cash on hand if there were people in need all around him? Even when the Good Jew is in debt, he gives freely to help another. When the rebbe's majordomo upbraids the rebbe upon discovering that a large sum has been given to a hasid to help him pay his bills, the rebbe only turns the occasion into an object lesson.[27]

The Chernobiler and Ruzhiner dynasties acted largely in the manner of the Good Jew. There was less emphasis on study and prayer than on the overall balance of Torah, worship, and charitable actions. The Good Jew did not have to stress his miracle-working ability. This was an implicit by-product of his being a Good Jew.

The Seer

Just as the Good Jew followed the talmudic model, so the Seer followed the prophetic model. The Seer of Lublin and his disciple, R. Zvi of Zyditchov, were such seer types. When someone asked them for advice concerning a match, they would look—clairvoyantly—to see the bride or groom and, on that basis, decide whether or not the match was a good one. This vision was considered possible "in the light of the first day of creation" when Adam sinned and this light was hidden from the world. It was made available to the tzaddikim for their use. In this light, it is possible to see from one end of the earth to the other.[28] The Besht, the prototype for all rebbes, kept the Zohar on his desk and "when he needed to see, he would look into the Zohar and see."[29] The Ruzhiner would say: "Let us recite a few chapters of the Psalms and our sight will clear, and then we shall see."[30]

Stories like these are the mainstay of the hasidic faith in the rebbe. Such stories are currently even told about the masters of the present.

The Miracle Worker and Healer

The Ba'al Mofet

The rebbe was seen as a *ba'al mofet*—master of the (miraculous) sign or marvel. *Mofet* (pl. *moftim*), the sign come to pass—the synchronicity experienced as extraordinary coincidence and beyond expectation—was promised to the true prophet.[31] Yet, as the opponents of Hasidism were quick to point out, a false prophet could also give such a sign.[32]

These signs were assumed to be produced by practical Kabbalah. The Besht, working a combination of the sacred acronyms of the *Ana b'koah* prayer, was able to achieve miracles.[33] Though knowledge of these combinations was considered essential,[34] the working of miracles by pure faith was considered more elegant.[35] Only fools thought that they could gain this knowledge from books.[36]

R. Ber of Radoshitz based his entire ministry on *moftim*, declaring that it was his task to utilize them for the sanctification of God's name.[37] Other rebbes agreed that it was necessary to use such signs from time to time.[38] During his training a disciple may be too busy learning other things from his master to learn how to perform the *mofet*; it is nevertheless essential that he gain this knowledge.[39] Once he becomes involved in guiding hasidim, he will need to know how and when to perform *moftim*. It is emphasized, however, that their use should not be indiscriminate, for "only a very great tzaddik can effect them without upsetting other levels in a person's balance."[40] "Not everything the Besht could do may we do."[41]

Some very great rebbes, aware of the ultimate benefits of a particular difficulty confronting a hasid, may not wish to alter his situation; instead, they will refer him to a lesser rebbe in the hope that the other, being less farsighted, will effect the change.[42] The hasid's request for a *mofet* shows little faith in God's plan.[43] Hasidim consider it weak and shameful to ask the rebbe to perform one. The rebbe's teachings are the central reflection of his purpose, not his signs. "I give you the cream [of the rebbe's teachings] and you want stories [of *moftim*]!"[44] one hasid rebuked another. He who thinks that miraculous signs can promote real change, bringing one to repent, is wrong.[45] One good deed was considered of greater value than a hundred *moftim*.[46]

A concerned mother who came to R. Shneur Zalman of Liadi, was told a miraculous story describing how the Magid had acted in a similar instance; the very telling of the hasidic tale was instrumental in the miraculous resolution of her case.[47] Generally rebbes had little to do with women, although many women were attracted to them through hearing tales of their miraculous powers. They would send their husbands to be taught by the rebbe. If, after making a few visits herself, a woman did not send her husband to see the rebbe, he did not wish to see her again, as his chief concern was teaching the men.[48]

Even though miraculous signs could be effected by study and involvement in *posqim* (halakhic decisors and authors of responsa) as well as by practical Kabbalah, the greatest *mofet* of all was to take a simple person and make a hasid of him.[49]

MIRACULOUS EXPECTATION

For the master of signs, it is essential to transform the time–space–person equation into miraculous expectation. Historically, as soon as reports of miraculous doings have spread, people have seen a fissure in the usually unvarying web of reality and were thus likely to embark on a pilgrimage. The hope—most often unconscious—is that some concessions from the harshness of life could be gained. The hasid hopes that, at a particular juncture in time, space, and person, the unyielding fabric of reality would give way to the supernatural.

THE NEED FOR PLAY

Miraculous expectation and surprise lie at the heart of man's amazement in art and his need to engage in play. From time to time we desire to encounter not only Kierkegaard's teleological suspension of the ethical, but also a temporary suspension of the natural order thus to gain a special value.

Expectation and report mutually reinforce each other in dynamics similar to those of positive feedback. The need for play, for the miraculous, originates somewhere between the instinctive and the learned. In such interplay, conditions prevail in which the magical and miraculous can be effected. However, when a sign has come to pass, this atmosphere is often attenuated, and some rationale of natural causation is offered by a skeptic. Recounting tales of miraculous signs has been not only a propaganda device, but also, like the drawing of a magical pentagram, an essential preparatory step in working the miracle. R. Israel of Ruzhin said: "I know no longer where and how to light the fire, or what words to say; but I tell the story, and it works also."[50]

THE MIRACULOUS AND MERIT

Hasidism did not innovate the search for the miraculous. From the time that Joshua made the sun stand still, the existence of the Holy Man was part and parcel of Jewish expectation. The *mofet* existed to prove the truth of the message of the prophet.[51] Had Israel not marveled at Moses' miraculous powers, the Exodus would never have happened. The expectation, based on another, redeemed order of being, marked the beginning of redemption. The redemptive feature of the sign is one of the justifications for its hasidic use. Persons beset with problems have a limited set of expectations. Often they have exhausted all avenues of action in the natural order of things. This serves only to confirm and reinforce their problems. But as soon as they can stretch their horizon, they are capable of therapeutic redemption through miraculous expectation.

To work a miracle, the rebbe must have a balance of merit in his account. The scandal of the miracle demands a rationale in consonance with the believer's world view. God's caprice in "favoring whom I shall favor"[52] needs to be explained in terms of some moment of great merit. When R. Barukh of Mezhibuzh referred some hasidim to a drunk whose blessing proved potent, he had to explain the source of this merit in terms of a heroic act of virtue. When R. Abraham Joshua Heschel of Apt could find no such merit in an innkeeper whose blessings were miraculously potent, and the latter confessed that he had taken God on as a partner, R. Abraham pointed to the talmudic laws of partnership in order to explain the efficacy of the innkeeper's blessings.

From a Torah perspective, the supernatural order of the miraculous is essentially "natural." In fact, this idea is so firmly implanted in the Jewish folk mind that it gave rise to jests during Israel's War of Independence: "There were two causes of our victory, one natural and one supernatural. The natural—God helped; the supernatural—so small an army won over such a large one." Or, "Don't rely on miracles! Recite psalms!"

After the fact, the "miracle" had to be fitted into the rational scheme of things. Divine grace was not altogether gratuitous. It demanded some acts of merit, not only on the rebbe's part but also on that of the hasid. The hasid had to commit himself to the miraculous scheme of things in order to render it "natural." If he was lacking in merit, he could not rely on miracles but had to recite psalms.

In short, the *ba'al mofet* (master of signs) was sought because of his reputation. Expectation was reinforced by report. The ba'al mofet was the answer to the expectation of a hasid in need. The ba'al mofet's greatest desire was to bring his hasid to spiritual regeneration—to *t'shuvah*. "He who repents becomes as one who is newborn." On the spiritual plane, this amounts to the resurrection of the dead. Even when a hasid had another rebbe as his master, the master of signs was still properly accessible to him. To seek his help was permissible within the hasidic milieu.

The Healer

The roles of healer and miracle worker are interrelated, at least in the popular mind. There were some rebbes who took to the healing ministry as a result of their pastoral work, and there were some, though not many, who took to their pastoral work as a result of their healing ministry. They recognized that healing involved the whole man. The rebbe, in the roles of healer and miracle worker, is still active in the present.

HEALING: AN ETHICAL CONCERN

The Bible sees the causes of sickness in ethical terms. Health is reward and sickness is punishment. To be healed is to be reconciled with God. The tzaddik serves as an instrument of reconciliation. The master of signs acts as if the disease were only a backdrop for God's saving power. The healer acts as if disease is self-inflicted. The patient needs to be healed, but not only symptomatically; the cause of the disease, which is sin, must be removed as well.

Healing depends on repentance. The biblical "I shall heal them from their savagery"[53] refers to the healing of repentance. Menasse, the King, was healed by his penitence.[54] Na'aman, the Syrian general, was healed when he followed the counsel of Elisha.[55] The cure was a miracle to which he contributed by changing his life. Pleading with Elisha, Na'aman said that he may prove unable to utterly abandon his idolatrous mode of life, but promised that his intention would never swerve from a commitment to the God of Israel.

The story of Na'aman and Elisha is a good model for understanding hasidic healing. Elisha healed to enhance, increase, and sanctify Divine reputation. The Besht also traveled to heal a young woman for this reason. Second, Elisha made his healing dependent on some act of collaboration on Na'aman's part. The rebbe does likewise. Third, Elisha expected a change of heart, as does the rebbe.

REFERRAL

Some rebbes were in the habit of referring their hasidim to specific physicians. Some of them diagnosed illnesses and sent the hasid to the physician for therapy. It is important to note that the services of a physician, when utilized, were required only for therapy, and not for diagnosis or prognosis.

The rebbe did not see himself as a physician or miracle worker unless he could exact from the hasid some change for the better in his religious or moral life. He wanted to serve primarily as a spiritual director. If the hasid was ready to follow his direction, he would exert himself in order to make life easier for the hasid.

The Gaon as Helper

The *gaon* is not like the ordained rabbi. The rabbi is qualified to decide what is permitted and forbidden, as well as on matters of life and death. The gaon is the pure, not applied, researcher in Torah. His power stems from his total immersion in Torah thought. He *is* a Torah. His study is a fragrant oblation to God. His merits are immense. In Jewish cosmology, it is assumed that if the gaon and the likes of him would not study, the world would cease to exist. For this reason, the gaon has often been approached to help individuals. In fact, among non-hasidim, the gaon has been one of the few targets of appeals for help. R. Ezekiel Landau was no friend of Hasidism; yet even hasidim speak of how he helped by offering the merit of his study on behalf of some sufferer. Such stories were also told of the Gaon of Vilna. Some rebbes, contrary to the usual order of Hasidism, did the same.

The person in need of help shrewdly counted on his nuisance value to exact the transfer of merit. By pleading insistently before the learned gaon, who was eager to resume his studies, the suppliant would finally get the *gaon* to relent. Generally, there was little communication between the gaon and the suppliant. The gaon had nothing to teach the suppliant that would speak to his condition. To be rid of him—the sooner the better—would create an increase in his own merit through his resumed studies. Nonetheless, the gaon would later tell of the greater insight he was granted from heaven as a reward for his concern and compassion.

The Son or Grandson of the Tzaddik—Parental Merit and the Sacred Graveside

All the rebbe's transactions are merit transfers. The rebbe, for whom the world was created,[56] and for whose sake it is sustained,[57] has all the merit he needs to effect sufficient grace for all his followers. If he could assist during his lifetime, when limited to the body's space and time, how much greater his help could be after his demise.[58] Were it not for the intercession of the saints in heaven, earth could not exist for even one moment.[59]

Parental merit is linked to the promise of redemption. Rabbi Barukh of Mezhibuzh made the parental merit of his grandfather, the Besht, the issue of much of his ministry. In Poland and Galicia, the term *eynikl*, grandson, came to denote a derivative rebbe. The rebbe's grandson did not need to claim heroic virtue for himself. He could, however, act as his ancestor's proxy and by his merit. Rebbes who had a unique contribution to make would value their pedigree for less than their own achievement and merit. R. Nahman of Bratzlav saw himself as being a *hidush*, independent of his great grandfather, the Besht. Not many children and grandchildren dared to make real innovations. Instead, they saw themselves as their parents' deputies, zealously guarding the rules of the ancestral heritage.

Hasidim are ambivalent about this aspect of their rebbes. At times they cannot wait for their rebbe to introduce change, while at other times they accuse him of straying from the ancestral path. One rebbe addressed the core of this ambivalence: "I am just like my father. He did not ape anyone; neither do I."[60]

The rebbe's direct descendant is basically at the service of the more conservative hasidic element. He acts in a scenario of ever more constricting rules. Since he cannot take the responsibility of updating the conventions established by his illustrious forefather, he retreats to the safe middle, away from the growing edge. Persons in need of help nevertheless come to him with confidence. He, after all, will not embarrass them as much as his ancestor—who was a rebbe by his own achievement—might have done. He will be content to cement their loyalties to the ancestral dynasty and its forms and practices. However, inevitably these forms will become devoid of charisma—a fact he cannot escape while acting in this role.

Much of the ministry of one who works on ancestral merit centers about prayers offered at the ancestor's graveside. Graves have been mankind's favorite holy places. The catacombs of Rome were only a transfer of the liturgy from the Cave of Makhpelah and Rachel's Tomb. If the church is not at a graveside, the reliquary turns it into one. So too does the naming of the church in honor of a particular saint pledge his merit to the worshiper. Similarly, the grave of the tzaddik has become the goal of pilgrimages, and many a cure and miracle have been reported as the result of such a pilgrimage.

Rebbes reported the occurrence of many visions and communications with ancestors[61] and teachers as the result of graveside visits. This inspired and reinforced hasidic belief in the transfer of ancestral merit to the hasid's account. The present-day hasid still feels that he can gain access to the rebbe via his descendants.

The Block Rebbe

By "block rebbe" we mean the relatively recent American phenomenon (1900–1940) of a hasidic rebbe, generally of the *eynikl* variety,[62] who practiced his ministry in the Bronx or Brooklyn or the Lower East Side in New York. These rebbes used their insight primarily to help those living on their own block. Often the block rebbe assumed a patriarchal stance, sharing, as a grandfather would, in the joys and sorrows of the neighborhood. He would help by intercession and reassurance, counsel and guidance. His clients would be both Jews and Gentiles. While the block rebbe was generally supported by one or several *landsmanschaften*, his clients did not have to be his European *landsleit*.

Block rebbes are now generally on the wane. The lack of a large hasidic constituency, which had reduced block rebbes to mendicancy, proved discouraging to the rebbes' children. They did not train for and perpetuate their parent's calling. Prior to pastoral counseling by modern rabbis, these block rebbes filled an important helping role for the immigrant population.

The Kabbalist

Kabbalist, mystic, and *ba'al m'qubal* all refer to one who has become adept in the secret lore, the Kabbalah. His studies centered on books like the Zohar and the writings of the Ari. His prayer was not the ordinary pronunciation of the words, but a secret code of permutations of holy names. Because of the kabbalist's belief that he served as a lamp lighter to bring about the effulgence of the Divine Spheres, the predominant view was that the kabbalist held the keys to bring about the influx from above. Who better than the kabbalist could bring about health, wealth, and progeny? Small wonder therefore that all kinds of practical powers were said to reside in him. If he managed to see "the light that illumined the world from end to end" and that "God reserved for the righteous," he could see and hear what others could not.

A rebbe's image depends on the reputation he has among the hometown esoterics. He is a great rebbe if he manages to impress and direct them. He will not do this by being kind and gentle with them. Instead, he wants to give them new light and revelation. The kabbalistic hasid wants his rebbe to be an open channel to the innermost part of the Torah. He wants access to ever new revelations. For the thirsting soul, the puzzle as to how the Infinite creates the finite, and how and why the Infinite is concerned for humanity, is never satisfactorily resolved. The way in which answers are newly wrung from eternal ineffability, expressed in the language of Torah, captured in the vessels of mitzvot, and experienced in meditation, is of utmost importance to such a hasid.

The speculative aspect of the Kabbalah, which gives access to the *mysterium fascinans* and leads the soul to the threshold of the *mysterium tremendum*, finds spokesmen and seekers in every age. In Hasidism, each great rebbe is seen as the repository of Kabbalah. Rebbes reveal to hasidim, both in the public lecture and in the privacy of the yehidut, the arcana that speak to their condition.

The key difference between the contribution of Hasidism and that of the Kabbalah was that these arcana became accessible to experience with the advent of the Besht. When R. Dovber, the Magid of Mezhirech, came to the Besht, the latter asked him if he had studied the Kabbalah. When R. Dovber replied in the affirmative, he was asked to interpret a particular passage in the Lurianic *Etz Hayim*. When the Magid had exhausted the academic exegesis, the Besht stood up and repeated the passage. This time the Magid actually saw the realities discussed in the passage.[63] This is what made him into a disciple. What was merely an esoteric game of verbal arrangements had, in Hasidism, become a profound experience. The arena of Kabbalah now shifted from the theological to the psychological realm.

Habad continued this tradition. With R. Shneur Zalman, there began a new era of reconciliation of rationalism and the esoteric. Even the academic Kabbalah gained in the process. For those who wanted more of the imaginative, R. Nahman of Bratzlav became the master. R. Israel of Kozhinitz, R. Hirsch (Zvi) of Zyditchov, and R. Isaac of Komarno were the mentors for those who wished to follow the path of the classical Kabbalah.

The Moreh Derekh: The Guide in Serving God

Of all the functions ascribed to rebbes, by themselves and others, the *moreh derekh* was the favorite. A latter-day rebbe, R. Arele Roth, wrote to his disciples forbidding them to call him anything else but *moreh derekh* in serving God.

The Besht and his successors saw the spiritual direction of their hasidim as the central function of their work. R. Levi Yitzhaq of Berditchev described the rebbe's work as representing a living tractate on Love and Awe before God. We have already noted that no book could give direction in this area; a living master was necessary. Although the rebbe taught the way of Love and Awe in public discourses, these served mainly to provide a framework for thought and to increase motivation. The real prescription for this work was given by the rebbe in the yehidut and in recipes and tracts designed for specific subgroups. R. Dovber of Lubavitch wrote ten works, each one for a different personality type.[64] While some rebbes directed their flock freely and intuitively, refusing to systematize their direction, others reduced direction to a science. Habad's most prolific writer of manuals of spiritual direction, R. Dovber of Lubavitch, describes his task as moral guide as follows:

> . . . I certainly have a duty and obligation to expound and explain thoroughly, in full detail, the various matters concerning the methods of worship in mind and heart, each thing in its place, stage and manner, so that he who has lost his way may not be confused and confuse others. This is in order, too, that a permanent edifice be built in the soul with regard to the light of the Torah she receives, so that it might all be planted firmly and become deeply rooted, tied with an enduring knot never to be severed . . .[65]

The Rebbe: The Head of Thousands and the Tzaddik of His Generation

Rashey alafim, the head of thousands, is a Biblical designation of leadership.[66] If he has no other merit than that of a Jephthah assuming the leader's mantle, the rebbe is still, for his generation, like Samuel in his.[67]

Israel is an organic whole. The rebbe is the head of the organic hierarchy. Other helpers are the nerves and the organs. Moses is vertically the head of Israel's totality in history, and the rebbe is horizontally the Moses of his generation. To each hasid, the rebbe is the head of all Israel, and he considers himself fortunate in having found the real chief of his generation. To be connected to the head in an organic fusion is of great healing power. Activity and verbalization are important, but the organic connection transcends any other in value and power.

In the hasidic world-view, all energy influx comes to the world via the rebbe. Those who refuse to accept the rebbe as head still stand in need of being nourished through him. A hasid receives his energies from the rebbe in a direct and loving manner. A mitnaged receives his energies in a roundabout way.[68] To receive energies indirectly is in itself a disease. To be aligned with the rebbe in a positive way is the first step toward healing.

To see the rebbe as a guide is to see him in an active function. To see him as the head of the generation is to see him in his salvational and existential function. Moses, in the Kabbalah, is the majordomo of the King.[69] The Magid saw himself in the role of Moses, as illustrated by the following story.

> When the Magid's beloved disciple, R. Aaron of Karlin, was away from home, the Magid foresaw his death should he return. Wishing to keep R. Aaron from returning, he used all sorts of ruses to prevent the return. When he was unsuccessful and R. Aaron died at home, the Magid's disciples upbraided him for not telling R. Aaron explicitly to stay. The Magid explained that he who is the King's majordomo cannot talk of what he sees.[70]

Moses' brother Aaron, on the other hand, is the majordomo of the supernal Queen. He is the great reconciler who loves peace and pursues it.[71] Some rebbes saw themselves as disciples of Aaron. This is more the function of the Good Jew. Both prophet and priest are in the service of God. Moses stands in the service of the divine paternal principle, and Aaron in the service of the divine maternal principle. Where the tzaddik seeks to balance his ministry between both principles, he does not fall into excess. Tzaddikism is a function of the preponderance of either too much fatherliness or too much motherliness.

Secondary and Occasional Helpers

Other Rebbes

Both the popular and the sophisticated helper need to refer to other helpers when the occasion arises. At times a rebbe will send a hasid to another rebbe, perhaps because he does not find it possible to empathize freely with the hasid. He may express this as an inability to accept the hasid without judging him, or as an inability to descend to his level. Not wanting to abandon the hasid, he sends him to a colleague.

A hasid may himself seek the occasional help of another rebbe, while in no way wishing to sever his ties with his own. He may find himself in the vicinity of another rebbe, or he may deliberately seek him out. If he does not wish to sever relations with his own master, he must pursue these external encounters with great delicacy, as indiscretion could result in banishment from his master. The rebbe feels that the hasid who does not follow his own master exclusively is fickle. The fickle soul will always look for easy shortcuts, seeking to recapture the "honeymoon" of the initial discovery. But in spiritual courting alone there is, for all the delight, little progress and an ephemeral goal.

Admonishers and Masters in Song and Dance

ADMONISHERS

At times, when the rebbe needed to dislodge a hasid from a "set"—a psychological fixation—he would send him to a *mokhiah* (chastiser, admonisher). The rebbe who finds that the disturbed moral condition of a hasid has become chronic must then induce a crisis in order to render the condition acute. This he does by sending him to a *mokhiah*. The full impact of his moral plight must be demonstrated to the hasid who has lived with it for many years. Because this defect has by now become strongly reinforced, it seems normal to him. The *mokhiah*'s job is to shock the hasid into seeing himself from a different perspective.

The "holy brothers" R. Elimelekh and R. Zussia spent several years in exile. They would seek lodging with a sinner and at night, in bitter tears, confess their sins until the host was moved to confess himself and accept a penance. At times, a rebbe would send a hasid on such an errand. The hasid would, by his constant example, stir the sinner to repent.[72]

MASTERS IN SONG AND DANCE

If verbal means failed to induce the crisis, a melody might. The Besht appointed one of his disciples to become a cantor. Cantor Mordecai of Zasslav traveled with his choristers, stirring people to penitence. Sometimes neither word nor music could induce the crisis, but dance could. R. Yitzhaq Isaac of Kalov (the Kalover Rebbe) was a specialist in this area.

The Mashpiy'a

Where constant vigilance and supervision were called for, mostly in the case of younger hasidim in training, the rebbe would send a postulant or novice to the *mashpiy'a*. Literally, *mashpiy'a* means influencer. In hasidic yeshivot, the *mashpiy'a* is the teacher of Hasidism. (For the teacher of Talmud and the manifest part of Torah, the term *rosh yeshivah* is used.)

A *mashpiy'a* often lived in a different locale than the rebbe. He saw it as his function to prepare the young hasid for his first yehidut. After immersing the young hasid-to-be in "six months of the oil of myrrh" (the work of penitence and purgation), he would then immerse him in "six months of spices and perfumes" (the work of individual spiritual grooming). Only then was the young man ready to "appear before the King."[73]

After the rebbe received the young hasid and gave him his direction, he would return him to his *mashpiy'a* or send him to a different one so that he might acquire the discipline the rebbe prescribed. The rebbe often appointed his son to act as *mashpiy'a*. This was the son's apprenticeship for the rebbehood.

The Shudar

Besides the mashpiy'a, the rebbe had another assistant—the *shudar* (pl. *shudarim*). *Shudarim* were called *shlihey d'Rabanan* or *shlihey d'Rahmana*. Both of these words are contracted into the abbreviation *ShuDaR*. The shudar was an emissary or envoy of the rebbe. His duty was to raise funds for causes that the rebbe supported. R. Shneur Zalman, for example, undertook heavy financial obligations toward the first hasidic settlers in the Holy Land. He sent his greatest hasidim, highly advanced souls, greatly accomplished in the service of God, to raise these funds. The rebbe assigned each such envoy a quota. The rebbe's envoy would come to a town, reside there for a time, repeat the rebbe's discourses, and counsel hasidim. During his stay, he would conduct several farbrengens. There, at the *shtibel*-conventicle, he would work through with the hasidic group the criticism he was moved to make as a result of watching them in their life situation. At times the rebbe gave his envoy specific tasks involving him in the spiritual direction of a hasid.

All types of helpers mentioned here are in the hasidic tradition. They are known to give help and are sought by those who need them. At times, they bring their ability and willingness to the attention of the public by direct action or through reports their clients spread to others. Together they represent an entire spectrum of help offered.

Chapter 4

How a Rebbe Is Groomed

I could have brought the Messiah, but instead I betook myself to mend you.

R. Nahman of Bratzlav (*Nahal Nove'a*)

I have no need for mending—I am complete. But you need to be mended, and I have come to help. But I can help only those who come to me.

R. Nahman of Bratzlav (*Nahal Nove'a*)

When R. Mendel of Vitebsk arrived in the Holy Land, he had with him a man who was his secretary-shamas. Once the secretary was overwhelmed to hear his master pray, "Dear Lord, how well known it is, and clear before you, that my secretary is a much holier man than I and by rights he should be the master and I should be the disciple."

A few minutes later R. Mendel called the secretary and gave him some menial task to do. The secretary could not keep from voicing his amazement at this double attitude; whereupon R. Mendel of Vitebsk said: "Yes, this is true. This is the transaction that I must have with God concerning my position and your position; but once I have assumed the role of master I must follow it through without equivocation."

(M. Kleinman, *Or Yesharim*)

How does an aspirant, operating within the hasidic frame of reference, become a rebbe? In answering this question, we will assume that the rebbe undergoes prior training, although the supposition is more fiction than fact. In the section below, we will also discuss the personality types best suited to rebbehood. Having drawn such a portrait, we will then be in a better position to view the various stages in the "training" of a prospective rebbe, the tests he must undergo to prove and strengthen his vocation, and the "gifts of the spirit" with which he is endowed and that aid him in functioning as a rebbe. Throughout our discussion, we will bear in mind the dangers inherent in the call to rebbehood. The rebbe must not reveal his vocation prematurely, as this would bring a host of problems in its train. Nor must he misuse those powers that have been granted to him in order that he may serve God. In short, the burden of responsibility that the rebbe bears—both as trainer and as trainee—is considerable. A young rebbe-to-be is always under the close and severe scrutiny of parents, relatives, fellow hasidim, and the rebbe. We will discuss the problems that a young trainee faces as a result of such scrutiny, and the ways in which he overcomes them. Finally, we will discuss the preparation of the rebbe-in-training for coronation.

REBBES: BORN OR MADE?

What is Meant by "Training"

It is clear that the rebbe needs to be trained for his work. Yet the word training has technical overtones. Grooming—like preparing, dressing, sprucing up, making presentable, preparing like a bridegroom—is closer by connotation to the actuality of the rebbe's preparation.[1]

77

We have no record of an incumbent rebbe's criteria for selecting a prospective rebbe from among his disciples. Nor do we have any record of a rebbe describing the explicit principles according to which a rebbe-to-be was trained. No rebbe ever went so far as to elaborate how he himself was trained. If only some master had spelled out the principles for selecting, training, and testing suitable disciples, we would know much more. However, no such stipulative statement is available to us. Therefore we must, utilizing the information we possess, reconstruct—though fictionally and ideally—a method of selection, training, and testing. In doing so, the reader should bear in mind that the image is a composite drawn from the anecdotal material at our disposal. It is not a profile of the *ab initio* selection and training of any rebbe. Obviously, we can claim no access to the supernatural guidance to which the rebbe lays claim in choosing, grooming, and crowning his disciples.

Imagine that, on the basis of our knowledge of the hasidic method, we were to institute the office of the rebbe. Imagine also that it is our task to find a person or persons who would serve as rebbe. Imagine that we would have to train him, or set up a training situation for him. How would we proceed?

Personality Types

From our reading of the literature, it appears that the guidelines for selecting disciples were based to some extent on a view of the optimal personality-type for a rebbe. Using the basic typological framework of body, mind, and soul, we will discuss the personality types best suited to the role of rebbe.

To some extent, the principle of selection is a projection of the trainer-rebbe's self as the optimal type. Hence, the Good Jew will look for different characteristics in his disciples than, for example, a rebbe of the Kotsker school. Here again, we refer to the categories enumerated in the previous chapter. Not all the categories mentioned there apply to our present discussion. Types like the gaon and the kabbalist cannot be discussed under the present categories, since their prerequisites are largely "academic" ones. Furthermore, they did not engage in the training of aspirants for rebbehood. Their disciples were not trained but taught. The gaon taught the manifest part of the Torah and his particular analytic and systematic approach to it. The kabbalist taught the esoteric part of Torah and the conceptual system by which it was to be appropriated. The types we are about to discuss differ from the gaon and the kabbalist in that they did take particulars of personality into consideration in the selection and training of their disciples.

The Good Jew

Among all the helpers in the hasidic milieu, the Good Jew is the general practitioner. His manner of listening and receptivity to the hasid in need is warm and fatherly. More than any other hasidic helper, he places himself into his hasid's situation and responds with compassionate concern. In doing so, he represents to the hasid the merciful God who is aware of his predicament and is ever willing to help.

In looking for a disciple, a Good Jew will, in all probability, feel most attracted to a disciple who shows the same inclinations. He will look for a man willing to run the risk of relaxing his self-control so as to enter into the emotional world of others. In selecting a disciple, the Good Jew might, like the Ba'al Shem Tov (who told the Magid a story in order to see how he would react), tell a story of a hasid in a predicament in order to see whether his disciple can feel the hasid's predicament, or whether he merely concerns himself with the abstract and conceptual aspects of the story.

For the disciple to demonstrate that he can empathize is not enough. The Good Jew also looks for certain characteristics of mind in his disciple. Unless the disciple is able to recover some kind of conceptual insight from a given emotional reality, he will be capable only of feeling and not of helping. The mind, therefore, that the Good Jew seeks in his disciple combines both feeling and intuition. The soul-type he looks for in his disciple is more maternal than paternal. This last is necessary to ensure that the Good Jew not be judgmental and limited in his acceptance of the future hasid.

Pronunciation, inflection, and local habit in gestures and clothing play a significant part in facilitating communication, and for this reason ethnic compatibility is a factor in the selection of the Good Jew.

The training of the Good Jew is directed primarily toward actualizing and exercising his inherent faculties with deliberation. The major scene of his activity is liturgical and celebrative. The rebbe will train his disciple in leading services. It is important that the disciple project and arouse infectious enthusiasm and ecstasy among the other worshipers. Without wavering from his own intentions in prayer, he must be sensitive to what is taking place around him. This dual awareness can be acquired by training. R. Arele Roth, in his talks to his disciples before prayer, makes this clear:

He who leads a congregation in prayer should be shown such a way that, singing well, and observing the melodic modes, he will at the same time lift up his broken heart to the Most High, and guard himself from pride. Once our friend . . . told me that until I returned to Satmar from the Holy Land, he was hired to lead the congregation in the great house of study. There he had to sing well, and he had no inkling at all that it was possible to pray and sing without self-consciousness. Now, in our house of study, he has already learned that it is possible to pray and to lead the congregation at the desk, chanting in the specific modes, and yet to be far from self-consciousness.[2]

The disciple is expected to absorb his master's modus operandi, and (within certain limits) is permitted to innovate and elaborate (mainly within the area of composing new melodies).

A Rebbe of the Kotsker School

As opposed to the consoling, charismatic type, the ideal of the Polish school is the person who lives in "perpetual crisis" before God. The Kotsker describes this state of unremitting tension.

He who seeks to be a rebbe must ascend dizzying heights and descend to vertiginous depths—all in order to seek the truth. He must constantly beat down doors—even if his heart bursts and his body disintegrates! Heaven and earth may crumble, but he must not give way. A rebbe who is not prepared to break his own head and skull, how can he teach others?![3]

The affective attributes necessary for serving as a Kotsk-type rebbe are a combination of acute awareness and empathy with the emotional extremes the rebbe hopes to arouse in his hasidim. The rebbe must not content himself with thinking that he understands these feelings in his hasid merely because he himself stimulated them. So high a premium did Kotsk place on individuality that the rebbe had to continually bear in mind the fact that his hasid, as an individual, responded to his stimulation in a unique way. The rebbe's empathy had to extend to an understanding of the uniqueness of his hasid's own feeling. Instead of operating on the level of warm, human interaction, a rebbe of the Kotsker school projects the image of the lonely man and expects his hasid to be able to manage as a "lonely man." When rebbe and hasid do communicate, they do so in momentary flashes. The rebbe communicates in hints rather than in lengthy discourses on his thoughts.

A disciple capable of responding to such a rebbe will most likely be a solitary person, given to constant soul-searching and self-scrutiny. He will develop intuitive abilities more than those of systematic thought. Engaged in violent battle with his own "shadow," he will be harsh and abrupt with himself and others.

Ethnic compatibility is of lesser importance, because communication is more crisis oriented. On the other hand, where the Good Jew does not need to demonstrate his prowess in Torah, the Kotsker type depends on talmudic idiom and insight for his "hints," and thus for his basic mode of communication.

The training of a disciple of the Kotsker school consisted, to a large extent, of unlearning much of what he had previously assumed to be true. All authority was to be concentrated within the disciple and would not reside in what he had been taught to venerate. As an old Kotsker hasid said to a young newcomer, "For a white beard, you are willing to sell your God?" The disciple's models were not the saintly holy men, but Pharaoh, the King of Egypt, who, despite all the plagues God visited upon him, did not budge from what he thought was right.

The disciple was expected to pursue talmudic study and to hide all "pious" mannerisms that may have brought the simple folk to admire him. When his fervor tended to spread out, he was to contain it and direct it upward. "We are here to raise heaven higher,"[4] was the Kotsker's admonition. The fervor that the disciple had to develop was not of the open, flaming kind, but the white heat of the center of the brand. "God wants the fire on the altar to burn with a small *mem*."[5]

When the hasid of the Kotsker school came to the rebbe, the rebbe snapped at him with questions: From? To? Why? How? Only the most earnest and unvarnished stutterings of the hasid were accepted. All embellishment and artifice were tossed back at him with a mocking gesture.

The Ascetic Hero[6]

Neither crisis nor paternal benignity is the forte of the ascetic hero. He concentrates on control and power. He is "the mighty man who subdues his inclination"[7] in the service of God. The more unusual his austerities, the greater his power in heaven and on earth. The ascetic hero will be attracted to a disciple who manages to transform the counsel he receives into rigorous self-discipline. Athletic types will predominate. Instead of giving himself to feeling, such a disciple will be more acutely aware of sensing. Since his teaching is primarily functional, he can either be one who reasons systematically, or one who grasps things intuitively.

The disciple of the ascetic hero is taught that he must make every effort to discipline himself in order to function well in all situations:

> . . . the foundation of all effort is that it does not make any difference whether one is up or down. One is like a woodchopper working for his wages. A woodchopper does not care if it is summer or winter, cold or warm: he always does what he has to do. This is the secret that enables one to eradicate all kinds of narrowness, blocks, and aridity of the heart. One can, through the very effort of the flesh, through effort and prayer, manage to manifest the hidden light that is contained in the block.[8]

The disciple is directed by this maxim of the rebbe:

> . . . one should never say: "I am not with it today." I tell you here, in this holy place, that if anyone ever again during his life says "I am not with it now," he is not my disciple. At least for that moment, he has withdrawn from the group, and he is not to be reckoned as my disciple, because, to my disciple, this phrase does not apply.[9]

R. Elimelekh of Lizhensk, the ascetic hero who bathed in icy water, rolled naked in the snow, and sat on ant hills, instructed his disciples to practice discipline in the following manner:

> 1. When you are free at any time from Torah, especially when you are sitting alone in a room without doing anything, or when you are lying in your bed and cannot sleep, you ought to meditate on the positive commandment: "And I shall be sanctified in the midst of the children of Israel." You must create in your soul the image (describing it to yourself in thought) of a great and fierce fire burning before you, its flames reaching the heart of heaven. And you, for the sake of sanctifying His Blessed Name, break the hold of your nature, and cast yourself into that very fire. Since a good thought is reckoned as a deed by the Holy One, blessed be He, the result of this meditation will be that not only are you not wasting your time, but you are also fulfilling a positive commandment of the Torah.

> 2. When reading the first sentence of the *Sh'ma* [Hear, O Israel] and the first blessing of the *Sh'moneh Esreh* [*Amidah* prayer], you ought to meditate as mentioned before. Moreover, you ought to *intend* that even if all the nations of the world would inflict the greatest pains on you and skin you alive in order to bring about your denial of His Blessed Unity, you would much rather suffer all these pains than, God

forbid, accede to them. You ought to describe this in your knowing and thinking as if they were actually doing all this to you, as if you experienced it all fully. It is in this way that you will be able to achieve what you ought to in the reading of the Sh'ma and the Amidah prayer.

3. Even at the time of eating and procreating, you ought to have the same intention. As soon as you begin to feel sensual pleasure, visualize and experience this image and then say in your mouth as well as in your heart that you would have greater joy and pleasure in the observance of the commandment: "I shall be sanctified" than from the pleasure you derive from the sensual enjoyment. This you will say to yourself time and time again.

As a proof of this, you must get your soul in such readiness that if they were to grab you in order to murder you in the midst of your eating or procreating, and would inflict grave pains on you, you would find greater joy in the sanctification of His Blessed Name than in this sensual pleasure. Be very careful, however, that these intentions and statements are made in great truth. These things must become engraved in absolute truth upon the tablets of your heart and in its very depth and center. Do not attempt to deceive yourself or the Most High.[10]

The soul of the ascetic hero is that of the mythic dragon-slayer in pilgrimage toward his individuation. Because his mode of communication is basically that of one who imparts strength to his followers, he demands great austerity and deliberateness of his disciples. His activity is concentrated in the areas of fasting and fervent, mighty prayer. Ethnic considerations are of little import, since his ascetic strength transcends and supersedes ethnic categories.

The ascetic rebbe trains his disciples to be "constant holocausts" (one of the ritual sacrifices in the Holy Temple of Jerusalem) before God in order to gain merit for Israel. This merit is dispensed to their followers in the form of tangible blessings.

The Habad Leader

While, to some extent, the attributes of the preceding three types are expected of the Habad rebbe, he is also expected to be a systematic teacher of Habad philosophy. According to Habad, "A rebbe's task is to teach Hasidism according to the spirit of the times, according to the needs of the people, and to accept 'ransoms.'"[11] The central scene of his activity is neither the tish (table) nor the amud (prayer desk), but the cathedra from which he "says Hasidut." He chooses as a disciple one who records his teachings "as he says them and as he means them."[12] Verbal and conceptual ability are at a premium. The mode of communication being very rapid, the pronunciation of the White Russian locale is an important factor.

Habad rebbes invested their greatest effort in hasidim who appeared to possess the proper "psychic mind and heart stuff for the [hasidic] doctrine and its acts."[13] Hasidim who "see each thing with a pure clarity, even things which at first glance cause the heart to become enflamed . . . have the ability to remove the heart's excitement and to inspect them with the mind's eye."[14] Only then can one "explain to the heart what it shall desire, and the heart in turn can bring into life that which the head understands."[15] Habad disciples have to have this special kind of understanding: but even this is not enough. A rich, lively, and detailed imagination is necessary so that the results of study and meditation can be translated into life. As the name Habad suggests, the mythic life of the disciple moves between the poles of the *wise child* and the *old sage*.

The training of the Habad rebbe is directed primarily toward absorbing all previous Habad doctrine, absorbing Habad elaborations by rebbes and hasidim, and acquiring an immense repertory of authentic hasidic tales to be used as illustrations at farbrengens. The farbrengen is the training arena of a Habad rebbe-to-be. While not too much freedom is given to the trainee to elaborate in the area of discourses, he has almost unlimited freedom in the area of song and informal talks.

The above typological considerations have their limits, in that they strain toward general types. Many rebbes, however, were unique in their combination of typologies or did not fall under any of these categories. Others, highly individuated persons, did not become rebbes as a result of being trained by others for rebbehood, but because their followers, appreciating their individuation, adhered to them. Dynastic rebbes, by definition, were not chosen but begotten, and therefore cannot be included within our typological framework.

The Rebbe's Ambivalent Attitude toward His Trainee

The rebbe who sees his function as that of training disciples can find no greater satisfaction. Yet there is a very real conflict involved. On the one hand, the rebbe needs to be able to see, in the progress of his disciples, that he is fulfilling his task, at least to some degree. On the other hand, when the rebbe allows his disciple to take over some of his own activities as a preparation for the future, and the disciple performs these functions well, the rebbe may begin to feel useless.

At the onset of Hasidism, this duality was not as manifest as it later became. Rebbes were more intent on training others than on maintaining their inherited position. The movement was new and live, the impetus was strong, and the disciple could not make any grave errors. In the early phases, the new and untried did not represent so much of a threat. Hasidism was prepared to upset the old structure. Later on this was no longer the case. What the opponents of Hasidism once protected, the rebbe and his hasidim now had to protect. Once the element of conservation became important, the rebbe could no longer permit the apprentice, so full of new ideas, to take over responsibility without himself being subject to conflicting feelings.

In Hasidism, the rebbe assumes the position of the father figure. He is guide and advisor, as well as someone to be feared. The congregation of hasidim assumes the role of "mother."[16] The rebbe therefore stands in the way between the rebbe-to-be and his own congregation. Hence, the oedipal situation: "If I were married to my mother (the congregation), I would be able to make her happier and lead our life better than this."

Thus, for a disciple to lead a congregation during the lifetime of his master—to even want to do such a thing—constituted lèse majesté. Yet several masters in Poland rebelled against this dictum and led congregations during the lifetime of their own rebbes. R. Elimelekh began the leadership of his group in Galicia, with the blessings of his master, Rabbi Dovber of Mezhirech. R. Elimelekh gave his blessing to his disciple, the Seer of Lublin, to lead a congregation during his own lifetime. Toward the end of R. Elimelekh's life, relations between them had become quite strained. Rabbi Ya'aqov Yitzhaq, the Seer of Lublin, likewise attracted Rabbi Ya'aqov Yitzhaq of Pshysskha, the Yehudi, as his disciple, and delegated the younger men of Lublin to his care. In order not to embarrass the Seer, the hasidim of Lublin did not refer to the Pshysskher by name, but called him the Yehudi. The fact that the disciple bore the same name as his master served to heighten the Lubliner's subconscious feelings of threat.

Rabbi Ya'aqov Yitzhaq, the Yehudi, did not outlive his master, but had already raised some disciples who were the Seer's "grandchildren," and who themselves became masters. When Rabbi Simhah Bunim, the disciple of the Yehudi, passed on, Rabbi Mendl of Kotsk assumed the leadership, though he was already quite outstanding as a rebbe-to-be in the days of the Seer. R. Mordecai of Izhbitz broke away from the Kotsker Rebbe during his lifetime. He did not wish to maintain his rebbe's way for himself and others. Nor, on the other hand, did he want to break the relationship. The conflict was between loyalty to a rebbe who had served him well, and the inner authenticity he taught him so well. They managed the conflict by living (and leading) away from the Kotsker Rebbe, and visiting him from time to time as disciples, bringing their hasidim along. In this way they could also claim to prepare their hasidim for their rebbe's teachings.

The rebbe was not fooled by his apprentice's tactics. Bent on preserving the old patterns, he had to be sure that there would not be any serious innovations on the part of the apprentice. Only when the apprentice was fully in the mold of the old, could the rebbe permit him to act. Yet, knowing his apprentice, he had to permit him some freedom. This freedom reinforced the ambivalence.

On another level, the ambivalence also manifested itself in the relationship between the rebbe-to-be and his fellow hasidim. Originally, the hasidim in whose midst the apprentice lived were more generous than their later counterparts. They too had loftier aspirations. They did not feel themselves convicted by the aspirant. On the contrary, he reinforced them in their own aspirations. But the latter-day hasid meets antagonism when he attempts to break through the peer lines and aspires upward. Once the rebbe publicly lifts his disciple out of the peer group, the other hasidim are challenged. The only response that will not incriminate them is to claim that the disciple's rise in station is due to his loftier soul. In this way, they can deny any real claim against themselves.

The modern aspirant may be discouraged in his aspirations by hasidim who accuse him of ambition and opportunism. "So you want to be a rebbe? Have you found fault with our rebbe that you can't wait?"

TRAINING

The rebbe's training can be viewed as a course of study derived from books, personal hearing and repeating of Torah, observation of and service to his master, and closely monitored *avodah* coupled with frequent yehidut, a supervised practicum.

Study of Books

A future rebbe's studies are the subject of great scrutiny by his trainer. The trainee will ask what he is to read and will be given special volumes of material generally not accessible to others. The rebbe had a number of volumes that he shared only with his disciples. R. Shneur Zalman had some volumes in his library that were off limits even to his disciples. These books were marked "Under Rabbenu Gershom's ban in this world and the next,"[17] and even his own son did not dare to read them. When a fire consumed a considerable part of R. Shneur Zalman's library, he asked his son if he could at least mention one item from these books so that his father might remember the rest. But R. Dovber replied that he had not dared to read them because of the seal. R. Shneur Zalman rebuked him, saying, "For Hasidut one should risk even the life of the world to come."[18] Hasidism's founder, Israel Ba'al Shem Tov (the Besht) was given for study the writings of R. Adam Ba'al Shem. So significant was this event in the life of the Besht that it became the subject of many hasidic tales.[19]

The rebbe examined his student on his reading from time to time and elucidated various passages. Among Habad leaders, a favorite reward for satisfactory completion of a theme of studies was the master's interpretation of an exoteric passage in an esoteric manner.

Study by Hearing and Repeating Torah

Among Habad rebbes, another means of instruction was employed. Oral instruction through special and private discourses was given to the trainee. The disciple would rehearse these discourses and then repeat them to his master, who would correct him and explain difficult passages.

The trainee would also request others to repeat discourses to him that they had heard prior to his birth or during his early years. He would insist on hearing not only their content but also a description of the setting in which they were given, so that he might live through the entire scene as if he had personally attended.

Although it was understood that both book learning and oral learning were essential to the disciple's training and development, generally the oral method was preferred because of the immediacy of its impact. When hearing a discourse from the rebbe or from a hasid well-schooled in Torah, a disciple could often understand an interpretation more deeply and thus gain greater insight into its meaning merely from the intonation of the trainer's voice. In addition, the oral discourse intensified the rebbe–hasid relationship and thus was specially prized by both. The rebbe could use such a discourse to show his approval of a disciple's progress. He never wasted a discourse on a hasid or disciple who would not be deeply receptive to it. To do so was considered the equivalent of masturbation.[20] Knowing the high value the rebbe placed on his discourses, the disciple was doubly encouraged when he received one.

Study by Observing and Serving the Master

Since the rebbe-to-be was expected to perpetuate the ancestral rules, he could not rely on mere verbal instruction. Many of his master's actions were internalized by the rebbe to a degree that precluded verbalization. The disciple's only recourse was to observe his master closely. He had to learn to distinguish between incidental and permanent elements of his master's conduct. If he inquired about what he observed, he would often be rewarded by his master with a tale of the origin of a custom or wont. Observing his master, the disciple saw him as a "supernal mirror." To know the divine became a matter of observing the master. "I have the sense that he was the *Eyn Sof* in a physical body,"[21] said R. Menahem Mendl II of Lubavitch in describing his own master and father-in-law during the week of mourning his death. This was not a theological principle; it verbalized the process through which he intently studied his master. As noted by Robert Katz, such intent observation is often accompanied by empathic submuscular movement.[22] The master's speech is very often listened to with unconscious subvocal speech movements of the hasid. All this leads to interiorization.

"What do you learn from your master?" To this question, R. Leib Sures replied: "I come to see how he ties his shoelaces."[23] In order to do this, the disciple is not content to be a disciple. He wants to become the personal attendant of the rebbe so that he may observe him at closer range. Once, while receiving a posthumous visit from the Besht, the Magid had R. Shneur Zalman as his attendant. It was a great privilege for R. Shneur Zalman and he told his descendants that he was both frightened and pleased by the honor. R. Zvi Elimelekh of Bluzhev once voiced the complaint, "When my grandfather served as rebbe, he still had some older hasidim who watched his every move and wished to know his intention every time he moved his spoon this way and that. Today no one cares except my Hungarian [R. Arele Roth]."[24]

The rebbe-to-be had to be very intent on observing his master; but he was not to mimic him. Close observance of the master is especially important among rebbes whose ministry centers around the *tish*—the table celebration. The table is like the altar, the rebbe is the priest, the food is the oblation, and the leftovers from the rebbe's plate—the *shirayim*—are the peace offering. The highly stylized meal is at once a liturgical act and an agape love feast. Periodically, the rebbe conducts the table together with his son or a disciple. This is the custom at the Bobover Tish, where the rebbe urges his son or another close relative-disciple to recite the *Eshet Hayil* (Proverbs 31:10–31) and to help with the distribution of the *shirayim*. Thus the rebbe can watch the trainee at work.

Study via Supervised Avodah, Frequent Yehidut, and a Practicum in Leading

Study of Torah is only one of the three pillars on which a rebbe's ministry rests. The others are in the category of *avodah*: prayer, worship, and acts of kindness. Therefore, in addition to his concern for the trainee's competence in Torah, the trainer will want to instruct the trainee and observe him at work in these areas.

The master instructs his disciple primarily at the yehidut. He gives him special tasks and asks him to report his progress from time to time. There are some acts that the trainee might be reluctant to discuss owing to self-consciousness or other inhibitions. Sometimes a master would surprise his disciple in acts of great fervor and devotion. A surprise visit from the master often makes it easier to discuss these matters after the initial shock and surprise subside.

When the master feels that his presence at a practicum session would inhibit the trainee, he will arrange the setting, assign the task, and withdraw. He may either observe from afar or wait for a report of the session. In this manner, rebbes have asked their disciples to take on the role of *hozer* (repeater of Torah), to lead the congregation in prayer, or to conduct the hasidic "table" or a farbrengen. (In Habad, the latter setting was the most conducive to unself-conscious acting, since conducting a farbrengen did not mean that the crown prince actually presumed to rule.)

Serving as his father's secretary, R. Yosef Yitzhaq was given the task of answering letters for him. These letters were later perused and constructively criticized by his father. When he was satisfied that his son knew what he was doing, he entrusted the counseling of the yeshivah students to him and made him the yeshivah's acting head. In making this appointment, his father delegated more responsibility to him. This gave the father further opportunities to train his son on the job. R. Shneur Zalman entrusted his son, R. Dovber, with leading the younger hasidim. This practice has continued to this day. R. Joseph Isaac, the late Lubavitcher Rebbe, entrusted several important functions to the present rebbe, his son-in-law, when he was in the process of training him.

The rebbe-to-be internalized the instructions he received at the yehidut. He meditated on them and expanded them to even wider significance:

"When my father placed this task on my shoulders," the Middle
Rebbe once said, "he said to me, 'The proper way to look at a Jew [in
order to direct him] is to see him as he stands in the primeval thought
of Adam Qadmon.'"

Three things did I learn from these, his words:

The soul as it stands in the primeval thought is on the rung of
"son." When it descends to become involved with a body, it stands
on the rung of "servant." But since I was charged to see him as he
stands in the primeval thought, I learned that the soul can be "son"
even in its lowest descent.

The soul as it stands in the primeval thought has such inherent
potentials that it can effect the task of *birur*—sorting out. These
potentials are reinforced and actualized in it so that the soul may be in
possession of the necessary powers to effect this work. But the
potential powers of sonship are hidden in it and need to be brought
into manifestation from the hidden potential source.

The soul as it stands in the primeval thought also includes in
itself all the souls which are yet to be made manifest by it in the
world's duration, up to the coming of the Messiah at the completion
of all *birur*. Although each soul is granted free choice in the manner of
its service, yet, the general disposition of this service is influenced by
such causes as parents in the parent–child relationship. Thus, a father
gives merit to his son, and then it may happen that the son's power
supersedes that of his father. On the level where the soul stands in the
primeval thought, all the details of its work here below are included—
whether it is to be active or passive, though in either mode, souls
receive passively from those above them, and in turn actively influence those below them.

Now the statement "The proper way to look at a Jew is to see
him as he stands in the primeval thought of *Adam Qadmon*" applies
not only to others, but also to one's own self.[25]

Sometimes a rebbe shares even his depression with his disciple.
R. Mosheh of Sambar once told how his master, the Seer of Lublin, said to
him: "People come to me in a depression and they leave with glowing faces;
and I myself remain in a depression, in a darkness in which there is no light
whatsoever."[26] In order to prepare himself properly for rebbehood, the
disciple needs to know that the master is not immune to depression.

In order to prepare his disciple for leadership, a rebbe may present
him with a dilemma and ask his advice in solving it:

The Kotsker once called two of his disciples into his study. "I have
two kvittlekh before me," he said to them. "One concerns a woman

who is in difficult labor. The other concerns a man who is mortally ill. It is the soul of the sick man that is to go into the child about to be born. If I pray for one, the other must die. Which one shall I pray for?" Ashamed to speak, one disciple kept silent, thinking, "If the rebbe does not know, who I am to make suggestions to him?" But R. Wolf Strikover, the other disciple, steeled himself and spoke: "Pray for the recovery of the man. Heaven has enough new souls to send down so that you can also pray for the mother and her child." The Kotsker was pleased with the answer, and said: "You have opened a door for me and invigorated me."[27]

THE TRAINEE AS POSTULANT

Testing the Postulant

Motivation and Determination

Since the position of rebbe is accompanied by status and glory, hasidim who are not suited to rebbehood, but who seek prestige (and who are blind to the attendant agony), might aspire to the rebbehood. For this reason, it is essential for the trainer-rebbe to test the trainee's motivation. In order to test a postulant's worth properly, the trainer must place all manner of obstacles in his path. R. Nahman of Bratzlav spoke of the obstacle encountered along the way with a certain wry love. "God is hidden in the obstacle. The wise man knows this; the fool turns back."[28]

R. Elimelekh of Lizhensk, who followed the model of the ascetic hero, was severe in his testing of disciples. At times he would not greet them; averting his face, he would wait for them to appear again and again, braving his "wrath." Only after the disciple had prove his tenacity by repeatedly seeking the Rebbe's presence would the Rebbe relent and accept him as an aspirant. R. Elimelekh once tested R. Naftali of Ropshitz by rejecting him with the caustic remark: "I don't want any thoroughbreds." Later, after seeing the strength of his determination, he accepted R. Naftali as a disciple.

The *bitush*—the verbal barb—and the counter-*bitush* are important means of sharpening true vocation. Sometimes the rebbe or an older hasid would expose a disciple in this way in order to test his vocation:

Once, during his father's incumbency, the Middle Rebbe, R. Dovber of Lubavitch, who was still in his teens, went to visit a small town.

There he found an older hasid whose manner of praying did not quite please him. When the young rebbe-to-be expressed his displeasure to the hasid, the older man grabbed him by his lapels and shook him furiously. "What did your father have in mind when he sired you, and what did my father have in mind when he sired me? How can you expect me to pray in your manner? As for you, you have not even begun to serve Him." Later, the hasid came to visit R. Shneur Zalman, his master and R. Dovber's father. R. Shneur Zalman greeted him and invited him to partake of refreshment, saying, "I want to thank you. You have made my Berl into a hasid!"[29]

There are a number of stories describing the tests used by rebbes. The Lubliner considered the greatest trial to be a temptation withstood, while R. Uri of Strelisk felt that an aspirant's patience had to be tested before he could become a rebbe. R. Moshe Leib of Sassov would ask aspirants whether they had yet reached the lowest rung in *ahavat Yisrael* (love of Jews): he pointed out that if they had, they could suck out the pus from the wound of a fellow Jew.[30] Buber reports that each Lublin postulant had to tell a tale about Lublin without mentioning the name.[31]

Sometimes personal and menial service constituted a test of the aspirant's worth, while at other times heroic acts of self-effacement proved the applicant's mettle. R. Zvi of Rymanov demonstrated his readiness for rebbehood by the manner in which he made his master's (R. Menahem Mendel's) bed. R. Arele Roth proved himself by his service to his master, the Bluzhover Rebbe, as did R. Bunim in his service to the Yehudi. The Zyditchover Rebbe so yearned to attend R. Barukh of Mezhibuzh's *Shir Hashirim* (Song of Songs) that he was prepared to die while listening, and R. Mendl of Kotsk demanded of his disciple, R. Yitzhaq Meir of Ger, to burn his talmudic writings as a test of his readiness for rebbehood.

Not all rebbes tested their disciples. Some rebbes were more eager for disciples and accepted them as soon as they showed interest. The Magid of Mezhirech, like his master, the Besht, accepted all comers, although he did so in a formal manner that was criticized by R. Pinhas of Koretz. R. Shneur Zalman likewise accepted all who came to him, testing them for knowledge and assigning them to one of the classes—*hadarim*—in his yeshivah. Yet, in spite of this fact, R. Shneur Zalman once tested his own grandson, R. Nahum. When R. Nahum, in preparation for his own wedding, was dressed in a new fur coat, his grandfather wanted to make a rip in it. When R. Nahum refused, R. Shneur Zalman said with disdain: "You won't amount to much."[32] R. Nahum did not become rebbe after his father, R. Dovber, died. R. Barukh of Mezhibuzh and R. Shlomo of Karlin courted every likely disciple and offered them all their knowledge if only they would remain. Yet for all their openness, these rebbes too did their own testing.

There were some rebbes who did neither courting nor testing, yet young rebbes-to-be sought their approval. These rebbes, like R. Barukh of Mezhibuzh, wanted to be "the head of all tzaddikim."[33] In this way, they undertook no obligation to train or test. R. Barukh's role was appropriated after him by the Apter Rav and by the Ruzhiner Rebbe (R. Israel) and his dynasty. When a young aspirant appeared, the Ruzhiner Rebbe would inquire about him, "He leads or travels?" (*Er fuehrt zu er fahrt?*). At times, the Ruzhiner Rebbe would honor a future leader. This honor was often indispensable to the aspirant's prestige.

Some rebbes, like R. Jacob Joseph Horowitz of Lublin, would not accept a disciple unless he would also spend some time studying under him. His academy was a finishing school for rebbes-to-be. Almost all the rebbes of Hungary, Galicia, or Poland had some training under him. Yet it seems clear that he did not so much train them as offer himself as a model.

In reading the anecdotal material of Hasidism, it becomes obvious that just as there is no one method of training disciples, so there is no one acceptable method for testing their vocation. Some rebbes placed more emphasis than others on putting the aspirant through severe tests, and still others ignored it entirely. Each rebbe had his own method of testing his disciple's motivation, and the method was often in keeping with the expectations inherent in the role played by the particular rebbe. The testing itself served a dual purpose. Those who did not have a true vocation were rejected. But more important, the testing served to reinforce the vocation of those who were "called" to rebbehood.

Self-Awareness

Another kind of test concerned itself with the postulant's self-awareness. The rebbe walks a narrow ridge. Knowledge of his exalted station must not give rise to a vertigo of pride. The lack of self-awareness, on the other hand, would disqualify him for the subtle work of guiding and advising others to help increase their own self-awareness.

DYNASTIC TRAINEES

The dynastic trainee endured even severer scrutiny than his non-dynastic counterpart, although his testing assumed different forms. In the case where the rebbe is born to the office, it is taken for granted that the father and mother made the act of conception a conscious and deliberate one. "These are the generations of Isaac, son of Abraham. Abraham begat Isaac." One rebbe, in explaining this redundancy, states that Abraham, the model of grace, deliberately begat Isaac, the model of rigor, for this was God's will.

The sanctification of the parents, at times complemented by an act of heroic charity,[34] is matched by vigilance during the mother's pregnancy, following the biblical pattern (Samson, Samuel). At birth, the infant is wrapped in a special swaddling cloth. Circumcision, the appointment of godfathers, and the naming are very important. Weaning, the first haircut, and the teaching of the *alef bet* to the child—all are matters of special ceremony and concern. (Later, the rebbe even atoned for the possible pain he had inflicted on his mother while nursing.) Teachers for the young rebbe-to-be are chosen with extreme care. The rebbe-father takes special pains to teach his son in private and instruct him in yehidut.

It is obvious, therefore, that a dynastic crown prince could not escape the awareness of his vocation. The little rebbe-to-be knew what he was and what he was to become. R. Israel, the son of R. David Moshe (the Magid) of Chortkov, in his youth was engaged in a talmudic disputation with a visiting gaon. Having proven his skill, he was scolded by his father, who explained that the Torah was not given so that he could show off. Often the young rebbe-to-be retorted hotly to such reproof. "How is it that you let yourself be led by the *yetzer hara* [evil impulse]?" R. Naftali of Ropshitz asked his son R. Eliezer (the future Rebbe of Dzhikov). "Could you not learn from him? He never weakens. He is always on the job." "How could I learn from him?" demanded the young R. Eliezer. In reply to his father he said: "The *yetzer hara* himself has no *yetzer hara!*"[35] The mother of R. Zvi Hirsch of Zyditchov would check her children when they returned from the synagogue to see whether they had prayed earnestly: she checked them for signs of sweat on their faces. Once she told her oldest son, R. Zvi Hirsch, that she had not found any sweat on him, saying, "Go and see . . . how your younger brothers are sweating. This is a sign that they have prayed in earnest. What about you? Just like a dry tree." Her son answered: "Mother, if sweat is a sign of prayer, then a horse is wiser than man; for only the lazy horses sweat when they run, but the good horses don't sweat at all."[36]

Young rebbes-to-be had a strong sense of their own authenticity. As inner-directed persons, they saw themselves as responsible only to God. Their colleagues and educators soon discovered how difficult it was to persuade them against their own opinion. "I was an orphan. No one taught me but God. Even before the Messiah I shall not bend, but insist that my teaching is true,"[37] R. Israel of Ruzhin is quoted as saying. At the age of six, R. Nahman of Bratzlav replied to his mother's accusation of religious laxity with the words: "I am a true *sar mera!*"[38] (one who forsakes evil). At times this attitude extended even to heaven. When he was not shown any new insights, R. Nahman wept until heaven relented and he saw.[39]

Rebbes-to-be would often hide their spiritual gifts, not only from outsiders but also from their own family. Parents and teachers treated them with great severity. R. Yomtov Lipa of Sziget was taken to the river by his father-in-law, who trained him. There his father-in-law chopped a hole in the ice, had him immerse in the river and, forbidding him to wipe off the water, had him dress and return to the House of Study to continue learning. This was all done in the urgency of preparing R. Yomtov, the future Szigeter Rebbe, to lead some day.[40] R. Joshua of Belz told his hasidim how terrified he was when, in his youth, he realized the full impact and meaning of leadership.

Once two children, the sons of R. Shmuel Schneersohn of Lubavitch, were playing at the game of rebbe and hasid. R. Zalman Aaron, then 7 years old, was playing rebbe, while his younger brother, R. Shalom Dovber, then 5 years old, played hasid. The younger brother girded his loins with a prayer sash and knocked softly at the door, and when asked to enter, approached his brother on tiptoe and said, "Master, please give me a *tiqun* for my soul." "What have you done?" the elder brother demanded. "I have stolen a pickle from Mother." At this point R. Zalman Aaron laughed, whereupon R. Shalom Dovber, in the heat of frustration, turned to his older brother and said: "You are not a rebbe. A rebbe never laughs at the distress of a hasid."[41]

Another time, the two brothers were playing the same game in the same positions. R. Shalom Dovber asked for a *tiqun* for not having recited the blessing after eating an apple. R. Zalman Aaron replied: "For the next forty days you are to recite a blessing out of the prayer manual after eating any food." "You did not do it right," his younger brother reproached him. "How can you say this?" R. Zalman Aaron argued. "I myself watched Daddy through the keyhole when a hasid asked him the same question, and I gave you his reply." "I too watched Daddy," R. Shalom Dovber replied, "But you don't do it right. Daddy always *sighs* before he answers!"[42] This childhood game proved prophetic, for it was R. Shalom Dovber who later became rebbe, and not his older brother.

The delicacy of a rebbe's calling and exalted position, balanced by an overwhelming responsibility, sharpened the awareness of the rebbe-to-be. His discipline was rigorous. His gifts were earned before he came to use them. What Gerald Heard calls the "heroic-ascetic" stage bestows upon the aspirant occult powers. It is in the nature of the hero that he earns his spurs. The trials of the chivalrous age can be compared to those of the tzaddik. He who has changed the darkness into light and the bitter into the sweet is given the Daughter of the King.[43] The rebbe-to-be is a knight errant, and the battlefield is the scene of his early combat with the evil impulse.

This romantic view stands at variance with contemporary sentiments concerning proper professional preparation, but for the hasid it was the reason for his affiliation with the rebbe. Where a favorable prehistory of a rebbe is not available, and some still remember him as a child who was worse than other, more pious lads of his age, the rebbe will not be forgiven, even though he has in the meantime proven himself to be a real and good rebbe for those who follow him.

When a rebbe has completed his son's training, he allows him to make his debut. He sends him incognito to other rebbes, who have to discover his presence among their hasidim. He sets him the task of guiding others and assisting him in his work. Sons are generally not "crowned" during the lifetime of the father, though on some occasions they have been.[44]

NONDYNASTIC TRAINEES

The nondynastic trainee faced certain difficulties that the dynastic heir did not. How was he to know whether his ambitions were identical with God's plan for him? The dynastic heir had fewer problems with his peers. They knew who he was and what his vocation was to be, and therefore did not force him into the peer structure. The nondynastic rebbe-to-be either had to risk the ridicule reserved for outsiders or for those who aspired to a station beyond their due, or wear the mask of conformity and later surprise his peers by revealing his true vocation.

Nondynastic rebbes-to-be had no less a sense of their own authenticity than did their dynastic counterparts. "Don't argue with me," the Kotsker Rebbe once said to his m'lamed, (tutor of small children). "I still remember the Sinai experience."[45] This he said when he was only four years old. So sure was he of his worth that when he was refused a consideration by his parents, he said confidently, "I shall pray to God and He will help me."[46]

Only the very young rebbe-to-be was allowed such acting out. After the age of ten, the shtetl culture expected him to conform to his peer group and to the norms of the shtetl as a whole. It was at this stage that the young aspirant had to "go underground" until the time came for him to reveal himself in his true vocation. To expose his vocation prematurely would give rise to all sorts of problems.

The young rebbe-to-be was unwilling to make his vocation known until he was able to bear the responsibility that such a pronouncement brought in its train. If he were to announce himself prematurely, he would only make enemies for himself.[47] Hasidim resenting his audacity would talk against him. Older rebbes, likewise, would resent his action, considering him foolish, and would not give him their support. The young rebbe feared the influence of the "evil eye" of the older rebbes, whose support was essential to his ministry. In addition, he usually would not want to embarrass older hasidim who had worked longer and harder, but had achieved less. A premature announcement was bound to cause them embarrassment. Thus, the aspirant usually waited for an auspicious moment to make himself known. In fact, the way was usually paved for him by an older rebbe who had supported and trained him, and who would help him gain the endorsement of the hasidic community by offering his own "stamp of approval."

At times the rebbe-to-be was faced with a severe test precipitated by the envy of his fellow hasidim. A disciple was not to teach his own Torah until he was "crowned." Even after his "crowning," when he came to visit his rebbe, he had to know his place. Envious fellow hasidim slandered R. Zvi Elimelekh to his rebbe, R. Naftali Zvi Horwitz of Ropshitz, claiming that he was overambitious. Thus, he found himself caught between the Scylla of refusing to obey his rebbe's command to say Torah in his presence, and the Charybdis of saying Torah too well. He managed by being short and to the point, and yet making it, by implication, impossible for the Ropshitzer Rebbe to punish him. As he sat at the table with his master, they discussed the power of God that is in everything, and R. Naftali of Ropshitz said: "I can remove the life of God that is in this cup." He did so, and the cup became a heap of dust, thus implying to R. Zvi Elimelekh that he could do the same thing to him. He then said to R. Zvi Elimelekh: "Ribetitcher Revel [Little Rav—a pejorative], say Torah!" R. Zvi Elimelekh was shaken; yet he answered: "These are the things that God said to Moses. He said: 'Remove your *na'al*, your shoes from your feet,' because the Sages have said 'Disciples of the wise can bite like a fox—*neshikhah*, sting like a scorpion—*aqitzah*; and strike like a snake—*lehishah*.' From this we learn that the wise have the power of *Na'A'L*. And this is what God said to Moses at the thornbush: 'You want to be a leader of people; then remove your Na'A'L. Despite the fact that you have it in your power to bite, to sting, and to strike, don't become accustomed to this, and don't employ these means against anyone in

Israel.'"[48] Without resorting to lengthy discourse, R. Zvi Elimelekh passed the test of obedience, while at the same time disarming the rebbe.

Another disciple was once asked by his master to deliver a Torah discourse in his presence. He said: "Behold: 'Listening is better than sacrifice.' Listening to a tzaddik whose life is a constant sacrifice is better than my speech." Like R. Zvi Elimelekh, he showed the skill and adroitness necessary to rebbehood.

Acquired Knowledge and Wisdom

Another kind of testing concerned itself with acquired knowledge and wisdom. Usually the master was unwilling to transform a "simple Jew" into a disciple. It was enough that the master celebrated his virtues. He would hold the simple Jew up to his disciples as a model, but would not accept him as a disciple. The required level of scholarship was not the same as that expected of the disciple of a mitnaged (non-hasidic) gaon. The rebbe did not seek expertise in the handling of the text, but rather a kind of inner preparation that enabled the disciple to deal with the text as guiding and applied Torah and as the mind of God. To translate this expectation into a more modern idiom: If the master felt that the disciple managed to extract the proper mythic dimensions from the text, he was content to take him on. When R. Zussia of Anipoly was first being tested on his erudition by the Magid and his disciples, he did not translate the text of the first Mishnah *Mi-eymatay kor'in et sh'ma b'arvit* as "From when does one read the Sh'ma in the evenings?" but rather "Out of *eymatay*— awe and trembling—does one read the Sh'ma." This was proof enough for the Magid and his disciples, and R. Zussia was welcomed.

Internalizing the Teaching

Another testing device was to observe what the disciple did with the teaching he received. Either the master himself would observe or fellow disciples would report to the master. The purpose was to see the way in which the disciple was prepared to integrate a teaching into his life.[49] Did any of his acts indicate that his symbol system had expanded as a result of the teaching? Was the disciple prepared to wait and work with what he got before he sought further instruction? Would he internalize a teaching just enough to hold it now and then work it out later, or would he promptly forget it? On the other hand, was he overtrained and inflexible, and thus unfit to become a rebbe?[50] All these questions had to be answered by observing the trainee in action.

Other Tests

Kvittel reading and soul-seeing are also part of the prospective rebbe's training.[51] The Besht once tested R. Gershon Kittover to see if he could help him in his work with deceased souls. After he had shown him what *kavanah* to use, R. Gershon followed his instructions and, suddenly faced with the uprush of countless souls, he fainted. Rebbes often told stories of how their own rebbes mended souls at night. It was considered a great privilege for a disciple to be allowed to witness this process so that he might learn how to mend souls himself.

Another way of testing was to see what questions a disciple would raise with his master, or what answers he would offer to questions raised by the master. "A man came to see me and he asked. . . . What would you have told him?" Such a question put the disciple to the test. Did he understand what the real problem was or was he taken in by the description of the problem? The rebbe also had to be sure that the disciple was not squeamish. He would have him meet a person afflicted with a gross problem to see how the disciple reacted under the stress of facing a person who had committed a grave sin.

Being a rebbe demands both a certain unshakeable firmness and a warm, empathic accessibility. The rebbe's firmness was not to be utilized in a peremptory manner and had to be accompanied by his empathy and his compassionate "presentness." R. Sholem of Probisch, the father of R. Israel of Ruzhin, warned his son to be sparing in his use of power:

> He [R. Sholem] once had a vision in which his soul ascended to the mansion of a great and holy tzaddik. Though R. Sholem knew who the tzaddik was, he did not want to mention his name. Instead of wearing his crown like all the other righteous ones, his crown was set on a table. R. Sholem was told that the crown was made of all the Torah and all the mitzvot of that tzaddik but *because he ruled in this world with insistent caprice, he did not deserve to wear the crown in paradise.* When R. Sholem of Probisch came back from his experience, he called his son, the Ruzhiner, and told him the whole story. "I am telling you this story because the time may come when you will need it."[52]

Habadniks relate how R. Shneur Zalman tested R. Aaron of Starosselye in his use of power. R. Aaron failed because of his authoritarianism. When R. Aaron later came to complain about his lack of feeling in prayer, the rebbe told him that this was due to the aforementioned flaw. "He who is harsh with God's children finds God being harsh with him."

Another means of training and testing is the use of approval. The aspirant needs to check his progress with his master. In the beginning, the master will usually give approval freely, but at later stages, he will withhold it. When a disciple came to complain to R. Menahem Mendl II of Lubavitch that he no longer received the approval he had received previously, the rebbe said: "This is not because you are doing wrong; but why don't you free yourself·from my approval? Who pats *me* on the back for doing right?"

Just as approval is used for positive feedback, so disapproval is used for negative feedback. At times the severity of the rebbe's reproach is greater than the occasion demands. The aspirant's defense against overly severe criticism may be the real issue of the test.

Having weathered all this, the disciple may now be sent out by the master to act on his behalf. The Magid of Mezhirech often appointed his disciples to act as his proxy. When R. Zussia preached, the Magid feigned anger in order to see how R. Zussia would act. When R. Shneur Zalman came to his colleague's defense, the Magid expressed pleasure at the way in which R. Zussia acted, at what he said, and at the comradeship of the two disciples. He once sent R. Aaron of Karlin to a town. R. Aaron thought that he would soon return. When the Magid suggested that he take his Sabbath clothes along, he thought it unnecessary but complied. He later found that he had to stay and administer a number of divorces. Here again, the Magid encouraged his disciple, this time R. Aaron, by expressing pleasure at the manner in which he discharged his task.

R. Nahman often sent his disciple, R. Nathan, on journeys to act on his behalf. Either R. Nathan himself or others would report to R. Nahman later, and he would express his reaction to the work done. On such occasions, the rebbe treats his disciple as an equal, as the following story illustrates:

Once, when R. Zvi Elimelekh of Dinov was young, he journeyed to see the Master of Lublin. On the way, he met a man who was traveling on a wagon with four horses. The owner of the wagon was rich. He asked R. Elimelekh where he was going, and R. Elimelekh answered: "To the Rebbe of Lublin." So the man said: "I too am going. Come with me and we will travel together." As they were traveling the man gave R. Elimelekh a little *lekakh* and shnapps because he said he was very hungry; whereupon R. Elimelekh said to him: "Because you have so invigorated me, I will say a good word for you to the Rebbe of Lublin." The rich man thought that this was some kind of joke. "How can this poor young man help me?"

When he arrived in Lublin, the rich man went to his inn. R. Zvi Elimelekh went directly to the Lubliner Rebbe. After a few hours, the rich man came to see the Rebbe. When he arrived, he saw that the door was closed, and, looking through the keyhole, he saw R. Elimelekh talking with the Lubliner. He was amazed at this.

Finally, the Rebbe opened the door and the rich man entered and gave his kvittel to the Lubliner, together with the ransom money. Since the rich man did not have any children, he had written this on his kvittel. When the Rebbe read the kvittel, he said: "I see that you will have children, but they will not live very long." The man was greatly shaken and almost fainted from pain. Then the rich man looked at R. Zvi Elimelekh in order to see if he would make good his promise. So R. Elimelekh said: "Would the Rebbe read the kvittel once more?" So the Lubliner read it again, and he said the same thing. R. Elimelekh asked him to read it a third time; and still he said the same thing. So R. Elimelekh said: "Well then, why don't you pray to the Lord that his children will live longer?" Then the Lubliner Rebbe said: *"You have invigorated me. You have opened to me a new way with your words."* And thus, the Rebbe blessed the rich man with children that would live long, and his blessing was fulfilled.[53]

The Dinover Rebbe may have perceived something the Seer of Lublin had overlooked. Such perception is important at the yehidut. It may be that it is not acquired by training, but comes as a gift of the spirit.

Gifts of the Spirit

Hasidim believe that the rebbe is given a number of gifts to assist him in his difficult work. They believe that the rebbe has achieved a reparation of his soul in a former life and has now come to repair the souls of others.

Part of the rebbe's endowment was in the realm of enduring relationship with kindred souls. Some of the rebbe's friends also agree to be reincarnated. They will be his colleagues. Another part of the endowment consists of special miraculous faculties, which are described in the following pages.

Clairvoyance

Many a young rebbe—the Seer of Lublin in particular—received the gift of clairvoyance congenitally. This precocity was the occasion of many tales. Often the tales related how the young rebbe-to-be renounced this gift during his youth, preferring not to use it while in training. When the gift became necessary, he would acquire it anew. At other times, a gift was bestowed upon a prospective rebbe when his master wished him to do some particular service, as when the Yehudi was given the shirt of his master, the Seer, in order to be able to read the incarnations of the souls of hasidim.

The Reading of Souls and Thoughts

The rebbe had to be able to read the incarnations of his hasid: he had to know the purpose of the present incarnation. At times, these visions would come to him spontaneously; at other times, they would come only when sought. Sometimes the young rebbe-to-be had to be "shown" how to seek them. R. Shneur Zalman suggested to his son, R. Dovber, that he visualize a Jew as he stood in the primeval thought of Adam Qadmon. This exercise helped him to focus on the soul's prehistory. The Besht wrote in a letter to R. Yitzhaq of Drohobitch:

> Know that for each soul one is to mend and raise to its root, one has to know all that has happened to it—all the incarnations from the time of the Genesis on—and then one can mend it. But if one does not know enough, then one cannot bring about any good effects, but, heaven forfend [one brings about the contrary]. Thus did I receive [the teaching] from my master. But if you are aware of this, I empower you, and you will succeed; for I trust the great justice of your heart, that *you will listen, and you will hear for what [purpose] the words [are intended]*. It is not enough to pay attention to the soul telling of her incarnations, for my master taught me that the soul tells only of her last incarnation. I leave it to you to elaborate. If you are the master of souls, you will understand it all in its fullness. And the Holy One, Blessed be He, will gather our dispersed so that all the souls will complete their body, and then the complete redemption will come soon. Amen.[54]

The ability to read souls was an essential gift in the diagnostic part of the yehidut. It included the ability to read a kvittel, and, via the kvittel, the soul's record in the Book of Life. This meant that, to some degree, the rebbe read the person's future as it was contained in the Book of Life. With this came the ability to read of a person's sins and virtues in the Book of Life. As a reader of souls, the rebbe was able to read a person's acts on his forehead and to interpret the significance of what he saw.

A rebbe also had the ability to read the thoughts of his hasidim. We have no data on the question of whether telepathy was taught or subjectively acquired. However, there are many tales describing how rebbes taught disciples to "read kvittlekh." One rebbe promised a young hasid whom he admired and whom he wished to steal from another rebbe that he would make him into a rebbe and teach him how to read souls and understand the language of birds and trees.[55]

Telepathic Contact with Other Living Tzaddikim

Another gift in the category of supernatural awareness is the telepathic contact the rebbe has with other tzaddikim. R. Pinhas of Koretz once sent a letter to the Magid of Mezhirech, thanking him for thinking of him at the time of the shofar-sounding—"As soon as you did so there, I felt it here."[56] He also wrote to one of his disciple-friends, R. Yeshaya of Dynawitz, telling him how he accompanied him on a "journey"—*aliyat han'shamah*—correcting some errors R. Yeshaya had purportedly made in discerning the visions he was shown. Since R. Joseph Isaac Schneersohn discusses the first letter in detail with his hasidim, we have further corroboration that telepathic power is accepted as a reality among hasidim. Prerequisite to this gift is a "sense of the imagination that must be rich and detailed."

The Vision of the Prophet Elijah and Other Departed Masters

To meet Elijah the Prophet is another gift of the spirit. The Magid was amazed at his disciple, R. Shneur Zalman, for having, unbeknownst to him, experienced this twice. The Magid reports his amazement in a letter, in which he describes how the Besht appeared to him and told him that his disciple had met with Elijah. Elijah's visit is usually connected with a vision of instruction on a point of doubt in the mind of the adept.

The tzaddik may be visited not only by Elijah but also by his own ancestors and by the Besht. Furthermore, to the adept, not only the souls of the righteous departed, but also those of the dead who require reparation, may appear. The rebbe must learn to control this faculty so that he will not be overcome by it and faint (as did R. Gershon Kittover when the Besht opened him to thaumaturgic vision). During the Festival of Booths the Magid, in training R. Shneur Zalman, told him to remain in his *sukkah* (booth) for a visit by the Ba'al Shem Tov. He ordered R. Shneur Zalman to be calm and observe the event as if it were the most natural thing. Later, when R. Shneur Zalman was imprisoned, his ability to invoke the presence of exalted souls helped greatly to sustain him in his suffering. R. Joseph Isaac Schneersohn reports similar visions during his imprisonment in Moscow.

Controlled Ecstasies

While a rebbe cannot afford to be completely out of touch with his hasidim at any time, he must be able to enter ecstasy at will. However, the gift of ecstasy must be brought under control. Thus, during the course of his training, the rebbe learns to control his gift. When he is in a state of ecstasy, the rebbe may be beside himself, his eyes bulging; or he may be motionless and unaware even of having his shirt changed. He may sweat profusely; yet there are no physical causes for exertion. R. Shneur Zalman once entered into ecstasy with his friend, the "Angel" (R. Abraham, the Magid's son). When he felt that R. Abraham was in danger of being consumed by his state, he brought him a roll and milk in order to revive him. R. Zussia brought his brother, R. Elimelekh, out of ecstasy by covering up the mezuzah.

Cosmic Insight and Coronation

The Rebbe Moves the Aspirant to Cosmic Insight

Like Siddhartha, who gave to Govinda the experience of the vision of the All,[57] the rebbe wants to impart the central vision to his disciple. By effectively guiding him in meditation, he enables his disciple to see that "There is no One except He."[58] When R. Isaac of Homel left R. Shneur Zalman after a yehidut, he wrote to a friend: "I was ready to run out into the street and shout from the rooftops, *Eyn od Mil'vado* [There is no one aside from God]! Why did I not do so? A reason deeply hidden in my mind prevented me."[59] "The entire purpose of all teaching and teachings is that the absolute hiddenness of the undisclosed core of the luminary of the soul be made manifest."[60]

In the Lurianic scheme, the pneumatic keys are manipulated by the use of *shemot*—names. By manipulating and combining sacred names, the hidden can be revealed. When a rebbe revealed to his disciple the "names" for his last and final *yihud* (unification), the disciple had completed his training.

Rebbes were not content, however, to parade their psychic powers. "I can make you into a 'seer' in half an hour. So what?"[61] To remain socially effective while unification was achieved; not to lose track of the Above and the Below; and to act in a way that consistently bound both worlds together—these were proof that the disciple had attained leadership. In his old age, R. Naftali of Ropshitz, when he could no longer act simultaneously on many levels, refused to talk. R. Shneur Zalman rebuked his son for being so absorbed in meditation that he could not hear a child's cry.

As Joseph Campbell uses the term *myth*, the rebbe acts on the mythic level. The level of signification is cosmic; yet if he were to behave as if that level were the only reality, he could not be a rebbe. On the other hand, if he did not have access to the mythic cosmic level, he could not be a rebbe either. To be aware of and operative in both levels at the same time—this is what the aspirant has to demonstrate to his master's satisfaction.

The aspirant demonstrates his attainment of the unification of mind and will by the way in which he now understands the fabric of time and the act appropriate to a particular time. He understands the mystery of both the changes and the sameness that the Messiah is to bring. He is no longer, like a lower-level hasid, arrested in verbal and discursive meditation—he has reached the point of constant contemplation coupled with redemptive action. This means that he lives with the constant of truth as it is caught in the paradox of the eternal opposites of the reality of God and the reality of creation. When the aspirant demonstrates that he can shape Beauty in his emotions, and contain Love and Awe at the same time, he has grasped the emotive *yihud*. On the ethical continuum, the aspirant shows that he has attained functional unification by living the ethical life in a free-floating yet structured covenantal situation, in which interpersonal love does not frighten him but rather moves him to ethical action and compassion. His compassion is not limited to one litigant only. The apocryphal story of the rebbe who said to both litigants, "You are right!" and to his wife, who pointed to the contradiction, "You too are right!" is illustrative of ethical *yihud*. True compassion results from the attainment of unification on the three levels of Ethics, Truth, and Beauty.

The aspirant now knows the life he needs to live in this world. To make this very clear, some rebbes would tell the aspirant a story. This story was to be the life-myth of the aspirant. At times he would wonder how far he had progressed along the myth. The aspirant knows that he cannot live his life-myth freely without having left the hold of the world. The Messianic helper leads his charge out of his involvement in the world only to lead him back to it again, to help him live in the world with insightful involvement. In the *yihud* experience, the aspirant has accepted his call to rebbehood. The *yihud* has shown him that he at once is the

Caller, the called, and the call. The *yihud* has also shown him that through
the texture of time there is a oneness of the different seasons: Passover and
the redemption from slavery, Yom Kippur and the redemption from sin
and guilt, Shavuot and Sinai and the redemption from ignorance of God's
purpose. As these merge, so too the fast of the Ninth of Av, commemorat-
ing the destruction of the Holy Temple and the beginning of the exile,
merges with its own other meaning, and the birthday of the Messiah
merges in the *yihud* of time and eternity. In the *yihud* exile and redemption,
the Law of Sinai and the forgiveness announced by God with the giving of
the second tablets received on Yom Kippur, become all one. In that
yihud the aspirant, the rebbe, and the cosmos are one unbroken unity.

Expansion of Consciousness

We have seen that the capacity for the expansion of consciousness—
aliyat han'shamah (ascent of the soul)—is part of the rebbe's training. This
was illustrated by the letter of R. Pinhas of Koretz to his disciple and
colleague, R. Yeshaya of Dynawitz, telling him that he followed him
telepathically on an ascent of the soul, and that, because of his yet
imperfect attainment, he missed a few points.[62] During the ascent, it
would have been harmful to criticize. To do this to another or to oneself is
a sin against the holy spirit. Thus, R. Pinhas of Koretz waited to criticize
R. Yeshaya later in a letter. "At the time of the ascent, one is not to
squelch the joyous flow."[63]

The ascent of the soul is an exalted form of repentance. Having been
raised so high, one can, for the first time, see what damage sin has
wrought.[64] The master and disciple have to empty themselves completely.
Ego loss is a condition of the ascent.[65] The one in ascent cannot take credit
even for the self-castigation and fasting that brought him to this exalted
level.[66] Therefore, the rebbe considers his ascent a gift of the spirit.

To have achieved vision on high is not enough. What is an end for
the contemplative person is only a means for the activist. The rebbe is an
activist. His ascent proves itself in terms of his acting out in a salvational
manner.

When the Disciple Is Ready

When the disciple has achieved his *yihud* and sees himself as re-
oriented along the time-space continuum in a dynamic way, the rebbe
pushes him into his work as rebbe. He informs the disciple of his readi-

ness—"I have already taken care of you."[67] In speaking of his disciple, he says: "He is already a Good Jew."[68] He calls him to the Torah and reads with great emphasis: "A prophet like you [Moses] will I raise up." Their communion has reached such profundity that the disciple, miles away, knows what Torah the master teaches and repeats it to his own circle.[69] The rebbe is proud of his disciple: "He steals the whites of my eyes. Everything I have, he has."[70] Or, "Forty years we are rebbe. You [the rest of the hasidim] take only the skim milk, and he [the disciple], the cream and butter."[71] In private, the rebbe may say to his disciple: "Go with your strength and save Israel."[72] Or he may tell him: "I have nothing more to teach you. Become a rebbe."[73] He may teach the disciple kvittel reading as a final act,[74] or in public give him a staff and a *gartel*.[75] He may call him to read from the Torah at *shishi*[76] [the sixth portion reserved for the tzaddik].[77] Now the rebbe-to-be knows that he has become a rebbe.[78] His power is so great that its abuse may lead to the spilling of blood.[79] The distance between master and disciple has become obliterated. The master has only to crown his disciple. This he may do in public or in private.

Coronation

We have an interesting description of a dialogue preceding a rebbe's coronation:

When, after the demise of the Middle Rebbe, the hasidim wanted to appoint R. Menahem Mendl Schneersohn I as their rebbe, he refused and pointed to an uncle, the Elder Rebbe's son, R. Hayim Abraham, who also refused to accept the position and pointed back to R. Mendl. Heading the delegation of older hasidim, R. Hayim Abraham went to plead with R. Mendl. When R. Mendl rose, R. Hayim said,

"Rebbe, please sit. I am only an uncle."

"How can I be rebbe? I don't know the mysteries of Torah."

One of the hasidim replied, "Did not our Sages first state: 'She gives him the kingdom' and then 'they reveal to him the mysteries.'"

"But if I am to be a rebbe, I should have received a hint from my grandfather!"

"Did you not receive a sign from him, either awake or in a dream?" one of the older hasidim queried.

"True. I had a dream. It was before he passed on, and I was sick. I cried out in my sleep, for I saw a Torah fall and no one could pick it up. The rebbe entered and asked, 'Why did you cry out?' When I told him, he said, 'Yes, you will raise it up.'"

Then the hasidim pressed him and he accepted the appointment.[80]

In the case of a dynastic rebbe who has not been officially crowned, an elder hasid may, at the crucial moment, turn a casual encounter into a yehidut and move the young rebbe to accept a kvittel as a sign that he has taken on the yoke of rebbehood. The following story illustrates this point:

> After the Rebbe [R. Shalom Dovber of Lubavitch] had passed on from typhus, my father too was sick from typhus and asked me to go to the Rebbe, his son [R. Joseph Isaac Schneersohn], and give him a *pidyon*, a ransom, asking him to pray for my father's recovery.
>
> When I came to the Rebbe, he asked me how my father was, and I answered, "My father has asked me to give this ransom for him." I held it out to the Rebbe, but he would not take it. He said, "I am not going to the tent [cemetery]. [During the first summer after his father's death, the Rebbe often went to pray at his graveside.] So what is the use of my taking the ransom now?" From his words, one could recognize that he was not ready to receive the ransom himself, in the manner of a rebbe. He had not even conceived that I meant for him to take it. He thought that I was asking him to read the ransom at his father's graveside; and since he was not going there at the time, he did not want to take it, hoping that someone else might go sooner.
>
> Then the Rebbe turned to me and said: "But you can't go either. You must not go to bathe." He knew that I was sick, and to go to miqveh before going to the graveside might harm me. "So send your brother. He is bar mitzvah already, isn't he?" My brother was fourteen at the time. All this he said to me, but he didn't take the ransom.
>
> R. Shmuel Gurarie, who sat by at that time, heard all these things, and he said to the Rebbe: "Are you going to send a small boy to the graveside? It is not fitting. What is the use of sending him?"
>
> And the Rebbe said: "Is it wrong for a child to go and intercede for his father?"
>
> "Oh, so a child is something?" R. Shmuel Gurarie replied. "You are also your father's child. . . . Take the ransom yourself." Then R. Shmuel Gurarie turned to me and said that I should give the ransom into the hands of the Rebbe. I gave it to him again, and this time he took it, and it seems to me that this was the first time he ever took a ransom.[81]

It was believed that the first ransom given to a rebbe would always be answered from heaven in the affirmative, as in the following story:

When R. Mosheh of Savran began his ministry, he arrived in a town for Shabbat. His *gabbai* went about town to announce the arrival of a rebbe. The townsfolk, however, ignored R. Mosheh in favor of R. Mordecai of Chernobil who had also arrived at the same time.

After an unencouraging Shabbat had been spent by R. Mosheh, R. Mordecai came to him on Saturday night and gave his ransom to R. Mosheh, saying: "I know you are upset that no one came, but after all, heaven did not want to assign the first kvittel to a commoner." After the townsfolk came to know of the Chernobiler's trust in R. Mosheh, they too came.[82]

In giving the first kvittel to a rebbe, a hasid establishes his contract (*hitqashrut*). The hasid expects that the mutual contract will continue beyond his master's death, as this is the implicit promise of many rebbes to their hasidim. In the first kvittel, *hitqashrut* becomes explicit. After the demise of the former rebbe, hasidim approach the new rebbe with a kvittel that explicitly states: "Hereby we tie ourselves body and soul by the five powers of the soul, to those powers of our-Lord-Master-and-Teacher, may-he-live-for-many-long-years."

Since the time of the Second World War, the hasidim of Karlin have not had a rebbe of their own. R. David Biederman of Lelov (the Lelover Rebbe) was very close in spirit to them. When the council of older Karliner hasidim met, they decided to become affiliated with the Lelover Rebbe; whereupon they gave him a *k'tav hitqashrut*, obligating him to be known as the Lelover–Karliner Rebbe. Generally, the obligations of the rebbe to his hasidim are not set up in a contractual way; but in this case, the Karliner hasidim insisted that their rebbe be formally known as the Lelover–Karliner Rebbe.

A rebbe's acceptance of a contract means that he commits himself to guide his hasid to greater perfection and to greater realization, to the point where he will not die without repentance.

Even after ordination, the older rebbe "patronizes" the younger. R. Hayim of Zans, by then an old man, asked R. Zvi Elimelekh of Bluzhev to pray for him that he might repent.[83] R. Joshua Dov of Belz would praise R. Zvi Elimelekh: "Such a young man, such an expanded mind, and yet he can contain it."[84] R. Shneur Zalman offered supporting opinions on behalf of R. Nahman of Brazlav, who was a much younger man. There are numerous such occasions in hasidic literature.

With his coronation, a rebbe is considered by his hasidim to have completed his training. At the same time, as far as the rebbe is concerned, he is just beginning. For all the help that he offers to other people, he will insist that he is still learning from them. He will meet with colleagues from time to time and learn from them. He will face ambivalent feelings of satisfaction and frustration when the time comes for him to train his own successor. Only then will he fully see what his master, in training him in the yehidut, has done for him.

Chapter 5

Techniques and Resources of the Yehidut

When a Jew comes and tells me of his worries, about matters of the body and livelihood, I listen carefully. His soul tells of itself in that quiet hour—of her worries and trembling. Therefore I must give a counsel that will help to solve both the physical and the spiritual problems. The body speaks for itself, and the soul speaks for itself; and he who answers must answer them in their relation to one another. Did not our Sages say (Avot 6), "The Sages taught in the language of the Mishnah, 'Blessed be He Who chose them and their Mishnah!'" Mishnah means talk on two levels—one word speaking to both body and soul.

The secret of life is flow, and everyone has to receive the influx of life in the same way as he has to give of the flow of life; and he who does not receive and give at the same time is a fruitless tree.

R. Zvi Hirsch of Zyditchov (E. Steinman, *Galicia*)

Every evening after prayer, the Ba'al Shem went to his room. Two candles were set in front of him and the mysterious Book of Creation put on the table among other books. Then all those who needed his counsel were admitted in a body, and he spoke with them until the eleventh hour.

One evening, when the people left, one of them said to the man beside him how much good the words the Ba'al Shem had directed to him, had done him. But the other told him not to talk such nonsense, that they had entered the room together and from that moment on the master had spoken to no one except himself. A third, who heard this, joined in the conversation with a smile, saying how curious that both were mistaken, for the rabbi had carried on an intimate conversation with him the entire evening. Then a fourth and a fifth made the same claim, and finally all began to talk at once and tell what they had experienced. But the next instant they all fell silent.

Emunat Zadiqim (in M. Buber, *Early Masters*)

THE YEHIDUT[1]

In this section we will discuss more extensive and specific definitions of the term yehidut, as well as the origins of the term and the synonyms used in the general hasidic milieu. We will describe the course of a yehidut and the setting in which it occurs. We will also explore the diagnostic procedure the rebbe uses, and we will study his involvement in the yehidut process, noting the ways in which the rebbe manages his involvement. We will examine the hasid in the process of the transaction; discuss how the rebbe views and interprets the hasid and his problems; how he reassures the hasid; and how he prepares him for the directive part of the yehidut— the etzah, the actual counsel. The process of the yehidut as a "turning point" will be viewed from close range. We will then study the prescriptions the rebbe gives the hasid to help him repent. We will also observe the rebbe in his dealings with psychopathology. Finally, we will sum up and evaluate the preparatory work the rebbe does prior to giving the directive counsel to the hasid.

Definitions of the Yehidut

Yehidut: An Expanded Definition

The greater ones among the Elder Rebbe's older hasidim used to say that yehidut means

clear (*Sheqalim* 6:2)
defined, set aside (*Yevamot* 62a)
unique, unified (Genesis *Rabbah* 4)

> This is to say that the intent of the yehidut is to clarify one's position, to define a way of service both in the forsaking of evil and in the acquisition of good virtues, and to unite oneself to the rebbe in complete union, renouncing one's self and will.[2]

Expanding on this, we see that the function of the yehidut is to clarify a person's role and being—the achievement of an identity. The chaotic person is not able to begin any work with himself, since this self is too fickle and shifting, having no stable locus in the universe. The yehidut anchors the hasid to a new self-image, which has, through the yehidut, become clarified and (for the sake of the work that is to follow) fixed. The work demands a new identity, which in turn requires the rejection of conflicting roles and the acquisition of factors to enhance one's true character. Therefore, the yehidut has to deal with the *way* in which this role and identity are to be established and maintained.

The motivation for continuing with this work cannot be rooted in the hasid. In order to become the person that the yehidut has defined him to be, he must work on himself as an object. Otherwise he would accept his problem-giving and chaotic self as an inevitability. The hasid has accepted a new view of his "I"; but this "I" needs a new "me." He begins to work on the new "me" by shifting his "I" to the rebbe. Now the rebbe has not only helped him to find the new "I–me" identity but has also given him the "how" in which this is to be done. Still, the process will remain incomplete until the hasid has the wherewithal with which to implement it. The knowledge both of the target of the work of transformation and of its function, must be implemented with the actual doing. The yehidut itself is already part of the execution, which is completed through the hasid's work. He now takes the rebbe's "I" as his own and thus shapes his "me." When the "me" is molded to the prescription, the "I" can merge into the "me." This coalescence is possible because the "I," in the process of shaping the "me," also introjected the rebbe into the new "me" structure. The new "I–me" is entitled to a new dispensation, and thus a new revenue can be drawn for the hasid by the rebbe. The new, changed person is entitled to a different dispensation—*mazal*—by the force of the minor–major premise equation: "If to change one's place changes one's mazal, how much more so does to change one's being change one's mazal." Since to change one's being is a conversion—a penitent return—a new dispensation is required in order for penitence, prayer, and charity to remove the evil decree. This is why one can expect all blessing and change for the better at the yehidut.[3] In short, a hasid comes to the yehidut "to salt and kosher his soul" and "to rid the heart of unfit leaven." The rebbe's task is to help his hasid achieve this purification. In order to do this, he utilizes all the means at his disposal.

The Setting Defined

Biyehidut also means in the privacy of the yehidut chamber, the room to which the rebbe retires (his study). The other contacts between rebbe and hasid are likely to be public, that is, in the synagogue or on the street, or at the banquet table, and therefore are not suitable to interaction on an intimate level. Or, on the other hand, they might not be deliberate encounters: hence, neither rebbe nor hasid is prepared to transact at depth. The word *yehidut* thus connotes the deliberate aloneness of the rebbe and the hasid.[4] Nevertheless, in non-Habad situations other persons were often present during the interview, and even among Lubavitcher rebbes, there were times when another person's presence was required at the yehidut. For example, in the later years of the Tzemah Tzedeq (R. Menahem Mendl the First of Lubavitch), it was often necessary for the *gabbai*, the rebbe's secretary, to attend. So too, in the latter days of R. Joseph Isaac Schneersohn, when he had become paralyzed and his language was impeded, people who could not interpret the rebbe's speech needed a translator; and so R. Eli Simpson, the rebbe's secretary, would enter with the person who sought counsel. This did not significantly disrupt the privacy of the communication, since the rebbe was not seen until the kvittel was written, and very often the person who wrote the kvittel was the rebbe's secretary; thus, he was quite aware of what was stated in the request, and his presence was welcomed.

Values

Hasidim have attached many values to the term *yehidut*. The most frequently quoted and most authoritative is based on the ascending scale of soul levels: *nefesh, ruah, n'shamah, hayah,* and *yehidah* (see Glossary). When a rebbe meets with a hasid, the *nefesh* of the rebbe meets the *nefesh* of the hasid, and the *yehidah* of both rebbe and hasid interconnect.[5] *Yehidah* is the name given to the divine spark dwelling in all human beings. This spark is in constant union with God; the spark *is* God.[6] Thus the yehidut represents the manifest unification of the spark with the Luminary, or of the particle with the whole.

When things are out of joint, we find ourselves in a world of separation. In the world of union, which is the *r'shut ha'yahid* (the domain of the Single One), everything is complete, and there is no evil.[7] The rebbe's study is the domain of the Single One. So great is this union that there can even be a totally silent yehidut.[8] The hasid who enters the rebbe's yehidut room therefore calls that room by many exalted names: private theophany,[9] the wedding chamber of hasid and rebbe,[10] the inner sanctum,[11] the holy of holies,[12] the supernal paradise,[13] and so on. Even the waiting room is celebrated by such names as the Lesser Paradise.[14]

Other Terms

Yehidut is a specific Habad term. Among other hasidim different terms were employed. In the Ukraine, the terms *pravven zikh*[15] (to celebrate) and *bentchen zikh*[16] (to be celebrated or blessed by the rebbe) were used. One of the reasons why the term *yehidut* was prevalent was that often other people were present at the time of the interview, and thus the process was not truly private. We use the term *yehidut* in order to avoid confusion, even though in Poland and Galicia the term was not generally used. There, the yehidut was divided into at least two encounters. The first thing a hasid did when he arrived in town was to go to greet the rebbe to "take shalom." The rebbe was generally seated at a table near the entrance to his room and the hasid would approach him and wait until the rebbe looked up from his book and offered his hand. (In Hungary the custom was for the hasid to kiss the rebbe's hand.) Some interrogation might then take place if the hasid had previously visited the rebbe's court. Generally, if this was not the case, the hasid waited until the proper time came for him to present his kvittel and pidyon (payment). After the Sabbath or the holiday, the hasid would come to the rebbe with his kvittel and ask the rebbe for his blessing. This was known as "receiving the parting blessing"—*birkhat hapridah*. If, however, the hasid intended to stay a little longer, he would present his kvittel earlier, and when he was ready to leave, he would come for the parting blessing. Simple people who came to the rebbe to seek help for specific problems (and not because they were hasidim who periodically visited the rebbe) called their encounter *poyelen bam rebbn*—to exact from the rebbe. Sometimes hasidim spoke of the yehidut as *arahn giyen* or *derlangen a kvittel*—to enter to give a kvittel—thus using a phase of the interview to denote the interview itself.

Phases of the Interview

The yehidut itself has several distinct phases. These phases are part of the yehidut's formal structure. Each has a distinct purpose in contributing to the meaningful pattern of the yehidut as a whole. Other than the exceptions indicated above and slight individual variations, the formal structure of the yehidut is generally maintained. This affords both rebbe and hasid an operational framework.

KVITTEL

The kvittel (literally a billet or slip of paper) is a note on which the writer requests the intercession of the rebbe. The kvittel text among Habad hasidim usually contains the following formula:[17]

> To His honored Holiness, our Lord, our Teacher and our Master, may-he-live-for-many-long-days:
>
> Please rouse the great mercies from the fount of the true mercies and graces for NAME AND MOTHER'S NAME.[18] [Here the condition of the person for whom intercession is made is given.]
>
> Soul ransom
> Pidyon
> [Here a sum of money is mentioned.]

Among other hasidim, the formula omits the address and the preface, giving only the name, the condition, and the ransom.

PIDYON NEFESH (SOUL'S RANSOM)

This is generally a cash donation given for the maintenance of the rebbe's household or for his charities.

ETZAH (COUNSEL OR ADVICE)

This is the direction to be followed by the hasid, the rebbe's solution to the problem.

BRAKHAH (THE BLESSING)

Most rebbes use a distinct formula such as, *Der oybershter zull helfn az*. . . . (May the most High grant that . . . come to pass).

In order to understand each phase of the interview as well as its relation to the whole, we need to do more than define our terms. For this reason, we will here expand our definitions of the kvittel and the pidyon nefesh.

Generally, the rebbe reads the kvittel[19] once with the hasid at the yehidut, and once when he intercedes for the hasid. If he prays at the ancestor's graveside, he will read the kvittel there again, and before the sounding of the shofar on Rosh Hashanah he may read it yet again.

When the rebbe has so many kvittlekh that it would be impossible to deal with each one individually, he may follow the example of the Apter Rav:

> [He] took all the petition kvittlekh and placed them in his pockets. Then, placing his hands on these pockets, he said: "I bless all the people whose names are included in these kvittlekh." In telling this story, the Chortkover wrapped all the kvittlekh that he had received together into one bundle and blessed them in the same way.[20]

On Rosh Hashanah, the rebbe petitions for a large number of people. In speaking of this, R. David Moshe of Chortkov related how his father, the Ruzhiner Rebbe, once met the Master of Savran and asked him, "What do you do on Rosh Hashanah when there is such a large number of people?" The Savraner replied: "In one quick glance, I see them all." Then the Savraner turned to the Ruzhiner and said, "What do you do?" The Ruzhiner replied: "All the souls of Israel are rooted in the heart of the tzaddik. Therefore, when a tzaddik prays and pours out his heart before the Lord, all of the people who are implanted in his heart are included in his prayer."[21]

In an emergency, a kvittel may be given in absentia.

> A story is told of a hasid who had previously been a Chernobiler hasid and who came to the Chortkover. The hasid explained that when he had been close to the Chortkover's father-in-law, R. Ahrele of Chernobil, he was able to write a kvittel at home, marking down his request, and the Lord answered him and helped him. When he inquired of the Chortkover whether he could now do the same thing, the Chortkover replied: "When you have any requests, just remember my name and the name of my mother . . . and, God willing, you will be helped."[22]

This is only possible, however, when the rebbe and the hasid have met before. As we shall see in the next section, the union has to be achieved in the yehidut confrontation. After this has happened, time and space no longer limit the relationship.

Hasidim not only give the rebbe a kvittel but also a pidyon.[23] There are some hasidim who give the rebbe a monthly or yearly retainer besides the pidyon, but the pidyon has a sacramental aura about it. Like a sacrifice on the altar, which is brought by the penitent to the Temple, the pidyon is given to the rebbe. The hasid sees in his rebbe an altar, a sacrifice without blemish, a High Priest offering the sacrifice by eating of the hasid's gift and raising it up to God in fervent prayer and study.[24] The gift of *t'rumah* (a contribution to the priest) was only a fiftieth of a person's income, yet it managed to raise the entire person before God. The pidyon is such a contribution and more: it is a true redemptive tool. The term *pidyon* occurs in Exodus (21:30), where it denotes the ransom money that is paid by the guilty party and has the power to abrogate the death penalty. Originally, in kabbalistic usage, the word referred to the entire procedure of esoteric intercession, although it was also used to indicate money given to the poor.

Halakhically, pidyon also refers to the redemption of the first-born son. The Torah stipulates the sum of five *s'laim*[25] as the pidyon amount for the child. One rebbe refused to accept any other money but that which he, a *kohen* (priest), received for his service. He claimed that the legitimacy of any other earning is questionable, in contrast to the sum the Torah states belongs to the priest.

Many rebbes have given all their money away to the poor and needy,[26] refusing to allow any money to remain in their possession overnight, since this constituted for them a lack of trust in God. Other rebbes were known for their "love of money." Yet although the Ruzhiner was known as a rich rebbe, he served as a distributor supplying the thirty-six hidden saints of the world with their needs.[27] Some tzaddikim of the Ruzhiner dynasty lived luxuriously and drove in glorious carriages. One of the tzaddikim who lived in great poverty once asked R. Israel of Ruzhin why he did not spend all his money on mitzvot. He replied:

> There are tzaddikim whose hasidim are such holy persons that the money they give, the tzaddikim can use only for mitzvot. Many of my hasidim are very simple people and the money they give me is good only for horses, straw for carriages, and tapestries. There are some good hasidim—and I have a large number of these—who are on a slightly higher level. Their pidyon money I use for my necessities—food and housing. The few hasidim I have whose money ought to be used for mitzvot are generally not too wealthy. You have very holy hasidim, this is why you cannot use their money for luxuries.[28]

The cycle of sharing between rebbe and hasid extends to food. The hasid brings food to the rebbe, who shares it with the hasid by giving him his *shirayim*—food favors. The hasid eats a morsel of the rebbe's food with spiritual relish and he learns to eat all the other food that he eats at home with the same dedication and fervor. The hasid knows that he receives his material and spiritual sustenance through the rebbe's blessings. In this sense he feels he eats *shirayim* all the time.

Why a rebbe would want money from his hasidim is to them a mystery. But this raises no basic question. Rather it stimulates their imagination to understand and to give reasons. The rebbe descends and the hasid ascends. That God should at times move the tzaddik toward the lower spheres is only the effect of His redemptive scheme. To Hayim Grawitzer, the hero of the novel by Fishl Schneersohn, it is all part of the mystery of the ever-turning wheel of circumstance:

> So it seems that here too it is the same wheel. Simple souls throw away their money in order to become raised to the level of the supernally holy ones. And one of these great holy men descends way down to money.[29]

There are times when a rebbe will not take a pidyon,[30] or if he takes it, will not use it. He may feel that this money or gift cannot be "redeemed" for a spiritual purpose. R. Ahron of Belz refused to use a gold watch that a hasid had brought him, because the hasid did not heed his counsel. Only on the day of the hasid's death did he use it, and thus caused the hasid to repent on his deathbed.[31] A woman brought the Belzer Rebbe a few yards of silk that she had received in reward for her illicit favors. The silk was left to rot.[32] R. Shneur Zalman returned a gift sent to him by a man who had obtained it through robbery.

The Union of God–Rebbe–Hasid

The many and various ways to describe the yehidut—"seeing a soul as it stands in the primal thought of Adam Qadmon," "the tie of *nefesh* to *nefesh, yehidah* to *yehidah*"—are an attempt to approximate the moment when two persons, rebbe and hasid, merge in the Infinite One. In this sense, the word *yehidut* can be translated as "the one-ing of God–rebbe–hasid." The rebbe no longer tells the hasid what he must do: instead the hasid comes to a momentous decision for himself. The hasid is, at that moment, being created anew; and with this new creation, the plan for his present life is again revealed. The purpose and the process, the network of relationships and responsibilities, all stand clearly before him. Still, the rebbe is said to be the seer, and not the hasid. The hasid cannot carry with him what he sees. Because of his lack of training, he is not experienced in piercing the amnesiac barrier obstructing access to the recovered–discovered material. The shock of becoming an object of God and of sharing momentarily with His mind; of being swallowed by it, and consumed; of experiencing cosmic consciousness and the complete and yet dynamic oneness of the All; of experiencing death and non-death, activity and passivity; of being Atlas and being crushed by the load, and at the same time feeling free and light; the experience of being carried; of being on fire and ground to bits; of being without breath, and of being only head without body—all this is too much for the hasid. Yet the hasid is there at the same place where the rebbe is, and at that same level. All contradictions are thus transcended, and in this sense, the rebbe–hasid juxtaposition or the perpendicular juxtaposition of

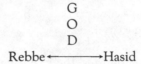

ceases to be anything but a merged unit in which the function of the hasid is to be helped, the function of God is to be the unmoved source of the energies, and the function of the rebbe is to be the one who remembers—and who so polarizes the random divine energies that they will be at the service of the hasid, and who so polarizes the hasid that he will be at the service of God.

In God's eternity, the yehidut is not an event, since it is always the eternal confluence of the All. In the hasid's experience the ontological, though not the phenomenological, yehidut has taken place. Generally, he does not transcend the person-to-person duality—the dialogical. His *hitqashrut* is often only symbolic, and he utilizes all possible symbols to make it real. But he seldom overcomes the awe and distance between himself and the rebbe.

The Yehidut—A Unique Encounter

Another meaning of the word *yehidut* is *m'yuhad*—set aside in a unique fashion. An impromptu encounter may turn out to be highly significant, but generally the term *yehidut* implies that both rebbe and hasid are specially prepared for the encounter. The meeting has its own formality and follows a generally predictable sequence. The purpose of the kvittel is to help the hasid recollect himself prior to the interview,[33] but the agenda for the yehidut is not restricted to dealing with the hasid's problems as presented in the kvittel. The kvittel affords rebbe and hasid a frame of reference from which to proceed. In order that the interview may proceed along the lines of the hasid's agenda, and in order to help the hasid overcome his awestruck reaction at finding himself in the presence of the rebbe, the rebbe begins the yehidut on the basis of the kvittel.

The Sequence Followed in the Yehidut

Generally, the following sequence of events is observed in the yehidut:

1. The rebbe prepares.
2. He informs the *gabbai* that he is ready to receive hasidim for yehidut.
3. The hasid prepares.
4. The hasid hands the kvittel to the rebbe.
5. The rebbe reads the kvittel.
6. The rebbe sighs.
7. The rebbe asks questions and the hasid replies.
8. The rebbe responds.
9. The rebbe offers the etzah.
10. The rebbe blesses the hasid.
11. The hasid departs.

In order to gain a clearer understanding of what actually happens in the process of a yehidut, we will explain each of these steps.

The Rebbe Prepares

In preparation for the yehidut, the rebbe reflects on his values and examines his intention and openness to his hasid and to divine guidance. He gives a sum to charity and prays that his counsel will help his hasidim. He divests himself of any previous concerns so that he will be ready to invest himself in his hasid. The rebbe will generally place an open book before him on a subject that bears interruption; and despite the fact that the hasid comes to the rebbe in a "crisis" situation, the rebbe will prepare to meet him not in an impromptu manner but with a face that expresses friendliness.

The Rebbe Informs the Gabbai that He Is Ready to Receive Hasidim for Yehidut

As the *gabbai* is often the person who writes the kvittel, the rebbe may consult him concerning the waiting hasidim and set up the order in which they are to be admitted. Rebbes have usually had a specific order of precedence for accepting their hasidim for yehidut. In some cases, those who came earlier have seen the rebbe sooner. Dignitaries have sometimes had precedence over regular hasidim. Curiously enough, some rebbes see non-Jews first, and then Jews. One rebbe explained that he did so in order to have the contrast between them work to the advantage of the Jew as the rebbe implored divine mercy for his hasidim. R. Mosheh Polier of Kobrin (the Kobriner) preferred young hasidim to be admitted first. Sometimes the rebbe may strike the name of one of the waiting hasidim from the list and may instruct his *gabbai* not to inform the hasid of this until the end of the yehidut session. This is not a capricious move on the part of the rebbe. He has observed this hasid at prayer and on other occasions and has come to the conclusion that the hasid is not yet ready for an interview, but that he might benefit from a period of preparation.

The Hasid Prepares

In preparation for the yehidut, the hasid will visit the miqveh and immerse himself in it. He dresses in his better clothes and girds himself with a *gartel*—a prayer sash. Upon arriving at the rebbe's court, he will either write his own kvittel or have the *gabbai* write it. There is a special attunement in the writing of the kvittel and in the reading of it. The writers write most often out of their "higher" mind. Knowing that they are writing for the rebbe's eyes makes them take their place on a higher level of awareness than usual. There is a sense in which they review their life from that height. Another way of stating this is that the interiorized rebbe, the one they have integrated as ideal master, guides the writing. Or, conversely, the rebbe reads the kvittel with the eyes of the hasid as he stands in the primal thought of Adam Qadmon.

The hasid generally has skipped the meal before the yehidut. He has the money for the pidyon ready as he seats himself in the anteroom. There he examines his conscience and reviews the events of his life since the last yehidut. If there is enough time, he will recite psalms.

Even if the yehidut is not to be a confessional, the hasid always enters the rebbe's presence as a penitent. He rethinks his values and centers them around the rebbe, recalling moments of great inspiration derived from the rebbe. In his imagination, the hasid already stands before the rebbe as he thinks of all these things. He is convinced that the rebbe can read his mind as he sits outside and waits. He feels the lack of privacy in his own thoughts. The sense of expectancy and receptivity toward the rebbe, the sense of yearning to be what the rebbe would have him be, prepares the hasid for the penitential process of the yehidut.

The Hasid Hands the Kvittel to the Rebbe

When the *gabbai* calls him, the hasid's heart beats faster: he tenses. With his free hand, he smooths his beard, adjusts his sash and hat, touches the mezuzah at the doorpost with a reverent kiss, and enters. He approaches the rebbe's desk and proffers the kvittel and the pidyon.

The Rebbe Reads the Kvittel

A generous look on his face, the rebbe takes the kvittel and the pidyon. The pidyon is usually put into an open drawer. The rebbe surveys the hasid. The hasid believes that the rebbe reads his forehead. The hasid's looks, his stance, his garb, his self-consciousness—all these are noted by the rebbe as he turns to the kvittel. Generally there is no word spoken yet, and the tension in the hasid mounts. The hasid usually remains standing before the rebbe and will refuse to sit in his presence even when the rebbe invites him to do so.

The rebbe looks at the name in the kvittel and uses a mnemonic device to remember it.[34] Having cleared his mind before the yehidut, the rebbe is flooded by impressions that take him to the root of the hasid's soul. Before he reads further, the real needs of the hasid are made clear to him, as well as the way in which these needs will be met. He beholds the soul before him as it has stood in the fullness of the divine thought and design, and looks at all the blocks and arrests that have kept the hasid from materializing this design. He looks deeply into the kvittel, reads it for its manifest content, and compares it with his estimate of what should have been written in it. He looks at the writing and notices if the kvittel was written by the *gabbai* or by the hasid himself. He takes note of what the writing tells him. He looks at the whole kvittel, shifts the focus of his eyes and looks again, and some constellations of letters form into new configurations—which may presage a shift from, for example, *mavet* (death) to *ma'ot* (money), or from *nega'* (plague) to *oneg* (delight).

The Rebbe Sighs

The rebbe becomes aware of the hasid's ancestors who have accompanied the hasid in spirit into the yehidut chamber. He marks the pleading of their needs in this descendant. Rapidly, he integrates all this in himself:

he becomes the hasid, and, standing in his place, sees how far the hasid is from being able to accept the right counsel for himself. The rebbe is flooded with immense compassion: he sighs. All this he raises in a short flash up to the point of unification with God, his own union in Him; and, looking at himself, he seeks to find his own experience, in a corresponding way, in that of the hasid. In a moment of decision, the rebbe mends this problem in himself and begins to question the hasid.

The Rebbe Asks Questions and the Hasid Replies

The hasid blushes at the rebbe's sigh. He is sorry to have caused the rebbe grief and concern for his soul. He feels as if he must apologize, but the rebbe begins his questioning. The questioning may remove rebbe and hasid far away from the explicit point of the kvittel. The rebbe may inquire about the hasid's business, his family, or his progress in his study and prayer life. The hasid replies to the rebbe's questions.

The Rebbe Responds

The rebbe may take one of the hasid's answers and repeat it to him, either in the same manner or with a different intonation. This elevates the conversation to the plane on which the etzah (counsel) can be given. If the hasid is ready, having followed the insight and having recovered from the shock of hearing what he really wanted to hear, the rebbe will proceed. If the rebbe sees no flash of recognition in a shifting of levels, he may try another route to bring the hasid to experience himself in the necessary way.

The hasid may have brought a simple, objective problem to the rebbe. If this is the case, a slightly different progression of events will be called for. However, the rebbe will still remember to "sell" the hasid some deeper insight—a word of Torah, a good custom—and then proceed to offer his counsel.

The Rebbe Offers the Etzah

Often the hasid does not receive the answer he expects from the rebbe. There is no guarantee that the problem he brought to the rebbe will have a solution. The hasid notices, however, that the rebbe is about to say something significant. The rebbe has shifted in his seat or has risen. His face takes on more authoritative lines. His voice becomes at once commanding and blessing; the hasid becomes especially attentive to absorb the rebbe's etzah.

When the rebbe has finished, the hasid may ask a few questions about something he has not understood. He may even want to argue with the rebbe. Generally, however, the rebbe maintains his position. Although the instructions may have been clear, the hasid may not understand how following these instructions can solve his problem. As he stands before the rebbe, he must make an act of faith. This he does, and inclines his head for the blessing.

The Rebbe Blesses the Hasid

Once more there is a shift in the rebbe's expression and manner, and the hasid, alert to this shift, strains to catch every syllable of the rebbe's blessing.

The Hasid Departs

When the rebbe has concluded, the hasid will utter a fervent "Amen" and start moving backward. Without turning his back to the rebbe, and without taking his eyes from the rebbe's face, he moves toward the door. The yehidut is finished.

The rebbe may make a few notations on the kvittel and place it where he can later use it to intercede on the hasid's behalf. The hasid may join a group outside in a dance, or he may sit quietly somewhere and fix the details of the yehidut in his mind, or perhaps even write them down. He may be surrounded by other hasidim who will eagerly question him with, "*Nu?* What did the rebbe tell you?"

The yehidut seldom deviates from this form.

The Setting of the Yehidut

The fact that the yehidut is a deliberate and planned encounter applies not only to the content of the yehidut but also to the setting.

Some rebbes prefer to see their hasidim during the day, while others prefer to do so at night. The overt reason given for choosing to see hasidim at night is usually that it is more convenient for those who must work during the day. However, there may be other reasons. Nighttime is more conducive to certain kinds of conversation. In the hasidic thought scheme, time has qualities that derive from constellations of the Divine Name. The nighttime constellations are of the Name A.D.N.Y., with the harsh decrees ruling until midnight, and then becoming sweetened by the foreshadowing of grace. Man's deeper self is more accessible at night; thus it is possible to deal with the more archaic levels. Intentional regression to primary states of being comes more easily at night.

The Lubavitcher Rebbe follows the pattern established by his late father-in-law and receives his hasidim after the evening prayers on Sunday, Tuesday, and Thursday nights. The appointments are set well in advance, and generally last from 9:30 in the evening until the early morning hours.

When rebbes were still located in small shtetls in Eastern Europe, such a strict regimen was not always followed. The hasid who came to see the rebbe generally came from out of town. He stayed at the rebbe's shtetl for at least three days, and often for a period of two weeks. There was less need to escape the urban tumult in order to prepare for the yehidut; yet the fact that the hasid had to travel some distance gave him more opportunity to prepare himself. The rebbe of the shtetl was generally more accessible to his hasidim than the modern rebbe.

The rebbe does not receive hasidim for yehidut at all times of the year. In Lubavitch, for example, it is customary for the rebbe to remain in seclusion for the month of Elul (the month before Rosh Hashanah) until after Simhat Torah (the holiday of Rejoicing in the Torah), a span of seven weeks. During this time, he may receive hasidim for special occasions, but these occasions follow a highly stylized custom and are not in the nature of a yehidut transaction. Similarly, from the beginning of the month of Nisan until after Passover, the rebbe does not receive hasidim on a regular basis. In emergencies, the rebbe can be contacted via his secretaries.

The yehidut itself takes place in the rebbe's yehidut chamber. If the rebbe is en route, a room is prepared for him and set up according to his preferences. Usually, the room is so arranged that the rebbe is seated at his desk with an unblocked view to the door. The distance from the desk to the door is not great. The room is not excessively bright: a lamp or candles are situated in front of the rebbe. The rebbe is seated in a throne-like chair. Another chair is located near the desk so that the visitor may sit (although, as previously noted, a hasid will seldom sit in the rebbe's presence). The room is usually lined with bookshelves.

The hasid has little time to note the composition of the room, the location of furniture, or other incidentals. His consciousness centers on the rebbe. Yet the subliminal effect of the room inspires a sense of competence and confidence, and an awesome intimacy. The general impression is that of a scholar's study.

How often does a hasid expect to go to a yehidut? In the early years of Hasidism, the contact between master and disciples (who later became rebbes themselves) was frequent. While a disciple lived at the rebbe's court, he came to see the master at least once a month. However, in the *Lyozhna Taqanot*, which describes R. Shneur Zalman's visitation policies, once in three years was the most frequent yehidut. Hasidim have been taught not to come to the rebbe unless they have a question that leaves only two alternatives open. If the question is referred to the *mashpiy'a* for resolution, the hasid may be told not to come to the yehidut at all.

At various high points in life—at bar mitzvah, before a wedding, and the like—the hasid comes for yehidut to learn a way of serving appropriate to his new life and to receive a blessing to succeed in this way. Apart from emergencies and rites of passage, a yehidut once a year has been considered the minimum in the general hasidic situation, and it remains so today. A favorite of many hasidim is to visit the rebbe on their birthday, or as close to it as they can.

The yehidut differs from other helping situations in several respects. First, the hasid is generally left to work through the rebbe's counsel with the help of the *mashpiy'a* or his fellow hasidim at the farbrengen. Second, the intensity of the yehidut is probably far greater than that of any other helping encounter. Third, it is probably less frequent and much shorter in duration.

Since the yehidut is obviously authoritative and implicitly directive, and since the hasid has faith that the rebbe's direction will work in his daily life on a morally heteronomous basis (he follows the rules of the *Shulhan Arukh* and the customs of Hasidism, and his behavior is generally decreed by norms from without), the yehidut itself is not a lengthy affair. If the yehidut takes much time, it is a sign that the hasid is ill-prepared. R. Shmuel of Lubavitch, in replying to a question as to why he spent more time with the rich than with the poor, said:

> The poor know that they are poor, and their need is clear to them; so
> we can quickly get to the point. It takes quite a while for the rich man
> to see his poverty; but once we get to the point where he sees how
> poor he is, it takes the same amount of time.[35]

The length of the yehidut can vary from five minutes to two or more hours on occasion. During the ministry of R. Joseph Isaac Schneersohn of Lubavitch (1880–1950), the average time was five to seven minutes. During the ministry of R. Menahem Mendl Schneersohn I, the average time was from a half hour to two hours. With the present Lubavitcher Rebbe, the time varies from five minutes to a half hour, with a first interview taking up to an hour. The time spent in a yehidut with other rebbes is similar in pattern.

THE DIAGNOSTIC PROCESS

In the diagnostic process, the rebbe has to deal with many coordinates and must locate the hasid along several continua. He must find the hasid's spiritual rung and plot his movement along this line. He must understand the hasid's body makeup and type. He must estimate the level of discipline the hasid has reached and know enough about his habits in order to counsel him. He must know what kind of mind the hasid has, whether it is given to abstraction or to the concrete, whether it is rigid or elastic. He must also be able to place the hasid in his social setting. He must know the hasid's financial capabilities and obligations. All these factors must be integrated by the rebbe before he can decide on the manner in which he and his hasid will interact.

The Kvittel as Symptom

As we have noted in discussing the sequence followed in the yehidut, the hasid, upon entering the yehidut chamber, hands the rebbe a kvittel. Even before the rebbe reads it, he has sensed all the data of the hasid's stance, his degree of tenseness, and the like. For a fleeting moment he *becomes* the hasid, and through his empathic identification is able to view himself as the hasid sees him. He now has a sense of the hasid's readiness and receptiveness, or lack of these. (The hasid may have arrived at an anticlimactic mood as a result of the inevitable delay caused by others who preceded him. The rebbe will then have to work the hasid back to the sense of expectancy, urgency, and willingness that brought him to the yehidut.) In sizing up the hasid, the rebbe may discern that this is someone who is at yehidut not because of his own wish and decision, but because his interaction with others has forced him to come. In this case, the rebbe may either dismiss the unwilling hasid and ask him to return when he is ready, or take advantage of the moment by attuning the hasid to his own attitude and helping him deal with it. If he decides to utilize the encounter, the rebbe will honor the kvittel and proceed with the first movement of the yehidut—the reading of the kvittel.

The rebbe reads the kvittel with a sense of anticipation. Will it be a complaining kvittel? This may already be indicated by its length. The longer the kvittel, the more wary the rebbe is. A hasid who brings many details of circumstance to bear on the yehidut is likely to have less insight into his condition and feel a greater need to defend himself against the rebbe. A short kvittel indicates a simpler approach, even where the needs are great. The hasid who writes a short kvittel shows more trust in the rebbe (and in God). A precise statement of numerous antecedents and causes indicates that the hasid has made a detailed evaluation of his position, and may not expect to be helped except on his own terms.

Still, a long kvittel is better than a lengthy oral exposition. The problem can be addressed more directly, in contrast to that of the hasid who works his story out in the rebbe's presence. However, the rebbe may, at times, ask the hasid to state what he wants despite the kvittel. And, because several days may have elapsed since the kvittel was originally written, the rebbe may decide that the hasid should relive the situation that prompted the request for yehidut. Or perhaps the hasid needs to be made to *feel* what he wrote on the kvittel. For unless he can feel it, there will be little progress made at the yehidut.

The rebbe delights in the *Ba'al Shemske* kvittel.[36] This is what the Apter, R. Abraham Joshua Heschel, called a kvittel that requested advice and a blessing in the service of God.[37] But such a kvittel would have to be genuine, and not merely a pro forma move on the hasid's part. To a hasid who presented a pro forma request to him, the Tzemah Tzedeq said: "Fool! Only this you lack?" But if the kvittel is sincere, the rebbe sees in it the vindication of his career. At one time, R. Shneur Zalman did not want to accept any other kvittlech, making it clear that his function was not to be a procurer of material blessings. This he held and taught to be the result of the simple faith that each one is apportioned that which God wished to apportion him. R. Menahem Mendl of Kotsk also refused to react to his hasidim's simple needs when they did not concern spiritual direction.

But the absence of such a *Ba'al Shemske* kvittel does not upset the rebbe. He expects these to be rare, and because of their rarity, all the more valuable.

If the kvittel relates to a matter of health, the rebbe is quick to commiserate and offer his intercession. If the kvittel concerns childlessness, the rebbe will likewise commiserate, although before he "promises" children, the rebbe will be relatively circumspect. If the kvittel concerns the hasid's livelihood, the rebbe is generally slower in his commiseration and intercession. He may feel that "Israel's poverty becomes him."[38] Having read the manifest part of the kvittel, the rebbe will then set aside the kvittel to return to it later. At this point, he turns his attention from the kvittel to the hasid's record.

Buber, in *For the Sake of Heaven*, offers a description that can help us understand the manner in which the rebbe "sees" his hasid. The description carries with it much of hasidic lore:

The Yehudi, having been appointed by the Seer to minister to the hasidim in his absence, went . . . in order to fulfill, as need arose, the functions of his office. At that very moment sundry strangers entered. He looked at them to see whether there were among them aspirants after the Rabbi's leadership [i.e., who wanted to have yehidut]. And now something came to pass that frightened him as nothing had done during all his life. He looked at one of those who had entered, a very ordinary person, and looked involuntarily upon the man's forehead. In the next instant it seemed to him as though a curtain were drawn apart. He stood at the brink of a sea whose dark waves assaulted the very heavens. And now they too were split asunder as the curtain had been and thus gave space for a figure, totally unlike the visitor, but with the same seal upon its forehead that was seen upon his. But already that figure was devoured by the waves; behind it stood another, different again but with that same seal. It too vanished and farther and farther the depths revealed figures after figures. The Yehudi closed his eyes. When he opened them again, nothing was to be seen but that ordinary man and the people about him and the room with its ordinary furnishings.

For a long time he did not dare to look at the next visitor. So as soon as he did so the same thing took place. Again a curtain was torn asunder and again waves rolled in the abyss and again vision succeeded vision. At this point the Yehudi mastered the disturbance of his mind and decided to obey the plain and open bidding that had been given him. He observed and sought to grasp every figure. He let it sink into the depth of his memory. He forced his eyes to remain open as long as possible. And suddenly when it came to the fourth and fifth visitor he noticed that a change had been accomplished within him. His vision penetrated the depths independently; with inhuman swiftness it pierced those realms it reached to the background of that row of figures and came upon the very being of the primordial.[39]

The record that the rebbe sees is the record of the soul's development through all its incarnations. It is the same record spoken of by *Avot* 2:1, which says that "all thine acts are recorded in the book." The rebbe must not be arrested by any of the figures until he reaches the level on which that soul stood in the primordial Adam Qadmon—the first vision God had of this soul. It is a vision in which all the potentialities of a soul are realized in divine fullness. The rebbe's task is to see that the hasid realizes this plenitude—if possible, in this present lifetime.

After the rebbe has seen the record of the hasid's soul, he recedes from this vision in order to be able to integrate it with the material he can observe, elicit through questions, intuit through empathy, and deduce from what is not said or shown in the hasid's life.

The Rebbe Locates the Hasid on the Mundane Continuum

Verbal and Nonverbal Indications

STANCE AND POSTURE

"And man became a living soul."[40] Onkelos translates "a living soul" as "a spirit that speaks." But it is not only the spirit that speaks; the body too speaks. And the language of the body is often more eloquent than that of the mind. When the mind is frustrated for lack of vocabulary, it will utilize the body to speak for it in gestures. For all the celebration of Israel's prowess in using the voice ("The voice is the voice of Jacob,"[41] and "As a worm's power is in its mouth so is Israel's. Thus it is written, 'Fear not worm of Jacob'"), verbal means are insufficient, and a Jew speaks in volatile gestures. The mind needs the body for a more genuine expression. The body speaks even when the face hides its message.

The rebbe listens to what the body says by noting its stance. Although the hasid's stance is one of awe and submission before the rebbe, as this is part of the protocol of the yehidut, the rebbe will observe whether the stance is usual or forced by the occasion. The proud man stands more self-consciously when he has to assume the stance of a supplicant; while the same stance fits the beggar like an old shoe. The habitual bearing of a man is observable even when he assumes another stance. The average hasid is not so consummate an actor that he can control his body language at will. The rebbe reads the hasid's unconscious body attitude like an open book.

THE HASID'S AURA

The Magid of Mezhirech once stated that "A small puncture in the body bespeaks a large one in the soul."[42] The soul surrounds and penetrates the body. According to the hasidic system, what inhabits the body is not the whole soul: it is too vast to inhabit the body.[43] Yet the soul is affected by the workings of the body and shows these in its aura. It replies to the rebbe's questioning gaze, laying bare the diseases of the body. Even if a hasid does not speak to him of his physical welfare, a rebbe may suggest that the hasid visit his physician for a checkup. If the doctor is unable to find any trace of the disease, the rebbe may suggest to the doctor where to follow up with a more intensive examination.

MANNER OF DRESS

The rebbe learns much about the hasid by the clothing that he wears. In a person's garments there is an entire science of physiognomy.[44] It takes little training today to distinguish between a Prince Albert–like Lubavitcher *shirtuck* and the Galician *bekkishe*, the Bobover overcoat and collar that resemble a Roman-collared paletot, and the golden, pinstriped *abayeh khalat* of Meah She'arim. Even the headgear is distinctive. The Polish hasidim wear high, rounded full fur hats (*shtreimlakh*), with the fur wrapped around the cap, while the Galician, Meah She'arim, and Hungarian hasidim wear sabletail *shtreimlakh*. There are further distinctions and subdistinctions in hasidic apparel. Thus, the hasid's affiliation is identifiable by the clothing he wears. If the hasid changes any aspect of the "uniform," he shows his criticism of or dissent from the group.

When the hasid comes to the rebbe, he will wear his better clothes.[45] Otherwise he opens himself to criticism from his peers. The rebbe is thus able to see the hasid's conformity or lack of conformity to the group norms. If the rebbe senses that the hasid is self-conscious in the garb he is wearing, he knows that the hasid is dressed in this manner only for the occasion, and that it is not his normal garb. The amount of wear and tear on the clothing indicates the hasid's financial state and is also an index of his character traits.

In short, the rebbe gains a wealth of information about the hasid merely from the seemingly insignificant factor of his apparel. He integrates this information with the rest of the knowledge he has acquired about the hasid in order to counsel him more effectively and according to his need.

SPEECH HABITS AND ETHNIC ORIGIN

If the hasid were to speak in one dialect and affect the garb of an ethnic group speaking another, this too would serve the rebbe as a clue to be pursued for understanding his hasid. But even if the hasid's garb and dialect correspond, the rebbe is still able to draw some generalizations that place the hasid into a cultural subgroup and thus have an important bearing on his character.

Allowing for individual differences, the rebbe chooses images that suit the specific ethnic temperament of his hasid. A Galician Jew would immediately elicit a different approach than a Lithuanian Jew. It may turn out that this particular "Galitzianer" is, in temperament, more like the proverbial "Litvak," but the rebbe will not lose much in making the first overture in the Galitzianer direction. If the rebbe's own cultural background embraces that of the hasid, their intimacy will probably be even greater.

Since much of a hasid's emotional life is rooted in his ability to regress to his haven–home–mother–father experience, the rebbe will use the hasid's ethnic origin to reinforce this loyalty. Thus, when this writer had an interview with the present Bobover Rebbe, R. Shlomoh Halberstamm, he was told the parable of the apple tree, after which the Bobover assumed an intimate manner of speech and said: "Your father is a Galitzianer, is he not?" Upon receiving an affirmative answer, he mused: "Toss a stick into the air, and it falls on its root."[46]

Whether or not the term for prayer, *davenen*, originates from *d'avinun*—"from our fathers"—remains open to conjecture, but it is certain that in order to pray to God, one has to identify with one's father and address God as "Our God and God of our fathers." Prayer is the verbal expression of the heart par excellence. The rebbe must know to which feeling level his hasid is attuned. This he comes to know by observing the hasid's manner of garb and speech.

The rebbe's diagnostic function is greatly aided by his ability to discern the hasid's ethnic roots and to empathize with them. By understanding the hasid's ethnic origin, the rebbe can also gauge, to a certain extent, the amount of warmth expressed in the hasid's family. People of different ethnic origin have different norms for demonstrating affection in the family. This knowledge will help the rebbe understand the hasid's natural temperament, and consequently will help him relate to the hasid in a constructive manner.

Obligations to Family and Friends

A number of problems dealing with conflicting loyalties stem from the hasid's diverse obligations to family and friends. For this reason, the rebbe cannot prescribe for the hasid unless he is aware of the hasid's obligations. A hasid who seeks a deeper contemplative life may find that the rebbe will interpret his yearning for more solitude as a wish to escape such duties as the parental obligation to "teach his children diligently." If the hasid is to remain at the rebbe's domicile for any length of time, the rebbe will inquire whether the hasid has his wife's consent. In assessing the appropriateness of the hasid's penitential donation, the rebbe will take into consideration the hasid's financial state in order to make sure that he is not imposing an undue burden on the hasid's family.

On the kvittel, the rebbe will generally find a list of the members of a hasid's family. The parents and children of the hasid are mentioned, each with what he or she lacks, so that they may receive the rebbe's blessing. The kvittel thus serves as a sociogram, mirroring the hasid's loyalties and conflicts, and expressing them in an overt request for advice or in the seemingly fortuitous apposition of family members in the order of the kvittel. The hasid who expresses the hope that his daughter will find a good match affords the rebbe material for further questions. He knows that the hasid is concerned not only about the match but also about the money necessary to provide his daughter's dowry. The rebbe translates the social problem into a financial one, and deals with each in relation to the other.

At times a hasid concerned for his friend's welfare may mention his friend's predicament to the rebbe. The rebbe will react to this request in a direct way by blessing the friend or by offering directional advice. He will also take the request into consideration in evaluating the hasid. A hasid's compassion and concern for others has positive value in the rebbe's intercession for this hasid.

The way in which a hasid judges his peers in the presence of the rebbe tells the rebbe much about the hasid's view of himself and others, and often provides the rebbe with a means of bringing the hasid to face himself with insight.

> To a hasid who complained about his friend, calling him a hypocrite, the Tzemah Tzedeq replied: "How long have you known him?" When the hasid replied that he had known the man twenty-five years, the Tzemah Tzedeq asked: "And all that time he has acted the same way?" "Yes," answered the hasid. The Tzemah Tzedeq then took a sharp blade and cut into the table, showing the hasid how the stain had penetrated through and through. "This table has been painted now for twenty years. Every year before Passover it is sanded and stained. The stain has now completely penetrated the wood. Is it not possible that this *tzavui* [hypocrite, painted one] is now authentically as he claims to be?"[47]

In refining the hasid's own judgment of his friend, the rebbe is able to bring him to insight. The very quality that served as a power for evil is turned into a power for good. The hasid's understanding of himself is deepened, and his sense of obligation to his friend strengthened.

The manner in which the hasid discharges his obligations serves the rebbe as an indication of whether he can be trusted with new and higher ways of service. The hasid's ability or inability to manage his finances tells the rebbe a great deal about his character. If the hasid was so poor at handling his various obligations that he was heavily dependent, a *shlemiel*, the rebbe could handle him in either of two ways. He could nurse him along at his present level, knowing that he could not be trusted with higher methods of service; or, if he felt that the hasid's dependence was merely a slothful escape, the rebbe could refuse to help him in order to force him to sink or swim on his own.

Vocation

Distance from worldly pursuits is a good thing for the hasid with a contemplative vocation, but not for the hasid whose career necessitates temporal involvement. The way in which such a hasid manages his worldly commitments tells the rebbe much, not only about his material life, but also about his spiritual life. The mature hasid discharges his obligations as efficiently as possible. He knows that although earning a livelihood requires sincere effort and exertion, it does not require all of a person's imaginative faculties. The hasid must always bear in mind where his real "home" is. All involvement in means merely as means is considered valid; but when the means capture the hasid's emotions, he is in danger of forgetting that his primary commitment lies in his role as a hasid. As such, all his emotions must be assigned to the service of God and subsumed under that heading. When the rebbe sees the hasid becoming absorbed in his material involvements, he needs to remind him that in forgetting the true end, he is treating the means as ends in themselves, and this contradicts his vocation as a hasid.

> A hasid once came to the Maharash, complaining that he found himself no longer able to study well. His prayers had become mechanical. The rebbe inquired of him where he resided [though he knew very well the circumstances of the hasid's domicile]. The hasid replied that he lived in Byeshenkowitch. When the rebbe inquired where the hasid did his business, the hasid replied: "In Riga." "And how many months do you spend in Riga?" the rebbe queried. When the hasid replied that he spent ten and a half months in Riga, the rebbe asked: "If you spend ten and a half months in Riga and only one and a half months in Byeshenkowitch, why do you say that you live in Byeshenkowitch?" "Rebbe," the hasid replied, "In Riga I am for business, in Byeshenkowitch I am at home." And suddenly the hasid understood the rebbe's meaning. He had forsaken his domicile in Torah study and prayer and had taken up residence in business.[48]

Today a rebbe can derive more information from the fact of a hasid's vocation than he could in the past, when there was little social mobility and when children, for the most part, had to assume their father's profession as their own. The father's vocation was considered the safest choice, since it eliminated any problems involving *hazaqah* privileges that established the son's legal right to a trade. Nevertheless, a son might, out of rebellion against parental authority, or for any other reason, decide that he did not want to assume his father's vocation even though he was truly suited to it. In this case, the rebbe would have to reconcile the hasid to his parental *hazaqah*.

The hasid's income does not concern the rebbe so much as its necessary concomitants and the problems it brings in its train. The rebbe has to help the hasid contend with the issue of luxury. Yet the rebbe must also recognize that luxury is relative: what passes for luxury and a sign of fiscal irresponsibility in a man of small means, may well be the regular and necessary ménage for the rich man. The rebbe may refrain from making sumptuary restrictions since, if the rich hasid were to become an ascetic, he would not give anything to the poor. To protect his hasidim from trying to outdo each other to excess, the Bobover Rebbe has imposed such restrictions. For example, there is a limit on the number of guests that may be invited to a bar mitzvah celebration, and the celebration is generally expected to be in the home.

Income levels naturally create certain specific dispositions, as described in the following passage:

> The division into income levels is a natural one, since it habituates persons to different styles of life, and the habits, after a while, become second nature. Riches and poverty are, by nature, diametrically opposed. A rich person is strong in:
>
> (a) self-confidence
> (b) a feeling of wholesomeness
> (c) broadness of heart
> (d) pride and arrogance
> (e) contempt of paupers and pride in his difference from them
>
> The poor, on the other hand, are:
>
> (a) weak in self-confidence
> (b) subdued
> (c) brokenhearted
> (d) oppressed
> (e) self-derogating
>
> These ten qualities that characterize the rich and the poor contain both desirable and undesirable elements. That which is undesirable

remains so whether it is of the nature of riches or of poverty. On the other hand, that which is desirable, whether of the nature of riches or of poverty, does not constitute a virtue in itself. For example, although self-confidence is a tremendous asset, for it is necessary to man in order to live up to his full potential, it nevertheless does not of itself constitute a virtue.

If self-confidence leads to a desirable end in the study of Torah and the observance of mitzvot, and in a virtuous life, then it is a virtue which has great usefulness. It reinforces one's knowledge of Torah: it reinforces the motivation to analytical thinking, and leads to growth in intellectual attainment. It aids in the control, persecution, and destruction of the vices, and the acquisition of the virtues. He who has self-confidence will not find it difficult to attain profound thinking and a higher level of virtuousness. However, all this holds true only when one utilizes the characteristic of self-confidence for that which is useful and good. However, if someone uses self-confidence to promote lower ends, as those empty souls among the rich are wont to do (those who have been blinded by their riches, concerning whom the Scripture states "that riches are kept to their owners' detriment"), then the characteristic of self-confidence becomes the foul source of all sorts of moral illnesses. The same holds true of the characteristics of brokenheartedness and self-abasement, which are great attributes and can set a person on the highest level of humanity when used for good and useful ends. But, if brokenheartedness is the result of poverty, it tends to repress the light of the mind and of feeling, and brings on dullness of the mind and depression of the heart.

The task of education and guidance is to heal moral illnesses and to strengthen moral health. Consequently, the manner of education that befits the rich is different from the manner of education and guidance that befits the poor. While both require that the process of education and guidance be carried out in a well-ordered manner, the approaches differ.[49]

If a hasid utilizes his financial position for the benefit of his fellow man, and thus in the service of God, he accrues great merit not only for himself, but for all Israel. A young woman who received long overdue back-pay amounting to $5,000, an amount greater than the family savings (and by that time, there was a large family to care for), received her husband's consent to turn this sum over to the rebbe. The money was used to establish a loan fund for yeshivah teachers, enabling them to collect in cash against promissory notes for their salary. The woman's act amounted to heroic virtue and became an example to the entire hasidic community, even though the rebbe did not divulge the donor's name. Such virtue becomes more than a diagnostic means in the rebbe's understanding of his hasid. It is a potent source of merit that the rebbe can exploit in the arousal of divine grace and mercy for all Israel.

Though a certain amount of arrogance may be expected of the rich, the index of arrogance must not exceed the hasid's financial position:

> A rich man at a rabbinical lay conference dedicated to political action, defied the rabbis publicly. In rebuking him, one rabbi said: "King Solomon said: 'The rich answered with arrogance.' But your arrogance, it would seem, greatly exceeds your wealth."[50]

Habit Patterns

A man's station in life determines his habit patterns. Habit patterns are of characterological significance. In order to help the hasid, the rebbe needs to be able to understand his habit patterns and distinguish them from innate, unlearned dispositions. Such unlearned dispositions are placed by the rebbe under other categories.

> Habit patterns exert a tenacious hold on man, both in themselves, and in their interaction with other forces that influence man. Although they are learned rather than innate reactions, they become so strong as to be almost instinctual. As the proverb would have it: "Habit becomes second nature." Besides being strong in itself, it is strong in the effects it creates. Habit exerts a strong effect upon every facet of man, from the limbs of the body, to the powers of the soul.
>
> Any action that exerts its influence upon the powers of the soul assumes one of two modes:
>
> (1) The action that operates within the mode of nearby influences, such as the action of the mind, which is a nearby influence of intimate closeness, for it explains and communicates the manner in which the thought is to be understood. This is applicable to matters concerning learning and conduct. Whenever the mind influences, it does so deliberately and with ease.

(2) The action whose influence is from afar and by imperative, such as the action of the will, which comes through the dominion of imperatives.

Habit operates in the latter mode. It works through imperatives and through domination. As the saying has it: "Habit *rules* everything." It does not concern itself with the things upon which it acts; nor does it concern itself with whether it relates to the limbs of the body in smaller things, or to the powers of the soul in greater things. Wherever habit is active, it works through domination and without consideration for that which lies outside its sphere.

    Habits are like all other qualities of men, and like all other powers of the soul. They are always instrumental. When they are utilized in the service of the good and the useful, they become beautiful. When they are used for the low and despicable, they become evil. Thus, we can speak of habits that are good and habits that are evil. And it becomes evident, therefore, that education and guidance for the purpose of strengthening habit must itself be well ordered and habitual. Contrary to the nature of habit itself [which does not concern itself with the specific], education and guidance concerning habit must be very specific . . . in order to strengthen and beautify the good habits, and destroy and uproot the bad habits so that they are obliterated.[51]

The rebbe's task necessitates that he understand the hasid's habit patterns in such a way that it will be clear which habits require strengthening and which are to be obliterated. He must be able to understand the hasid's basic needs as well as his true vocation. Only if he understands this will he know which habits are in the service of the hasid's life's vocation, and which are destructive to it.

Environment

In locating the hasid along his life continuum, the rebbe must first be able to locate him environmentally. What is normal for a hasid living in an urban environment is not normal for a hasid living in a rural setting:

This difference, at first blush, seems to be extraneous and irrelevant, but, in reality, it is not so. The place of one's domicile, whether it be in a rural or an urban area, exerts a fundamental influence on one's style of life. It influences all branches of life, from the intrapersonal area of the development of one's talents and the manifestation of one's soul powers, to the interpersonal area of one's style of life as it concerns the members of one's own family, their education, guidance and conduct.

Consequently, all branches of one's life and that of one's family depend on the conduct and style of life resulting from the environment in which a person and his family find themselves. If the influence of the environment itself is so great, even greater is the influence of the social mores of the environment. As a result, the difference of environment—the rural lending itself more to harmony and tranquility—is of great relevance and importance.[52]

By incorporating the environmental factor, the rebbe can judge whether the hasid's particular lifestyle is appropriate or not. Any rebbe who counseled a Warsaw merchant who had to travel to Danzig and Leipzig in the course of his business, in the same manner that he counseled a hasid from a small rural village, would have missed the mark. Just as R. Shmuel of Lubavitch found that a hasid's specific environmental context afforded the rebbe an opportunity for insight,[53] so did other rebbes utilize rural models for rural hasidim and urban models for urban hasidim.

The Rebbe Looks at the Hasid's Spiritual Life Space

A preponderance of one behavioral mode over all others is usually considered more of a vice than a virtue. The division between the generous and the lecherous is only a hairs-breadth. One is Abraham, the other is Ishmael.[54] One is holiness, the other is *q'lipah* (evil). Wisdom itself is a great virtue; yet there is only a hairs-breadth between wisdom and apostasy. The pious man is very close to the fanatical murderer. R. Naftali of Ropshitz observed: "Generosity alone is a lecher. Cleverness alone is an apostate. Piety alone is a murderer. The integration of all three is a hasid."[55]

It is not enough that the rebbe locate his hasid on the continua of intelligence, generosity, and religiosity. He must also determine to what extent each of these influences and limits the others. The rebbe seeks to determine not only the static point at which the various lines intersect, but also the range of the field within which the hasid moves. This range is circumscribed by innate, habitual, and balancing factors that have a primary lien over the learned factors. Habits motivated by the *yetzer hatov*, the inclination for good, arrive later in life than those motivated by the instinctual *yetzer hara*, the inclination for evil that is humanity's heritage at birth.[56] For this reason, the "poor child"[57] must be more "clever" than the "old and foolish king."[58] Rebbes are fond of celebrating the perspicacious hasid who knows the wiles of his instincts and has learned to channel his blind urge in the service of God.

The hasid's spiritual life space indicates how well or poorly he manages his instincts. The amount of Torah learning he has acquired is the index of his wisdom. His observance of the minutiae of Torah is the index of his piety. His ability to give himself to spontaneity is the index of his generosity. Finally, the level of his integration of all these is the index of his prayer life.

Education in This Life

Rabbinic tradition holds that the fetus in its mother's womb is taught the entire Torah; but the angel who is with the child in the womb uses the shock of the moment of birth to make the child forget all that he has learned. Thus, when a child learns Torah, he has a déjà vu experience, but no recall without study. The hierarchy of sophistication in Torah study extends from the level of the *am ha'aretz*, the simple ignoramus, to the gaon, the prince of Torah. It is an ascending scale in which the categories of the simple householder (ba'al habayit) alone range as follows: the one who barely knows how to read *Ivri* (the Hebrew letters); the *T'hilim* Jew (who spends his time reciting the psalms); the *Ayin Ya'aqov* Jew (who spends his time studying the talmudic legends); the *Humash-Rashi* Jew (who spends his time studying the Pentateuch and Rashi's interpretations); the *Mishnayot* Jew (who studies the Mishnah); and the *Hayey Adam* Jew (who studies the book of law concerned with daily living). When a Jew has attained the ability to study Talmud by himself, he is in the category of the *lamdan*, or "learned one." Here the *baqi*, the well-oriented one who has studied much and remembers much, is in competition with the *harif*, the incisive thinker. Their study centers on Talmud and *Tosafot*, *Rishonim*, *Aharonim*, and *Posqim*.

According to Hasidism, the study of Torah has great reparative merit. It would be a sin for the talented Torah scholar, who can give pleasure to God by learning, to fast and castigate himself if such asceticism would weaken his Torah study. At the opposite end of the scale, for such a man to engage in more than occasional secular work would constitute an error and a misapplication of his talents. Even if a hasid's talents lie in other areas of divine service, his life is considered badly out of balance if he neglects Torah study. The ignorant man, who neither knows nor cares to know, could not be a hasid. Torah is the sustaining food of the soul.[59] Intelligence and attainment in the study of Torah are not as important as exertion and effort. This is why the formula of the morning blessing is not "to achieve in the study of Torah," but "to exert oneself in the study of Torah."

A hasid's movement through the incarnational levels depends on his study of Torah.[60] The salvational model demands that the individual study the entire Torah. Since many souls have, in previous incarnations, acquired much of the exoteric teachings of Torah, souls in these latter generations stand in greater need of acquiring the esoteric teachings of Torah. A hasid who occupies himself with study on a lower level, when he is capable of study on a higher level, is not fulfilling his function.

Torah is one of the pillars on which the world stands. The world, *ha'olam*, was interpreted by R. Shneur Zalman as denoting that which is hidden, *he'elem*.[61] Thus, one of the pillars on which God's hiddenness stands is Torah. And the purpose of creation—God's hiding in order that He may be found—is realized in Torah. He Who has given Himself to man in the Torah can be found in it.[62] And so the whole purpose of life revolves around the study of Torah, the finding of God in Torah.

Intellectual pursuits other than the study of Torah are not to be followed unless they are in the service of Torah. Unless channeled in the service of God, such pursuits are fraught with danger. They contaminate the soul's mental functions and lead man astray.[63] Any hasid who is considering the pursuit of secular studies must raise this consideration with the rebbe, who will counsel him as to the advisability of such a course of study. Secular study for its own sake is considered unworthy and is shunned because of the dangers following in its train. It is only when such study is in the service of Torah and vocation that it even becomes a question for consideration with the rebbe.

In spite of this fact, the rebbe, in communicating with his hasid, will utilize whatever conceptual models the hasid possesses in his intellectual arsenal. He will seek to establish the hasid's conceptual coordinates, and, in order to produce insight and motivation, will address him in the language of his intellectual pursuits. Generally, the rebbe prefers to speak on the level of the hasid's highest conceptual mode, for he is the hasid's master and teacher, and seeks always to raise the hasid to higher levels of intellectual attainment and integration. Yet, in a case where the intellectual interferes, the rebbe will avoid the language of the learned in order to show the hasid the need for ethos or pathos. The hasid who overintellectualizes may be shocked to find that the rebbe will utilize reversal tactics in order to help him gain insight into himself.

A Habad hasid once came to visit R. Mendel of Kotsk. In the course of their discussion, the rebbe, dealing with the hasid's prayer life,

asked him what the Sh'ma meant to him. The hasid replied with a
lengthy discourse of book learning. Impatiently, R. Mendel interrupted him and said: "That's all very well. This is what it means to
your head. But what does it mean to your *puppik* [umbilicus]?"[64]

The rebbe was aware that the hasid's involvement with prayer and its
significance was overly intellectual, and he was concerned with making the
hasid aware that mere intellectual involvement left much to be desired.
The hasid's whole being must be involved in his service of God. A mature
hasid did not allow a great distance to remain between his intellectual and
behavioral attainments. He knew that it was essential that the two levels of
Torah and mitzvot be in harmony.

Level of Observance and Commitment

The Mishnaic formula *yatza y'dey hovato* ("he fulfilled his obligation") is not enough for the hasid, who, by talmudic definition, must do
more than the Law requires of him.[65] The hasid equates mere fulfillment of
the Law with automatism. The execution of a mitzvah demands of the hasid
a high level of intentionality; he interprets *im kiven libo yatza* as, "if he
intended in his heart" (he transcended the exile). To merely extricate
himself from the grasp of obligation was considered ungenerous to God.
Such mitzvah action left the hasid earthbound. Study and prayer needed an
active arousal of Love and Awe in order to raise the hasid to higher levels.[66]

In order to locate the hasid diagnostically, the rebbe has to know the
levels of his observance. Here we are not referring to the observance of
those mitzvot that obligate all of Israel. It goes without saying that gross
deviation from the halakhic norms is not tolerated. Generally, halakhic
deviations pointed to a "disease of the soul." This area of the hasid's need
was of great concern to the rebbe, who wanted to work through this
problem before discussing anything else with the hasid. Nowadays, the
task is more difficult. A hasid who comes from a nonobservant environment may need strong motivation before he can undertake fuller observance. For this reason, it may be necessary for the rebbe to provide this
motivation by first leading the hasid to higher levels of inner life. As a
result of a more intense involvement in service, the hasid may feel a real
need for fuller observance as an indication of his deeper involvement. He
may then be more ready to make a fuller outer commitment, having
established his inner commitment. Thus, we cannot understand the
rebbe's prescriptions solely by seeing them against the models of the past,
when the Jewish community, by and large, was completely halakhic in its

behavior. By these standards, it would seem incompatible for the rebbe to prescribe meditative techniques prior to a hasid's full participation in the halakhic life. Yet conditions have changed, and the hasid who comes to the rebbe from the periphery of Jewish observance may be following his attraction to the inner spiritual life. If this is what brings the hasid to the rebbe, the rebbe will have to deal with him in such a way that he will feel his inner direction has been strengthened. The more the hasid is able to feel this, the greater will be his potential for halakhic involvement. In the past, the rebbe often had to urge his hasid to higher and more generous levels of observance on the basis of Halakhah in order to justify to him the esoteric way. Today, the reverse is true for the convert to Hasidism. The esoteric is his motivation for observance. Previously, when the authority of Halakhah was self-evident, it was utilized to reinforce the esoteric quest. Today, however, many Jews find halakhic authority a problem, perhaps the very problem that brings them to the rebbe. For this reason, the situation of the past is reversed, and the rebbe uses the esoteric as a building block and as a means of reinforcing halakhic involvement.

Besides adherence to halakhic norms, the hasid's commitment demands adherence to certain hasidic norms. Solomon Poll, in *The Hasidic Community of Williamsburg* (1962), sets up the sociological scale of garb as an index of hasidic commitment and status. R. Joseph Isaac Schneersohn speaks of hasidic *"befits"* as the norms for the initiates.[67] These norms deal with everything from such externals as garb (white shoes and socks) to the wearing of *Rabenu Tam t'filin* (a second set of phylacteries), to commitments with regard to study and meditation.[68] A *tamim*, an alumnus of the Lubavitcher Yeshivah, must study hasidic writings for at least an hour each day (this, in addition to his halakhic obligation to set aside time for study), and must frequent the miqveh, the ritual bath. A regular hasid who had not studied at Lubavitch is required to study and to immerse himself in the miqveh only Mondays, Thursdays, and Sabbaths. Similarly, the standards for special dietary considerations for Passover and the year round differ from *tamim* to hasid.

Spontaneity and Intentionality

Kavanah, intentionality, is one of the classical hasidic terms. No other term so strongly points to the core of Hasidism as does this one. Kavanah can also be translated as devotion. "Prayer with kavanah is prayer to which one has surrendered." The pace and the content of the prayer have fully taken over the hasid's being. The paradox is that kavanah implies both spontaneous surrender and deliberate intentionality.[69]

Kavanah operates in different ways, depending on the capabilities of the hasid. To the hasid who is capable of little deliberate action, kavanah implies great effort and energy involvement. Any deliberate act will require a great investment of energy. Such a hasid will be in greater need of the rebbe's help in order to properly direct his energy. The literal meaning of kavanah is "to direct outward." Part of the rebbe's task is to help his hasid direct his energies outward and upward in the service of God. It has been said that the ultimate meaning of the art of kavanah is to direct one's heart to God.

Hasidism has been praised for the spontaneity it imparts to its followers. Yet this sense of spontaneity does not contradict the necessity for intentionality.

> When R. Shneur Zalman took leave of his master's son, the Angel, he was urged to "beat the horses so they will know they are horses." The next time R. Shneur Zalman took his leave, the Angel urged him "to beat the horses so that they cease being horses."[70]

This story is an illustration of the hasidic metaphor employed to describe the master's method of instructing his hasidim. The rebbe must work at achieving deliberate control over his "horses" so that they will know their place. However, having achieved this level of control, the next step is to achieve that spontaneity whereby the horses are no longer horses, and, having been transformed into human beings, can be trusted to act spontaneously in their own capacity.

Deliberateness corresponds to the use of the will, and spontaneity to the use of delight. While "there is nothing higher than delight [as a motivation], there is nothing stronger than the will [in fulfilling the motivation]."[71] Generally, the problems that the hasid brings to the rebbe can be attributed either to the function of the will or to the surrender to spontaneity. Lying, for example, is deliberate, and passion spontaneous. Here the functions of deliberateness and spontaneity are obviously misused. The rebbe's task is to help the hasid redirect those energies of the will that are being utilized in lying. Similarly, he must help the hasid redirect those energies that are being devoted to acts of passion so that they may be used in the service of spontaneity and surrender to God.

The yehidut, as we have pointed out, is not a casual encounter. The entire process of the yehidut takes the intentionality of both rebbe and hasid for granted. The setting of the yehidut is deliberate, as is the process. Yet, at the same time, the process is also initiated by the hasid because his own lack of deliberateness is the problem that necessitates the yehidut. If the hasid could execute his decisions and follow them through with all the deliberateness that this requires, he would not have to seek out the rebbe for help in this direction. The hasid is aware of his past inability to implement his deliberate plans. He is conscious of his own instability, because he knows how often he has been unable to energize himself into action even after deciding which form his action is to take. He comes to the rebbe and pours out his bitterness over his own fickle nature. He despairs because he knows what he wants to be, and yet is unable to translate this desire, sincere as it may be, into deliberate action. He is caught in a conflict in which his evil impulse and God are at polar ends of the continuum. He expresses the full agony of his position: "Woe is me from my Creator; woe is me from my inclination."[72] Overcome with despair, he comes before the rebbe, accusing himself of all the faults he can remember—all at once. All the failures he has accumulated burst in upon him and he feels that he is the worst of the worst and completely unsalvageable. His condition is further aggravated by the fact that he is in the presence of the rebbe, who presumably suffers from none of the symptoms that plague the hasid. The distance between the hasid's "is" and his "ought" is at that moment so greatly increased that it reaches well-nigh infinite proportions. The hasid may be unaware of what he is doing, but, in his bitterness, he turns to the rebbe and accuses him of having placed him in this terrible predicament. His despair is so great that he feels that unless the rebbe performs some feat of magic to save him, the rebbe deserves to die for having caused him so much stress. The following anecdote serves to illustrate the point:

> R. Shmuel Munkes, one of the Elder Rebbe's hasidim, was present when they came to arrest the Rebbe. At first the Rebbe was confused by the imminence of death and managed to escape through the window. He was making his way toward the woods when R. Shmuel blocked his path and said to him: "What do you fear? If you are a rebbe, then no bullet will penetrate you. And if you are not, then you deserve to be shot for having robbed your followers of the capacity to enjoy this world without pangs of conscience."
>
> The Rebbe turned and surrendered to his captors. He approached them in his *t'filin* [phylacteries], but they backed down in terror. Later, when his hasidim asked why the gendarmes had been so intimidated by him, the Rebbe replied: "It is written: 'And all the people of the earth shall see that thou art called by the name of the Lord; and they shall be afraid of thee.' And our Sages explain that 'these are the *t'filin* in the head.'" When the hasidim replied that they too wore *t'filin* and this had not disturbed the gendarmes, the rebbe

explained that the Sages had made reference to the *t'filin* that are *in* the head, and not those that are worn *on* the head.[73]

To R. Shmuel Munkes, the resentment expressed toward the rebbe was highly conscious. He meant, in effect: "If you are a rebbe, then the miraculous is available to you, and you can act to save yourself and others. If you are unable to do this, then you are no better than we, and you deserve your predicament and its fatal consequences, for you have so often held us in the double bind. This then is poetic justice." The rebbe, with his phylacteries "in the head" (i.e., internalized), manages the miraculous by maintaining toward the world a deliberate and intentional attitude that inspires awe and terrorizes both his captors (those who would restrain him) and his hasidim.

Later, we will analyze a few of the gambits operating between rebbe and hasid, and show how the rebbe manages to lead his hasid back to the point where he will be able to disentangle himself from his predicament. However, at this point, the rebbe is more likely to say: "Why do you make demands of me? Make them of yourself!" In this way, the rebbe refuses to accept the hasid's inability to act on his own. If he were to do so, he would have succumbed to the hasid's intimidation. To merely bail the hasid out of his difficulty is not to help him in any significant way. In fact, such action on the part of the rebbe will, in all probability, hinder the hasid's progress and thus negate the purpose of the yehidut.

To sum up, the rebbe can work with his hasid only to bring about a real change in his life if the hasid is willing to take the responsibility of following the rebbe's guidance intentionally and deliberately. Overcome by the weight of this responsibility, the hasid may want to play the role of the helpless child who expects his father to do all the work. The rebbe must shift the responsibility back to the hasid, who must mobilize his own faculties of will and delight to serve his need. The rebbe will usually help by breaking the work down into manageable sections so that the hasid need not be daunted by the task confronting him.

The Hasid's Prayer Life

Of all the resources the rebbe needs to implement at the yehidut, the most sustaining is the hasid's prayer life. The rebbe could not complete his diagnosis of the hasid's spiritual life-space without having an accurate picture of his prayer life.

A hasid's prayer life is filled with paradox. His preparations for prayer must be very careful and detailed; yet when he prays, he must be able to forget his concentrated effort and see in his prayer only the wonder of God coming to meet him. The hasid has learned from the rebbe how crucial preparation is. It enables him to establish the proper setting of place and mind, triggering the anticipation that gears the hasid for the emotions he should feel during prayer. In the liturgy, the hasid again follows a predictable routine, yet he knows that its very predictability means that the onus for infusing it with kavanah, with newness and spontaneity, is up to him. If prayer were only the result of the hasid's preparation and effort, it would be a mere hoax, and the hasid would be abetting the hoax. Yet it is clear that without control of the conditions of prayer, very little would happen.

Hasidism considers prayer an end in itself, so much so that R. Pinhas of Koretz said: "Prayer is not to God; prayer is God Himself."[74] Yet prayer is also a preparation for the mitzvot the hasid is to perform during the day: it imbues him with the strength and motivation to perform the mitzvot. Thus prayer in itself is an end, but this end can be used as a means to other ends.

A vital part of the rebbe's task is to teach the hasid the proper manner and intention of prayer. Each rebbe offers his own instructions to his hasidim.

> Said the "Yud" (Rabbi Yaakov Yitzchak of Pshysskha): "Do you wish to know what is proper prayer? When you are so engrossed that you do not feel a knife thrust into your body, then you are offering prayer aright."[75]

> Said the Koretzer: "It is written: 'Lift up thy voice as a Shofar' (Isaiah 58:1). As the Shofar cannot emit any sound except when blown by man, no man can raise his voice in prayer except when the Shekhinah prays through it."[76]

Prayer is a socially acceptable means of regressing to a more primal, nonintellectual expression. The language of prayer turns us into children. We are urged into what psychologists call an "oral regressive" state to "taste and see that God is good. Happy is the strong man who *hides* in Him."[77] Such a man can, though he is now a strong man, becomes like a child before God.

Any real change in the hasid's personality can only be accomplished through prayer. In prayer, the hasid melts back into the undifferentiated God and emerges again with the good in him reinforced, and, ideally, the evil in him transmuted. The rebbe will teach his hasid about the higher and lower unification,[78] but the hasid himself must achieve this unification in prayer.

Two diametrically opposed aspects of the self are self-remembering and self-forgetting; yet both have to be achieved in prayer. In the depth of meditation, the hasid must forget himself, concentrating only on losing himself in complete union. The hasid who wants to mock the mitnaged explains how the latter reads the Sh'ma: "Hear O Israel, the Lord is One (and there is no one else who knows this except me alone)." The hasid, on the other hand, knows that he himself must become lost in the One. Yet in the higher moment of prayer, the Amidah, the hasid must ask for rain and healing, and, in order to do so, he must regain his self.

In his prayer the hasid must beseech God to "enlighten our eyes in Thy Torah and cause our hearts to cleave to Thy commands. Unify our hearts to love and revere Thee." Yet most of his prayers are recited not in the singular but in the plural. In prayer, he must bring about his ego loss and regain a renewed ego. The best prayer, therefore, is the communal prayer in which he is not the focus, but where he has merged into the group mind. Yet, when he reaches the *tahanun*, the confession, he is again the individual who makes his examination of conscience.

As well as being a time of surrender, "the time of prayer is [also] a time of warfare."[79] Like Jacob when he struggles with the angel, he must prevail against God, his own self, and his evil impulse.

In his prayer life, the hasid must engage in a pretense, yet he must not be taken in by it. In this process he becomes like the tzaddik. Prayer is the moment that allows the hasid to reach the higher mind even though it is not his own essential state of being. In this state, "extraneous" thoughts may come to him. These thoughts are not really extraneous to the hasid, as they would be to the tzaddik. However, the hasid must, in order to pray properly, forget that they are really his own thoughts; he must label them as intruders and discard them in order to continue soaring in the highest regions of his imagination.

During prayer, the hasid must achieve full divestment of his worldly attachments; yet he is subject to criticism if he does not heed the cry of a child.[80] His mind must adhere to the divine, angelic, and spiritual aspects of the very letters of the prayer in which he is immersed;[81] yet he must pray with his prayer desk in mind.[82] He must find something new—a new insight, a new depth—in each prayer; yet he must resist the temptation to treat his prayers as homiletic workshops, always seeking new and clever readings.[83] He must be able to view history *sub specie aeternitatis*, and yet feel the deep distress of the people for whom he intercedes.

The effects of the hasid's prayer must manifest themselves in increased compassion for others. He must emerge from his prayerful communion with God with a living word to be realized in the work of the day, one that for this day becomes a multidimensional motto. More Love and Awe for God must be manifest in the discharge of His commandments.

The hasid who can manage all this has achieved a high degree of receptivity. Prayer becomes for him the laboratory where he can prepare himself prior to the yehidut and later implement the counsel he receives from the rebbe.

But what of the hasid who cannot manage all this? He comes to the yehidut without the necessary tools. In the early days of Hasidism, the hasid was generally well prepared and came to the rebbe, after having been trained by his *mashpiy'a*, as a well-instructed novice. The main points of prayer and self-scrutiny were already a functional discipline for him. When the hasid came to the rebbe, the rebbe would test his level of competence and prescribe for him a way that would meet his needs. Even today, no matter how unprepared the new hasid is, he has seen and experienced hasidic prayer. Often it was the quality of another hasid's prayer that precipitated the new hasid's conversion to Hasidism. Because the rebbe works in the midst of a community, never in a social vacuum, and because the yehidut is set in the context of the liturgical day at the rebbe's court, the hasid cannot escape this confrontation with hasidic prayer. But the rebbe needs to discover how much of this prayer life the hasid has adopted for himself, how much he still needs to pretend in prayer, and to what extent he is fooling even himself.

After we have established the theoretical framework for prayer, we will need to deal, to some extent, with the specific counsels offered by the rebbe. Here, we wish only to add that, in the case of a more advanced hasid, the rebbe will want to discover from which of the five soul levels the hasid's prayer originates. He will want to know to what extent the energies of the prayer are derived from holiness, and to what extent from the energy system of evil. During the process of yehidut the rebbe may discover that some hasidim hold erroneous notions about prayer. He will therefore set himself the task of rectifying the situation by publishing his views in a book or by giving his hasidim a "pep" talk before prayer. The diagnosis of the individual hasid's prayer life is the rebbe's primary concern.

The Rebbe Looks at the Hasid's Inner Makeup

The Hasid's Soul Makeup

A hasid considers himself not a "body that has a soul," but rather a "soul that has a body": his soul is his essential being. In exploring the hasidic world-view, we dealt with the composition of the soul as it parallels the composition of the worlds. In treating the rebbe as the general soul, and the hasid as a part of that soul, we were dealing with the divine soul. Similarly, in discussing the rebbe as he looks at the hasid's various incarnations and attempts to integrate them, we were again dealing with the divine soul. The animal soul, on the other end of the continuum, is the "substance" on which the divine soul impresses its "form." Rooted in the world of *tohu*, it is actually higher than the divine soul in origin, though not in function. The animal soul has great power, and at times is characterized by comparison to a particular animal. Thus, Habad speaks of the animal soul of a sheep, a goat, and an ox, and prescribes separate ways of dealing with each. In prescribing for his hasid, the rebbe thus takes into consideration the hasid's particular type of animal soul.

Where the divine soul sets the high watermark of the soul's attainment in this and all other lives, the animal soul represents the low watermark. There is no way in which a soul can, by its own efforts, transcend the limits of its origin. A person may experience a moment of grace as the soul of a tzaddik invests itself in him, but this influence soon wanes, and the soul returns to its original state.

For all the importance of the divine and the animal souls, Habad stresses the need to understand and to work with the rational soul. This is the intent of the *Tanya*. If the rebbe were dealing primarily with tzaddikim, his first consideration would be the divine soul, because a tzaddik must identify completely with the divine soul. If, on the other hand, his hasidim were largely *r'shaim* (wicked), his first consideration would be the animal soul, since to be a *rasha*—a wicked one—is to regard oneself as identical with the animal soul. Most hasidim who come to the rebbe are neither righteous tzaddikim nor wicked *r'shaim*. The third category is that of the *beynoni*—the man in between. Although he does not sin behaviorally, he does harbor evil thoughts, though he attempts to eradicate them. The hasid who comes to the rebbe may not be a *beynoni*, but in order to profit from the rebbe's counsel, he assumes the stance of the *beynoni*, "for it is the measure of every man."[84] The *beynoni* is managed by his rational soul. In order to utilize one's intellect in the service of God, one has to work with the rational soul. The rational soul is thus the ultimate arbiter of the hasid's behavior. The fact of man's free choice necessitates the use of the rational soul. Only the rational soul is empowered with the ability to choose, to make decisions. The inclination for good and the inclination for evil may influence man, but they make no decisions.

The rational soul is also called the *l'vush*, or garment. This garment is produced by the spiritual intentions of the parents at the time of their procreative act. The proper intention and sanctification of the parents determine all acts of a person as he is invested in this *l'vush*.

The stance of the *beynoni* is that of the person who has conscientiously and deliberately decided never to derive life energies from any source other than God. This means that he considers each sin as idolatry, since at the moment of sin all one's energies derive from the evil energy system of *q'lipah* and not immediately and directly from God. The decision of the *beynoni* must be constantly reinforced at great emotional expense. It is this world of the *beynoni* that the rebbe must enter in order to be able to help his hasid.

By temporarily abdicating the position of tzaddik, the rebbe no longer has the center of his being in the divine soul. Assuming the posture of the *beynoni*, he moves from a region that is "beyond reason and knowing" to a region where conscious and deliberate action can occur. In doing so, he is moving from the simple, God-centered, divine soul identification to a conflict-ridden dialectic field, in which the hasid and his problem are contained. This shift enables him to empathize more deeply with his hasid, and therefore puts him in a better position to help him with his problem.

The rebbe's identification with the stance of the *beynoni*, and thus with the rational soul, does not mean that he disregards the hasid's animal and divine souls. On the contrary, the pull of both these souls on the rational soul is what creates the hasid's stressful situation. It is this situation that the rebbe addresses.

For the rebbe, the diagnosis of the hasid's rational soul is the most taxing one. The divine soul can be seen in the hasid's aura. The animal soul can be perceived in the hasid's constitution and stance. But to invest oneself in another's rational soul is the most difficult task. The literature itself does not offer much data concerning this investment. If it did, we would have the best possible transfer point of the rebbe's diagnostic technique. Auras cannot be read by the average person, and the Yehudi's shirt is not available to us. The rational soul, which roughly corresponds to the Jungian ego behind the the persona, and even more to the Freudian ego, is the crucial entity in the counseling process.

We have dealt with many aspects of the rational soul under other headings. A hasid's environmental conditions, his education, his habit patterns, and his intentionality are all functions of the rational soul. Here we are chiefly interested in the concept of the total form of the rational soul as given to a person by his parents at conception, and as nurtured in the early stages of life before the *yetzer hatov* and the divine soul make their manifest (conscious) appearance. Since the child spent a longer time in the mother's womb than in the father's body, the mother's influence is not only genetic but also environmental. (This is another reason why the kvittel is written in the mother's name.) In order to utilize his empathic investment in the rational soul in the service of the diagnostic process, the rebbe must draw upon both conscious and unconscious *ruah haqodesh*.

The Hasid's Habit and Decisional Patterns

As noted above, Hasidism considers habit patterns as functions of the rational soul. Hasidic literature speaks of habit patterns in a manner similar, at least in rudimentary form, to the way psychology treats Freudian defense mechanisms. Not wanting to be the battlefield for the evil and good inclinations, the rational soul seizes upon certain habit patterns that it perpetuates. In doing so, it allies itself with the instinctual workings of the animal soul.

Decisional patterns, particularly those involving the greater temptations—lying, incest, adultery, apostasy, blasphemy, and murder—may originate in the divine soul. The Jewish soul will not and cannot be severed from God. In modern terms, the anxiety of being severed from God through these temptations is greater than the anxiety over death. The rational soul will not undertake the responsibility for these decisions; the responsibility must rest on the shoulders of the divine soul. Unlike habit patterns, which are the result of repeated action, decisional patterns are the result of a deep will on the part of the person involved. Obviously, there is some area of overlap inasmuch as the hasid must decide whether or not to perpetuate his habit, even if his only decision is a refusal to make a decision; and the deep decision, when reinforced, becomes habit.

In cases of great and intense conflict, where two or more decisions or habits are in opposition, the hasid needs the help of the rebbe in order to free himself. The rebbe must help the hasid make a choice. He must free the hasid's motivational energies. This he does by either of two methods: by establishing in the hasid a higher insight into the primary decision involved or by exacting from him a deeper obedience and commitment that supersedes the level on which the conflict arises. This is why part of the diagnosis of the rational soul includes the evaluation of the hasid's personal commitment to his rebbe.

The Hasid's Past Lives

We have already mentioned the fact that, in order to help the hasid in a meaningful way, the rebbe must be able to see the hasid in this particular incarnation not as an isolated entity, but as a product of his past lives. It remains for us to deal with the problems that the belief in reincarnation creates for the rebbe. These are treated below under the headings of unfinished tasks and transtemporal influences.

UNFINISHED TASKS

Unfinished tasks may, in a manner of which the hasid is unaware, haunt him until such time as he completes them. Unless he fulfills these tasks, he may be unable to continue with the tasks of his present lifetime. The following story illustrates the problem of unfinished tasks:

> At a wedding meal the bridal pair had just pronounced the blessing over their food. Both bride and groom swallowed the first bite and choked to death. The distraught parents came to the celebrated kabbalist, R. Isaac Luria, and poured out their grief. Luria consoled them and told them that the bridal couple had almost completed their life tasks in the previous incarnation, but had not yet merited to eat in a sacrificial manner. When they had recited the blessing at the wedding meal, they had eaten the first bite in the manner required for their fulfillment. Once they had done this, there was no more work for them here. Thus it was the work of divine mercy to take them from this life before they could spoil the gains of all their past lives. The parents listened to the rebbe's explanation and were consoled.[85]

Another illustration of the way in which unfinished tasks are handled is the following story told of R. Mendl of Kotsk:

> The mother of a great Talmud prodigy came to the Kotsker in tears over her son's severe illness. Attempting to arouse R. Mendl's pity, she pointed out her son's great achievements. But R. Mendl only replied: "He has scarcely begun. He has not yet produced anything of worth." The mother left the rebbe, and, thinking that he had rejected her plea, broke down in great lament. One of the great hasidim of the Kotsker, seeing her plight, sought to console her. He explained that R. Mendl had utilized the argument that her son had scarcely done anything, in order to prolong the son's life. And with this the woman was consoled.[86]

In Hasidism there is a great dedication to the life process. If there is a task to be completed, it needs to be completed in the service of life:

> A rich man once came to make the acquaintance of the Besht. He explained to the Master that he had no particular problem that

required the rebbe's blessing, but that, having heard many great and wonderful stories concerning the deeds of the Ba'al Shem Tov, he had decided he must meet this man. In reply, the Besht asked the man if he would mind hearing another story. The man was eager to hear the story, and so the Besht began:

There were once two men who had grown up together as friends. However, when they reached manhood, they found themselves in very different circumstances. One was a wealthy man, and the other very poor. The poor man, in order to save his life, asked help of his rich friend. The wealthy man did not hesitate, but offered his friend half his fortune. Now, with time, the situations of the men reversed, and the one who had before been wealthy was now very poor, while his friend, to whom he had given half his fortune, had become a very wealthy man. Sure that he could receive help from his now wealthy friend, the poor man sought him out and explained to him his difficulty. But instead of helping him, the wealthy man ran away in order to avoid having to part with any of his fortune. However, time once again reversed their situations so that the poor man became rich and the rich man became poor, and they were once more returned to their original situations. Now, the friend who had before refused to part with his fortune began to feel the distress of his own situation, and went to his friend begging forgiveness. The man who was now wealthy readily forgave his friend and offered to help him out of his difficulties, but this time he insisted that the friend give him a note as insurance against any time when their fortunes might again be reversed. The poor man gave him a note, and the rich man once again shared his fortune with his friend. Needless to say, as time passed, the two men again suffered a reversal of fortunes, but, true to form, the man who had written the note refused to honor it and his friend remained penniless.

The two men died. When they came before the heavenly tribunal, the full sinfulness of the one friend's life weighed against him and he was sentenced to hell, while his friend was to go to heaven. However, the one who was to go to heaven would not accept the plight of his friend, and he explained to the heavenly court that, in spite of the manner in which his friend had treated him, he still loved him and did not wish to see him condemned to hell. The decision of the tribunal was that the only way to avoid this was to return both men to earth, so that the sinful man might have an opportunity to atone for his actions. And so the sinful man was returned to earth and established himself as a rich man, while the other was but a beggar.

When the beggar knocked on the door of the rich man, begging for sustenance, he was pushed rudely away and refused any aid. And so the beggar died.

At this point in the story the rich man, who had come merely to make the Besht's acquaintance, jumped up, an amazed look on his face. "Yesterday," he said, "I turned away a beggar. Was he the beggar of your story, and am I that rich man?"

No answer was necessary, but the Besht nodded. The man was overcome with repentance and was anxious to know how he could make amends for his sin. The Besht explained to him that his friend, the beggar, had a widow, and that he was to go and give three quarters of his fortune to that widow in order to atone for his sin.[87]

Every man has to fulfill his life task, according to Hasidism. The Besht himself was reincarnated, according to hasidic tradition, so that this world might partake of his fragrance. So inexorable is this cosmic law that Hasidism saw the sufferings of the Jews under the Inquisition in terms of debts they had incurred in previous incarnations. Once this precedent was established, the next step was inevitable—the European Holocaust was interpreted in the same terms. Those souls who had committed idolatry atoned by way of a violent death.

A hasid who came to R. Shneur Zalman of Liadi, complaining of his unhappy marriage to a shrew and requesting the rebbe's permission to divorce her, received the reply: "There are souls that have incurred such immense reservoirs of sin in past lives by their idolatrous lives that they need to die a number of violent deaths. For you, there would not have been a sufficient number of reincarnations before the advent of the Messiah; so heaven had mercy on you and gave you this wife. Each time you feel you can't bear it any longer, you die another 'death' and come closer to your atonement."[88]

Since unfinished tasks remain as outstanding debts and, in the course of world history, have to be paid, it is essential that the rebbe, as part of his diagnostic process, establish what the hasid's unfinished tasks are. After he has established what these tasks are, the rebbe must help the hasid complete these tasks in order to fulfill the purpose of his present life.

INFLUENCES FROM PAST LIVES

Sometimes a hasid, having gained a particular skill in his previous life, remains satisfied with his skill and refuses to progress on to the next task. The rebbe must then help him by explaining that his skill is actually a past achievement, and that his refusal to move on is a desire to rest on his laurels.

This is not easily done. The rebbe has learned to appreciate a soul's attraction as a definite good. A soul is attracted to the important tasks in its life. "Let a person ever study where his heart desires"[89] is a maxim not only for the rebbe but for all conduct.

By what criteria will the rebbe know whether a soul has completed its task and wants to idle in the momentum of the past, or whether the soul is being attracted to its next task? The answer lies in the problem of right effort and resistance. Past achievement and its aftereffects show themselves in the hasid's unwillingness to exert himself. The soul satisfied with the past is rigid in its achievement and sees only one way. This rigidity and lack of generosity or exertion in the service of God are seen as the work of the evil inclination. The rebbe knows that if he were dealing with a genuine attraction to something new, the striving would have less structure. There would not yet be a definite pattern. The soul, in its encounter with the rebbe, would seek to give form to the new striving. It would experience all sorts of hesitations as a result of the urgings of the evil impulse, which would attempt to mire the soul in the conservative and less demanding pattern of behavior. But when a hangover from the previous life keeps the soul in a stranglehold, the resulting pattern is rigid, there is little generosity, and the soul has a tendency to a sort of constipation. Sometimes there are genuine borderline cases in which a soul needs to work through a pattern harmonious with, but not identical to, that of the last life. Such a case is more difficult to deal with on both the diagnostic and prescriptive levels. However, the rebbe's insight and training equip him to assess the clues that he finds in the hasid and to evaluate the hasid's stance.

The Rebbe Integrates the Parts into the Whole

Early in his career, a rebbe usually spends more time with his hasid in yehidut than he does later, when he has become more proficient at his calling. This is because, in his early career, the rebbe had to integrate all the factors of a hasid's inner makeup by slower, more conscious and deliberate methods. As he became more experienced, he learned to shift more of the responsibility to his unconscious *ruah haqodesh*, the spirit within him. As he became more proficient, his empathic investment grew deeper, as did his ability to focus on the needs of each hasid who came to visit him.

The conscious and deliberate level is the only one on which we can follow the rebbe as he integrates the various factors of the hasid's makeup. Body and soul, habit and attraction, status and family, earning and obligations, this life and past lives, animal, rational, and divine souls—all these are integrated by the rebbe. It is not enough for the rebbe to integrate all the factors of the past and the present: he must also be able to predict the hasid's future performance. To demand more than the hasid can produce will be harmful to the hasid's development. In addition, the rebbe's integration will still fail unless it is a dynamic rather than a static appraisal of the hasid. R. Joseph Isaac Schneersohn emphasized the fact that man, unlike all other creatures, is of a compound nature, and the inspection of the craftsman must deal with all the features in a dynamic rather than a static manner, seeing man as he moves in all the directions of his compound nature. The repair must not aim at static perfection, but must keep to such tolerances as make effective movement possible.

The rebbe must complete his integration on all levels before he is able to prescribe for the hasid. Only then will his prescription be meaningful.

WHAT CHANGES CAN BE EXPECTED FROM THE HASID?

The Hasid's Receptiveness to Change

The fact that the hasid often comes to the rebbe as a last resort and in desperation does not always mean that he will be receptive to change. On the contrary, the hasid may merely wish to utilize the rebbe's services to protect his habitual role and behavior. In this case, he comes to the rebbe like a child to his father, asking him to play the judge, and, in doing so, justify his ways. Hasidim have often seen their rebbe in this role, and it has often been for this very reason that they sought his help. If they felt that the rebbe would attempt to change them, they would think more seriously before coming to the yehidut.

If the hasid has faithfully acted on the dictates of his conscience and the law, and has followed the instructions of the rebbe, but finds himself in a crisis as a result of his obedience, the rebbe must take the hasid's part and utilize his own charismatic powers in order to undo the decrees of God or to implore Him to issue another decree. In doing so, he reinforces the popular expectation.

If the rebbe always collaborated with the hasid as he is, he would never be able to induce change in him. Yet most of the time the rebbe will not play judge, unless he can, in the process of the transaction, move the hasid to a higher level. Even when the rebbe does not make an explicit demand, the implication remains and is reinforced that the hasid is expected to improve. This is unavoidable, since the entire dynamic of the yehidut centers around the hasidic concept of *teshuvah*.

The rebbe utilizes a number of social tools in order to keep his hasidim open to change. In his public lectures, he maintains a sufficiently antinomian stance, and, both in public and in private, he reinforces the image of his own unpredictability. His hasidim are generally moved to exclaim: "His footsteps are unknown." Like Peretz's Litwak, the rebbe goes daily to heaven "if not higher." "Who can understand his ways?" To the citified Warsovian hasid who was addicted to urban conformity, the Kozhinitzer, R. Arele Hopstein, was an unfathomable enigma. Through his antics, R. Arele made risk and change the norm for his hasidim.

The rebbe's unpredictability and authority over the hasid do more to open the hasid to change than does the normal stance of the helper vis-à-vis his client. Even so, the hasidic framework obliges the rebbe to move with his hasid only through such options as are sanctioned by Torah Law and the hasidic wont. A direct and definite transgression of the halakhic order would remove rebbe and hasid from the relationship of authority and movement.

One of the major causes of anxiety over change is absent in Hasidism. The hasid always has the reassurance that his change will be acceptable. Any social unpleasantness that might occur owing to the hasid's change in role is mitigated when the hasid announces that he is acting according to the rebbe's decree. Even the great Torah academician who, at his rebbe's behest, becomes a coachman for the benefit of his soul, can be brought to overcome his reluctance once he is reassured of his acceptance among his fellow hasidim. In short, the hasid's role change does not kill him socially. Only in rare cases will the rebbe impose "exile" on the hasid. When this occurs, it does mean social death for a certain period. But even here the "resurrection" is assured, and, inherent in it is the social approval that comes upon the revelation of the social mystery.

In the society of other hasidim, the hasid can afford a significant role change, since it is all chalked up to "repentance and the rebbe." Nevertheless, the rebbe cannot take the range of the hasid's removal from his former habits for granted. He may, as part of his counsel, set up a series of incremental moves in order to "dilate" the hasid enough so that he will be able to accommodate the larger change. Generally, however, the rebbe need not be overly concerned. His authority and the hasid's wish to comply, his blessing and the side effects that the hasid desires, are in favor of the hasid's progress. The rebbe's reputation is not at stake. The hasid who will not or cannot comply with the rebbe's counsel knows that the failure will be attributed to him and not to the rebbe.

The hasid's openness to change is reinforced not only by his relationship with the rebbe but also by his relationship with his *haver* (friend). This relationship involves an extremely important social contract. The friend is the person with whom the hasid planned the yehidut and with whom he will share the rebbe's counsel. By sharing with his friend the rebbe's statements and his reaction to them, and the insights that he has gained, the hasid ensures that the friend will be on the side of his conscience and memory. By acting as a daily reminder of his task, the friend becomes the rebbe's surrogate.

The hasid who follows R. Elimelekh's advice and sees himself in the rebbe's presence every day, who envisions the rebbe repeating his counsel in an awesome voice, will continue to move in the direction of the etzah's fulfillment. This the rebbe knows and takes for granted. In integrating all the factors he knows about the hasid, the rebbe will also take into consideration the hasid's possible tendency to overplay his counsel in such a way that it reaches absurd proportions (in the same manner as a reaction formation). The hasid may be moved to do this in an unconscious wish to prove the rebbe wrong. From this position, the hasid feels that he cannot lose. If he overacts on the rebbe's counsel, he is "entitled" at least to the success of the rebbe's blessing for having so assiduously carried out his task. In order to avoid this trap, the rebbe may put a limiting rider on his counsel.

There are times when the rebbe finds it necessary to use verbal shock as a means of therapy. However, he will never attempt to use this method unless he is certain that the hasid will be able to withstand it and be receptive to any change it may bring about. This means that he must first test the hasid. If the hasid responds with insight to the rebbe's seemingly off-the-subject remark, the rebbe can change the subject immediately in the direction of the remark. He has effected both his test and the next move: the preparation of the hasid for the etzah. If the hasid does not respond well, the rebbe may change his tactics and bring the hasid to the same insight by a more circuitous method.

The rebbe's position of authority leaves the hasid no real operative choice but to accept the rebbe's interpretation of his problem and the counsel he prescribes. The only other recourse would be to switch rebbes—a step that, in the hasidic world, would elicit extreme social sanctions. The hasid may attempt to short-circuit the rebbe's counsel in more subtle ways, but if he has any insight into his own situation, he will realize that in so doing, he sabotages only himself. If the hasid does not realize this, the rebbe will make it clear.

The Process of Change: Abrupt or Gradual?

Depending on the insightful capacity of the hasid and his freedom for role change, the rebbe now has to integrate the prognosis into the diagnostic procedure. A gradual process is often more desirable, because fewer situations are upset and less energy needs to be invested at any one time. The spread of time allows for a better and deeper integration of the change. In addition, the family of the hasid can collaborate better and with less disorganization, restructuring themselves along with the hasid in order to accommodate the change. This process takes a great deal of time, and there may be instances where the process is so slow that it comes dangerously close to stagnation. In such cases, the problem that the hasid seeks to change is only reinforced.

It is for this reason that R. Joseph Isaac Schneersohn divides problems into two categories. Wherever a new mode of behavior has to be learned, it is advisable to proceed in slow stages. Wherever a gross evil has to be eliminated, however, there is no benefit in waiting, and only danger in slow withdrawal.

Where a habit has reached the proportions of addiction, it may be necessary to impose a complete and severe withdrawal much like the "cold turkey" method used for drug addicts. In cases of diseases of "matter," the method followed involves "breaking the habit, imposition of the will, and abstinence." In cases where the powers of the soul are afflicted, the method is "guidance, education, and habituation."[90] With a *ba'al t'shuvah* (a penitent) who knows the proper halakhic way, but has fallen below the norms, the general principle will be to proceed on the first level of withdrawal in an abrupt manner. However, the acquisition of proper habits and functions is to be established in a more gradual manner. Just as each hasid brings with him the solution to his own problem, so each solution dictates the method and pace with which it is to be carried out.

The hasid who wishes to seek the rebbe's counsel must be prepared to "bare his soul" in the yehidut chamber. The rebbe will plumb the depths of the hasid's being, whether the hasid wishes it or not. In order to see the hasid as he stands in the primal thought of Adam Qadmon, in order to understand the hasid's life task and in order to follow the hasid's problem to its root and source, the rebbe utilizes all the special techniques at his disposal. The hasid may block the rebbe, either consciously or unconsciously. He may be ashamed of his real problem, or he may be unaware of the true nature of the problem. He may try to hide some of his more unpleasant character traits. All these things will make the rebbe's task more difficult, but they will not prevent the rebbe from penetrating the hasid's "mask." Once the "mask" has been penetrated and the hasid is willing to cooperate with the rebbe's diagnosis, the rebbe is in a position to give the hasid his etzah, the action-directive by which his problem can be solved or alleviated.

Chapter 6

The Dynamics of the Yehidut Transaction

The manna revealed a man's sins; therefore it was considered "the bread of shame"—we could not bear it. A rebbe must not shame his hasid by revealing his sins.

R. Israel of Ruzhin (E. Steinman, *Rishonim Aharonim*)

The world thinks that to take a ransom (to bless another) is a difficult thing, belonging only to great rebbes. The truth is that every Jew can do this by saying a word of praise about his fellow, but it must be said in sincerity. Hundreds of angels wait on Rosh Hashanah for a Jew to say a word of praise about another Jew because they know how God loves to hear the praise of Israel.

R. Shmuel Schneersohn of Lubavitch (*Toldot*)

R. Michal was reputed to be able to read the thoughts of people, and to be able to read on their foreheads the damage they had done to their souls. Once R. Michal came to a city where many people came to see him, their caps pulled low over their foreheads. When R. Michal saw them, he said: "It is foolish for you to do this. The eye that can see the interior can look past the cap."

Once R. Michal preached to a congregation: "One is to hear my words." Then he added: "I did not say, 'you must hear my words,' but 'one is to hear my words,' because I too must listen to them."

(E. Steinman, *Galicia*)

THE TRANSACTION

On the simplest level, the yehidut is a transaction that occurs because one party—the hasid—has a need that the other party—the rebbe—can fill. From this simple description it might seem that the rebbe is the active party and the hasid is the passive one. This is not so. The hasid too must actively contribute to the yehidut. In other words, mutuality is essential to the transaction. The hasid must be ready to surrender himself to the process of the yehidut. If he is not fully prepared to do so, the rebbe must help free him to participate fully in the transaction.

Relationship

Acceptance

It is crucial to the yehidut transaction that each party—both rebbe and hasid—accept the other as he is. The hasid is prepared to accept the rebbe as "rebbe" because he has learned about him from others. But it is very difficult for the hasid to accept the rebbe as a person. The rebbe has fewer difficulties accepting the hasid as a person, although some qualifications in this acceptance are implicit in the relationship. The rebbe's acceptance of the hasid implies that both he and the hasid are included in the community whose sole purpose is to "do Thy will with a perfect heart."[1] Even if the person who comes to see the rebbe is unwilling to see himself as a member of this group, the rebbe will not permit himself to ignore his own motivation for involvement.

For the rebbe, acceptance of the person who comes for help and the hope that he will become (if he is not already) a member of the hasidic

God-serving community go hand in hand; yet the latter is deemphasized by the rebbe in favor of total acceptance. He is aware that the person seeking help may not be able to see himself in the role of a hasid. If he were to make this condition explicit, the seeker might not wish to continue the relationship, since he is, at this time, unwilling or unable to share the rebbe's value structure.

We have here a pedagogic formulation of acceptance that is temporarily satisfied with low-level extrinsic motives. Noble motives on the part of the hasid are the result and not the precondition of the rebbe's acceptance of the postulant. The rebbe's love and acceptance of the postulant is predicated on the frankly persuasive principle that Abraham utilized with the strangers he fed.[2] Because "the task of education and guidance is to heal moral illnesses and to strengthen moral health,"[3] the rebbe cannot rely on the undivided help of the postulant (the one in need of strengthening) in the transaction. He accepts that part of the hasid in need of help, as well as the hasid's tendency to self-love (but only in order to circumvent it). The entire energy system of the yehidut transaction, on the parts of both rebbe and hasid, is one of love and empathy; and, in the same way as the rebbe would rid himself of all the destructive and evil characteristics were they his own, he is, for the sake of that love, committed to help the hasid eradicate them in himself.

Love of a Fellow Jew

"Thou shalt love thy neighbour as thyself," said R. Shneur Zalman, "but not more than you love yourself." "What you don't accept in your own self, you should not accept in your neighbor." In any candid transaction arising out of *ahavat Yisrael* (Hasidism always uses this term in speaking of love, since the love of one's fellow Jew is a positive command in the Torah), there are two inclinations for good battling one inclination for evil, and the inclinations for good are sure to prevail.

This great love was celebrated by the Magid, who was heard to say that he wished he could love his own children as much as the Besht loved even the most wicked in Israel (and the love of the Magid for his son, known as "the Angel," was proverbial). R. Moshe Leib of Sassov related how he was taught by two peasants at an inn that to love means to know what the other one lacks. No love of God is possible unless the love of Israel acts as the instrument for that love. Such statements concerning the love of Israel could be multiplied many times. R. Abraham Joshua Heschel of Apt wished to be known as the Ohev Yisrael—the "lover of Israel." This he considered to be the supreme epitaph.

This great love energizes the rebbe–hasid relationship, and each experiences this energizing on his own level. The hasid sees in the yehidut the same mythic love experience that the rebbe celebrates for him in the description of divine love. The *Tanya* teaches that if such a love as men share causes them to cleave to one another,

> How much more so when a great and mighty king shows his great and intense love for a commoner who is despised and lowly among men, a disgraceful creature cast on the dunghill, yet he [the king] stoops down to him from the place of his glory, together with all his retinue, and raises him and exalts him from his dunghill and brings him into his palace, the royal palace, into the innermost chamber, a place such as no servant or lord ever enters, and there shares with him the closest companionship with embraces and kisses and spiritual attachment with all heart and soul—how much more will, of itself, be aroused a doubled and redoubled love in the heart of this most common and humble individual for the person of the king, with a true attachment of spirit, heart and soul, and with infinite heartfelt sincerity. Even if his heart be like a heart of stone, it will surely melt, and his soul will pour itself out like water, with soulful longing for the love of the king.[4]

The rabbis of the Talmud explain that the injunction "to fear the Lord your God" is intended to include the disciples of the wise. The hasid applies this same equation to include the rebbe as well. If the rebbe is the head of the children of Israel (Rosh B'nai Yisrael—RBY), then the hasid is his limb, and the love and obedience of the limb for the head is boundless. The Habad principle "the head rules the heart" becomes, by extension, the principle of the hasid's love and obedience to his rebbe. The guiding principle for the rebbe—*ahavat Yisrael*—is the vessel to *ahavat HaShem*—the love of God. In other words, the love of God is contained in the love of Israel. The hasid's love for the rebbe is the sublimation of *ahavat Yisrael* (which is expressed when hasidim relate to one another) and follows the same direction as *ahavat HaShem*. While the rebbe concretizes his love of God in his love for his hasidim, the hasid sublimates his love of God in his love for the rebbe.

We cannot comprehend the love between rebbe and hasid without looking at the less obvious aspects of their relationship. Outwardly it seems that all the polarities are contained, so that the hasid's Promethean rebellion, which is often unconsciously directed toward God, is also directed toward the rebbe. All the father ambivalences are directed toward the rebbe. The hasid is grateful for the paternal care, but at the same time angry that he needs it. The transference situation that applies in other helper–helped relationships, manifesting itself in both positive and negative ways, also applies here. This is not part of the hasid's general awareness and will not usually be raised by the rebbe to the level of conscious discussion. While the rebbe is generally more aware of his own negative transference than the hasid is of his, the rebbe clothes the negative feelings he may feel for the hasid in terms of annoyance over not being able to study Torah and pray at his leisure.[5]

The love energizing the relationship between rebbe and hasid, and which, by its existence, makes possible the depth and scope of the yehidut, is atypical. It cannot be compared to other counselor–client relationships or to any other love relationships. In short, rebbe and hasid partake of a unique love relationship. Its singularity is largely due to the fact that it is not directed toward the manifest object of the love. The rebbe's love of God is manifested in his love for his hasid: the hasid's love of God is manifested in his love and devotion for the rebbe. The love relationship would not be possible without the overpowering love of God, which consumes both rebbe and hasid.

The Rebbe as an Archetypal Model

Earlier we referred to the rebbe as an archetype. In order to grasp the nature of the transaction between rebbe and hasid, we will flesh out the details of the projection in the section below.

The rules of the rebbe–hasid transaction are implicit in the relationship. The hasid has heard how the rebbe, in recalling his own rebbe or ancestor, speaks of them as being "in the supernal model," an "absolute soul." He has heard that the "*rabbeyim* lived in the supernal image."[6] Therefore, when he enters the yehidut, he knows that he stands before an archetypal model that is, in an essential way, completely inaccessible to him.

Though remaining inaccessible himself, the rebbe makes the divine accessible to his hasid. Some of the hasid's life problems are rooted in his relationship with God; yet the hasid cannot work his problems out with God, at least not directly. And this is where the rebbe, as an archetypal model, serves the hasid. He functions as a conjunctive person: he responds to the hasid's problem by answering, scolding, and even by giving the needed "pat on the back."

The conjunctive function of the rebbe is of great importance in the transaction between rebbe and hasid. Against the "divine" role that the rebbe assumes, the hasid can work out his problems with some assurance of definite results. When the rebbe assures him of children and health, the hasid knows that the rebbe, like Moses, is the mouthpiece of God and that "the Divine Presence speaks through the throat of Moses."[7] If the rebbe were not there to intercede with the divine, the covenantal relationship between the hasid and God would not be concretized. None of the accessible means of communion with God are equal to the mediation of the rebbe. In the presence of the rebbe, and in the demands he makes on his life, God becomes real for the hasid. The rebbe stands, as it were, in *loco dei*, and his pronouncements have the authority of a fiat.

As the archetypal model, the rebbe serves not only the hasid's being but also his becoming. He is both the human archetype and the divine; and as such he reminds the hasid of his own potential, of what he can aspire to become. As a human archetype, the rebbe gives direction to the hasid's striving.

The Rebbe as an Accessible Model

In order to establish the rebbe's authority, Hasidism must place him hierarchically above the hasid. Yet in order to maintain his effectiveness, the rebbe cannot be too far beyond the hasid's reach. Though he may have evolved into the most exalted personage, the rebbe needs to have started at the lowest rung so that hasidim can learn from him. The functional tension between the rebbe's exaltedness and his popular involvement is always present. A rebbe will state that it was hard work and not an exalted soul that brought him to his present station. But the hasid, in order to defend himself from the rebbe's challenge, places him back on the pedestal. The rebbe's reminder, "You need not think that a rebbe is that much greater than you—it is enough if you think him a handsbreadth higher"[8] is accompanied by the hasid's rejoinder that this handsbreadth is qualitatively impassable. This defensive attitude is evident not only in the aspirant but also in his community. The hasidic community will not let a hasid transcend its own plane of being. If he succeeds in doing so, he is a challenge to them, and they will have to invoke a rationale for his escape from earthboundness. In order to do this, they will speak of the exalted level of his soul. If he becomes a rebbe after his master's demise, it only serves to substantiate their claim that he was not an ordinary soul to begin with. If one were to point to an aspirant's humble beginnings, the community would merely reply: "At times the soul of a very exalted person becomes the son of the very least on the rung of holiness."[9] All the possibilities are covered so that the rebbe's accessibility as a model does not become too great a source of anxiety for the individual hasid or community. At times the rebbe, for reasons of his own, collaborates with this attitude. He may do this because he does not want his hasid to suffer undue anxiety, or because he does not want the hasid to aspire to heights that are beyond his present reach. Or, the rebbe may do this simply because he wishes to foster Tzaddikism.

Although the hasid may never aspire to copy the rebbe in his inner being—this he considers too remote—he is expected to copy certain aspects of the rebbe's behavior. The fact that the hasid is not given much access to the rebbe's inner life reinforces the attitude that the rebbe's speech and actions (at least on some levels) may serve as accessible models, but not his inner life. Thus, R. Noah of Lechowitz replied to his son when he asked if hasidic masters numbered among the thirty-six hidden saints of the world: "Child, what kind of a face would we have if all that were to our being would be what is manifest?"—implying that for all his manifested rungs, there was still so much more that was hidden.[10] Or, after R. Zvi of Zyditchov once enumerated his achievements, R. Naftali of Ropshitz exclaimed to the Apter: "What humility! He mentioned only the very lowest ones."[11]

In spite of the implicit understanding that only the rebbe's manifest behavior is accessible to the hasid, there are exceptions. Where a hasid aspires to greater discipleship, the rebbe's inner life may be made accessible to him.

Whenever the rebbe acts specifically as rebbe, as in saying Torah, bestowing blessings, receiving kvittels, the simple hasid must not even emulate his behavior. Whenever the rebbe acts as an exalted "servant of God," the *disciple* may venture to emulate him. Generally, the hasid remains in the posture of adulation, seeing in the rebbe a person who points him in the direction of divine service. Whenever the rebbe acts as a hasid, as in visiting a senior rebbe and deferring to him, he is the model of hasidic etiquette and custom, and a hasid must not venture beyond the behavioral modes set by the rebbe's own conduct. In this way, the rebbe creates and formulates hasidic custom.

Where conscious copying is suspected, hasidim react adversely. The more unconscious the copying, the higher the moral rating.

The rebbe who looks at a hasid as he enters the yehidut can gauge his level of adherence to hasidic custom by his clothes and behavior. It may serve as a visible index of the hasid's willingness to follow the rebbe's advice.

In relating to the rebbe, the hasid is aware of the areas of accessibility and nonaccessibility and responds accordingly. The rebbe's partial accessibility is both a challenge and a cause for anxiety. It challenges the hasid to realize his potential, but also makes him anxious about the gulf between

the rebbe's achievement and his own. The rare hasid who truly responds
to the challenge will become a disciple. By and large, hasidim will mini-
mize the rebbe's accessibility in order to decrease their own anxiety.

The Rebbe Interacts on Many Levels

Interaction with Himself

The hasid comes to the rebbe with high aims. Often the rebbe feels
chastised by the hasid and the purity of his aspirations. The hasid's highest
soul level, that of his "delight and will," which is located in his *yehidah*,
has great significance in the yehidut. In order to be able to raise the hasid,
the rebbe must meet him by locating the lowest of his own levels beneath
the highest of the hasid's levels. This creates a disparity. The hasid's
"ought" reaches higher than the rebbe's "is," and serves as an inspiration
to the rebbe.

Many rebbes have confessed that they needed their hasidim for
inspiration. Often a hasid's simple concern for another inspires the rebbe.
The rebbe is always on the lookout for good points in his hasidim that
may be used for intercession to exact benefits for the entire community of
Israel and for individuals in need of help.

In each individual who comes to him to seek his help, the rebbe sees
the possibility of a new insight:

> Once R. Shalom of Belz sat at the table [*tish*] and a woman came and
> wept before him about her plight of barrenness, and begged his
> blessing to conceive. The rebbe blessed her and she went. The rebbe
> sat for a while, lost in meditation. Then, turning to his hasidim, he
> said: "You saw this woman. She has already come several times, and
> each time I blessed her. Yet she came again. So I bethought myself:
> 'She comes to me, and all I am is flesh and blood; yet she continues to
> come. How much more ought we to come and place our requests
> before Him Who is the King of Kings!' Out of this meditation did I
> also beg for her." And with God's help she was blessed with chil-
> dren.[12]

Even the proverbial "nudnik," the unlettered nuisance who interrupts the
tish, has a positive value for the rebbe, as the following story illustrates:

> Rabbi Levi Yitzhaq often welcomed at his table an honest and un-
> taught man whom his disciples regarded askance because they
> thought him incapable of understanding what the rabbi said. And

what business has one who boils pitch among those who compound ointments! But because the man was good-natured and simple, he either did not notice the attitude of the rabbi's disciples, or did not let it ruffle him, so that finally they asked the tzaddik's wife to show the lout the door. Since she did not want to do this without her husband's permission, she reported to him the misgivings and the request of his disciples. The rabbi replied: "When the Seven Shepherds will one day sit at the holy feast: Adam, Seth, Methuselah to the right, Abraham, Jacob, Moses, to the left, David in the middle, and a poor untutored man, Levi Yitzhaq of Berditchev, goes up to them, I believe they will nod even to that lout."[13]

Thus, even the simplest hasid teaches the rebbe something. Yet the more complex the hasid, the greater will be the rebbe's involvement with him, since it will occur on many more levels.

Interaction with the Hasid's Various Selves

The rebbe who meets a hasid who has deviated from the straight and narrow path will ask him: "Where are you?" This question "Ayeka?" which God asked of Adam, has perennial reverberations in the hasidic universe. The hasid who came to Kotsk and was asked by the rebbe "From where?" felt challenged to the quick, as if Aqavyah ben Mahalalel (in the third chapter of *Pirqey Avot*) had asked him to consider the three ultimate questions: where from, where is, and before whom? The rebbe confronts the hasid in this abrupt manner in order to have him choose one of his selves for the sake of the interview.

The rebbe cannot transact anything of real significance if he deals only with the hasid's pious self and not with the self that makes the real decisions. If the two selves happen to be identical, there is no problem. The rebbe, however, knows that there are very few people who act as authentic selves. In hasidic parlance, a person who, under God, is fully autonomous, is referred to as an *atzmi*, an absolute self. In speaking of his father, the late Lubavitcher rebbe referred to him as an *atzmi*. A hasid will be flattered if the rebbe refers to him as a *p'nimi*, an interior person. The *p'nimi* acts out of deep inner compunction: he is never fickle. A contract made with an *atzmi* is the most serious one. The worst contract is one made with a hypocrite. Among hasidim he was outside the pale. But a close neighbor of the hypocrite was the *hitzon*, the opposite of the *p'nimi*. He was considered capable of feeling emotions that he would readily show, but that were shallow and did not commit him to action. A yehidut with a *hitzon* was difficult because of the immediacy of his response, which soon vanished because it was momentarily sincere but shallow. The rebbe, receiving the appropriate response from a *hitzon*, could be sure only of the *hitzon*'s ease of responding, but not of any appreciable change in his life. In order for the *hitzon* to become a hasid with whom the rebbe could transact significantly, the rebbe would first have to produce in him a greater depth and a larger inner life. Even in a person who was closer to the *p'nimi* than a *hitzon*, the rebbe had to establish contact with the "manager" of the person.

The teachings of Habad were directed toward the *beynoni*, the man who is managed by his rational soul. A contract with the divine soul, which obligated the *beynoni* at Sinai and to which he was adjured at birth, was one that only the divine soul—and not the whole person—could honor. There is no point in attempting a transaction with the animal soul, since it is bent on seeking only its own pleasures. The only real contractual partner is the rational soul. Neither the divine soul nor the animal soul can alter behavior. All behavior is the function of the go-ahead signal of the rational soul.

Yet the rational soul experiences problems of its own in dealing with identities and roles. The roles of father and husband differ, and both are distinct from those of merchant and hasid. When the hasid meets with the rebbe, he faces him as a "hasid," but his problem may engage another part of his personality. A hasid who was unhappily married wanted to ask the rebbe about the advisability of a divorce. Several times he came to the rebbe, and each time, the hasid in him monopolized the conversation. He had to return yet another time, and this time the rebbe recognized that he was now dealing with another person and so he focused immediately on the divorce.

The rebbe must deal not only with the many facets of a hasid's being, but also with the many significant persons the hasid has introjected. When a young hasid came to the rebbe about a problem that the rebbe knew was not his own, the rebbe asked that he send his *mashpiy'a* to him. The rebbe then berated the *mashpiy'a* for projecting his own problem onto the hasid. Here we are not dealing with a genuine case of introjection. The young man had been coached for his yehidut by the *mashpiy'a* which had projected, and the rebbe was able to discern this projection.

Parental vestiges in the hasid are not so easily dealt with, since the hasid may be unaware of their existence. Another reason is that the rebbe will not wish to remove these parental vestiges completely, since they are often of great help to the hasid. The hasid could not say "My God and God of my fathers" if he did not have a good parental deposit in himself.

What is important here is that the rebbe separate the hasid from his parental introjections if they interfere with his progress.

The rebbe can deal with parental or other influences in a more direct manner. He may report to the hasid that he has spoken with the discarnate soul of the father or any other ancestor and has gotten him to agree to the counsel he is about to give the hasid. That the rebbe can do so is not questioned by the hasid. Hasidim are familiar with many such stories. A story is told, for example, of how the soul of the Ari appeared to the Besht and they argued over an interpretation of Torah. The Ari finally agreed to the Besht's interpretation.[14]

Occasionally a hasid may decide, for reasons of his own, to change rebbes. This is a rare occurrence, and when it happens the hasid usually fears the wrath of his former rebbe. In this case he will seek the protection of his new rebbe. But his problem may not be that simple. In all probability, he will have incorporated many of his former rebbe's values, and these may be a hindrance to him in his relationship with his present rebbe. Thus, the rebbe will first have to deal with these assumed values before a meaningful transaction can ensue.

In addition to dealing with the hasid's many selves, the rebbe is aware of the fact that he must grapple with the hasid's dark side if he is to help him. The hasid may have committed a considerable number of sins, and each sin has brought him deeper into the realm of *q'lipah*. The rebbe must protect the hasid from the onslaughts of this realm. By personifying the hasid's sins in terms of evil entities, the rebbe faces the demonic aspects of the hasid. He must wrestle with the hasid's vices and free him from their hold.[15]

The rebbe must also interact with the hasid in the transcendental realm, opening for the hasid such gates and channels as the hasid needs to have opened for him. If the hasid is in need of healing, the rebbe has to seek healing for him from the realm of health. At times, the rebbe may find his path blocked. In such a case, he will have to open a channel for the hasid by devious means. A hasid who suffered from a fatal disease traveled from master to master and gained no help until he came to R. Pinhas of Koretz, who wished him great wealth. The rebbe later explained that although he found the gates of health blocked to him, he was able to open the gates of material abundance and thereby secure a new lease on life for the hasid.

Interaction with the Hasid's Life Process

The rebbe's involvement with his hasid commits him to interact not only with the hasid's present but also with his past and future. His empathy must therefore include both the hasid's being (a composite of his past and present), and his becoming (his movement toward his future). To understand the hasid's problematic being, the rebbe must be able to view him "in situation": he must be able to see him as a particular person with a particular problem. To see either (the hasid or his problem) in isolation would yield only a distorted view.

The rebbe sees the hasid's problem in terms of process. (This too is a legitimate use of the word *gilgulim*—reincarnations.) In the process of life, there are many moments of crisis.

> Therefore is man named "one who walks" and not "one who stands on one place." He must rise from rung to rung and not remain fixed at one station. Between one level and the next, before he can reach the higher one, he must "fall" from the previous rung. But it is written [and thus are we assured] "though he fall, he is not removed." The fall is not a real one, and in comparison with others, he is still higher, but in comparison with his erstwhile state, it is a fall.[16]

The hasid experiences a "death" in his need to regress from his former rung and being. This is part of his grooming for the next level. Yet at the moment of his fall, he feels that he is forever arrested on this fallen level, and comes to the rebbe in the desperation of his plight. At this point, the rebbe must use his empathy in order to ask himself what it feels like to be forever arrested at this particular stage and to fear that the predicament is permanent. He must be fully able to feel the hopelessness and despair the hasid feels, yet he must not allow the hasid to give way to despair. The rebbe knows that the hasid's condition is not permanent, for he knows that "man is judged every day," and this means that tomorrow will be a different day and a different judgment.

> Once the Besht's disciples asked him concerning the contradiction between "Man's budget is granted to him from Rosh Hashanah to Rosh Hashanah" and "Man is judged every day." The rebbe replied by knocking on the window and calling the watercarrier, Yuckel. "Yuckel, tell me how are you today?" the Besht asked. "*Oy*, rebbe," Yuckel replied, "I am old and my shoulders are weak; and the children are studying Torah and not one thinks of helping me. My wife is old and sickly, and my sons-in-law conduct themselves like rabbis, and all that on my shoulders, rebbe. I don't want to sin, but I feel depressed by all my woes."
>
> The next day the Besht again called him over, and again he asked him, "How do you feel today?" Yuckel chuckled and said: "Rebbe, you know I am a lucky man. I have fine children, and sons-

in-law who study Torah, and my wife, she is such a darling and keeps house well, despite her being old and sickly; and to think of it—all this is borne on these old shoulders! Yes rebbe, I am a lucky man. May God be praised for His abundant graces."

After the Besht dismissed Yuckel, he turned to his disciples and said: "See, not a single thing has changed. Yuckel is the same and his budget unvarying, but today he was judged differently."[17]

By dealing with the hasid in this manner, the rebbe plots him on a course: he helps the hasid see himself as part of a process, rather than as a static being. In this way he can be assured that what seems terrible and impossible one day, may find its resolution the next. The hasid's problem is but a station on the way.

The rebbe faces the hasid in three ways, but these ways are not separable. Each is an intertwining thread in the ongoing being of the hasid. The rebbe faces the hasid in his manifest being as a person in trouble; he faces him in his interactions with his own many selves; and he faces him in the dynamics of becoming. The rebbe also faces the hasid simultaneously in another dimension: that of the divine ontological moment. It is the "way in which a soul stands in the primeval thought of Adam Qadmon." It is a moment in which a particular life has achieved its specific destiny, although the momentum of the dynamics of becoming will not allow the soul to hold on to the moment. At this ontic juncture, that soul's particular plan and destiny are worked out as they stood in the primal thought. As S. Y. Agnon stated:

> A person has three beings. The first being is the way in which a person perceives himself, the second is the way in which a person is seen by others, and *the third being is prior to the first, and it is the being by which he was created by Him who created him.* If a person merited and did not damage the being which his Creator made him, then that being overwhelms the other two, and then even his shadow inspires grace and beauty.[18]

The third being is the soul as it stands in the primal thought. The rebbe, then, must be able to interact with the hasid in the dimension of this moment, which has ongoing significance. Viktor Frankl considers the interaction on this level "the finest maxim for any kind of psychotherapy," and here he quotes Goethe:

> If we take people as they are, we make them worse. If we treat them as if they were what they ought to be, we help them to become what they are capable of becoming.[19]

The rebbe is therefore involved in a dual set of tensions: (a) the tension between total identification and objectivity, and (b) the tension between the hasid's problem as a vexing static condition and as a point in the hasid's dynamic movement. In more traditional, hasidic terms, the tension is between (a) the goals and purposes of this incarnation, in which the problem brought to the rebbe occurs; and (b) the goals and purposes of the person's reincarnational life, in which the problem figures as a point on a curve. The rebbe's manifold tensions in feeling the problem with the hasid also help unlock the rebbe's creativity in helping the hasid.

Interaction through Arrangement Making (Sidur Seder)

Another important function of the rebbe's interaction with his hasid lies in arrangement making. By arrangement making we mean a restructuring of the hasid's loyalties, responsibilities, and priorities. The purpose of this restructuring is to liberate the hasid from a web of tensions that holds him at dead center. The arrangement need not be a final action directive for the hasid; it is efficient if it acts in such a way as to divert the tensions that are restricting the hasid's movement. The hasid may require help in making a series of progressive rearrangements, each one freeing him for the next task. Arrangement making is thus a temporary restructuring that extricates the hasid from tensions that are crippling his movement.

The ruse of arrangement making is often necessary because the person in need of help is unable to shift his precarious economy by himself. The arrangement of his defenses is set in such a fashion that he believes the slightest move threatens to topple the entire economic structure of his psyche. The rebbe's first step is to help the hasid shore up his defenses. This he does by distracting him from his present position, where, at tremendous cost to his psychic economy, he must guard and protect all possibilities. Here the rebbe's task is not as difficult as that of other helpers in the same position. The hasidic structure enables the rebbe to call upon the hasid's faith in him. Because he is able to demand this trust from the hasid, the rebbe can more easily deflect him from his care and anxiety. In placing himself in the rebbe's hands, the hasid is able to let down his defenses because he trusts that the rebbe will protect him. Any insight the hasid may gain from seeing his problems restructured in such a way, will provide only a temporary framework for movement. This framework will, in all probability, have to undergo several adjustments until a clear "objective" insight, replacing all the temporary insights, is reached. Each adjustment is a stage in a series of distractions aimed at bringing the hasid to the point where he can act without tension on the instruction that the rebbe wished to give him in the first place.

The process we have described is mentioned by R. Nahman of Bratslav in his discussion of the method of helping those weaker souls whom he called "eggs."[20] He explained that because their outer protection is so weak, it can easily crack. Figuratively speaking, such "eggs" have both a rounded and a pointed end, the rounded end representing insensitivity, and the pointed end representing sensitivity. In order to help such a soul, the rebbe must be able to "turn" him so that his "sharp end" will be directed toward those areas in which sensitivity has positive value, and his "round end" will be directed toward those areas in which sensitivity is undesirable. Since it is not advisable to turn such souls all at once, the rebbe must do so gradually. (This, R. Nahman explains, is one of the reasons why the Messiah has not come. The tzaddikim want to redeem even those weak souls called "eggs," and this cannot be done quickly.)

This method of arrangement making is based on Maimonides' Theory of Education, which proceeds from lesser to higher values by providing an ever-ascending scale.[21] The rebbe's ability to assist his hasid in a gradual ascending movement is part of his understanding of the hasid's life process.

THE MANAGEMENT OF FEELING

The rebbe cannot diagnose by external and mechanical methods. He uses no questionnaire, no projective tests. He is the diagnostic instrument, the one who reads the scales, integrates the readings, and plans a course of help. Yet, he too is subject to the human condition. He is affected by what he sees, and this can cause distortions. In order to be an effective helper, the rebbe has to know how to transcend these possible distortions. This can only be done by constant effort and vigilance.

How does the rebbe become sensitized to his hasid, and how does he maintain this sensitivity? How is he able to so empathize with his hasid that he can truly feel his problem, without entering into the same blind alley in which the hasid finds himself? In other words, how is he able to maintain his inner distance without blocking his empathy? Does he know when the subtle balance between involvement and distance is upset? How does he separate client from client in the maze of his own involvement with their problems? What role does the hasid play in the transaction? How can he help or hinder the rebbe in the achievement of their mutual goals?

In this section we will trace the rebbe's interaction with the hasid, his investment in and empathy with his hasid, the ways in which investment and empathy can become blocked, and how the rebbe removes these blocks. We will also show how the rebbe clears his mind of "interference" from one yehidut to the next (divestment) and we will discuss the responsibilities he undertakes as he prepares to prescribe for his hasid.

Investment and Empathy

Investment is the literal translation of the hasidic term *hitlabshut*. Figuratively, the term expresses the rebbe's action in "clothing" himself in the garments of the hasid's thought, word, and deed. These he examines from within, thus fulfilling the command in *Pirqey Avot*: "Do not judge a man until you have arrived at his place."[22] The rebbe takes this command literally. He assumes the place of the hasid and enters his consciousness, while at the same time retaining a hold on his own consciousness.

The Rebbe's Investment

Imagine a person who has undergone surgery and is asked how the treated part of his anatomy feels. Let us say that it was his foot. In order to answer the question meaningfully, the patient must become "all foot." If he remained "all head," he could not really answer the question about his foot. Yet at the same time he must bring the feeling of his foot to the attention of his head. If he is to do something about the foot, he cannot consult the foot about the course of action, but must consult the head. Still, a decapitated head cannot answer the question about the foot.

According to the hasidic view, the rebbe is the Head of the People. He feels what they feel. He is the head and can advise the foot about the proper remedy.

The field of interaction between rebbe and hasid coheres because they are bound to one another in a relationship that is known as *hitqashrut*. In the yehidut, *hitqashrut* becomes more intense and profound, and *hitlabshut*—investment—enters the picture. In *hitqashrut*, the hasid and the rebbe remain who they are. In *hitlabshut*, the rebbe becomes the hasid for the moment. *Hitlabshut* is more than trial identification. The rebbe has already received the kvittel, and in the process of *hitlabshut*, he sees the hasid in his abiding and recurring personal essence. *Hitlabshut* provides the rebbe with a basic area of empathy and understanding: from here, he can proceed to establish the external information he needs in order to help his hasid. This field of empathy enables the rebbe to experience the hasid's problem on a subtle level within himself.

> When the men of our covenant [euphemism for hasidim] enter into yehidut and reveal the things that plague their hearts in their inner-most being, each one according to his state, then each thing they tell me I must find in myself in its subtle form, or in the subtle form of the subtle form. It is impossible to answer him [the hasid] and give him something to mend his ways and truly order his life until one mends this matter first in oneself, and only then can one give an etzah and a tiqun.[23]

The process of investment is very debilitating for a rebbe, who must interview a large number of hasidim each day. "Yehidut is very expensive in health," one rebbe explained, because

> Yehidut is a continuing investment and divestment. . . . the invest-ment of becoming the other and the divestment in order not to be the other any more, but to invest oneself in the next one, is a great psychic exertion.[24]

The burden of the rebbe is great. Since the rebbe participates in the hasid's world view, he sees the hasid's problems in terms of evil decrees that have to be removed, rigors of law that have to be sweetened at their root. The rebbe cannot simply tell the hasid that he must learn to live with his problem. Even if this is necessary because there is no immediate solution available at the root of the hasid's soul, the rebbe still has to reach much higher. He must reach into a previous incarnation of the hasid in order to show him why he must now agree to live with his problems because of their reparative value.

What is the element that provides for the identification of rebbe with hasid? It is obvious that here one is not dealing with objective problem solving. The rebbe has to feel in himself the pain of his hasid. Where the natural impulse of a man in his position might be to laugh at the hasid's problem (which, viewed from a vertical perspective, might seem insignifi-cant), the rebbe, through the process of his identification with the hasid, will sigh at the hasid's agony. The rebbe is able to identify fully with his hasid because, at the moment when he gives the hasid his undivided attention, he is also giving his undivided attention to God, and the one makes possible the other. This paradox is difficult for the modern reader to comprehend, yet there are many hasidic tales that illustrate just this point.

R. Naftali of Ropshitz, who was very fond of joking and punning, one day, in his later years, decided that he was not going to talk anymore. His family was very much upset: they addressed him, but they would receive no answer from him. Finally they sent his son, R. Eliezer of Dzhikov, to see what was wrong with his father. R. Naftali explained:

"At one time I was able to keep two things in my mind at the same time. I would joke with a person while at the same time attending to some very high unifications in the mind of God. Now that I am old, and am able to think only one thought at a time, I do not want to talk, because to talk would mean that I cannot be in the presence of God."[25]

A latter-day rebbe, R. Kalonymus Kalmish of Piasetzno, was once asked if his great involvement with his hasidim did not prevent him from pursuing his work. By way of reply, R. Kalonymus pointed to a pad on his desk on which he had marked down some deep kabbalistic insights. He explained that every time one of his hasidim left his presence, he tried to understand the hasid's problem in terms of a kabbalistic problem, and the solution that he offered was in terms of a solution to the problem in Kabbalah. In this way he managed to be active in his own vineyard, writing and studying, while at the same time tending the vineyards of his hasidim.[26] This illustration emphasizes the rebbe's belief concerning the problems of his hasidim. He believes that every problem is a special message from God. This fact enables him to learn at the same time as he is helping his hasid. It means that he is not merely pressing the hasid's problems into a previously established gestalt.

One of the most difficult problems of the rebbe (R. Shmuel of Lubavitch considered it the most difficult) is that he must continually invest and divest himself so completely that there will be no transfer of person or problems from one hasid to the next. Often rebbes would use the moments in between each yehidut for intercession in order to remove any incubatory element from their conscious mind. Thus, they would be able to meet the situation of the next hasid in terms of its own structure.

Empathy

In order to bring the relevant material of Hasidism to bear on the process of investment and divestment, we need to digress for the moment to the process of empathy as discussed by Robert Katz. He cites Theodor Reik's outline of the process of empathy. This process may occur in the following order: (1) identification; (2) incorporation; (3) reverberation; and (4) detachment. It is possible that the order may change, or—and this is more often the case in the psychological realm—the phases may occur simultaneously.

Presumably, the rebbe is a master of the empathic process. Since too much awareness of the process may inhibit the engagement of emotion in the other,[27] the rebbe will deliberately regress in the service of his empathy. Yet he is not anxious about his need to regress, since he trusts that the "unconscious holy spirit" will help him maintain the proper frame of mind, enabling him to detach himself when necessary.

In order to lose his "objectiveness," the rebbe draws upon his experience so that he can discover the hasid's problem on a subtle level in himself. To refer again to the words of Robert Katz:

> Only when we detect something familiar in our own experience, do we appreciate the quality of the other's experience which we have internalized. "I personally feel I only 'understand' if I can detect in my own mind the germ of a similar feeling as the one which I try to understand, given that a similar thing should happen to me" (Lumeij 1957, p. 22).[28]

Hasidism, at its inception, was erroneously identified with Sabbatianism. In Sabbatianism (and in many other gnostic systems), a person must *actually* experience the experience of the other. The rebbe, on the other hand, knows that this is not necessary. If it were, the whole therapeutic process would place the helper in terrible jeopardy. All that is necessary is that the helper find the same problem in himself on "a subtle level." Discussing this from the angle of empathy, Katz explains the above statement:

> It is important to note the important qualification that Lumeij introduces. It is not essential that we experience the actual event. We can imagine the event and anticipate what our own response might be. *We have within ourselves the potentialities of every human response. Because we share this common emotional endowment, we are able to understand from within ourselves what the meaning of the experience of others might be for them.* We could not recognize the other's experience unless we had some *a priori* knowledge of it.[29]

Hasidism has its system of correspondence and its system of the evolution of the higher cause down to the lower effect. Since the tzaddik can be held responsible for the sins of his generation,[30] we understand that the experience of the body follows the more subtle experience of the head. On the subtle level, the rebbe has had the same experience, and he must find it and raise it to the conscious level. If he is unable to raise it to consciousness, he will fear that he is repressing his subtle involvement, and that it may be "evil that is hidden in the depth of the depths."[31]

The rebbe's subtle experience is both the same and different from that of the hasid. To the rebbe, his subtle experience has the same meaning as the hasid's gross experience has to him. In the hasidic system, the rebbe's subtle experience contains the hasid's gross experience as cause contains effect. Therefore, as far as hasidic ontology is concerned, the rebbe's experience is not merely symbolic: rather, it is identical with the hasid's own experience.

Despite the fact that this is an expensive process in terms of the rebbe's health and emotions, the rebbe gains a great deal in the form of his own perfection. The hasid stimulates the rebbe and enlarges the rebbe's scope. The rebbe lacks some experiences in his own life. When the hasid brings his problems to the rebbe, and the rebbe invests himself in them, he empathically experiences the hasid's life. Had the hasid not brought his problems to the rebbe, the rebbe would not have had occasion to plumb the depths of his range of subtle experience.

The rebbe's investment in his hasidim is reinforced on a deep level by the fact that he makes his living from the honoraria that his hasidim provide. The rebbe must protect his investment in his hasid, and his hasid's investment in him. This is the significance of the pidyon for the rebbe. The pidyon is a retainer, and the rebbe must act as an agent retained by a client.

The Hasid's Investment

The rebbe's investment in the hasid is facilitated by the hasid's reciprocal investment in his rebbe. According to custom, the hasid who comes to yehidut has already heard the rebbe's discourses and has made the concepts and values discussed in them his own. While these may not yet be fully internalized, working parts of the hasid's consciousness, they are nevertheless part of his upward strivings.

Just as the rebbe experiences difficulties in his investment in and empathy with his hasid, so the hasid experiences difficulties in his investment, even greater than those of the rebbe. In coming to the yehidut, the hasid may so absorb the atmosphere of the rebbe's court before his interview, and may so empathize with the rebbe during the yehidut that he sees himself as he supposes the rebbe sees him. Thus, the hasid's self-image will not be the one he normally carries, nor will it reflect the way in which the rebbe perceives him; rather, the image is a fictitious product of the hasid's mind that is reacting to the ambient influences. Such an image can block the productive interaction between rebbe and hasid. R. Mendl of Kotsk, concerned about this phenomenon, taught the following maxim:

> If I am I because you are you, and you are you because I am I, then you are not you and I am not I. But, if I am I because I am I, and you are you because you are you, then I am I and you are you and we can talk.[32]

Whatever good the hasid derives from the yehidut must arise from an authentic interrelation with the rebbe.

In Habad this interaction is seen in terms of the rebbe's lower level descending below the hasid's higher level. Thus the relationship is established. The hasid's strivings, the level of the *yehidah* of his soul, where his capacity for delight and the power of his will reside, reach upward toward the rebbe, and even higher into the Divine Will. The rebbe, on the other hand, by the power of the *yehidah*, can descend even to the lowest levels and yet remain fully aware on the highest level of awareness. Both of these *yehidah* movements—upwards and downwards—are aspects of *m'sirat nefesh*—self-sacrifice. The hasid is prepared to change his entire mode of life, and the rebbe is prepared to descend into the hasid's private hell.

Investment and Anxiety

The rebbe knows that his efforts to reveal secrets to his hasid may cost him even the lives of his own children; yet he also knows that he cannot do anything but act in the way he must, since this is his raison d'être.[33]

At the moment when he must invest himself most deeply in his hasid, the rebbe may experience a temptation to escape this involvement and settle down to solitary study and prayer. But he has been told by his master that involvement with the hasid is in the service of his own life. If the rebbe fulfills his own task too soon, he may have to die, as there will no longer be any purpose for his life on earth.[34] Thus, the hasid distracts the rebbe from his thirst to become lost in God, and in this way, keeps him alive.[35]

The rebbe, having allowed himself to become aware of his hasid's attitude toward him, is bound to the relationship. Awareness and empathy cause positive feedback, which increases the mutual empathy. The hasid relates to the rebbe more fully, and the hasid's empathizing with the rebbe stimulates the rebbe to invest himself ever more deeply into the hasid.

It is almost as if the rebbe acted against his better judgment. Each time he opens himself to the hasid, he opens himself to pain. "I feel his pain even more than he does," R. Nahman of Bratzlav said of one hasid. "He can at least become distracted from his pain, but I cannot."[36] Herein lies the rebbe's problem. He must consciously and deliberately enter the realm of the hasid's pain. It might seem that this repeated exposure to pain would make the rebbe phobic of hasidim and their problems. But phobias plague only those who successfully escape pain and thus reinforce the need to escape. The rebbe, by immersing himself in the hasid's pain and fear, extinguishes the dread.

The rebbe is also willing to expose himself to such pain because of his love for the hasid. The pain and the joy of meeting one beloved, and of interacting with him, have the effect of canceling each other to some extent. Furthermore, some of the pain and dread are already diminished when the hasid comes to see the rebbe. This is the function of the hasid's empathy. Like the mature patient who goes to his physician and assumes the physician's clinical detachment in order to discuss his symptoms and prognosis more accurately, the hasid comes to the rebbe with his symptoms readied and described in the kvittel, eager to hear the rebbe's prescription. To prevent a situation in which the hasid, in his confusion, might present a petition unsuited to his spiritual rung, the *Lyozhna Taqa-noth*[37] demanded that the hasid write his kvittel at home. The kvittel thus serves the purpose of bringing the hasid "back to reality." This is especially significant in view of our earlier discussion of the hasid's mental self-image, which may impede investment and communication. When the rebbe has the kvittel before him, he can ensure that the hasid's "real" problem is discussed, rather than the problem the hasid has come to see as his own under the influence of the environment at the rebbe's court.

The rebbe cannot become completely lost in the hasid's pain, since the hasid, by his presence, demands that the rebbe help him in an objective fashion. Because the hasid comes to the rebbe prepared to change certain conditions of his life, the rebbe must work in the direction of the results he and the hasid envision. This factor serves to change the focus of the interaction, diverting it from identification and investment to the objective result, and thus facilitates the psychic distance between rebbe and hasid. At the same time, the rebbe, having attained this psychic distance, cannot prescribe for the hasid's real condition unless he sees it as that of a person in a specific situation. Therefore he must situate himself in the hasid once more by reinvestment.

It is important to understand that the movement that we are here describing is not that of the rebbe vacillating between two different poles of consciousness: the rebbe expands his consciousness to encompass both poles. This causes great tension. Yet, the greater the tension in the rebbe and the more willingly he maintains it, the more creative his insight into the hasid's problem, and the wider his scope of counsel will be. As Katz explains:

> Part of our self is fused with the identity of the other. Yet another part of our feeling and thinking is capable of responding to this experience as the external thing it is.[38]

The creative tension arising from the rebbe's embrace of these two poles enables him to find a fresh approach to the etzah.

Investment in Prescription

Even when the rebbe is ready to give the hasid a prescription for his condition, he must be invested in the hasid in order to see the prescription in terms of the hasid's life situation. The story of R. Michael of Zlotchev bears repeating here (Kahane 1922, p. 66). He once gave a harsh penance to a simple Jew who arrived late Friday afternoon from a business trip and barely made it home in time for the Sabbath. It was not until he found himself in a similar situation, and the Besht pointed out to him that the contrition of the simple Jew was as great as his own, that R. Michael realized that his penance had been too harsh. Thus, the rebbe must himself taste the discipline he prescribes in order to know what it can do for the penitent. This he does by investment. The rebbe's investment in his hasid at the time of prescription must take into consideration one important factor: halakhic etiquette, according to which one seeks a severe ruling for oneself and a lenient one for others. The rebbe who would himself be prepared to work through a severe regimen must not burden his hasid with the same. It is not necessarily a lack of generosity that may cause a hasid to find a regimen given by the rebbe too harsh. There may be some very real and worthy commitments that he, in his life situation, cannot ignore, though they may stand in conflict with the rebbe's prescription. The rebbe will therefore privately acknowledge the hasid's generosity in wishing to follow his counsel, and yet will not ask him to strain other relationships that also make demands on his resources.

The rebbe may know that his hasid feels an exaggerated guilt over a sin that is not as severe as the hasid feels it to be. Here the rebbe faces a dilemma that he cannot, but by his own empathic investment, resolve. If he gives the hasid a penance in consonance with his guilt feelings, he will be able to help the hasid overcome them. However, in order to help the hasid properly atone for his sins, the rebbe must be able to make him aware of the relative lightness of his transgression. In this way, the burden of guilt can be channeled into areas where it is better employed. The hasid who feels great guilt about a ritual infraction, but is lax on interpersonal ethical levels, needs to be helped to see his guilt where it really exists.

There is another reason why the rebbe will not accept the hasid's harsh estimate of his own guilt. Ultimately, the interaction between rebbe and hasid should achieve in the latter a more mature view of good and evil.

> Truth is a middle path. It wants not to turn to the right by making things more difficult, by finding unreasonable faults and sins in oneself which one has not committed. Nor does it want to turn to the left, to ease one's sense of duty due to self-love in the doing of good works. Both of them, left and right, are false ways.[39]

When the hasid is able to achieve a more mature view of good and evil, the proportionally true weight of an infraction will become known to him. If the rebbe has weighed his guilt harshly, the hasid will be resentful. He will react by saying: "I did not know then how ill or good my acts were. But the rebbe did know, and he let me suffer needlessly." This will shake any real confidence and trust the hasid has in the rebbe, and jeopardize future transactions and growth. The hasid's resentment is bound to result in at least a partial rejection of the rebbe's hierarchy of values. On the other hand, if the rebbe does not help the hasid atone for his guilt, the hasid will, in all probability, become involved in a greater sin in order to justify a greater penance. Or, he may take out his aggression by projecting his own guilt onto others. In either case, he will have found a way of dealing with his excessive guilt feelings. The rebbe can help the hasid overcome his guilt feelings in a positive rather than a negative manner. However, short of complete empathic investment, the rebbe will fail the hasid in his prescription, and the hasid will be forced to utilize his own resources to deal with his guilt feelings.

By the time the rebbe is ready to prescribe for his hasid at the close of the yehidut, he may have at least partially distanced himself in order not to become "lost" in the hasid. If this is the case, he will have to become reinvested in the hasid to be sure that his prescription is truly relevant to the hasid's condition. By doing so, he will be able to "see" the effect of his etzah on the hasid's life. Only then will he be able to prescribe in the sure knowledge that his counsel speaks optimally to the hasid's present life situation, while at the same time taking into account his ongoing life process.

The Rebbe Faces the Possibility of Missing the Mark

In spite of his natural and hereditary endowment, his gifts of the spirit, and his acquired skill and wisdom, the rebbe still faces the possibility of missing the mark in relating to and empathizing with his hasid. The rebbe is aware that two opposing forces operate within him: (1) logic and reason, coupled with reality testing, and (2) his unconscious *ruah haqodesh*, coupled with his intuition and empathy. The faculty of reason tends to thwart the workings of the unconscious processes that are so vital to the rebbe in yehidut. In addition to effectively analyzing the hasid's problem in situation, the rebbe must so liberate his intuitive and empathic processes that he will be able to empathize freely with his hasid. "The effective empathizer succeeds in getting an inside appreciation of his client."[40] However, there is some danger in yielding to unconscious processes. There is almost no recourse to reality testing. "The participation may have been so engrossing and so irreversible that the practitioner overidentifies with the client and disqualifies himself for the disinterested analysis that is necessary."[41]

The Kabbalah and the teachings of Hasidism have taught the rebbe the need to utilize his *hush hatziyur*, his imaginative faculty. Hayim Vital and R. Nahman of Bratzlav refer to this faculty as the holy *m'dameh*. R. Nahman warns that the *m'dameh* of the person whose mind has not yet been cleared of the troubling "yeast" is unreliable. Such a person will tend to project, while assuming that he is actually empathizing.

> What is essential to our understanding of empathy is the idea that it is the experience of another person that we take in rather than an experience of our own which we project onto another. In this phase, we introduce into our own consciousness something that is partly alien and foreign to us. It is another way in which we reduce the social distance between ourselves and others.[42]

If the rebbe becomes anxious about entering into the strange and anxiety-producing realm of the hasid's sin, if we cannot conceive of himself as being involved in even the most subtle aspect of that sin, he will be blocked in his investment and powerless to help the hasid. It is often possible to descend into a familiar hell; but one that is unfamiliar is more hellish. Or, as stated by R. Nahman: "A rebbe must be able to go to any of the twenty-four supernal courts to plead for his hasid. If he does not know the court at which the case is to be tried, or if he does not know the way to the court, he cannot help his hasid."[43]

The rebbe is the model for the hasidic community and his teaching is the norm of the community. The form of signature he uses, "the insignificant one," stresses self-derogation; yet he is also authoritarian—he "calls the shots." He is ethnocentric (Russian vs. Polish, Polish vs. Litvak, Galician vs. Hungarian, etc.), fundamentalist, and stresses conformity to the highly specialized hasidic "ought." All these factors militate against a high degree of empathy. Yet the rebbe needs this empathy, and in order to attain it, he has to draw on his love for all Israel and for his fellow-man. This love, which extends to the greatest sinner even more abundantly than that of a father to his child, can again lead the rebbe to become overengrossed, and the rebbe must guard against swinging to this pole.

Because of his capacity for empathy, the rebbe is able to gain information from the hasid that would otherwise remain undisclosed. This fact, in addition to the rebbe's vertical position vis-à-vis the hasid in the hasidic hierarchy, creates yet another difficulty in the rebbe–hasid relationship. If the rebbe uses the knowledge he has gained through empathy in a judgmental manner, it will undermine his relationship with the hasid. If, however, he is able to overcome the judgmental tendency, the mutual empathy between rebbe and hasid will flow more freely. The following hasidic stories illustrate this point:

The Turning Point

A respected woman once came to ask the advice of the Rabbi of Apt. The instant he set eyes on her he shouted: "Adultress! You sinned only a short while ago, and yet now you have the insolence to step into this pure house!" Then from the depths of her heart the woman replied: "The Lord of the world has patience with the wicked. He is in no hurry to make them pay their debts and he does not disclose their secret to any creature, lest they be ashamed to turn to him. Nor does he hide his face from them. But the Rabbi of Apt sits there in his chair and cannot resist revealing at once what the Creator has covered." From that time on the Rabbi of Apt used to say: "No one ever got the better of me except once—and then it was a woman."[44]

The Golden Scale

Rabbi Naftali, a disciple of the Rabbi of Apt, who later became the Rabbi of Ropshitz, asked a fellow pupil to find out what their teacher thought of him. For half a year his friend made every effort to get the rabbi to say something, but he said nothing about Naftali, nothing good and nothing bad. So his fellow disciple told Naftali, "You see, the master has a golden scale in his mouth. He never passes judgment on anyone, for fear he might wrong him. Has he not forbidden us to judge even those who are supposed wicked through and through? For if anyone were to wrong them, he would be wronging God himself."[45]

Both these stories that are told of the Apter Rebbe illustrate how he had to learn, painfully, not to misuse his empathic understanding by passing judgment. The beauty of the first story lies in the fact that one of those whom he would judge was the very one to teach him the lesson. The second story illustrates how this lesson became intrinsic to the rebbe's manner of relating to his hasidim.

At times the rebbe may think that he is invested in his hasid and is fully empathizing with him, when he is not. The rebbe will not generally admit that he has "missed" the hasid's reality in his investment, and, since implicit belief in the rebbe is part of the hasidic behavior syndrome, the hasid will not admit that the rebbe has missed the mark. If the rebbe has not invested himself properly in the hasid, the hasid will maintain that the rebbe has seen something in him that he is not yet aware of himself. Thus, the rebbe's "miss" becomes a "hit" as a result of a self-fulfilling prophecy: the hasid will live up to the rebbe's expectations of him.

The rebbe may realize that he is unable to invest himself in his hasid as fully as he wishes. At this point he may, like the Middle Rebbe and the Tzemah Tzedeq, interrupt the yehidut and go into seclusion in order to fast and pray. This, he hopes, will bring him to recover his own repressed material, so that when he becomes aware of it, he will be ready to resume his interview, having discovered the condition of the hasid as it obtains in him on the subtle level. Mending it in himself, he has found a solution that he can recommend to his hasid.

Psychoanalytically considered, the rebbe is anxious that his lack of empathy with a particular hasid may be due to his own repression of evil. He fears that unless he finds the evil within himself, he will not be able to prescribe, since any prescription will necessarily involve a projection of that evil of which he is unconscious. Hence, the following paradox ensues. The rebbe is not properly empathizing with his hasid. When he prescribes, he fails to prescribe for the hasid because he is too busy prescribing for himself; yet he is unaware that he harbors this evil, even in its subtlest form. The paradox is that while unaware of his own condition, he prescribes for it.

The skilled rebbe will avoid such situations. Instead, by placing himself in the presence of God in a penitential manner, and by fasting and examining his conscience, he will become distracted from his problem.

Then, by reciting psalms, the rebbe will allow his own problem to confront him as an instrusion into his psalm chanting. It may be that one of the sentences will suddenly trigger a new insight, or that an idea will rise as an extraneous thought disturbing him in his chanting. In this sense, the inclination for evil contributes to its own defeat via the rebbe's ruse. As R. Nahman observed: "I don't know how anyone who does not know the mystery of the High Priest and the scapegoat can accept a pidyon."[46] The reference here is to the scapegoat that is sent to "*Azazel* into the desert" in order to divert Satan and to obtain atonement.

If the rebbe finds that, in spite of all his efforts, he is still unable to empathize with his hasid, he will refer him to another rebbe. R. Levi Yitzhaq of Berditchev once interrupted an interview and sent a hasid away. The hasid had been illicitly involved with a woman, and, as the hasid put it: "We waited until she had completed her seven clean days." The hasid then went to R. Shneur Zalman, who was able to help him. The passionate R. Levi Yitzhaq could not empathize with one who had been deliberate in his deviation from the law, while at the same time trying to satisfy the law. Had the man sinned in a moment of passion, he could have helped him. In this case, it was a matter of temperamental incompatability that upset the rebbe's empathy. If the hasid had not waited the seven clean days and had sinned in passion, R. Levi Yitzhaq could have helped him by prescribing an equally passionate surrender to God and His purposes. This he actually did on another occasion when he met a man on the street who had a reputation all over Berditchev for his amorous pursuits. R. Levi Yitzhaq said to him: "I envy you. You have so many acts of love on your conscience. If only you would turn to God with your passionate love, he would turn all your sins into merit, and you would be greater in His eyes than many a saint."

In spite of his natural gifts and his awareness of his own mission, the rebbe faces many pitfalls. These are all the more dangerous because of the great depths and the many levels of his vision. The rebbe must have the capacity to maintain a delicate balance between the two poles of the investment continuum: he must rid himself of all factors and attitudes that would inhibit free empathy and investment, while at the same time guarding carefully against become overengrossed in the hasid.

Countertransference and Divestment

Countertransference

As an effective empathizer, the rebbe can trust himself and his reactions. As rebbe, he need not be defensive. He can enjoy his inner security precisely because he knows where, on the subtle level, he himself is vulnerable. This enables him to identify freely. When the rebbe sighs, he shares his hasid's anxieties. This he does freely and without fear of contagion. His self-scrutiny keeps him from falling into the traps laid by his own needs. He manages his countertransference without allowing it to beguile him.[47] Therefore, rebbe and hasid can speak freely of their love for each another. Each has a strong emotional investment in the other. So ideal is this love that, according to a popular hasidic saying, "had King Solomon known of rebbe and hasid, he would have written the Song of Songs about them instead."[48]

While the bond between rebbe and hasid rarely assumes any of the manifest forms that are normally associated with an expression of love, there are a great many stylized gestures that express this love. When the rebbe teaches, he "inseminates" the hasid, who then gives birth to the rebbe's seed in the form of Torah and mitzvot. In the hasidic system of correspondences, to teach someone who does not absorb the teaching, or who is unworthy, is likened to masturbation and results in a nocturnal emission on the part of the rebbe. Hence, the hasidic interpretation of Psalm 25:14: "The secret of the Lord is [to be imparted only] to those that fear Him and His covenant. [By the means of the member in which the covenant is sealed] will He let him know."[49] The rebbe who feels such love for a hasid that he is moved to kiss him, will sublimate this feeling and instead give him a special teaching discourse. Sometimes the rebbe will show his love by sharing his food and wine.

The love between rebbe and hasid can at times be fierce and jealous. This accounts for the sense of crisis when a hasid leaves one rebbe for another. To do so arouses the rebbe's *q'piydah*—wrathful contempt. The rebbe feels that the hasid has in a sense spurned him and has demeaned the love between them.

Divestment

The rebbe's love for his hasid does not blind him to the hasid's realities. He does not permit his vision of the hasid to become clouded by his love for him. He is trained to love the hasid in "the manner of Abraham," a love governed by reason and by a commitment to God, and not with "the love of Ishmael," in which the reason behind the love is obscured. In other words: Abraham loves in order to bring souls to God. Ishmael loves *because* he loves, and he possesses in his love. "His hand is on everything, and the hand of everyone is on him."[50] For the rebbe, the criterion by which he judges his love for the hasid is the extent to which he is content to leave the hasid in the hands of divine providence. By so doing, the rebbe should have no difficulty disengaging his attention and emotions from the hasid. Here again, the statement of the Middle Rebbe applies: He is to look at each soul in the way in which it stands in the primal thought of Adam Qadmon. The rebbe sacrifices the hasid for the sanctification of God's name. This process is somewhat akin to the process in which R. Elimelekh counsels his hasid to cast himself, in his imagination, into a fierce fire for the sake of God. In *hitpashtut*—divestment—the rebbe can "drown the hasid in 'grace' or in 'fire.'"[51] By surrendering the hasid to the fire, the rebbe frees both himself and the hasid from the attachment. The proper perspective is then reestablished, and both rebbe and hasid belong once more to God and not to each other. The manipulative and possessive aspects of their love are removed, so that rebbe and hasid are realigned to face God instead of each other. In this posture, the rebbe regains a greater degree of objectivity.

Although it is vital to the yehidut that rebbe and hasid empathize with each other, it is equally vital that neither assume the other's role. The rebbe must not do what the hasid should do for himself, and the hasid must not presume to do the rebbe's task. It is considered as destructive to try to raise a hasid beyond his level as it is not to help him at all. Under these circumstances, the hasid's progress will, at best, be of very short duration, and his fall may cause him great harm.

The act of divestment allows the rebbe to distinguish what the hasid, "according to his own rung," must do, so that his prescription will truly alleviate the hasid's condition.

When Divestment Is Blocked

We have almost no material on the possibility of the rebbe's "hangover" from hasid to hasid. We must, however, assume that the process blocking investment may also hinder divestment.

If, in confronting a hasid, the rebbe notices a confusion of persons before him, he will be aware that he is still speaking to the previous hasid rather than to the one who now stands before him. If he can negotiate an immediate switch back to the hasid who confronts him, he will do so. If not, he will, as in the case of blocked investment, terminate the interview and work through his involvement. The best method of overcoming the block is to "recite a chapter of the Psalms" for the hasid with whom he is still involved, and then leave him in God's hands. If the divestment is still not achieved, the rebbe may turn to more introspective methods and perhaps seek solitude and penance. If he is still not ready to resume the interview, he can summon the presence of special persons who, by being available to hear other things from the rebbe, can divert him and free him from his blocked divestment. Or, he may call such persons in order to tell them an analogous story, which gives him the possibility of working things out.

Only when the rebbe has achieved total divestment is he ready to empathize with and invest in the next hasid. When he finds his divestment blocked, he must use every means at his disposal to free himself so that he can once more be at the service of his hasid and of God.

The Abreactive Process

The Role of the Rebbe

It would be so much easier to confess to God if His countenance could be seen. We would be able to see how angry He is and would be able to suggest ways of making amends. But in the absence of any divine feedback, we have great difficulty rousing ourselves to weeping and sorrow over our sins. Yet if we cannot rouse this grief, we are charged with a burden of unexpressed regret that remains to plague us and possibly lead to the repetition of sin. In order to avoid this, we need someone who can mediate the divine to us. As early as the time of the Temple, worshipers confessed before the priest as he brought the sacrifice to God. The same situation, translated into contemporary hasidic terms, exists today in the yehidut.

We are here concerned with the abreactive element of the yehidut, as it relates not only to guilt feelings but also to a host of other pent-up feelings that the hasid may face and for which he needs the help of another person. In the rebbe, the hasid has found the person-parson[52] par excellence to help him unburden his feelings.

According to Habad, any expression that derives from the level of thought does not require the presence of another person to strengthen and validate it. However, any expression on the level of feeling does demand the presence of "another." This "other" helps in the expression of joy or sorrow: the joy is thus multiplied and the sense of sorrow deepened. This is why, according to Hasidism, it is only when new guests attend the meal of a newly married couple that the seven nuptial blessings of joy may be recited.

The rebbe acts as a catalyst for the hasid. If he laughs, his hasidim guffaw. If he dances, his hasidim skip and jump. Whether the feeling is joy or sorrow, anxiety or frustration, the rebbe's presence usually causes the hasid to feel more strongly and to express his feeling before the rebbe. This is not to say that the expression of emotion may not be impeded. The rebbe may also restrain such expression. There are many kinds of rebbes, and what a hasid would express before a *"guter Yid"* (Good Jew), he would not reveal to a kabbalistic rebbe. Some rebbes are much more accessible to the expression of feeling than others. The hasid takes his cue from his rebbe's own expression of feeling. Even the most benign rebbe, whose mien and manner invite the expression of feeling, inhibits this expression on the part of his hasid by the simple fact of his position. Yet this threshold can be overcome. In fact, the suddenness of an emotion rushing past inhibitions and causing the hasid to burst into tears, exonerates the hasid. The outburst that he tried unsuccessfully to contain, has washed him in its torrent, and he experiences a feeling of relief. Having initially tried to control himself, the hasid regards his inability to suppress the outburst of feeling as a sign of its emotional authenticity.

Often a hasid is unable to connect his weeping with any part of the content and context of the conversation that preceded it. He cries because "the spark had approached the Luminary,"[53] because the "cut-off limb" has regained its feeling and connection and only now has begun to feel the pain. Although the hasid may search for a suitable rationalization, the salient fact is that he did cry. The seasoned hasid will tell the novice that this is because the yehidut is like the days of penitence, and he who does not cry on these days, according to the sixteenth-century kabbalist R. Isaac Luria, does not have a complete, undamaged soul. A hasid seeks the rebbe in order to mend his soul—hence, his tears.

Because of the implicit rules of the rebbe–hasid encounter, the rebbe will not console the hasid when he weeps. (There is little tactile contact between rebbe and hasid. Some hasidim do not even shake their rebbe's hand; and the rebbe, seated behind his desk, seldom comes forward to offer his hand.) Thus, the hasid's weeping will work itself out without the rebbe's help. Often, as a result of the hasid's inhibitions rather than his management of his emotions, the weeping will be postponed until after the yehidut.

In spite of the social sanctions involved, the rebbe will generally not restrain the hasid who feels that he must work through any phase of his inner life with his rebbe. The hasid feels closest to God in the rebbe's presence; he feels he can tell the rebbe what he would not tell anyone else. Because the rebbe's values are those that he prizes most highly, he will be more repentant in the face of the rebbe than he would be before anyone else but God Himself. For the rebbe is the embodiment of the divine and therefore his values represent the ultimate in signification. The fact that the hasid can confess before so great a personage as the rebbe affords him much-needed emotional relief.

Deliberate Abreaction

The hasid may feel that he lacks authenticity and reality if he finds himself blocked from feeling in the rebbe's presence. It is likely that when he was preparing for the yehidut, his anxiety was great and his feelings were awakened to the point of weeping. But by the time he stands before the rebbe, he may have worked himself dry. Furthermore, there are a great many delightful encounters as the hasid comes to the town of his rebbe. Friends are met and much fellowship is shared with them. All this, along with the joy of the rebbe's table, may have caused another kind of feeling to take over. Or it might be that the exertions of the trip, coupled with the many new and (to a young hasid) awe-inspiring faces, have so numbed the hasid that, during the yehidut, he cannot experience the feelings he had anticipated. This may result in his telling the rebbe, probably more out of chagrin than out of self-awareness: "The sins I confessed, I have not truly regretted. Even as I speak of them now, I do not truly repent, but still feel pleasure in recounting them. And even the chagrin that I now feel concerning this is not genuine, and therefore my telling is not sincere, and even . . ." At this point he may faint.

The rebbe does not interfere with this process. The chances are that the hasid has now gained greater insight into the nature of his problem, as well as the nature of Hasidism and what it was trying to teach him all along. For the rebbe to interfere with the process and show the hasid where he has strayed, rather than letting the hasid work through the insight himself, would short-circuit all that rebbe and hasid are trying to achieve.

The hasid may not be able to face his inner maze insightfully. He may lack the capacity to pursue the process fully and may become arrested in asking the rebbe for a counsel for his deadness, dullness, and aridity. The rebbe has often taught the hasid that the arousal of the supernal mercies is always effective, even for one who is completely without emotional life. The less the hasid feels, the more he is to be pitied. So high does his plea reach that "He restores the dead to life in great mercy."[54] The hasid who suffers from emotional deadness and dullness—*timtum halev*—and is unable to set his plea for the supernal mercies before God, places it instead before the rebbe who is palpably accessible to his pleadings. This the rebbe will endure and reinforce. The rebbe may sigh and even weep with the hasid; and this is sure to bring about the hasid's abreaction. When the rebbe weeps upon reading the list of a person's sins, pitying the sinner's soul—"How low he has fallen"—this opens the hasid to weeping.

Delayed Abreaction

AFTER THE YEHIDUT

Even if the hasid has restrained himself during the yehidut, he will feel free to give vent to his feelings afterward. The example set by other hasidim, coupled with his own heightened expectation, allows him to burst into tears or to express himself in dance. In the days of the "old rebbe" (Lubavitch), hasidim engaged in a yehidut dance after their encounter with the rebbe. Then, a hasid would often be dancing and weeping at the same time. The rhythm of the dance and his body movement freed him to express his pent-up emotions. The hasid danced with his eyes closed, lost in his own feelings, at times punctuating the occasional phrase of a hasidic song with an outcry of intense emotion or with the stamping of his foot. In the absence of the emotive expression afforded by the dance, the hasid may simply seek a secluded corner in order to give vent to his feelings. But even this expected reaction may be delayed until the hasid has the opportunity to celebrate the next farbrengen, or perhaps until the next prayer session.

AT PRAYER

The first prayer session that the hasid attends after leaving the yehidut affords him another opportunity for delayed abreaction. The rebbe's words will have stimulated a particular mind-set in the hasid. Immersed in this particular set, the hasid listens with "new ears" to each word of the liturgy, especially to those words that the rebbe speaks. The rebbe's words will reverberate within the hasid and take on new meaning and significance. This is especially true if the rebbe has, during the course of the yehidut, helped the hasid arrive at a new insight, for then the hasid will construe and constellate his universe according to this new insight. Since the liturgy has so many possibilities for raising the level of the meaning of the text, and the hasid may be freed from its simple and manifest meaning, he will find many phrases speaking to his own condition. Any one of these phrases may serve as the key to delayed abreaction and unlock the flood of feeling. Furthermore, any inhibitions that are social in origin do not usually interfere in prayer, and the hasid can feel free to pour out to God all the feeling that he has hitherto repressed. This does not contradict the fact that, prior to the yehidut, he could not pray with feeling. Seeing the rebbe and receiving his blessing may have removed the block. Moreover, the yehidut may have prepared the hasid for a yehidut-with-God experience that can occur in prayer.

AT THE FARBRENGEN

While most hasidim would by now have experienced their emotional release, there are some who require a greater audience and setting, as well as the stimulation of alcohol and song in order to effect the release. The farbrengen serves this purpose. We refer here to the hasid–hasid farbrengen, and not the one over which the rebbe presides. The *mashpiy'a*, who is now the main speaker, may question a hasid directly about the yehidut or may stimulate such discussion by relating a yehidut experience of his own. The point here is not to embarrass the hasid, but rather to celebrate the rebbe's virtues in public. "But for the rebbe, where would I be today?" may serve as an opening gambit.

Having imbibed (often the hasid who has been to yehidut offers the liquor as a *tiqun*), the hasid may, after a "heart *nigun*," begin to relate his own story—what brought him to the rebbe, what he wrote on the kvittel, and so on. From here on, the hasid will act out the yehidut. When he reaches the point where he is relating the rebbe's questions, and finally, his answers and the blessing, he may break into the long-delayed abreaction. Such an abreaction differs from the one experienced in the rebbe's presence, in that it involves the active participation of his fellow hasidim. The hasidim do not always participate in an affirmative manner. The hasid may find that the others will chide him or rebuke him, and this may trigger his emotional release. Any rebuke that a hasid receives at the hands of his fellow hasidim is generally given in an encouraging manner, since no hasid wishes to negate the rebbe's impact on the hasid who has come from the yehidut. Seeing how deeply other hasidim have reacted at their own yehidut, the hasid is drawn into a setting in which his own reaction is scrutinized for its appropriateness. If appropriate, it is reinforced; if not, it is restructured.

AT HOME OR AT WORK

If all previous occasions have failed to trigger the hasid's abreaction, he may find that, either at home or at work, someone will say a word that will trigger it. Believing that each person—even a Gentile—can be an emissary of Providence, the hasid may hear a word, seemingly unrelated to the yehidut, that will illumine for him the insight or feeling he has previously blocked, and will allow him the necessary release. Thus, Rabbi Jacob Joseph of Polnoye, who left a yehidut with the Besht without being won over to the hasidic way, saw the Besht's point of view only when he passed a Gentile on the road who asked his help in extricating his wagon from a muddy ditch. When the Polnoyer said: "I cannot help you," the Gentile replied: "It is not that you cannot, you will not." Only then did the Polnoyer understand what he had not wanted to face previously, and he knew that the Besht was right.

The Secret Confessed

THE CONFRONTATION

A secret demands to be revealed, and the soul is forever involved in confessing. The Besht once pointed out to his hasidim and disciples that a person often revealed an act that he had committed during the night by a slip made during the day. The disciples and hasidim, however, expressed their disbelief, until a man appeared before the Besht and betrayed himself in just such a slip. The Besht, through further interrogation about the slip, was able to get the man to confess. Rebbes are alert to such clues. By tracing the clue to its source, they compel the hasid to reveal what he has suppressed.

Since the rebbe has access to the hasid's "file" and the hasid, in coming to the yehidut, tacitly invites the rebbe to "read" him, the rebbe will at times utilize this access to confront the hasid with the unconfessed. By doing so, the rebbe robs the unconfessed of its compulsive power. Once the hasid has confessed his sin, it can no longer exert a repetitive function over him. The dictum "Sin brings on sin" is true only as long as the sin remains unconfessed. Once the hasid has admitted the sin, he has initiated a new chain: "Mitzvah brings on mitzvah," and he has severed the bonds that tied him to the chain of sin.

When the rebbe feels that the hasid's compulsion to sin is so strong, his habit of good so weak, and the hasid's relationship with him so tentative that it would be disastrous to confront him with his sins, he will refrain from doing so. Instead, he will work toward building a relationship that may some day make it possible to stage such a confrontation or elicit the hasid's own confession. R. Uri the Seraph of Strelisk was sent by his dying master, R. Shlomoh of Karlin, to R. Moshe Leib of Sassov in order to learn when not to confront a sinner. R. Moshe Leib explained:

> What you say, I also saw; yet if I had told him [the sinner] this right away, he would not have been able to give up his sin, and he would no longer be able to come here. Thus, his way to t'shuvah would have been blocked to him. But if I show him love, he may some day

consider: "If only the rebbe knew how sinful I am, he would not show me such love. I must become a better man so that I may deserve his love."[55]

There are times when a rebbe will flagrantly confront a hasid, even though by shaming a man in public one may forfeit one's share in the world to come. R. Meirl of Premishlan once publicly confronted a hasid, whom he called to the Torah and to whom he read the opening line of Genesis 12:1, in which Abraham is commanded to leave his home and depart for the Holy Land. Rashi comments: "Here [outside the Holy Land] you will not merit children. There you will." In a characteristically cautious and incisive manner, the rebbe of Premishlan deliberately mis-read the passage, punning: "Whore! You will not merit children. There, repenting as I show you, you will." The man fainted and was later a penitent.[56]

Whether a rebbe will confront a hasid directly and publicly, as did R. Meirl of Premishlan; or confess a sin as his own and in this manner confront him, as did R. Zussia; or, like R. Moshe Leib of Sassov, patiently wait for the hasid to seize the opportune moment for confession—this will depend not only on the particular rebbe's skill as a counselor, his sense of responsibility to his hasid, and his long-range view, but also on the features of his own personality. Some of these features may be conscious, while others, which represent the root of his soul, may not be accessible to his consciousness.

REGULAR VERSUS SPONTANEOUS CONFESSION

Although confession before a *talmid hakham*, a Torah scholar, is anchored in halakhic precedent, and in some cases the rabbinical court convened during the month of Elul to help penitents who came and confessed their sins, confession was not instituted on a regular periodic basis in Hasidism. This does not mean that rebbes did not hear the confessions of their distressed hasidim, but merely that they did not generally encourage periodic confession. R. Nahman was the only rebbe who wished to make confession a regular part of his counseling work. It goes without saying that the objectionable (to Jews) feature of absolution played no part in the process of confession. (Though even here we must refrain from categorical denial, since rebbes did tell hasidim that, after due penance, their sin was atoned for and should no longer plague them. They did not act as priests, however; rebbes cannot call upon a superabundance of grace such as was won for the Christian sinner by Calvary. On the other hand, Yom Kippur and other penitential graces are available to the rebbe and the hasid.)

In spite of R. Nahman's practice of inviting hasidim to confess their sins to God in his presence at periodic intervals, regular confession did not become a feature of Bratzlav Hasidism. But R. Nahman also counseled private confession. He encouraged hasidim to learn to pray in the vernacular so that in their private prayer they could pour out their hearts to God. This practice survives to this day.[52] Thus, protecting their need for confession, they learned to include it in their private prayer. They could no longer confess before the talmid hakham because their rebbe did not live long enough to make this a regular feature of his ministry, and his children did not continue his ministry after his death. It is for this reason that the Bratzlaver hasidim are known as the "dead hasidim"; for, since R. Nahman's demise, they have had no living rebbe. Perhaps the practice of regular confession proved too radical for most hasidic groups, since the Bratzlaver hasidim are the only hasidic group without a living rebbe. Those practices of R. Nahman that survived, albeit in modified form, and that made their appearance in other hasidic groups, were often not credited to Bratzlav. In any case, the confession that R. Nahman had emphasized was not among them.

Although few rebbes actually make confession a regular part of the yehidut, a rebbe may counsel confession as a means of exorcising certain compulsive behavior syndromes. R. Shalom of Belz, when asked by a young man how to deal with his compulsive evil (sexual) thoughts, counseled the man to tell everyone about them. In a great flood of weeping, the young man complied and was never again plagued by such thoughts. It is taken for granted that if a hasid does not take the aforementioned example of the young man and the Belzer Rebbe seriously, he will entrench the obsessive tendency of his thoughts. This occurs because the dynamics of obsessive thoughts are maintained in tension and movement by (a) the conflict they create; (b) the secrecy that the hasid maintains about the conflict and the content of his thoughts; and (c) the projection of the conflict upon others, and, if this does not succeed, the consequent loss of temper. All these factors reinforce the guilt feelings. The idea that God sees into our thoughts is a reality for the hasid who is working to establish kavanah (intentionality) in himself. Hence, he experiences guilt and shame over the recurring invasion of his mind by these obsessive thoughts. The act of confessing these thoughts, either to others or to the rebbe, helps rid the hasid of the entire syndrome. Should an evil thought reoccur, the hasid is able to treat it lightly, even to laugh at it: having shared it with another, it no longer holds a secret fascination for him.

The rebbe must beware of allowing his hasid to confess prematurely. Grief, shame, and guilt play their part in helping the hasid work toward greater personal integration and socialization, and the rebbe must be careful not to allow the hasid to abreact before the process has had a chance to work itself out. Nor will the rebbe agree to become the arbiter of the completed process, since he wants the hasid to dedicate his intentions to God and not to him. The rebbe whose manner is warm, and who is consequently most accessible to his hasid, must guard against becoming the object of all the hasid's love and devotion. Instead, he must deflect the hasid's devotion from himself toward God. This can be accomplished in two ways—the way of the mirror or the way of the transparent glass. The rebbe who does not deflect the hasid toward God may find himself the target of the hasid's ambivalence. Any momentary satisfaction the rebbe may derive from being the object of the hasid's devotion will be paid for by the rebbe's own disintegration.

Any important insight gained in the realm of kabbalistic and hasidic Torah interpretation was to be kept in incubation for nine months. Only then would it bear fruit. Similarly, the premature divulgence of a secret resolution robs it of its motivational power, and the rebbe may rebuke a hasid for reporting or confessing a resolve that has not yet ripened into consistent action. On the other hand, rebbes were delighted when hasidim withheld from them information regarding their own high attainments and such information came as a surprise.

The Unconfessed

The scrupulous man may attempt to repress unconfessed sins, and here the rebbe faces a dilemma. If he forces the confession, the penitent may not have the emotional strength to work out the penance. Or, it may be that the hasid has not yet severed his liaison with the sin object. If this is the case, the rebbe is taking a serious chance in attempting to force the hasid's confession. The sin object may still hold greater attraction for the hasid than his relationship with the rebbe. On the other hand, the rebbe's action in forcing the confession may prove to be just what the sinner needs in order to make him realize that his attachment to the rebbe is more important than his attachment to his sin. Such a realization will strengthen his relationship with the rebbe, and any subsequent measures that the rebbe prescribes will have greater effectiveness. The rebbe must, therefore, rely on his conscious or unconscious *ruah haqodesh* to guide him to the most effective action. It may be that the rebbe will not force a confession, because he realizes that the unconfessed is about to appear, but in disguise.

Guises Under Which One Confesses

One of the devices most often used to mask personal confession is the introduction of a third party.

> A sinner who wanted to atone came to the rebbe of Ropshitz to learn what penance he should do. He was ashamed to confess all his sins to the tzaddik and yet he had to disclose each and every one, for otherwise the rabbi could not have told him the proper form of atonement. So he said that one of his friends had done such and such a thing, but had been too ashamed to come in person and had commissioned him to go in his stead and find out for him the purification for every one of his sins.
> Rabbi Naftali looked smilingly into the man's sly and tense face. "Your friend," said he, "is a fool. He could easily have come to me himself and pretended to represent someone who was ashamed to come in his own person."[58]

R. Naftali could have permitted the hasid his anonymity; but then the basic element of true confession would have been lacking. The rebbe did not turn the tables on the hasid in order to embarrass him. The embarrassment was secondary. R. Naftali's primary concern was the hasid's need to own up to his sins in the presence of another person. In other words, the cathartic effect on the hasid's affect system was of primary importance.

The Secret and Neurosis

Part of the neurotic person's problem is that he or she has a blind spot. On the whole, such people are capable of dealing with reality; but there is one area in which their view of reality is distorted. If we define neurosis as a psychic imbalance caused by the freezing of defenses that are no longer useful into a limiting pattern, we can see that any helper, in dealing with the neurotic, has two major tasks: First, to help the person gain insight into the fact that his defenses have outlived their usefulness. Second, to set up reality-testing conditions that will help break the limiting habit pattern. This has been learned from the research of psychoanalysts and behaviorists. But existential therapists have yet another insight into neuroses. They consider them aggregates of bad faith. It is therefore essential that a person be brought to see his or her own acts of bad faith.

Closely related to bad faith is the unconfessed secret, which has its own dynamic power. The constant repression of the unconfronted and unconfessed is very costly and can show itself in the neurotic tendencies of the person who must sustain this cost. Thus if a hasid's lack of trust leads him to feel that he must maintain his defenses at all costs, even though they may have outlived their usefulness, he may work himself into a state of neurosis that will make it impossible for him to lower his defenses and confess to the rebbe. It is the rebbe's task to bring the hasid to the point where he can forsake his limiting defense pattern in favor of a more useful life pattern. Only then will the hasid be able to free himself for confession.

Sin and Sex

Sin and evil inclination are often merely the guises of sex, and those sins associated with sex usually arouse stronger guilt feelings than most other sins. Therefore, the rebbe's method of counseling the penitent who comes to him confessing a sexual sin is very important. At the same time, the rebbe is faced with a difficult task. The rebbe can serve as an accessible model for many human actions. But sex is not a publicly demonstrable act. If it were, hasidim would be careful to study their rebbe "as he ties his shoes" in his sexual life. In the absence of an accessible model, there is recourse only to the verbal negation of the sexual sin. The positive active model is unavailable.

This is not to say that the hasid does not hear from the rebbe about the glories of the cosmic *hieros gamos*. Sex has a bifurcated value: it is negatively charged by verbal instruction, and positively charged by instinct and the supernal model. The hasid finds himself in a field that fluctuates between the two poles, and the resulting tension causes him to experience great guilt feelings about any sin that is sexual in nature, or any sexual action that he fears may be considered a sin. It is not difficult to understand, therefore, why sex is often the subject of confession at the yehidut. The hasid's greater guilt feelings about sex produce in him a greater need to abreact, and he feels he must unburden himself of his guilt before he can allow himself the much needed release from emotional tension.

Sin and Forgiveness

Persons who experience guilt feelings usually find it difficult to forgive themselves or to accept forgiveness. However, when the feeling of guilt is heightened by the sanctity of the person who is the channel of exoneration, the forgiving process is easier because the full cathartic effect, in all its absolutive power, comes into play after a heightened awareness of sinfulness. In Protestant terms this is the dynamic of conversion, of being "born again." It is also part of the dynamic of the Sacrament of Penance in the Catholic Church. A similar set of dynamics operates in the hasidic sphere, though the manifestations are different.

In the realm of the hasid's subjective experience, the rebbe acts as the absolving agent, releasing the hasid from the burden of his own guilt. On the objective and dogmatic levels, the rebbe does not actually absolve the hasid from sin. However, the feeling of absolution is implicit in the hasid's sense of relief when he realizes that the rebbe accepts him as a person and has prescribed a purgative and reparative penance. The absolution becomes real to the hasid inasmuch as he accepts a penitential regimen to deal with the guilt. Even when the hasid's guilt is not occasioned by actual sin, the rebbe's reassurance is still an essential factor in the counseling process. R. Dovber of Mezhirech (the Magid) was plagued by guilt feelings for having thought critically of the Ba'al Shem Tov in the Master's presence. He was so pained by his conscience that he experienced great distress; finally he had to be shown a vision in which Moses, teaching little children about Abraham's disbelief in the divine promise, explained that such thoughts are occasioned by the body, "for even the body of a very holy person is still only a body and can bring on involuntary thoughts."[59] Only then did the Magid find relief from his oppressive guilt. The vision acted as his reassurance.

At times the hasid's guilt feelings are occasioned by his own need to feel guilty. In this case, no amount of reassurance can help, since the object of reassurance is to remove the hasid's guilt feelings, and the object of the "guilty one" is to experience the guilt feelings. For this reason, it is very difficult to deal with a person who is greatly beset by scruples. Spiritual directors consider scrupulosity a disease of the soul. Hasidism, at its inception, gave rise to a dual attitude with regard to scrupulosity. In a world where people had been competing with one another in the observance of minutiae, Hasidism did much to dilate attitudes and deflect them away from scrupulosity. At the same time, Hasidism also raised sin from the episodal category of the final judgment to the level of a cosmic catastrophe. Because of the cosmic implications of sin, the rebbe often had to act as the one who reassured from the standpoint of *halakhic* categories. We find such a statement of reassurance in the teachings of R. Moshe Leib of Sassov. "If you believe that you can cause damage, you must also believe that you can repair."[60] R. Nahman also speaks to his hasidim from this position. No matter how great the damage, it is never great enough to cause a person to be cast out of the universe. Despair does not exist.

Abreaction is an essential part of the yehidut process as a whole. Whether the hasid's abreaction occurs during the yehidut, immediately after the yehidut, or at some later time, depends partly on the rebbe's expectations (and the hasid's awareness of them) and on the tactics he uses during the yehidut, and partly on the hasid's own conscious or unconscious motivation to repress or confess his sins. The relationship between rebbe and hasid is a dynamic one, and the dynamics of their relationship affect the way in which the abreaction manifests itself, as well as the time and place in which the abreaction occurs. The expectations of both rebbe and hasid are reinforced by the expectations of the hasidic community. Regardless of the circumstances that surround and give rise to the abreaction, and regardless of the way in which the abreaction manifests itself, the essential factor is that the abreaction does take place. Otherwise, the terrible burden of the hasid's guilt feelings would be too oppressive to allow him to continue in a meaningful life pattern.

Insights Produced in the Transaction

Not Every Yehidut Need Yield Insight

If the hasid comes to the yehidut to receive the rebbe's blessings, and the course of action that the hasid must follow is clear, the rebbe need not strive to produce insight in his hasid. However, sometimes a hasid will come to the rebbe with a problem produced by an insight he has gained. This insight may have been produced in a transaction between the hasid and the *mashpiy'a* or the hasid may have received the insight himself. Once the rebbe has offered his advice on the problem, the course of yehidut is simple and short.

The rebbe may not be satisfied (as was the case with R. Shneur Zalman) to merely give his stamp of approval to any unilateral action taken by the hasid. Having received the hasid, the rebbe may feel that he must contribute something to the equation of the hasid's life. He will therefore teach the hasid a "word" so that he will be enriched by his contact with the rebbe. The "word" may have many purposes: reinforcement of motivation, the modification of the hasid's posture in life, the enlarging of the hasid's pattern of concern, or the urging of concentration on the task at hand. The rebbe may test in the hasid the possibility of more fervent or expanded religious behavior, or he may steer him toward greater achievement in the realm in which he is weak. If the hasid's achievement on the level of ritual is high, the rebbe may steer him toward greater ethical observance. In short, the rebbe will want to interact with his hasid in such a way that the hasid will leave the yehidut a richer, more fulfilled person.

Even if the rebbe will not want to produce any particular insight in the process of the yehidut, he will still want the yehidut to be an uplifting experience—that is, one in which the hasid rises to higher levels of awareness and understanding. The anxious hasid may be so preoccupied and engrossed that this will keep him from achieving the light and joyful manner that allows him to work best. In the formal setting of the yehidut, even a hasid who is generally good at upleveling—shifting his attention to a higher level of awareness—may become constricted. The rebbe will therefore seek to create an ascendant movement in almost every transaction (unless, for some reason, ascent at this particular stage may prevent the hasid from movement, either in a therapeutic or a motivational sense).

Upleveling, *ha'ala'at hamidot*, is any movement away from constriction and emotional or situational captivity. Since, in the hasidic doctrine of correspondences, rebbe and hasid operate on more than one level, any act, feeling, or transaction ought to touch as many levels as possible. Upleveling thus consists also of involving as many higher levels as possible in the hasid's life, and making them relevant.

Upleveling may include the seeking of lower levels corresponding to the hasid's concern. Thus, a rebbe may reply to a hasid who raises an abstract problem of interpretation: "Petachl! [Literally, *fool*—said without rejection, almost as a term of endearment, and therefore usually in the diminutive.] Nothing else troubles you but that?" When the rebbe, at this time, points to a corresponding life situation in which the same problem occurs, and which is more relevant to the hasid's life, he is still involved in an aspect of *ha'ala'at hamidot*. The process refers more to the expansion of levels than to moving up on the hierarchy of values. Downleveling—that is, shifting one's attention to a lower level of awareness—robs the hasid of a multilevel range, restricting him to one level of concern.

One of the purposes of upleveling is to make the primary and secondary processes harmonious. As the rebbe causes the hasid's consciousness to expand, it will go beyond the level of verbal constructs. This is what makes the rebbe's and the hasid's gestures more significant.

One of the ways in which upleveling is discussed in hasidism is in terms of a concept that we have mentioned before—the "sweetening of the decrees." This cannot be accomplished on the superficial level of the conflict; thus, the conflict must be raised to its source. Hasidim say that when a rebbe laughs it is a sign that he is sweetening the hasid's decrees. By making the predicament seem ludicrous, he robs the power of Satan of its tragic hold. The hasid, however, may see little reason to laugh, and may say to himself: "Maybe the rebbe laughs. So he sweetens the decrees. But you, fool, why do you laugh? The decrees are on you!" (The joke is on you.) Still, if he laughs along, the hasid may be able to "ascend" with the rebbe.

Another instance of the rebbe's upleveling is when he works for signification: declaring, for example, that there is Judge and Justice, there is meaning, and *this* is the meaning.

Properly utilized, upleveling does several things: First, it expands the hasid's awareness. Second, it raises the hasid's posture from difficult, heavy, despairing, depressed, and pessimistic, to easy, light, hopeful, elated, and optimistic. This is important even when no further insight is needed beyond the harmonization of levels. Third, it prepares the hasid for the possibility of insight, which may be the next move in the transaction. Each method operates in such a way that there is a softening of the hard lines that separate one level from the next, and movement is thereby initiated once more.

Some Cases of Yehidut Are Solely for Producing Insights

Any person who comes to see the rebbe with a particular problem will require insight into the true nature of his problem; insight regarding its purpose in terms of his potential; and insight regarding its cause, and therefore also its cure. The creative tensions that the problem produces have their place in the inner world of the person experiencing the problem. They are part of his life-space and mind-consciousness feeling. At times, he is made victim of the tensions simply because he does not understand the role in which he is being placed. Because this is not the role that he wants to play, he is temporarily immobilized and filled with despair. Generally, tensions are produced when a person is expected to act in ways in which his or her inner person does not wish to act. Or, a person may be expected to act by two different significant persons in diametrically opposed ways. At times, the conflict is produced by two or more attractive choices, any of which, if chosen, would mean the forfeiting of the other(s). Or the reverse may occur. People may face a number of undesirable alternatives, and, in order to extricate themselves from the bind, they may have to choose at least one of them.

If the hasid's problem is real—that is, if it is not a subjective problem that exists only in the hasid's mind—it can be solved only by the hasid's facing it and experiencing its brunt. At times, however, the problem is purely subjective and exists only because the hasid's mind lacks insight into the reality behind the problem; hence, the formulation of a workable solution is obscured. The hasid may expect the rebbe to help him in a magical, manipulative, authoritarian (parentlike or Godlike) way. Since the rebbe sometimes acts in this way and such action has been recorded in hasidic tales, the hasid's expectation may have been reinforced before he came to the yehidut. However, the rebbe will often feel that to produce a life-enriching insight in the hasid is far more significant than to help him in a way that fails to produce insight and understanding. A hasid may complain to the rebbe that the *yetzer hara*, the evil inclination, is pursuing him. He will ask the rebbe to *do something* in order to rid him of his evil inclination. But the rebbe will in all likelihood reply (as more than one rebbe has done): "You have not yet reached such a high level that the *yetzer hara* pursues you. Rather, it is you who are pursuing the *yetzer hara*." In this way, the rebbe forces the hasid to face his rationalization for what it really is. In another case, when a hasid came to the rebbe because he had a problem concerning his livelihood, the rebbe asked him: "Why don't you pray about it?" When the hasid replied that he was unable to pray, the rebbe exclaimed: "Now you have a serious problem!"[61] Instead of altering the hasid's circumstances according to his expectation, the rebbe thus utilized the hasid's manifest problem to help him gain insight into a deeper and more serious issue.

It is important to remember that in the rebbe–hasid relationship, any insight gained at the yehidut is more than a mere matter of intellection or emotion. Every insight contains an implicit obligation to action. Thus, if the rebbe can help his hasid gain insight into the real source of his problem, he will have produced through the transaction an action directive. The very nature of the hasid's allegiance to the rebbe implies that he will accept this directive as binding.

Insight into the Problem

When the hasid is not aware that he has a problem, the rebbe must help him realize this. The hasid may have come to the yehidut only in order to seek the rebbe's blessing. The rebbe may ask the hasid about various facets of his life that, to the hasid, do not seem problematic. The rebbe will help the hasid gain insight into problems of which he may be unaware or that he may be repressing.

> When a hasid came one morning to R. Israel of Vishnitz for his regular visit, the rebbe surprised him by asking him to *daven Minhah* (to pray the afternoon prayer). Since the visit was made in the morning, the hasid, a simple householder, was surprised by the rebbe's request, and expressed his surprise to the rebbe. The rebbe then said, "Never mind. Tell me about your business affairs." Again the hasid was surprised that the rebbe would withdraw his request in this manner, particularly since the rebbe knew all about his business affairs. Nevertheless, after some urging by the rebbe, he recounted for him a typical day. He ended his account by saying that in the evening when he went home, he recited the evening prayer twice. When the rebbe questioned him about this, he admitted that since his lumber business made it necessary for him to be out in the forest during the day, he neglected the afternoon prayer, and, in its stead, recited the evening prayer twice. The rebbe then repeated that he must *daven* the afternoon prayer. Only then did the hasid understand the rebbe's previous injunction.[62]

> A hasid who was a salesman, and who on his travels took some liberties with the kashrut laws, came to the present Lubavitcher Rebbe, complaining of the dysfunction of his digestive system. The rebbe told him that he must be more careful to see that his food was truly kosher. Although this advice answered the hasid's need, the rebbe added that the hasid should check his mezuzah at home. Upon doing so, he found that a letter was missing from the phrase, "as thou goest in the way," thus rendering the mezuzah unfit for use (non-kosher).[63]

In this last story, the rebbe used a double entendre in order to give the hasid a deeper insight into his problem. The Besht was fond of giving his hasid an additional sign or *mofet*.

A hasid who comes to the rebbe may be suffering from an anxiety unrelated to any specific problem; rather, it stems from the general economy of his emotional life. To such a hasid the rebbe will point out that, for a Jew, anxiety arises not only from the threat of the instinctual urges of the body, but also from the threat of the suppressed instinctual urge of the soul.

When the hasid places his anxiety in the service of needs that are extraneous to his real problem (as the rebbe sees it), the rebbe will point out that the hasid "asks what he needs and does not ask what he is needed for." Reversing the order of things, the rebbe thus makes the hasid aware of his real problem. Instead of looking for the mature task at hand, the hasid was looking for infantile paternal security.

A hasid may be able to go to the *mashpiy'a* to ask about a particular problem, and the *mashpiy'a* will deal with the problem as the hasid presents it. The rebbe, on the other hand, will want to deal with the real problem, and not merely the symptomatic one.

Insight into Process

INSTANT WISH-FULFILLMENT VERSUS PROCESS

One of the ways in which the hasid seeks to trap the rebbe, whether consciously or unconsciously, is by attempting to cast the real and sustained work in his lap and by relying on the rebbe's parental "magic" to produce what he himself ought to produce. But the rebbe will not do the hasid's work for him. This may come as a shock to the hasid, and, faced with the burden of his own task, he may attempt to complete it in one fell swoop. When he finds that he is unable to do so, he despairs and returns to the rebbe to complain. It is at this point that the rebbe must help him gain insight into the slow functioning of the process.

Insight that makes for a dynamic point of view is not easily acquired. Once acquired, it needs to be rediscovered from time to time, since the process of verbalization and discursive meditation is not given to the dynamic view and tends to displace it. The liturgical routine is an aid in overcoming inertia, and the rebbe may borrow models from the dynamics of the liturgy in order to bring the hasid to see the dynamics of process more clearly. Insight into the dynamic quality of nature is profound and mystical: it is impossible to capture this insight within the framework of a verbal construct. The verbal construct stultifies the insight. Verbal expression is capable only of drawing moments, and not duration. The dynamic becomes static when expressed in words; but the world is not static. "The world is a spinning die. . . ."[64]

However, the dynamic view requires its complement. For all the insight of the dynamic view, it does not afford the hasid sufficient information about the order, time, and moment of his deliberate action in the process. Order and succession are an essential part of the insight that the hasid must gain in the yehidut. Being a conscious and moral being, he must use the intelligence acquired via his *sensory* feedback for goal-seeking *motor* purposes. He cannot rely solely on a process of nature to lead him in the direction of his goal. Rather, he needs to appreciate the amorality of the process, and exploit its dynamics for moral purposes—that is, to serve God. At the same time, his service must take process into consideration. He must not carve against the grain. The rebbe, in his teaching, will often stress that an understanding of the difference between the static and the dynamic is the key to understanding the difference between Mussar and Hasidism, between *before* the Besht and *after* the Besht.

Buber has shown us that some of the rebbe's methods of involving the hasid in the process of life are similar to those of the Zen master. He compares the teaching of a Zen master with that of R. Moshe Polier of Kobrin:

> After the death of Rabbi Mosheh of Kobrin, the Rabbi of Kotsk asked one of the disciples of the deceased what had been the most important things for his master. He answered: "Always just what he was engaged in at the moment." And the abbot of a Zen monastery is asked, "One of the first patriarchs has said, 'There is a word which, when understood, wipes out the sins of innumerable aeons.'—What is this word?" He answers, "Right under your nose!" The disciple asks again, "What does that mean?" "That is all that I can say to you," replies the teacher.
>
> The two answers, the hasidic and the Zen, are almost identical in essence: the key to truth is the next deed, and this key opens the door if one does what one has to do in such a way that the meaning of the action here finds its fulfillment.
>
> The teacher, therefore, is the man who does all that he does sufficiently, and the core of his teaching is this, that he lets his disciple take part in his life and thus grasp the mystery of the action. Rabbi Mendel of Rymanov used to say that he had learned Torah from every limb of his teacher, Rabbi Elimelekh. The same, only from the other side, is now expressed by the Zen teacher. When a disciple who serves him complains that he has not yet been introduced into the wisdom of the spirit, he answers, "From the day of your coming I have always instructed you in the wisdom of the spirit." "How so, master?" asks the disciple, and the teacher explains to him, "When you have brought me a cup of tea, have I not taken it from your hand? When you have bowed before me, have I not returned your greeting?" The disciple bows his head, and now the teacher elucidates further for him, "If you want to see, look straight into the thing; but if you seek to ponder over it, then you have already missed the goal!"[65]

When R. Shalom Dovber of Lubavitch stresses the difference between the *oved* (one who serves with the devotion of the heart) and the *maskil* (one who serves with the contemplative intellect), he too contrasts dynamism versus the static (verbal) approach. The hasid who asked R. Shalom Dovber which holy day was the most important one, received the reply, "The one that is now." R. Leib Sures refers to the same process when he relates that he came to the Magid to learn "how he ties his shoelaces." The story of R. Jacob Joseph of Polnoye, who came to light the Besht's pipe, is in the same vein.

PROCESS AND ROLES

When the hasid has gained insight into his habit structure and into the tensions that cause him to assume conflicting roles in the course of his interpersonal interaction, he can then do *t'shuvah*. Habit does not yield to deliberate interruption until its dynamic quality, which causes it to be called second nature, is recognized. As long as habit is unconscious and mechanical, and its dynamic nature is unrealized, one cannot repent.[66] For this reason, the rebbe must help his hasid gain insight into the problem of inappropriate roles—a soul's errant behavior.

There are times when the rebbe must move a hasid to an inappropriate role in order to groom him for a particular task. When R. Shneur Zalman said to R. Yosef of Byeshenkovitch, "For the sake of your soul it is better for you to become a coachman than a rabbi," this was R. Yosef's initiation into the dynamics of guiding other souls. When the process of initiation had been completed and the insight appropriated, the "coachman" was told to become a mashpiy'a but this was only after R. Yosef had proven himself in a "crisis" by bringing an errant Jew to repent.

Sometimes a temporary role change serves the dual purpose of bringing the hasid to an important insight and enlarging his repertoire of empathy. One redeeming process that often opens the hasid to such insight is the mitzvah of *hakhnasat orhim* (hospitality). A hasid who becomes a host may be forced by uncouth guests to accommodate himself to their pace and behavior in order to make them feel comfortable. By assuming the role of host, the hasid has the opportunity to view life from a new angle and garner new insights from his new role.

In some instances a rebbe might counsel a hasid to live in exile. This too represented a temporary role change. Wandering incognito, the penitent-pilgrim virtually kills his persona, casts off his name, and, wearing garments that are inappropriate to his station and manner, learns to enlarge his repertoire of empathy. Exile was one of the favorite modes of early hasidic training. Even the Besht had to spend some time in exile. Once, after he had become known, he spent the Sabbath in the home of a seemingly uncouth person who was, in reality, a hidden tzaddik and wanted to help avert a harsh decree that had fallen on the Besht.

There are many other examples of temporary changes in role, such as the following:

> A stingy rich man who came to the Magid to receive his blessing was told to eat the richest and most expensive foods, and this would help him overcome his stinginess. When his hasidim were at a loss to understand such counsel, the Magid explained that only by eating in this manner could the man understand the true meaning of charity. By seeing the great difference between his present rich and expensive state and the former meagre fare to which he had subjected himself because of his own stinginess, he would also be able to understand the difference between his former state and that of the poor man, and that "the poor have a real need for bread."[67]

Sometimes a hasid attains insight into his inappropriate role by way of a pointed remark made by the rebbe:

> A hasid who came to the Tzemah Tzedeq to complain about the treatment he received at the hands of his fellow hasidim, received the reply, "Who asked you to spread yourself all over the bet hamidrash so that everyone who needs to step in needs to step on you?"[68]

INTEGRATION OF PROCESS AND ROLE INSIGHTS

It is not within the rebbe's province to work through with the hasid his newly acquired process and role insights. The hasid must accept the responsibility of working them through with the help of the *mashpiy'a* or a fellow hasid. Once the inappropriateness of his attitude toward process and role is shown to him in the yehidut, the hasid can manage the integration by recalling the yehidut experience. The rebbe may have made a note on the hasid's kvittel and returned it to him. In this case, the hasid will read the note just before going to bed, at the time when he says the final prayer before sleep. Then he will scrutinize himself in light of the notations made by the rebbe, and thus set the stage for the necessary corrective actions. The hasid is aware that, at some time, he will return for yehidut with the rebbe, and at that time, the rebbe will expect a report of the progress the hasid has made in the direction of the insight he gained at the last yehidut. With this thought in mind, the hasid works for his own improvement in a deliberate manner.

Insights into Problem Solving

A person who finds himself beset by a problem that demands his attention is forever casting about in his mind for a possible solution. Sometimes the most immediately available solution is rejected because it demands a certain sacrifice. A hasid who comes to the rebbe with a particular problem may not require insight into the dynamics of the life process. His problem may be more specific. In this case what he requires is a workable solution to the problem. The problem itself may be so much a part of the hasid's life at this point that in itself, it constitutes a solution to other life problems; and to remove it without first taking care of the other subproblems would cause the hasid excessive anxiety.

The rebbe cannot be caught in the bind of the therapist whose client protests that no real help is available to him because none of the solutions put forth is workable. The rebbe's position places him on a different level of authority. The hasid who comes to the rebbe cannot claim that a particular suggestion or solution will not work. The rebbe's suggested solution carries with it the sanction that it is the *only* workable solution. The rebbe's counsel thus becomes a new possibility; it is exempt from the failure of former attempts that were unaccompanied by the rebbe's prayerful concern and blessing.

The rebbe is not responsible for working through the solution with the hasid. He is responsible only for bringing the hasid to insight into the solving power of the solution. This he can do in a number of ways. He can be directive and point out to the hasid the reason he cannot realize the value of the solution. Perhaps the hasid's lack of faith is responsible. Another method is to use adroit Socratic questioning as a means of eliciting the insight from the hasid himself. Or, the rebbe can ask the hasid, with a steadiness that prevents the phobic averting of his attention, to focus on the worst possible result of adopting the solution. By testing the realities in his mind, the hasid can then see that the conditions causing his aversion are not so terrifying after all. Without the rebbe's help, the hasid may never have managed to look at his aversion and thereby rob it of its terrifying effect. With the help of the rebbe, the hasid can examine the proposed solution in the light of reality, placing the obstacle-obstruction-aversion in the proper perspective, and then working out the solution that he previously discarded.

REINFORCING MOTIVATION AND
EXPLORING THE DEFENSES

Reassurance

One of the most necessary and most frequently used means of help is reassurance. The anxious client comes to see his helper, and the first thing that passes between them is reassurance. This need not be verbal. The client's anxiety has given rise to a cycle of behavior that culminates in his seeking help. All the preparations of making an appointment, anticipating the help that will be offered, and finally arriving at the appointed hour and place serve to reduce the client's anxiety. The arrival at the office completes a satisfaction circuit in the client, and this alone offers reassurance. This sense of reassurance is reinforced if the client sees the relieved and radiant faces of satisfied clients as they leave the consulting room. Soon he too will see the helper and he too will be relieved of his burden.

The hasid who has been nurtured on tales of the rebbe's greatness and his ability to help on all occasions feels sure that this help becomes effective from the moment he begins his journey to the rebbe. The first basic movement of the hasid toward the rebbe, the writing of the kvittel, serves as reassurance, for now the rebbe has been notified of the hasid's need for help, and surely he cannot help but respond. This feeling of reassurance is increased by a concatenation of good regression memories of past encounters. Even the name of the town that has become part of the rebbe's name carries with it its own reassuring magic. The friends whom the hasid encounters in the town also reassure him that no matter how serious his problem, the rebbe can help him. The assurance of his friends does not fully succeed, however, since the hasid knows that their reassurance is based partly on their own hope for the efficacy of the rebbe's blessing. Nothing short of the encounter itself can fully reassure. Since the rebbe *knows*, the hasid hopes to be able to read in the rebbe's facial expression the "prognosis" of his mission.

Regardless of how much reassurance the hasid may have received before coming to the yehidut, he will still have a certain sense of anxiety and apprehension in first confronting the rebbe. This is where the rebbe's acceptance comes into play. Only the hasid's assurance that the rebbe has accepted him will suffice to quell his anxiety. Elsewhere we have discussed acceptance as it functions between rebbe and hasid in providing a basis for the mutuality and trust essential to the yehidut process. Here we wish only to deal with acceptance as a function of reassurance and the reinforcement of motivation.

The rebbe expresses his acceptance in a number of ways, from his initial greeting "Peace be upon you," and the handshake and smile that go with it to his recognition of a hasid who he calls by name, and to his warm welcome to a hasid who has come for the first time. All these are basic forms of reassurance. The reading of the kvittel is another form of being received. It signifies the rebbe's acceptance of the hasid as a person in a life situation with a problem. The rebbe may then further encourage the hasid to voice his anxiety by inquiring about his welfare.

When the rebbe begins to question the hasid in detail, other forms of reassurance enter. The hasid now becomes involved in the process of the rebbe's evaluation. If the problem is one of guilt, the rebbe can, through his authoritative position, help the hasid see his guilt in the perspective of his entire life. The hasid may be overemphasizing or de-emphasizing his guilt, and the rebbe has to reassure him that the guilt has purpose in his life, and that once its purpose has been realized, the guilt can be overcome.

If the hasid's problem is one of health, the rebbe may reassure him, "Think well, and it will be well." With this, the hasid experiences not only the rebbe's acceptance of his problem, but also the divine acceptance that lies behind it. The hasid no longer sees his condition of sickness and despair as static and unchanging. Once more he is involved in a view of process, in which his personal crisis is not unyielding to divine grace.

The rebbe will not always reassure the hasid. There are times when, in the first moment of meeting, the hasid discerns a somber note. The rebbe, foreseeing no immediate change in the conditions that beset the hasid, or perhaps detecting a turn for the worse, may be unresponsive to the hasid, change the topic of conversation, or in some other way indicate that he is not accessible to acceptance. Usually it is not so much a matter of the rebbe's refusing to accept the hasid; rather, he withholds acceptance as a way to create deeper insight and interpersonal movement.

R. Elimelekh of Lizhensk was known to withhold his acceptance for this reason on a number of occasions.

> For six years and then for another six years, Rabbi David [Biederman] of Lelov had done great penance: he had fasted from one sabbath to the next, and subjected himself to all manner of rigid discipline. But even when the second six years were up, he felt that he had not reached perfection and did not know how to attain what he still lacked. Since he had heard of Rabbi Elimelekh, the healer of souls, he journeyed to him to ask his help. On the evening of the sabbath, he came before the tzaddik with many others. The master shook hands

with everyone except Rabbi David, but from him he turned and did not give him a glance. The Rabbi of Lelov was appalled and left. But then he thought it over and decided that the master must have taken him for someone else. So he approached him in the evening, after the prayer, and held out his hand. But he was treated just as before. He wept all night and in the morning resolved not to enter the tzaddik's House of Prayer again, but to leave for home at the end of the sabbath. And yet—when the hour of the holy third meal had come, he could not restrain himself and crept up to the window. There he heard the rabbi say:

"Sometimes people come to me who fast and torment themselves, and many a one does penance for six years and then for another six—twelve whole years! And after that, they consider themselves worthy of the holy spirit, and come and ask me to draw it down to them: I am to supply the little they still lack. But the truth of the matter is that all their discipline and all their pains are less than a drop in the sea, and what's more: all that service of theirs does not rise to God, but to the idol of their pride. Such people must turn to God by turning utterly from all they have been doing, and begin to serve from the bottom up and with a truthful heart."

When Rabbi David heard these words, the spirit moved him with such force that he almost lost consciousness. Trembling and sobbing, he stood at the window. When the Havdalah was concluded, he went to the door with faltering breath, opened it in great fear, and waited on the threshold. Rabbi Elimelekh rose from his chair, ran up to his motionless visitor, embraced him and said: "Blessed be he that comes!" Then he drew him toward the table and seated him at his side. But now Eleazar, the tzaddik's son, could no longer restrain his amazement.

"Father," he said, "why, that is the man you turned away twice because you could not endure the mere sight of him!'

"No, indeed!" Rabbi Elimelekh answered. "That was an entirely different person! Don't you see that this is our dear Rabbi David!"[69]

On his journey to Rabbi Elimelekh whom—after the death of the Great Magid—he had chosen for his second teacher, young Jacob Yitzhak, later the Rabbi of Lublin, came to a little town, and in the House of Prayer heard the rav of that place reciting the Morning Prayer with deep fervor. He stayed with him over the Sabbath and noticed the same fervor in all he said and did. When he came to know him a little better, he asked him whether he had ever served a tzaddik. The answer was "no." This surprised Jacob Yitzhak, for the *way* cannot be learned out of a book, or from hearsay, but can only be

communicated from person to person. He asked the devout rav to go
to his teacher with him, and he agreed. But when they crossed Rabbi
Elimelekh's threshold, he did not come forward to meet his disciple
with his customary affectionate greeting, but turned to the window
and paid no attention to his visitors. Jacob Yitzhak realized that the
rejection was directed to his companion, took the violently excited
rav to an inn and returned alone. Rabbi Elimelekh advanced toward
him, greeted him fondly, and then said: "What struck you, my friend,
to bring with you a man in whose face I can see the tainted image of
God?" Jacob Yitzhak listened to these words in dismay, but did not
venture to reply or to ask a question. But Rabbi Elimelekh understood what was going on within him and continued: "You know that
there is one place lit only by the planet Venus, where good and evil are
blended. Sometimes a man begins to serve God and ulterior motives
and pride enter into his service. Then, unless he makes a very great
effort to change, he comes to live in that dim place and does not even
know it. He is even able to exert great fervor, for close by is the place
of the impure fire. From there he fetches his blaze and kindles his
service with it, and does not know from where he has taken the
flame."

Jacob Yitzhak told the stranger the words of Rabbi Elimelekh
and the rav recognized the truth in them. In that very hour, he turned
to God, ran weeping to the master, who instantly gave him his help,
and with his help, he found the way.[70]

The hasid comes to the rebbe for reassurance about the ultimate
outcome of his problem, and, except in cases where the rebbe withholds
his reassurance for the purpose of bringing the hasid to a particular
insight, the hasid will not usually be disappointed. Basic to this reassurance is the rebbe's tacit acceptance of the hasid as a person of worth for
whom the world, with all its goodness and richness, was created. This
acceptance is further reinforced by the theology of the function of the
rebbe, which makes the hasid's journey to the rebbe an act of return to
God. Implicit in the hasid's act of return is the blessing he hopes to receive
from the rebbe.

The Nondisruptive Nature of the Yehidut

The yehidut is aimed at helpng the hasid function *in* the world, not
apart from it. It is not like a retreat in which the patient-client is in
quarantine. The yehidut is not to cause any disruption in the ongoing
social life of the hasid. Just as the secular helper must not "take the client

apart" in a way that renders him inoperative as a person, so the rebbe must not allow the process of the yehidut to debilitate the hasid socially.

> Any craftsman who is about to repair an instrument must, first of all, take it apart with great care and take pains not to break even the damaged part. After he has taken it apart, he carefully inspects each part. He is objective about the good and bad in it, and then divides them into the categories of "good," "possibly useful," and "damaged." He then further inspects each part separately to see if his first sort holds true. Then he chooses the means of repair: how to remove the damaged part; how to replace it; how to correct that which is still useful and make it completely good; how to strengthen that which is good. Finally, he will consider the order of repair: what to begin with and how to continue. It is only then that the repair will be fully and well done.[71]

This analogy is limited in its usefulness for an obvious reason. The person in need of help is not like a clock that can be taken apart and need not function during the time of repair. He is a man, and as such he must live and breathe and continue to function throughout the time of the repair. The sorting between helper and helped is only a mental act. In the relationship between rebbe and hasid, R. Moshe Leib of Sassov's counsel to the Seraph of Strelisk—to have patience with the sinner—must be heeded. Before the rebbe begins to attack the hasid's weak spots, he must strengthen the healthy aspects. The same dynamic obtains in the therapy of repentance. The first rungs of repentance—actual remorse and abandonment of sin—often cannot be reached until some form of higher repentance has been attained. The latter is what makes the "lower repentance" worthwhile and sustains it during the difficult purgative period. Hence, a premature catharsis can be damaging to the hasid. The energies needed to see the hasid through the uphill climb may be uselessly diverted. The level of repentance in terms of health, productivity, and spiritual attainment often depends on the energies the hasid is able to devote to the work at hand. These energies will be of a lower order when the hasid cannot build up his security for the time when he examines his inner structure. If he is not threatened from without (in which case he must guard the frontiers of his personal domain), the hasid will be free to enter into the process of examining his own inner being. If his defenses are in order—even if they are not the best and will have to be rebuilt—he must be able to trust them for the time being. Hence, the rebbe must study the purposes of the hasid's defenses, and when he knows what they were intended to do, he can then help the hasid reinforce them, if only temporarily. Later, when the hasid has grown internally stronger, he will be able to divert some of his inner energies to the defenses, so that he can become vulnerable again and build new defenses to better serve his new being.

Seeking the rebbe's help and counsel involves no stigma. In fact, the danger lies in the opposite direction. Like patients boasting of their therapists instead of working out their problems, hasidim sometimes boast of their rebbe. The rebbe, however, considers this a sign that the hasid is not doing the work required of him. Once the hasid's defenses have been strengthened, he is ready to do the real work himself. Among the factors that tend to shore up the hasid's defenses, allowing him to work through his problems, are the rebbe's teachings and counsel, the farbrengen, the *tish*, and in general, the fellowship of other hasidim. These same factors enable the hasid to manage his problems without disrupting his normal social life and obligations.

Problem Solving as Restructuring

Problem solving is often nothing more than a restructuring of the environment of the one in need of help. There are times, however, when the environment either cannot or should not be restructured.

The hasid is forever attentive to the rebbe's expressions. If the rebbe does not show the hasid any encouragement, does not bless him with the desired formula, the hasid knows that his situation is not amenable to change. He must face his condition as inevitable. Here again the process of shoring up the defenses enters in. The hasid's defenses need to be strengthened to the point where he will be able to manage his life in full awareness of conditions that will, in all probability, remain static.

There is an apocryphal story that illustrates problem solving in terms of the restructuring of environment:

> A hasid came to his rebbe, complaining of the lack of space in his small dwelling. Much to his surprise, the rebbe advised him to take in his goat and chickens. Later, the hasid returned to complain that following the rebbe's counsel had only made things worse. The rebbe then told him to remove all the animals from his house. The result was that the hasid returned to report how grateful he was for the rebbe's counsel. After removing the animals, he found that he had much more space!

This story really has a dual message. At first glance, the impact seems to be that a temporary restructuring of the hasid's environment provided a solution to the hasid's problem. However, when we realize that the restructuring was only temporary, and that there was no actual change in the hasid's environment, it becomes evident that the arrangement making was really in the service of teaching the hasid to be content with his lot.

There are other methods by which the rebbe helps the hasid live with the inevitable. The hasid sometimes needs a mental trick to help him when he is overwhelmed by his own adverse condition. When the rebbe tells his hasid that his condition is the result of a debt incurred in a previous incarnation, the hasid must learn to accept the inevitability of his state. When the rebbe tells him why he must accept his condition, in this case because he has incurred a debt, the hasid is better able to resign himself to its inevitability. Thus, the rebbe introduces the inevitable as a real factor in the hasid's arrangement making. The hasid is able to see not only the inevitability of his condition, but also its redeeming value as a forward movement in his life.

The hasid may or may not be aware of his need to restructure his environment. He may come to the rebbe specifically to ask his help in improving his environment, or, as is more likely the case, he may come to the rebbe with any problem that he is unable to solve. The solution the rebbe provides will be in terms of arrangement making. The rebbe scrutinizes the hasid's past arrangements and offers suggestions for better ones. These suggestions may be objective and directly manipulative of the environment, or they may be subjective and involve manipulation of the hasid's internal arrangement of priorities or of the social life-space he assigns to various persons and activities in his life. If the restructuring involves primarily the hasid's internal arrangements, the rebbe must first shore up the hasid's defenses so that he will be able to weather the attack on his inner structure. The rebbe's suggestions are received by the hasid in the same manner as directive insights, and operate in the same manner in terms of the restructuring of the hasid's life. To reinforce his suggestion, the rebbe will tell the hasid a story showing how another hasid had successfully incorporated the proposed salvational model into his life. This procedure at once reduces the hasid's anxiety. The fact of a successful precedent makes the counsel easier to follow.

Shock

Often a person in need of help cannot be gradually brought to see his own condition in all its complexity. At such times it may be necessary to shock him into a totally new view of himself and his condition. The hasid may have been made aware of his shortcomings in the past, but for some reason has not acted on this awareness. It may be that his own self-image is so hypnotic that he is unable to break its spell. Or he may have felt that those who alerted him to his shortcomings, possibly members of his own peer group, lacked the status necessary to lend weight to their opinions. Whatever the reason for the hasid's refusal to face all his faults, the rebbe's task will be to overcome the hasid's elaborate defenses; the rebbe will use the hasid's investment of faith and trust in him to make him face the truth, unpleasant and shocking though it may be. The rebbe's ability to bring the hasid to a more realistic self-assessment is enhanced by the warmth and acceptance of the yehidut atmosphere, which enables the hasid to relax his guard. Because the hasid sees in the rebbe's yehidut room a special haven, he feels secure enough to dispense with the usual "Who me?" reaction.

In order to shock the hasid into a realistic appraisal of himself, the rebbe attacks him on three fronts. R. Dovber, the Middle Rebbe of Habad, uses the image of military attack in order to show that victory is achieved not in the symmetric array of force against counterforce, but in an attack of three flanks against one. "Before the advent of Hasidism, one would attack base love with high love, base fear with high fear. Nowadays we attack base love with high love and high fear and high pity, and in this case, the base love yields."[72] In the yehidut chamber, the rebbe uses the same method, coupled with love, compassion, and awe, to induce in the hasid the necessary insight into self. If the hasid has already been made self-aware, but lacks insight into process, the rebbe may use shock to induce movement. In fact, insight and movement are really one and the same thing.

The hasid who, trusting in his own sterling character, feels sure that the rebbe will place him higher than the sinner, may be in for a shock.

> Once two men came to R. Yitzhaq of Vurky. A woman who had been widowed also came to R. Yitzhaq, demanding that he collect a debt owed to her by these two men. After listening to the arguments on both sides, R. Yitzhaq ruled for the woman, saying that within a year's time, the men must repay the debt. After the woman had left, the two men demanded of the rebbe: "Why do you believe such a slattern? Her husband has been dead for more than a year and people have been murmuring that she is pregnant." Whereupon the rebbe took hold of his beard and replied thoughtfully, "In that case, she will be in very great need in the near future. You must go and pay her what you owe immediately."[73]

In this story, the shock that results from hearing the rebbe's counsel is intended to have the important function of turning the hasid away from smug self-satisfaction to an area of real human concern.

The extent to which shock is used in the yehidut depends to a large extent on the school of the rebbe. Rebbes of the Kotsker school, for example, used shock more often than Habad or Ruzhiner rebbes. Shock was considered part of the system of expectation for a Kotsker hasid. "I need a rebbe who will flay the living skin from my flesh, not one who will flatter me," R. Yitzhaq Meir of Ger exclaimed.

Reassurance and shock are not necessarily used independently; more often they are used interdependently as part of the yehidut process. In this process, the rebbe works with the hasid in such a way that some parts of the hasid's makeup are strengthened and others are prepared for discarding. In making use of reassurance and shock, the rebbe must discriminate between what he desires to reinforce in the hasid, and what he wishes to extinguish.

The Rebbe Plays Up to the Hasid's Problem

At times it is necessary for the rebbe to enter into the hasid's problem on such a primary level that he embraces, for a time, the symbol system of the hasid. Usually the rebbe does not need to do this, since his role as teacher means that the hasid lives in his rebbe's symbol system. The rebbe, being the center from which all worship moves toward God, is the one who establishes both the outer setting and the inner set. But in the course of a yehidut with a hasid who has a special problem, the rebbe may have to reverse roles. This reversal acts in such a way as to free communication and give impetus to the therapeutic process which, because of the hasid's problem, has become static.

When a woman came to see R. Abraham Yehoshua Heschel of Kopishenitz with a problem requiring prayer, the rebbe was able to help her understand and to motivate her by comparing prayer to an audience with the President of the United States. By temporarily entering into the woman's symbol system, the rebbe was able to bring her to an understanding of her problem and its solution.

R. Elimelekh of Lizhensk was adept at playing up to his hasid's problem when he felt that this would, in itself, provide a solution to the problem.

A hasid came to R. Elimelekh confessing a capital sin. The Rebbe told him that he must atone for his sin by allowing himself to be executed in the manner prescribed by Torah, that is, by fire. This meant that the offender was to be executed by having hot lead poured down his throat. So great was the hasid's remorse that he was ready to brave this death, but R. Elimelekh explained that the execution could not be carried out until the man had actually been through the process of confession and remorse. After the hasid had been through a regimen of *t'shuvah*, the Rebbe called the hasid before others who were to be witnesses to his execution; but instead of pouring hot lead down the hasid's throat, the Rebbe poured honey. The hasid protested vehemently that he really wished to be executed; but R. Elimelekh pointed out that when a person has worked through all the necessary levels of *t'shuvah*, it makes no difference whether he receives lead or honey. Then the hasid understood what he was unable to understand before—that the rebbe wants the *ba'al t'shuvah* and not a corpse.[74]

In order to understand the import of this story, we must rely on R. Elimelekh's knowledge that anything short of this drastic method would fail to solve the hasid's problem and would leave him beset by guilt feelings. The hasid's own disappointment at not being executed points in this direction. Only an imaginative and daring rebbe would have attempted this method.

When the rebbe enters into the fantasy world of the hasid, he knows that it is not a true world. Yet, propelled by grace and charity, he can do little else. R. Nahman of Bratzlav tells the story of a man who imagined himself to be a rooster. Here again it was necessary for someone to enter into the hasid's symbol system in order to help. In this case it was another Jew who, assuming the rooster role himself, managed to move the hasid from the position of eating crumbs under the table to the point where he was once more able to sit at the table and behave like a normal person. All the while his friend maintained that they were both in reality roosters. Had he not done so, the schizophrenic identification with roosters would have prevented the man's return to sanity.

These cases are extremes; yet they point to a method inherent in much of hasidic counseling. R. Shneur Zalman of Liadi, in his last written fragment, writes:

How truly humble is the being of the soul. At the root of her operation, she is engrossed in the physical Torah, both for herself and for others. What is the work of charity but an approaching of mind to mind, and a counseling from far away [from the real truth in God], dealing with family matters, although most of these are just a pack of lies? Yet it is impossible to do it differently and still to do a kindness;

for truth is only in the Torah, and Truth said of man, "Create him not." But Grace said: "Create him for he is full of graces." Thus Truth is cast to the ground, and a world is built on a grace that is not true; for nowadays it is all done not with the Truth of Torah, but by [the rebbe's] approximating the mind of the one [the hasid] who must do the work, in order to gain his cooperation. Though it be far from the Truth, there is no other way, and this way is a very humble one; so all we can do is accept the facts as they are and do so in love and generosity.[75]

At the end of his life, R. Shneur Zalman was resigned to the fact that there can be no other way but to enter into the "lies" of family matters and give counsel out of a love far greater (in its redemptive value) than the Truth, which devastates man and says "Create him not."[76] R. Shneur Zalman knew that a rebbe must enter into the hasid's labyrinth and help him find his way out. The rebbe realizes that the labyrinth serves the hasid as a temporary defense against the problems of the world. This is precisely why the principle of grace is invoked and not that of truth.

When the Defenses Relax and Dreams Are Discussed

What is clearly a delusion in the man who thought he was a rooster, thus placing him in the category of the insane, is also present in the normal person. In the latter case, the delusion is not part of wakeful life but part of a dream.

Just as the rebbe will help the hasid who suffers from delusions, or whose waking problem requires the rebbe to temporarily assume the hasid's symbol system, so the rebbe will help the hasid whose problem manifests itself in dream form. In accepting the hasid's symbol structure, the rebbe enters with him into a subjective world in which the associative and imaginative faculties operate. The same is true of dreams. The hasidic system sees most dreams as emanating from the world of *tohu*—chaos. *Tohu* is not merely a jumble of images: it has coherences of its own. When the *m'dameh*, the associative and imaginative faculty, is clarified, some very profound matters become clear. Visions are experienced because of the workings of the *m'dameh*, and much of what Freud calls dream work deals with the sorting of symbols and associations in order to elicit the message that the self is trying to convey to itself. For this work, the hasid needs the help of the rebbe.

When a hasid comes to the rebbe to relate a dream, it is usually because of its disturbing nature. The hasid does not consider it folly to worry about a dream. He knows that the dream may have a message for him: it may be a premonition or a warning. If the dream has troubled the hasid, he needs the rebbe's reassurance of its innocuous nature, or, if the dream is a foreshadowing of events to come, the hasid will need the rebbe's help in taking countermeasures.

Not all dreams carry so much veridical or symbolic material. Erotic dreams, for example, will not be brought to the rebbe unless they are recurrent. Erotic dreams necessitate repentance, first of all because lost semen always demands a reparative act to redeem it, and second because a dream at night is the result of a thought during the day. Only such material as contravenes the deep inner will need seek to be resymbolized in dream form. According to R. Nahman, however, a dream in which there has been no fantasy content, but which nevertheless brings on pollution (i.e., loss of semen), needs no reparation. It is merely a bodily relief that does not involve the imagination, and for this reason, according to R. Nahman, it is as innocent as any other bodily secretion.[77] Since the hasidic system does not, in general, encourage celibacy, there is no need for the young married hasid to avoid sex, and in the proper situation, it becomes a mitzvah. Hence, very little is done about an erotic dream in itself: the rebbe's primary concern lies in the hasid's preoccupation with the dream and with the fantasy material.

In the time of the Talmud, the dream mystique received a great deal of attention. Formulae for the effective interpretation of dreams were prevalent. A bad dream was subject to regulation of "dream fasts" (the *Ta'anit Halom*) in order to avert the decree foreseen in the dream. Hasidism chose a different method of dealing with the dream. Rebbe and hasid worked through the dream together. The hasid's readiness to share his dreams with the rebbe allowed the rebbe to enter into the dream material and to deal with it by questioning the hasid as to what it represented in terms of *hirhurey d'yoma*—the thoughts and desires of the day. In this way, it was believed that the rebbe could help the hasid avert the evil decrees that the dream foretold.

Hasidim often dream of encounters with their rebbe. A hasid who dreamed that he was at a yehidut with R. Joseph Isaac Schneersohn, the late Lubavitcher Rebbe, wrote to him of his dream and of the dialogue that occurred, inquiring of the Rebbe whether he truly meant the words he had spoken in the dream. The Rebbe replied:

> In answer to your letter: The dream is caused by the thoughts of the day. As one thinks by day, so one dreams by night, and this is the good side of the dream if it is a good and proper dream. Yet it is

nothing but a dream, and this is the fault of the dream, for it is only a dream. This may lead to satisfaction with the dream alone, and one may be tempted to leave it at that. Moreover, there are those who take pride in their dreams, and this is but the ruse of the "clever one," the *yetzer hara*, who engrosses a person in all sorts of digressions, and to that end, even agrees to dreams of Torah and service. Yet his intention is clearly to hold the person back from that which is truly good and proper.[78]

There are times when good dreams are encouraged, yet always with the proviso that the real work is not to be ignored. R. Ahre Dokshitzer, a hasid, came to the Tzemah Tzedeq and asked what he must do to "grow in Hasidut." The rebbe replied: "Study each discourse well and meditate on it sixty times. What a person thinks of during the day, he dreams of at night. When does a person grow? When he sleeps. Study as I tell you and you will dream Hasidut and thus grow in it."[79] When R. Ahre Dokshitzer became an old man, his daughter once came to wake him to go to services. He resented the intrusion, but his daughter exclaimed: "Father, 'Today must ye do it. Tomorrow is the time of reward.'"[80]

These stories point to the ambivalent attitude toward dreams. On the one hand, the hasid is not to neglect his dreams, but rather to pay attention to what they have to teach him. Yet, on the other hand, he is to bear in mind that a dream is but a dream.

There is a great deal of dream material in Hasidism, but what is recorded is generally the rebbe's dream material and not that of his hasidim. When the rebbe dreams and finds his dreams worth recording, they are then seen as visions and usually taken very seriously, especially if a master who has passed on appears to his disciple or son and shares with him insights of Torah. Some purely symbolic dreams have also been recorded, but since the method of free association was not employed in the interpretation of dreams, and since these dreams belong to sacrosanct persons, they have little immediate value for our purposes. The chances are that those interested in Jungian symbolism would find it worth their while to pursue these dreams further.[81]

The counseling process that occurs in the yehidut is very intense; yet the yehidut itself may be of short duration. At the same time as we assert the uniqueness of the yehidut, we must bear in mind that its very unique-ness means that it is difficult to find a scale by which we can meaningfully compare it with other helping processes. It is for this reason that it has been necessary to study in some detail the dynamics of the yehidut transaction. Only by studying the yehidut as a deeply reciprocal transaction is it possible to arrive at some basis for understanding the counseling process involved, and for comparing it to other counseling situations, both religious and secular. Yet even here we must be mindful of the specialness of the structural and dynamic setting of the yehidut. The role of the rebbe is to a large extent unique and has great bearing on his manner of counseling as well as on the hasid's mind set in coming to the yehidut. The strong social sanctions that exist within the hasidic community play an important part in preconditioning the counseling situation. The depth at which rebbe and hasid are involved with each other, and the assumption of mutual love and trust, indicate that once the hasid's defenses have been reinforced there is almost no length to which both would not go in order to work through the hasid's life problem.

Chapter 7

The Etzah and
the Blessing

When a man conducts himself properly, he can see with an eye that is
not an eye, and hear with an ear that is not an ear. Therefore, when
anyone comes to ask for counsel, I hear how he himself tells me how to
answer him.

        R. Pinhas of Koretz (*Midrash Pinhas*)

Only the soft and gentle way in teaching, coughing and counseling.
        R. Nahman of Bratzlav (*Nahal Nove'a*)

*A constipated person cannot give simple one-sided advice; he vacillates
between "on the one hand" and "on the other hand."*
        R. Nahman of Bratzlav (*Liqutey Maharan*)

*If someone is asked an etzah he should say before replying, "Many are
the thoughts in the heart of man and the etzah of the Lord will prevail."
. . . When one knows that there is a way in which a decision is closer to
the virtuous ways of our Sages, one should advise that this way be followed as long as one knows that it will not bring great loss or harm. In
the case where there is no such indication, one should listen to one's
heart, for the Divine rests in the heart. . . . One who gives advice should
never give it second thoughts or reconsider. . . . When one gives advice,
one should never be precise as to why one chose one thing over the other
or about the means one is to take. . . . One should try very hard not to
give any advice at all, for silence is far better than talk. . . . One way of
giving an etzah is to consult the oracle of the Torah—that is, to open it
at any place and see what it says. . . . The way in which one is to give
an etzah is to always say that it is for the union of the Holy One, blessed
be He, and His Divine Presence—to unite the names YH and VH—and
in this way, he will prevail.*
        Shabbatai of Orshiva (*Segulot Yisrael*)

DEFINITIONS, SCOPE, AND FUNCTION

Scope and Definitions

Until now, we have observed the rebbe in his role as a diagnostician and in his therapeutic working-through of insight with the hasid. We now turn our attention to the directional aspect of his work—the etzah, and its relationship to the brakhah, the parting blessing.

The Place of the Etzah in the Yehidut

The etzah represents the climax of the yehidut. The preceding movements in the yehidut are all stages preparing the way for the giving of the etzah, which is the third of four basic movements—the "taking of shalom," the diagnostic process, the etzah and the brakhah. After the etzah, the transaction will be completed with the bestowing of the brakhah.

Etymology

In hasidic imagery the word *etzah* is a cognate of *etz*—tree. For the rebbe to give an etzah to the hasid is for him to turn or bend the hasid in the direction of more fruitful growth, just as a good gardener bends a tree for better and more fruitful growth. Thus, R. Nahman describes the rebbe as the "master of the orchard."[1]

Value and Variety of Etzot

The area of needs covered by the etzah is as large as life itself. Chapter 3 contains a detailed description of the range and variety of the hasid's needs. As this chapter unfolds, we will discuss how the rebbe helps the hasid meet these needs.

The etzah is considered more valuable than prophecy; for a prophet can only foretell what is already destined to come to pass, whereas one who is capable of giving an etzah can also make it come to pass. The results of the etzah are often miraculous. The less an etzah is accessible to common sense, the greater, according to Hasidism, is its miraculous power.

The rebbe's etzah has the power of a fiat. The hasid's acceptance of the etzah is the sine qua non behind the power of the rebbe's blessing. A hasid who does not accept the rebbe's etzah as an action directive can blame only himself for the ineffectiveness of the rebbe's blessing. The rebbe plants with the etzah and waters with the blessing, but the plowing and the basic groundwork are the hasid's responsibility. Since hasidim believe that the rebbe, in giving the etzah, sets in motion certain processes, the hasid's refusal to act and maintain the momentum will automatically thwart the new dynamics initiated by the rebbe to alter the particulars of the hasid's life. The etzah places the hasid under a probationary sentence.

Even if a hasid feels that the rebbe has made a mistake in evaluating his problem on the basis of the evidence he has presented, he is mistaken. The rebbe's seeming error usually turns out to be the truer assessment of fact. The hasid's trust in the rebbe usually means that he will not question even a seemingly impossible counsel once the etzah has been given. Even if the hasid supersedes this trust by attempting to reopen the discussion, the rebbe will, in all probability, discourage or even forbid such a move by a comment such as: "Let him [the hasid] not think that one answers because one thinks this or because one thinks that. One answers the way in which things are."[2] Inherent in the etzah is an "insurance" against the hasid's fickleness in carrying it out. Hasidic lore includes tales of the dire sufferings of hasidim who have asked more than one rebbe for an etzah, and then, rather than acting according to either etzah, have tried to effect a compromise between the two.

In some cases the rebbe, aware of a hasid's fickleness or of his need to contradict persons in authority and to act contrary to their advice, will steer the hasid in the "wrong" direction, knowing that the hasid's final action will be contrary to the action directive. Generally, however, this does not obtain. Hasidim joke about what one should do when a rebbe is not available and counsel is desperately sought. According to the joke, one should ask a mitnaged for his advice and do the opposite. Rabbi Simhah Bunim of Pshysskha interpreted in the following way the statement of the Sages that Abraham fulfilled all the biblical commandments before the Torah was given at Sinai: How did he know what to do? He questioned the idolaters of his day, and whatever they said, he did the opposite.

How the Problem Creates the Etzah

The rebbe himself does not take credit for the etzah. Like R. Pinhas of Koretz (quoting Bahiya ibn Paquda), he will say: "When a man conducts himself properly, he can see with a 'non-eye' and hear with a 'non-ear.' Therefore, when a hasid comes to ask an etzah, I hear how he himself tells me how to answer him."[3] This is a function of the rebbe's empathy with the hasid. Like Carl Rogers, who believes that the solution to a person's problem resides within the person, R. Pinhas believes that the hasid too brings with him his own solution. The rebbe need only help him discern the solution that exists in his own being.

Functions of the Etzah

The Etzah as Rearrangement

In previous chapters we have discussed the rearrangement of factors in the hasid's life as part of the counseling transaction. Many etzot are functions of this rearrangement of priorities, means, and ends.

THE SYMPTOMATIC RESHUFFLING OF CATHEXES

Because the rebbe has power of attorney over the hasid's life, and because of the priority of the hasid's tie with the rebbe over all other ties, the rebbe is in a position to rearrange the hasid's pattern of emotional investments. The rebbe's etzah acts to protect the hasid from the recriminations of those who would challenge his rearrangement of cathexes.

Both rebbe and hasid hope that the rearrangement of emotional investment will be threefold. First, it will be a matter of mutual decision; second, a matter of function; and third, a matter of priority in handling the new tensions and conflicts arising as a result of the reshuffling. The hope is also that the new arrangement will be less taxing than the previous one; yet it is clear to both rebbe and hasid that, in the beginning, the new pattern will tax the hasid even more than the old one. The rebbe will have to give the hasid sufficient reassurance to help him manage the transitional period. Otherwise the hasid is likely to prefer to slip back into his old pattern and resume his old tensions, rather than muster the effort necessary to manage the transition.

Generally, the critical tensions in a person's life arise not only from the social and environmental pressures that beset him, but also from the person's basic posture to the world—that is, the manner in which he takes his stand in facing the world. When the world impinges upon him in one posture, it creates the source of one kind of tension and strain, and thus gives rise to a particular pattern of behavior. Another posture may result in strain and tension that manifest themselves in an entirely different behavior pattern. The basic posture is thus responsible for the etiology of the problem and calls not only for symptomatic reshuffling, but also for an etzah dealing with etiology. The posture itself, according to Hasidism, is the result not only of the person's early life experiences but also of the root of a person's soul, which stimulated these experiences. Depending on where a particular soul is rooted, whether in divine grace or in divine rigor, there is already inherent in it a tendency that becomes amplified by the posture one takes and the attitudes with which one responds to experience.

A hasid's basic posture to life is a composite of his physical, mental, and spiritual constitutions as they confront the world. It is clear that when the Tzemah Tzedeq says to the hasid who complains of being stepped on, "Who asked you to spread yourself all over the *bet hamidrash* so that wherever one steps, one must step on you?"—he is dealing with the origin of the hasid's inclination for interpersonal conflict; in other words, with the hasid's basic posture in regard to life.

ETZOT DEALING WITH INTERPERSONAL GAMES

There are times when the rebbe must prescribe a reshuffling, not of the hasid's emotional investments, but of the interpersonal games in which he is involved. In such cases, the etzah the rebbe gives the hasid must act in such a way as to restructure the hasid's role vis-à-vis one or a number of persons. It is clear that the rebbe cannot do this until he has produced a certain insight in the hasid. However, it may be necessary for the rebbe to first impose the etzah before the hasid can be brought to insight. We have an example of this in the story "The Etzah" by Isaac Bashevis Singer, in which a quick-tempered man, who has made a virtue out of his own pedantic anger, is advised by R. Chazkele Kuzmir to act like a flatterer. Here we have a borderline situation between a pure case of genetic counsel and a case of role counsel. The rebbe does not advise him to *become* a flatterer, but merely to *act like* one. The person in conflict insists that he must reject this counsel because, having made a virtue of his own vice, to find another vice painted as a virtue puts him in an existential contradiction. The hasid must therefore object strenuously. But the rebbe insists, and the hasid, following his advice, takes on the etzah as a yoke, and, acting upon it, eventually restructures his inner being.[4]

Another case of an etzah dealing with interpersonal games is illustrated by the hasid who found himself in difficulty with the *poritz* (country squire). Thinking to impress the squire, the hasid had dressed in rags and pleaded the case of the pauper. In this case, the rebbe's etzah was that the hasid must dress himself in Sabbath finery and speak to the landowner in the manner of the rich.[5] The etzah worked. The posture of affluence inspired the squire's trust.

When the rebbe advises the hasid who has lived in peace and harmony with his wife, and whose wife has remained barren, to start a quarrel with her and then to become reconciled, he has substantially altered the husband's interpersonal games with his wife. The acceptance of the rebbe's etzah as an action directive may result in the wife's conception.[6]

ETZOT DEALING WITH GAME RULES

One might define structured behavior as a "game": move is reciprocated by move. The rules are the context of the dynamics by which the game proceeds.

Often the hasid's problem is not one of assuming the wrong role or of playing the wrong game, but of following the wrong rules. Halakhah is the cosmic game rule. What is permitted and what is forbidden, what are man's obligations to God and to his fellow man—all these are in the province of Halakhah and all the actions of a Jew are governed by halakhic prescription. In prescribing any etzah having to do with game rules, the rebbe is operating within a halakhic frame of reference. This does not mean that he is strictly bound by Halakhah: there are times when, for various reasons, he may see fit to supersede Halakhah. Because the rebbe is privy to the divine mind and will, he is in a position to supersede Halakhah without violating it; but he will not do so unless he is aspiring toward a higher good. Generally, he will remain within the halakhic sphere and will, in fact, expect his hasidim to observe the maximum letter of the law rather than the minimum.

The hasid appeals to the rebbe when he encounters conflicting rules. The rebbe's first move in dealing with such conflicts is to seek out the reason for the conflict. If an arrangement can be made to resolve the conflict by attending to one rule first and then the other, the rebbe will help the hasid make such an arrangement. On the other hand, the hasid knows that the hasidic value system is not identical with the normative halakhic one. Previous decisions of the rebbe, etzot he has given to other hasidim, have taught the hasid that what is a stricture for the non-hasid is not necessarily so for the hasid. For example, Halakhah forbids bathing and washing (beyond washing of the eyes and fingertips) on Yom Kippur. This means that a person who has a nocturnal emission on Yom Kippur cannot do what is normally required of him by law—to go to the miqveh. The conflict between the need to bathe for ritual reasons and the halakhic stand on bathing and washing on Yom Kippur cannot be resolved within the halakhic framework. Where the halakhist will rule against bathing on Yom Kippur, the rebbe will say: "Bathe, become clean, and then worship afterwards with fervor."[7] In doing so, the rebbe is advising an action directive at variance with Halakhah.

When a hasid comes to the rebbe with a rule conflict, the rebbe may approach the problem in a number of different ways. He might use an esoteric rather than the usual exoteric hierarchy. He can appraise the hasid's needs and rule that one demand takes precedence over the other. He may assess the hasid's intrinsic role and task or evaluate the needs of others, the community, the cosmos, or the hour. He might also trace the nature and origin of the conflict in order to discover what conscious or unconscious motivations may have led the hasid to place himself in the conflict situation. Or, the rebbe may act on the basis of a combination of these considerations. Having discovered the nature and origin of the conflict, and its relationship to the larger arena of the hasid's life, the rebbe may either rearrange the demands on the hasid or lead the hasid to understand why he is prone to conflict, and thus release him.

The Etzah as Preparation for the Mofet

Not all etzot are designed to deal with tangible ends. There are etzot designed to bring on crises whose ultimate purpose is the generation of faith. Here the rebbe prepares the field for working a *mofet*. Such an etzah may be highly specific or it may be a general etzah that acts as a form of reassurance, preparing the way for the sign.

A hasid who came to his rebbe in anguish over the fact that he was to go on trial in another town was given the following etzah: "If one is to be put on trial, it is only fitting that one travel to the place of his trial by first class." Although the hasid did not understand how this advice could help him, he did as he was told and purchased for himself a first-class train ticket. When the time came for his journey, the hasid found himself on the train, weeping profusely. When a kindly man who was sitting next to him asked him why he was weeping, the hasid poured out his tale. As it turned out, the man was the judge who was to try the hasid's case, and was himself on his way to the place of the trial. After hearing his tale, the judge instructed the hasid that, when the time of the trial arrived, he was to act as if they had never met, and reassured him that as long as he did so, all would be well.[8]

In this case, by taking the rebbe's advice, even though he did not under-. stand its application, the hasid helped prepare the way for the working of a sign. Sometimes a hasid who brings his problem to the rebbe will be told to travel to a particular town. Although the hasid may not be able to see how such an etzah can provide the solution to his problem, he will follow the rebbe's advice and will find that the answer to his problem lies in that town. Because the answer is unexpected and often miraculous in its manifestation, it takes the form of a *mofet*.

> A woman who sought the rebbe's help in finding her lost husband was advised, much to her amazement, to go and do her marketing in a neighboring village. Following the rebbe's instructions, she went to the marketplace, and there she found her husband.[9]

In other instances a rebbe will send a hasid to a particular town and instruct him to seek out in that town a specific person, who will help him with his problem. Generally the person is unknown to the hasid, and how such a person could help him with his problem is beyond his comprehension. But, once again, the hasid goes, and miraculously the problem is solved.

The practice of charity is another etzah offered to prepare the hasid to receive a *mofet*, and the more heroic and selfless the charity, the greater and more powerful is the hasid's merit. For this reason, the rebbe will hope that the hasid's sense of charity can be stimulated in such a way that he will act of his own accord. If it is necessary for the rebbe to demand that the hasid behave charitably, this detracts from the merit of the charitable act. A hasid who is in financial need may be counseled by the rebbe to give away what little money he has to some worthy cause. Although the hasid may feel that this will only increase his problem, once again the act may be the preparation for a *mofet*, whereby the hasid's wealth may be doubly increased.

When the rebbe knows of no other method to prepare the way for a *mofet* that might alleviate the hasid's situation by softening heaven's harsh decrees, he will often advise the reciting of psalms. "He who wants to soften the rigors of God, let him tell *all* his praise [i.e., recite all the psalms]."[10] "For all kinds of conditions, recite the entire book [of psalms] without a break."[11] This recitation should not be merely a matter of form. In order to ensure their efficacy, the psalms must be recited as if King David himself were addressing them directly to the person now reading them.[12]

The basic ingredient, without which the rebbe's etzah would remain ineffective in preparing the way for a *mofet*, is the hasid's own faith in the rebbe and in his counsel. This faith enables the hasid to accept the rebbe's etzah as an action directive even though he may not understand the advice. A common etzah used to be prayer at the graveside of a tzaddik. If the hasid had faith that through such prayer his condition could be altered, then the miraculous could occur. "If it were not for the prayers of the righteous [in the world to come], this world could not exist for half an hour."[13] Sometimes it would help if a hasid took some earth from the grave of a tzaddik. During an epidemic some hasidim would take a little earth from the grave of R. Dovber, the Middle Rebbe of Lubavitch, and sew a small packet of the earth onto a garment; and it is said that this helped immediately.[14]

According to R. Pinhas of Koretz:

> When great trouble befalls a person, and he has no hope left except that it come by the grace of the Most High, then he should do nothing save trust in the Lord. He should not take medicine, or pray, or go to the miqveh, but simply trust truthfully, and by this means will his salvation come.[15]

Faith then is the essential ingredient.

ETZOT DEALING WITH HEALTH

Physical Health

For the hasid, physical illness is no less a problem to bring to the rebbe than any other. He will usually seek the help of the rebbe before consulting a doctor, and if he does go to a doctor, it will probably be on the advice of the rebbe.

The rebbe often exhorts the hasid to consider his health to be as crucial an area in God's service as any other. "Good health is as important a positive command as donning the phylacteries."[16] It is important not only in itself, but also in its effect on the hasid's mental and spiritual health. For this reason, if the hasid is concerned about his physical health, the sooner he comes to the rebbe the better.

The Interaction of Body and Mind in the Etiology and Cure of Disease

"When a small damage occurs in the body, a large damage occurs in the soul."[17] So the Magid counseled his son when he admonished him not to fast. For the hasid, this dictum works both ways. It means that a large damage may occur in the soul because of a small damage in the body, and vice-versa; the malfunctioning of the soul can cause the malfunctioning of the body. In short, the states of mind and body exert a reciprocal influence. It is not possible to divorce the two entirely, since there is an area of overlap in which the dichotomy between mind and body is not clearly discernible. In such cases it is often difficult to differentiate between those ills and etzot that properly belong within the province of physical health, and those that belong within the province of mental health. Generally, one area is seen as the primary concern, and the other as the secondary one. Even here we have difficulty differentiating, because what seems to be the secondary concern may be causally related to the primary concern, and so the difficulty persists.

In dealing with health, the rebbe's etzah often included a *s'gulah*. The word *s'gulah* is difficult to render faithfully in English. In kabbalistic terms, a *s'gulah* refers to a charm, which acted as a kind of nostrum or panacea, and whose power is derived from forces higher than itself. The word *s'gulah* is also used to designate the power exuded by the charm.

> Charms . . . are not subject to change; they always retain their fundamental essence because they are related to the constellations, which have remained constant since the day they were placed in the heavens. This astral influence is observable in all creatures, especially in man; for the constellation under which a man is born determines his fortune. The Talmud itself states that everything depends on a lucky star—that is, on the heavenly constellations. It also states that wealth and wisdom depend on the proper conjunction of the stars. Man's diseases, too, are influenced by the constellations, for the Holy One, blessed be He, assigned them the power to accomplish tasks in the terrestrial regions whether for good or for ill. . . . Of course, one should not ascribe independent power and will to the constellations. All their power and will is derived from the might of their Creator

and Maker, who employs them just as the High Priests of the Holy Temple were kept occupied on the eve of Yom Kippur lest they fall asleep.[18]

Such is the kabbalistic–astrological understanding of the word *s'gulah*. With the advent of the hasidic rebbe, the word assumed a different connotation. No longer was it the astrological influences that were responsible for the potency and efficacy of the *s'gulah*, but the rebbe's charismatic power. Hasidim have often trusted in the rebbe's charisma far more than in the instrument itself. Those hasidim more intimately associated with the rebbe have come to trust in the rebbe more deeply and looked upon the *s'gulah* as a symbol of his power; while people less closely associated with the rebbe have depended more on the potency of the charm itself.

For the rebbe whose view of man is based on a psychophysical parallelism, or, better, interaction, the purpose of the *s'gulah* is not to help the body alone or the soul alone. Often these charms have been designed to facilitate the soul–body interaction, or to treat physical symptoms by attacking their moral concomitants.

Though it is not possible to universalize the rebbe's approach to healing his hasid, one thing is clear: he treats each hasid in an individual manner. Each case is unique. The rebbe has to help his hasid on many more levels than the doctor; yet at times the rebbe collaborates with medical authorities by acting in his halakhic capacity.

A case in point is a colostomy patient at the Mayo Clinic who refused to follow the doctor's dietary orders. He had relinquished all hope of living, and was halakhically forbidden to pray with *talit* and *t'filin*. He was referred to the chaplain, who, after consulting with the patient, established that he was ready to follow the counsel of the Lubavitcher Rebbe. The chaplain then placed a call to the rebbe's office and was later called by the rebbe's secretary, who spoke to the patient and explained that although it is generally not permissible for colostomy patients to pray in *talit* and *t'filin*, in this particular case, the rebbe's instructions were that he must do so. From this, the patient recovered his will to live, and from that time forth he was able to hold his own.[19]

Hasidic literature does not make it clear whether all rebbes had a system of healing in which one or another systematic schema held sway. Sometimes we are left with the impression that rebbes discounted all physical causes and means in the etiology of a Jew's disease; yet, at other times, their view of "mitzvah matter" as possessing a chemistry of its own invalidates any "spiritualistic" interpretation. For this reason, "spiritualist" and "materialist" are not good categories for understanding the healing work of the rebbe. For the rebbe, the moral and physical universes are one and the same thing, coexistent on the basis of a psychophysical parallelism. To the rebbe, the active and independent variable of all dependent variables is God's will. If an etzah is to help in any real way, it must be directed toward the end, "May it be His will that . . . ." However, it is also God's will that man have the freedom to choose for himself. To choose sin places the transgressor in the energy system of q'lipah, and demonic forces are unleashed that cause imbalances of health and disposition. The protective screen of mitzvot, which has been broken down by the sinful act, must be mended. Before restoring the balance of health and disposition, however, the rebbe has to erect a temporary screen to protect the hasid in his vulnerability. One means of doing this is the s'gulah.

Sometimes the rebbe will ascribe a hasid's ills to the overwhelming influence of his inclination for evil. This influence may result in various forms of psychophysical deviations from Jewish behavior norms. In order to offset the imbalance, the rebbe will—by means of reproof, by shoring up the will to health and life, by producing insight, and by redirecting the hasid's energies—help strengthen the hasid's inclination for good.

If a hasid's ills are the result of a heavenly decree against him, the rebbe's task is to remove the decree. This he does by various means. He may urge the hasid to repent, or he may argue before God on the basis of the hasid's merit, or, if one avenue of approach is blocked to the hasid, the rebbe may negotiate a blessing in another unblocked realm. Or, it may be that the rebbe will have to utilize a combination of means in order to remove the decree.

The cures for a hasid's ills were as manifold as the ills themselves. Each cause necessitates its own cure. Anything, prayer or herbal concoctions or the donating of money to charity, could act as the cure for a particular ill. The specific cures prescribed for particular ills are discussed in greater detail in the following pages.

The Will to Health and Life

STRENGTHENING THE WILL TO LIVE

In treating physical illness, many rebbes have realized that the true problem was that the hasid had lost his will to live. The etzah they prescribed was designed to stimulate the hasid's will to live. Often this was all that was needed to effect a cure.

Each rebbe had his own method of restoring the hasid's motivation to health. The Besht quoted the Talmud to a learned man, asking him,

"Do you enjoy pain?" The man answered in the words of the Talmud, "Neither suffering nor its beneficial effects." By appealing to the hasid in an idiom familiar to him, by bringing to light the answer that the hasid himself knew, the Besht was able to stimulate the hasid's will to live. R. Nahman of Bratzlav, building on the libidinal will to live, had an ailing hasid recite the Song of Songs.[20] The Rebbe of Kobrin disapproved of the dramatic healing scene because he felt that dramatizing the illness would reinforce it. His counsel was: "No signs! No storming prayers! A little Torah and a roll and milk is all you need!"[21] One rebbe counseled an ailing colleague who had lost his will to live: "Sure you can die and be in heaven, and this you will enjoy. But is it not better to live and give God joy here? Get well!"[22]

These are but a few examples of the etzot that rebbes might prescribe with a view to stimulating the hasid's will to health and life. In keeping with the purpose of the etzah, these etzot were directed not at the manifest symptomatic ills of the hasid, but at the root and source of the ills, in this case, the fact that the hasid had relinquished the will to live. Only when this will to live has been rejuvenated can the manifest illness be expected to improve.

SUGGESTION

The hasidic universe is full of suggestions. The heavens suggest the glory of God, and all the world is full of r'mazim—hints. Every creature is laden with significance, and the rebbe, in his teaching, reinforces this frame of mind. Gesture points to the significant, yet unspoken, realities that surround the rebbe and the hasid. The rebbe's speech is often purposely imprecise so that it may point to many levels at once.

Unlike the hidden "persuaders" in our world, the persuaders of the hasidic world are manifest. Persuasion is eagerly sought, and the hasid cooperates with it. According to E. Goodenough, all religion is a suggestive curtain,[23] a playpen designed to protect the individual from the incursions of the tremendum. From this point of view, the conditions of pain, disease, and distress that the hasid brings to the rebbe are generally the result of the incursion of the tremendum into his life. The hasid wards off this incursion with the help and support of the rebbe.

The narrower meaning of suggestion is something that borders on the therapeutic use of hypnotic suggestion. Unless the rebbe is dealing with a dybbuk, he rarely makes use of hypnosis. There are two basic reasons why hypnosis was not a desirable tool in the rebbe's healing process. First, for the sake of diagnosis, the rebbe does not need to resort to hypnosis. Second, for the sake of imposing a new course of action, the rebbe requires the hasid's conscious participation. Perhaps this is not far from the reasoning behind Freud's rejection of hypnosis.

Since the best posthypnotic suggestion remaining active in the subject is the one of which he or she is unaware, we cannot be sure that there were not instances in which the rebbe saw fit to use hypnosis. However, no such instances are reported in hasidic literature, and none are known to this writer. The basic assumption that all people must earn their own rungs makes it immoral to use posthypnotic suggestion in nontherapeutic situations.

In the hasidic hierarchy, the rebbe is supreme. The greater the number of hasidim who come to him, the greater are the tales told of him, the more power is ascribed to him, and consequently, the greater is the power of his every gesture and syllable to impress the hasid who seeks his help. This enables the rebbe to utilize a type of suggestion that differs from the therapist's posthypnotic suggestion. Since posthypnotic suggestion is usually unconscious, it is not as necessary for the patient to have absolute trust and confidence in the therapist. The rebbe's use of conscious suggestion necessitates an environment of trust. Because of the hasid's implicit trust in the rebbe, and the rebbe's hierarchical position as the trusted authority figure, conscious suggestion can be used effectively in the yehidut. The unconscious factors of guilt, which attracted the hasid's symptoms of distress in the first place, are the only possible inhibitors of healing; and since the rebbe brings the hasid to a cathartic confession and release, and encourages the mending of damages, the hasid is freed to accept the blessing that, in the hasidic belief structure, makes the healing imminent. Thus, the blessing itself is actually a form of suggestion serving to reinforce the positive conscious suggestions that the rebbe has made during the process of the yehidut. All this may be further reinforced by the giving of a *s'gulah*.

The more sophisticated the hasid is in hasidic lore, the more he feels the need to fit the rebbe's suggestion into his own conceptual system. In order to assist him and to increase the efficacy of the suggestion, the rebbe may accompany his blessing with an appropriate thought, a "word" from the Torah. This raises the blessing itself to the magnitude of Torah and empowers it with the same level of truth in the eyes of the hasid.

A woman who came to her rebbe because she suffered from an abnormal discharge was given the reassurance that she would be well. This reassurance was reinforced by the words of Torah: "Before the Lord you will be purified." By this she understood that she would be purified of her unclean flow.[24]

Heaven and earth may tremble—they too depend on the Torah—but the rebbe's suggestion holds firm. After hearing the rebbe apply the Torah *vortel* (word) to his particular case, the hasid is assured of his cure; and every time he repeats it to his peers, the rebbe's suggestion is reinforced.

There are times when the rebbe may see himself as powerless in the face of heaven's decree against his hasid. At such times, he will be eager to hear a new interpretation of a Torah passage that may illumine another avenue of help. This new interpretation may enable him to avert the heavenly decree. Sometimes the Torah thought that frees the rebbe to help a hasid or disciple comes from deep within the latter's own soul.

> The soul of the disciple shall be summoned in its depths so that out of it, and not out of the soul of the master, the word will be born that proclaims the highest meaning of the teaching, and thus the conversation is fulfilled in itself. "When I begin to talk with someone, I want to hear the highest words from *him.*"[25]

S'GULOT AS PSYCHOSOMATIC MEDICINE

Usually, the rebbe's assurance that "All will be well" or that "God will send you a speedy recovery" will satisfy the hasid's need. However, if the rebbe sees that the hasid craves something tangible as evidence of the blessing's potency, he may give the hasid a *s'gulah.*

S'gulot vary in range from herbal medicines and symptomatic palliatives to the occasional use of fecal mixtures that are sure to help because they are so horrible, or because they secure sympathetic magic, either by positive or by negative parallels. Because the hasid has implicit faith in the rebbe (as opposed to the secular patient whose faith relies on empirical substances), the substances used as placebos need not have any logical connection with the illness being cured. The rebbe considers his own faith and that of the hasid sufficient to invest the placebo with healing power.

S'gulot may have symbolic significance. Generally, rebbes have employed substances related to the Jew's sacramental life. Leftover *etrog* (citron), matzoh, wine, oil from Sabbath lamps, Sabbath foods and *haroset* were at one time the main ingredients of the rebbe's "pharmacopoeia." The necrophagous or fecal substances usually employed by other shamanic wonder-workers have had no important place in the rebbe's repertory (unless his insight into the patient pointed to their use, as in the case where the Rebbe of Strettin prescribed a snake's head and bat's head concoction).[26]

Torah Signification Magic. Whenever *s'gulot* are of a Torah nature, they are invested with "meaning" and thus they are said to help because of the Torah significance they have. Among hasidic masters, those who practice Torah signification predominate.

> The daughter of the Belzer Rebbe, practicing Torah signification magic, once suggested to a man suffering from a painful leg cramp that he give a box of candles to the synagogue. Later, when her father asked her why she prescribed this measure, she quoted from Torah: "A lamp unto my feet . . . is Thy word."[27]
>
> Another rebbe called a person with gangrene to the Torah and read to him: "Thy foot did not swell," and he was healed.[28]
>
> A story is told of the Holy Master of Dinov, how he once came to visit his son, R. David, who was lying in sickbed. During the visit, he instructed R. David to add the letter "yud" to his name, so that henceforth his name should be written, instead of "dalid, vov, dalid," "dalid, vov, yud, dalid." When the Master was asked where this solution was hinted at, he answered: "We find this in the Talmud, where, in Brakhot, our sages tell us: 'He gave him a hand—a yad' is to be interpreted as, 'He gave him a yud,' i.e., he added the letter yud to his name." And thus he raised him from his sickbed.[29]
>
> R. Zussia once suggested to a mother-to-be, who came to him because she feared a miscarriage, that she smell his hand. He explained this in terms of Torah signification: "No woman dropped her child from smelling the Holy Flesh."[30]

Sometimes the signification is not so much Torah signification as it is simple common sense. In such cases, the rebbe's etzah is based on a true understanding of primary gratifications. The Lubliner's counsel for impatience—"to smoke a pipe"[31]—may seem rather obvious and commonplace; but it is often the most obvious solutions that escape us, and it is often the commonplace that best speaks to our everyday problems.

The Significance of the Agency Behind the S'gulah. The rebbe is the healing agent in his own *s'gulot.* He uses charms, cameos, and amulets in a manner unlike his Sephardi or kabbalistic counterparts. Following the example of the Besht, rebbes felt that a charm or amulet need not contain God's name or the names of angels. It was sufficient that it contain the rebbe's own name. Even the enemies of the Besht found it impossible to object to his using his own name in this manner. R. Moshe Leib of Sassov did not use his own name for *s'gulot,* but did not need to use the name of God. He simply wrote on amulets the word "Shabbat"[32] and trusted in his own agentic power as sufficient to ensure the efficacy of the charm.

Since the rebbe's agency is often necessary for the remedy to be effective, the remedy is usually no longer potent when a rebbe is no longer alive.

> A man who had traveled to the Tzemah Tzedeq inquired as to a remedy for his wife's frequent headaches. The Tzemah Tzedeq told the man to instruct his wife to bathe her head in hot water. The man returned to his wife and she followed the Rebbe's instructions: every time she felt a headache coming on, she bathed her head in hot water, and each time her headache was relieved. So it was all the days of the Tzemah Tzedeq. However, after the Tzemah Tzedeq had passed away, the woman was again troubled by headaches, and again applied the trusted cure, but to no avail. When her husband came to R. Shmuel of Lubavitch and told him the story, the Rebbe smiled and said: "Well, if hot water does not help, let her bathe her head in cold water." When the woman followed R. Shmuel's counsel, she found that it helped. So it was all the days of R. Shmuel of Lubavitch. After R. Shmuel had passed on, the woman was free of headaches for a while; but once more they returned. When she tried bathing her head in cold water, she found that this did not help. When she tried bathing her head in hot water, she found that this did not help either. When her husband came and told his story to R. Shalom Dovber of Lubavitch, he, like R. Shmuel, smiled and said: "Well, try mixing the hot and cold water together."[33]

Beyond the humorous aspect of this anecdote, we find that the constant factor underlying the prescriptive variables is the agency of the rebbe. Obviously the remedy itself is far less important than is the rebbe's power to ensure its efficacy.

When the Besht had to go on a journey, he entrusted his daughter with the task of prescribing for his hasidim, stressing the importance of her agency in acting as his proxy. One of his letters to his daughter reads as follows:

> To my daughter, Adile, the righteous one who fears the Lord, may she live:
>
> Since I must remain a little longer on my journey, I therefore permit you to issue *s'gulot* from my book of prescriptions, which is in the possession of my trusted majordomo, rav and hasid, the saint, . . . R. Nahman, may he live, of Horodenka. However, do not send these through any third party, but *with your own mouth tell the* s'gulah *to the*

one who needs it. This is the word of your father who blesses you with all good forever.

Israel Besht of Mezhibuzh[34]

From his letter, it is obvious that the Besht considered the agency of his daughter indispensable to the workings of the *s'gulah.*

When the Besht's granddaughter was sick, he sent his daughter the following prescription:

> Take a teaspoon of good oil and put it into a glass. Mix some white ginger into it, adding a jigger of brandy and some soap. Leave the mixture stand for two hours and then rub the child's feet before sleep, and this will help.[35]

Here we have the prescription for an analgesic rub. Sometimes the active agency of a substance is not understood, and the miraculous power derived from God via the rebbe is emphasized. Thus, when penicillin was first discovered, the writer heard one hasid tell another older hasid about the event. The older hasid replied that he had once heard that the Besht had scraped off the rot from a cheese and rubbed it into the open wound of a person, and he was healed. He added the comment that the original point of the story was that the Besht was so great that he could even take rotting and poisonous substances, and, at his bidding, they would heal.

It is significant to note that the rebbe's healing prescription is effective even in cases where the patient is unconscious and unaware of the rebbe's agency. Patients in a coma and those thought dead were healed by the infusion of a potion of the rebbe's wine.[36] The explanations built on the patient's conscious faith participation with the placebo need to be overstretched to accommodate such cases. In ascribing no medical efficacy to the substances used in the rebbe's ministrations (or to the substances used in the doctor's medications), the hasid places the entire responsibility for his recovery in God's hands. The woman who said to the Rebbe of Radoshitz, "First I trust in God and then in the rebbe," was severely rebuked by the rebbe's reply: "First in God, and then again in God, and then once more in God."[37] In the final analysis, God is the only agent behind the act.

Healing by Trial. From the Torah, we learn that disease may be a form of punishment.[38] Hasidism also teaches that disease may be the result of a heavenly decree against the patient. The patient is on trial and the rebbe is his attorney. As such, he must be able to discover some merit that will enable him to plead his client's case before the Arbiter and Judge. Only in this way will the rebbe be able to remove the heavenly decree and effect a cure. Another way of looking at the trial is to see it as a device the rebbe uses to remove the guilt feelings blocking the hasid's will to health and life.

The rebbe is involved not only in acting as an attorney for the patient but also in negotiating a "new deal" for him. He must manipulate the heavenly tribunal's equation in order to effect the healing. Sometimes this manipulation involves a great risk to the rebbe himself or to his immediate family.[39] If the rebbe feels that he is powerless in the face of the heavenly decree, he will try to explain to the hasid why he must bear his burden and surrender to the will of God, and will help the hasid implement this surrender. This affords the rebbe another opportunity to negotiate with the tribunal by showing that not much more can be gained by the hasid's continued suffering, since the latter has already "kissed the rod that smote him."

Touch, Laying On of Hands, and Lahash. The rebbe's use of his hands in healing is illustrated in the following anecdote:

> When R. Shalom of Belz would touch a hasid's afflicted body and the hasid would be healed, he explained that the healing was effected because his fingers, active in Torah study, deserved such power. So R. Shalom of Kaminka testified before R. Israel of Ruzhin. "On what does he base this?" the Ruzhiner asked. R. Shalom Kaminker replied: "It is written: 'Yishlah *D'*varo V'yirpaem'—He sends forth His word and He heals them. The initials spell Yado—His hand." "And you, rebbe, how do you heal?" asked the Kaminker of the Ruzhiner. "By not touching," the Ruzhiner replied. "And where is this indicated?" "In the same words—Yishla*h* D'varo V'yirpae*m*. The final letters of these words spell *moah*—brain."[40]

Healing is a draining process for the rebbe. R. Nahman relates how he experienced depletion of his powers each time he healed.[41] Perhaps because of this tremendous depletion of energy, not every rebbe wanted physical contact. Lubavitcher rebbes do not even shake hands with their hasidim. Those rebbes who do use their hands in healing have not generally done so when the afflicted person is a woman. One source rules that once a woman is beyond a certain age, however, it is permissible for the rebbe to touch her in order to effect a healing.

The healing touch is usually accompanied by a *lahash*—a whispered formula or blessing. Hasidism shares with the rest of Judaism (and with

Christianity) a strong faith in the utterance and its curative power. We have little in the way of literature on the use of *lahash* in Hasidism. However, this writer knows of a case of meningitis cured by the mention of the Lubavitcher Rebbe's Jewish name and that of his mother. The Rebbe had first suggested that the name of his father-in-law, the former Lubavitcher Rebbe, be used as a *lahash*. When this did not work (and here again we see the importance of the rebbe's living agency), the Rebbe suggested the use of his own name and that of his mother. Another case of the use of a rebbe's name as *lahash* is reported in *Or Yesharim*.[42] At farbrengens, stories of dexterous manipulation by a rebbe with healing results are also current. R. Pesah Molastovker was healed of a broken skull by R. Shneur Zalman's manipulation. It is assumed that any healing by means of manipulation or the laying on of hands is accompanied by a *lahash*.

Healing by Medical Means

In Hasidism there have been two prevalent attitudes concerning the use of medical means and empirically tested substances for purposes of healing. There were some rebbes who felt that the use of medicines was unnecessary. They felt that the hasid need not place his faith in the empirical workings of medical prescriptions. All that was necessary was to remember that "I, the Lord, am your healer."[43] This attitude is very close to that of Christian Scientists. On the other hand, some rebbes themselves prescribed medicines or used the services of a physician for this purpose. One man, Dr. Bernard of Piotrikov (the Piotrikover Rebbe) was first a doctor and later became a rebbe. For his religious ministry he would not accept payment and often generously helped those in need; but in his capacity as a doctor, he required payment, feeling that it was a necessary part of healing that the patient pay.[44]

Still another attitude toward the use of medicinal substances was that of R. Barukh of Mezhibuzh. He explains that on the ascending scale from inanimate to animate (plant, animal, human), there are a number of things that are, by nature, good, healthy, and sweet. It is a simple matter to raise and redeem the sparks of these things. But what of the bitter things? How can they be redeemed? R. Barukh explained that it is into these bitter things that God put medicinal properties, so that they too could be utilized and their sparks redeemed.

Although there are a few rebbes who have earned degrees in medicine and pharmacology, even rebbes without formal training have written prescriptions. The prescriptions of R. Kalonymus of Piasetzno, for example, were honored by Warsaw druggists. All this takes for granted the rebbe's ability to make an accurate diagnosis. No hasid will be amazed at the readings ascribed to Edgar Cayce or other psychics who served as accurate diagnosticians. The hasid will cite a number of stories from his own experiences and those of his friends, where the rebbe accurately diagnosed a disease and prescribed the corrective therapy. In some cases the rebbe may even find it necessary to contradict the physician or surgeon whom his hasid has consulted.

This writer has a colleague in New England whose child had diphtheria. The physician consulted urgently advised a tracheotomy to ensure the child's survival. However, when the man called the Lubavitcher Rebbe, he was advised not to permit the unnecessary and disfiguring operation. The physician withdrew from the case and suggested that he return the next morning to sign the death certificate. He also threatened to take legal action against the father for his religious fanaticism, which he was sure would cost the child's life. How amazed he was when he returned the next morning to find that the crisis had passed and the child was convalescing.

In another instance, R. Jacob Isaac Schneersohn sent a woman who served as cook at the yeshivah to a famous surgeon and gave her a note to give the surgeon. The woman, intending to test the doctor, did not give him the note until after he had examined her and pronounced her well. After receiving the note, the doctor again examined her and, upon finding the rebbe's diagnosis correct, arranged for surgery, which was successful in removing a malignancy.

In cases of doctor–rebbe conflicts, rebbes will deal with the issue by quoting the Besht: "You looked at the sick man from the physical side, and I from the [more comprehensive] spiritual one."[45]

Instead of referring his hasid directly to a particular physician, the rebbe may tell the hasid only the place where he is to seek medical help: "Travel to . . . where you will find help."[46] Since this vague counsel was often given in other than medical situations, it was not at all strange to the hasid. Such counsel was a test of the hasid's faith in the rebbe, and it was considered wrong for the hasid to press the rebbe for further details. The hasid would merely follow the rebbe's direction, and when he returned after a successful mission, he would tell his peers of the rebbe's far-ranging vision.

As is the case in other areas of the hasid's life, the rebbe might also find it necessary to refer his hasid to another rebbe in problems related to physical illness.

A young man with consumption visited various rebbes, but was not helped until he was referred to R. Pinhas of Koretz, who prayed that he be given an ample livelihood. "Having opened the gates of sustenance," the rebbe said, "I managed to sneak in and open for him the gates of healing."[47]

For various circulatory ailments and diseases involving fever, rebbes have prescribed bloodletting and cupping. R. David Moshe of Chortkov prescribed bloodletting and cupping by means of leeches. The Besht and R. Pinhas of Koretz advised against bloodletting by means of opening veins unless one could be sure of releasing the bad blood on the first attempt. Otherwise "blood must be carefully guarded and preserved."[48]

Generally, though a rebbe may see fit to refer his hasid to a medical practitioner or to another rebbe who may be better able to help him, he will not refer the hasid to a non-Jew. R. Pinhas of Koretz became very angry upon hearing of Jews who went to a non-Jewish shaman, exclaiming that it was impossible to be healed by such a person, for they "cure" by replacing a small impurity with a larger one.[49] R. Shlomoh Shapira of Munkatch also forbade the removal of earth from the graves of non-Jews for healing purposes.

In Hasidism's moral universe of discourse, to be healthy is a mitzvah, to be sick is a sin: "The evil inclination gives rise to all kinds of new diseases, and each time God creates new medicines."[50] Since the rebbe is seen as having access to these new medicines, he can lead the hasid back to the mitzvah of health. The main purpose of the rebbe's work is to bring his hasid to repent. The formula recited in the night prayer indicates the intrinsic connection between health and morality: "May it be Thy will that I sin no more; and that which I incurred by sin, please erase in Thy great mercies, *and not through suffering and painful diseases.*" In the *Qitzur Shulhan Arukh* (the Abridged Code of Law), there is a section headed: "Laws Concerning the Care of the Body According to the Laws of Nature." Because the rebbe operates in a moral universe of discourse, these laws are often absent from his counsel. When the heavenly tribunal decrees health or disease, no healing can be effected until the rebbe has made arrangements for other means of satisfaction and reparation for the debt incurred by the sinner. Only when the rebbe has attacked the root of the illness can the manifest illness be expected to improve.

Death Counseling

The rebbe's task extends up to and even beyond the grave. When the rebbe knows that the hasid's illness is a terminal one, he must prepare the hasid to meet death. In fact, the terminal moment of life was the subject of a lifetime's preparation. Death counsel dealt with such things as attitude to leaving this world, preparation for entering the other world, lucidity and serenity at death, and preparation for judgment, heaven, and hell.

The rebbe served as a model for the confrontation with death. A rebbe's descendant would share with his hasidim the last insights reported by the late rebbe. An entire section of the hagiography of rebbes deals solely with their demises.[51] Some hasidim also had remarkable deathbed experiences,[52] and both rebbes and hasidim used them as models for the instruction and edification of terminally ill patients.

According to the rebbe,[53] even death is a mitzvah, and thus desirable when it comes. When R. Yitzhaq of Squira heard that his brother, the Chernobiler, could no longer don phylacteries, he knew that the Chernobiler's end had come. "A tzaddik," he said, "dies willingly when he can no longer fulfill any mitzvot on earth."[54] Rebbes would often offer a hint of their own approaching death so that their hasidim would be alert to the fact that they were preparing for death. Later, hasidim would regale one another with stories of their rebbe's preparation for death.

When R. Nahman visited a dying hasid, he said: "What? Worries over death? There is a much nicer world there!"[55] Clearly he was preparing the hasid to accept his death with serenity by assuring him of a better world beyond the grave. In another story, R. Nahman of Bratzlav offered to teach one of his hasidim how to die, on the condition that the hasid would return after death to tell him how it went.[56] Often the hasid facing death was reassured by the rebbe's promise to help him even after his demise. Such reassurance was possible, since both rebbe and hasid believed in the availability of posthumous help. Once the patient was assured that his death did not mean permanent separation from his rebbe, his anxiety was reduced. By asking the patient to check with him after death for further counsel, the rebbe was able to reassure the hasid that death was merely a state of transition.

After a hasid's demise, the rebbe must console the bereaved. "Your son already hears the rebbe, my father-in-law, teach Hasidut in heaven,"[57] the present Lubavitcher Rebbe consoled a bereaved father. "Your father teaches in heaven," R. Menahem Twersky of Chernobil reassured a rebbe's son. Many other such counsels—"Be glad you were a foster parent to so holy a soul,"[58] or, "If you knew how the one you mourn lives and mocks your weeping, you'd stop"—are offered by rebbes to the bereaved. The rebbe also advises them regarding burial and mourning procedures.

After death, the rebbe mends the souls of the deceased, recognizing his obligation to them because they have given him a pidyon. One rebbe who did not wish to help a deceased one was admonished by his disciple: "Either you help him or you won't be my rebbe!"[59] A baker, who had often furnished bread and cake to hasidim, was helped by R. Nahman after his demise.[60] R. Nahman, expecting his deceased hasidim to come to him for counsel even after death, was heard to say: "So just because he died, does that mean he can't come for Rosh Hashanah?"[61]

All these are merely examples illustrating how the rebbe was able to reassure his hasid and prepare him to meet death in the proper frame of mind. Even death had to be sanctified. The hasid, knowing that the rebbe's help extended beyond the grave, was able to face death serenely.

Mental Health

Psychopathology

The hasidic universe of discourse is sufficiently out of line with that of society as a whole to make the norms and categories of mental health and illness not quite transferrable from one to the other. What would be considered the peak of health, by hasidic standards, would in all probability be considered mental illness by secular psychiatric norms. Since the tzaddik, the model to which everyone ought to aspire, cannot function in evil, his sensory–motor responses are impaired: he may be unable to see or hear what is wrong or even to move his hand. Secular society would place him into a pathological category. Conversely, a well-adjusted product of our secular society, who would feel no urge to weep during the Ten Days of Penitence (from Rosh Hashanah to Yom Kippur), would be classified by the hasidic system into a pathological category.

As in the case of physical illness, Hasidism does not subscribe to a single-minded view regarding mental illness.[62] One master states that the usual state of man is insanity, and that only by the grace of God are we sane; another view holds that mental illness, like physical illness, is caused by the evil inclination that has invented all kinds of diseases. In the latter view, the normal state of man is sanity; sin, and consequently mental illness, are caused when the "spirit of folly" (*ruah sh'tut*) enters man. This spirit of folly represents a fall from consciousness, a fall from "right knowing." It is the spirit of forgetfulness and of involvement with the animal soul. It is this spirit of folly that causes man to fall from reason into a state where he does not discriminate between right and wrong. The spirit of folly covers the contradiction and obscures moral awareness. It is this same spirit that makes the thief pray that his thievery be successful. Sometimes the spirit of folly is referred to as a disease of the will.

Still another facet of mental illness is explored by R. Aaron of Karlin, who is reputed to have said: "There is no mental illness without pride. All mental illness is based on having one's own way." R. Shalom Dovber of Lubavitch expresses yet another view. He states that sanity is the result of *hitkal'lut*—the blending, merging, harmonizing of all things; while *hithalqut*—alienation, division, the inability or unwillingness to harmonize—is that which leads to insanity.[63] *Tiqun* (repair of the cosmos) is the world of integration; *tohu* (chaos) is the world of disintegration. *Tohu* is the source of insanity.

With the advent of the Ba'al Shem Tov, the Jewish attitude toward the institutionalization of asylums (*heqdesh*) changed. The *heqdesh* fell into disrepute. People vied with one another to fulfill the commandment of giving hospitality to strangers. Hasidim had lowered the barriers. The emotionally disturbed were no longer deemed so aberrant or deviant from the common way. The leeway within the family was generally great enough to encompass even those with emotional illness. It was not difficult to accept the fact that one member of the family had chosen to be silent, one to study day and night, and so on. The more dangerous deviations were not those based on idiosyncracies, but those that tended toward violent, lustful, or antireligious behavior. Even in cases where custodial care was necessary, no hasid would consider sending a child or a relative to an institution in which he could not be under the care of Jews and be assured of kosher food. Non-Jewish institutions were out of the question. All possible custodial care was given by the families of the disturbed. The mentally ill themselves shared the basic presuppositions of the sane community. Seeking the rebbe's counsel became the accepted course of action. Furthermore, it became an accepted fact that the rebbe's help was extended to those who were mentally ill even as it was extended to those who were physically ill, and that with his help, the ill person could become well again.

It is difficult to explain how the rebbe is able to cure the mentally and emotionally disturbed, since his methods are not easily accessible to our understanding. This difficulty is enhanced by the fact that the rebbe's conceptual models have been morally rather than etiologically oriented. Unlike the secular therapist who operates by insight, the rebbe operates by power. The rebbe's charisma serves as much to obscure his healing power as it does to explain it. The only statement we can safely make is that the hasid's relationship with the rebbe has carried with it an atoning relief, which has aided not only those problems that are ostensibly moral but also those that, within the hasidic universe of discourse, are intrinsically moral.

If the rebbe's conceptual models are difficult to pinpoint, it is equally difficult to discover a clear statement of his diagnostic terminology. The material gathered for this book is not based on case histories, but on religious tracts discussing the immortality of the soul, or on hagiographic celebrations of a rebbe's powers. These sources do not describe the patient's symptoms in sufficient detail for us to "diagnose" them. We found no material that, according to A. Hoffer's description,[64] dealt with schizophrenia.

Nevertheless, there are many reports of bizarre occurrences. Yet who is to say whether these reports describe saintliness or insanity? Perhaps the rebbe himself shared much with the schizophrenic. His sense of smell was keener than that of the average man, he heard more and he saw what hardly anyone else saw. The Besht spoke of two states of mind—the "expanded mind" and the "fallen mind." The fallen mind is the normal state of man. The rebbe was supersensitive to the significance and interrelationship of things, where others had difficulty seeing any connection. The Berdichever's (R. Levi Yitzhaq) ecstatic outpouring in prayer and his deep depression are symptomatic of the manic-depressive state of mind. In the hasidic system, protracted silences and withdrawals have not been labeled catatonic, but *hitbodedut* (solitude), and considered completely within the normal range of behavior. Religious observance given to meticulous detail has not been labeled compulsive-obsessive, but instead considered *z'hirut* (carefulness), and thus held in high esteem.

Rebbes were often deeply touched by the utterances of "madmen." R. Nahman was convinced that there must be some good in mental illness. "If one can reach such profundity through insanity, it too is necessary."[65] The dybbuk confirmed much of Hasidism's eschatological affirmation and served in this way to bring people to repent. Many an exorcist was himself emotionally moved by the possessing spirit.

At times a rebbe's helping function as diagnostician has had halakhic significance. By placing the client into a favorable setting he can also redeem him and another person from a legal bond, as illustrated in the following story:

> There lived a *m'lamed* (teacher) in Klimovitz, and he told the following: "Once after Pesach, I had no teaching job, so I decided to spend Shavuoth in Lubavitch since I had never been there on that day. So off I went on foot. In Lubavitch, I had a relative, so I had a place to

stay. After Shavuoth all the guests went to see the Rebbe in yehidut. I did not rush and waited for a few days. I heard that a woman had come to Lubavitch with her brother-in-law who was going to give her *halitzah*. However, since he was held to be a fool, he was incapable of giving her *halitzah*, which meant that she would never be able to remarry. She already had visited many rabbis, and had hoped that they would permit her to take *halitzah* from him, but not a single one of the rabbis permitted her to do so. And each one added to the long list of responsa that she carried with her. She came to R. Eliezer Mosheh of Pinsk. He too looked at all the responsa that came before him, and he wrote what seemed to be the truth of the situation, namely, that the man was incapable of rationality and therefore he could not permit her to receive *halitzah* and to remarry. When he saw her pain and that she still was young, and had spent so much money on these travels, for she had also taken her disturbed brother-in-law with her and a man to guard him, R. Eliezer Mosheh said: "Listen, dear woman, I will give you counsel. Go to Lubavitch to the Tzemah Tzedeq. First of all, he is a great gaon in learning, but he is also a tzaddik, and I think that you will find your help there." So she went to Lubavitch. When they told this to the Tzemah Tzedeq, he said that he should first make sure that all the people that wanted to see him in yehidut had done so, so there should not be too many people left about when the woman came to see him. He should see that all the others had traveled home. The teacher, realizing that he was in no rush and that something was about to happen, decided to stay in Lubavitch.

The Rebbe said that he wanted to see the disturbed man. When they brought him, the Rebbe said: "What do they call you?" So he answered, "Is that any of your business?" And he asked him again: "Tell me what they call you." So the man replied: "First you tell me what they call you, then I will tell you what they call me." So the Rebbe replied: "They call me Menahem Mendl." And the man said: "They call me Mosheh." So the Tzemah Tzedeq said: "Listen Mosheh, I will ask you for a favor. You know where the market is?" "Yes," he said. (He had already been in the market, and had broken several wagons and caused some other damage as he always was wont to do, and for which the poor woman had had to pay compensation.) So the Tzemah Tzedeq said: "Go to the market and here are ten kopeks. Buy for me two kopeks' worth of tobacco for smoking, two kopeks' paper for cigarettes, two kopeks' worth of matches, and for two kopeks some snuff; two kopeks you owe me as change. *Nu*, Mosheh, will you do this for me?" "Of course, what do you think I am, a thief? Don't worry, I will bring you your change." And immediately he ran between all the people who stood there, and went out through the window. He ran to the market, into one of the stores and shouted, "Quickly, quickly. For two kopeks this and for two kopeks that." And he remembered all the things and brought back the change to the Tzemah Tzedeq, saying: "Nah, I brought you what you wanted and here are the two kopeks change. See, I'm no thief," and he ran away. The Tzemah Tzedeq said then that they should set the time for the next Wednesday to perform the *halitzah* ceremony. The woman was filled with joy, and contributed charity to all the poor in the city, and after the *halitzah*, she went to the Tzemah Tzedeq and asked him in the name of R. Eli Mosheh of Pinsk to write his responsum along with the others, because R. Eli Mosheh had asked her to bring him the Tzemah Tzedeq's answer. She thought the Rebbe would tell her to come back in several days, after which he would have prepared the responsum, for this was the way in which all the geonim up to now had treated her. The Tzemah Tzedeq, however, said to her: "Good. Right away." He took a small piece of paper and wrote: "It is written in the Yerushalmi—A fool who knows how to give change, is not counted a fool in the legal sense." (It is important to note that all the geonim she visited had looked at the responsa of the previous geonim and then had written their own. The Tzemah Tzedeq had not even bothered to read them.) When she came to R. Eliezer Mosheh of Pinsk and he saw the little note of the Tzemah Tzedeq and she told him the whole thing, he was amazed and said to the people who were with him: "What do you think of that? How many times have I studied that Yerushalmi, but if one studies Torah for her own sake, as does R. Mendl, one has eyes that are luminous." [R. Kahan, *Shmu'ot VeSipurim*, p. 34]

Hasidism speaks of the mentally ill under two basic categories. The *shoteh*, the feebleminded person, is considered incapable of executing any valid act: this is the legal category of mental illness. The *m'shuga*, the disturbed person, is the person who manifests deviant behavior: this is the social category of mental illness. From the foregoing discussion, it is obvious that Hasidism has had its own norms with regard to mental health and illness, and that these norms may be the direct antithesis of those held by society at large. The only major area of agreement between them is the attitude toward self-destructive or antisocial behavior. The hasidic community has been as concerned as any other with deterring and restraining these forms of behavior. Either the *shoteh* or the *m'shuga* could, at some time, manifest destructive behavior. When this has occurred it was a major concern for the friends and relatives of the hasid involved. There are many manifestations of self-destructive or antisocial behavior. Abusive language, nonobservance of Jewish Law, indecent exposure, and apostasy have been among forms of behavior that have shocked relatives and friends into bringing the disturbed person to the rebbe for help. We can see that, even though there may be agreement between the hasidic and secular worlds as to the undesirability of antisocial behavior, the behavior forms that properly belong under this category often differ, as do the means of dealing with them. Inasmuch as Hasidism has—at least in the past—considered "possession" the prime cause of deviant behavior, so its method of dealing with the aberrant has consisted largely in bringing the possessed one before the rebbe so that the demon might be exorcised.

Possession

The patient who is brought to the rebbe because he is thought to be possessed by demons is a sight attracting much attention. In this climate, the paranoid and the hysteric have had easily available models of abnormal behavior to emulate. The rebbe has had to be able to distinguish those who were actually possessed from those who were only feigning possession in order to utilize a socially acceptable model for their aberrant behavior.

From a reading of the relevant literature, it is possible to draw a composite picture of a possessed one. The one who is possessed may develop a marked loss of appetite, a strong introversion, a loss of the libidinal will to live, and may be overcome by convulsions. When urged to eat or to behave normally, he may become abusive and hostile, verbally attacking his family, and, in general, washing their dirty linen in public. He may refuse to say a holy word or to touch a holy object. When these behavior forms first manifest themselves, the hasid's family will react much like any other family, worrying that the hasid is not his usual self: "He acts as if a dybbuk were in him." The hasid is not constantly under the thrall of the dybbuk, however, and when his other personality, the one known and loved by the family, does manifest itself, he will complain of the attacks of the other "strange" self and the sufferings he has to undergo at its hand. When the family becomes convinced that he is indeed possessed, they will take him to the rebbe.

In dealing with the patient before him, the rebbe will endeavor to negotiate with the suffering spirit that is possessing the hasid rather than with the hasid's true self. The rebbe questions the dybbuk and generally accepts as truth whatever the dybbuk has to say about his own origins. During the course of his questioning, the rebbe will discover that the dybbuk was a person who committed a terrible sin, and, as a result, was not permitted even to go to hell but was condemned to wander without any place of abode. Wherever he roams, he is persecuted by demons and angels of wrath and can attain no rest unless he enters a living body. If he enters the body of an animal, he suffers from animal privations and from his own loneliness, but even this is better than the incessant punishment inflicted by the demons. Only once he has entered the body of an animal, and that animal has died, is the dybbuk permitted to enter a human being. Most human beings are well protected against possession. However, in the case of one who is possessed, it is understood that he has committed some sin (generally not as heinous as the dybbuk's own) that has removed the angelic protection and made him vulnerable to possession. Or, it might be that a mezuzah or a set of phylacteries, which acted as a protective mitzvah, were damaged, and thus the person was made vulnerable.

A public exorcism is an impressive occasion. The rebbe emphasizes the importance of *t'shuvah* and calls upon those assembled to repent of their own sins. At times the dybbuk exhibits clairvoyance by naming names and places of persons involved in sin, and thus expedites confession and repentance. On rare occasions, the dybbuk may refuse to reveal his identity and the reason for his present state, but usually he cooperates, and the information he reveals provides a powerful motivation for *t'shuvah* to those assembled.

However, when the rebbe orders the dybbuk out of the person who is possessed, the dybbuk is recalcitrant and refuses to leave. This is understandable, for the dybbuk has nowhere to go and demons await him. The rebbe can sympathize with the dybbuk's plight, but he is still committed to help the one possessed. For this reason, he threatens the recalcitrant dybbuk with dire results should he continue to disregard the injunction to leave. He commands the dybbuk to leave via the small toe (or else the spirit's exit place will afflict the possessed one for some time afterward), and then out through the window. When the dybbuk complies, the mark is visible on the small toe, and, if the window was not open, there remains a bullet-holelike opening as a visible sign of the dybbuk's departure. The patient is then returned to a protective situation, his anti-demon barriers restored. The patient has been made well, and the rebbe emerges triumphant.

So it is when the dybbuk complies with the rebbe's first commands and is intimidated by his threats. However, the dybbuk rarely departs at the rebbe's first demand, and the rebbe's threats seem no worse than those awaiting the dybbuk should he comply with the rebbe's demand. Prior to Hasidism, the exorcist relied solely on his power and authority to order the dybbuk to leave. He threatened and banished, but seldom offered the dybbuk the help he needed in his own struggle. The hasidic rebbe has often shown great compassion for the possessing spirit, offering to help him by making amends for his sin so he can achieve peace and rest, as long as the dybbuk would agree to leave the body of the possessed one. The rebbe offered the study of Mishnah and the recitation of the Kaddish, as well as other intercessory means in order to help the dybbuk. At times, a rebbe might even ask a dybbuk how he might best help.

The obvious point is that the dybbuk must not continue to inflict pain. He should yield to the purgative effect of the work of the demons within him and thus accept his fate in order to hasten his redemption. This could prepare the dybbuk for the next stage, in which he would, through *t'shuvah*, make reparation for his own sin and thus be relieved of his discarnate state. It must be remembered that the exorcism is usually a public affair. The hasidim who assemble to witness the banishment of the dybbuk know that even a soul that had committed so great a sin and that was condemned to wander could atone for its sin and be redeemed.

There is no doubt that the dybbuk phenomenon can be interpreted largely in terms of psychopathology, but this is not our concern. The purpose of diagnosis is to pave the way for therapy. For the rebbe, the hypothesis of the dybbuk has yielded a successful therapy. The parapsychological phenomena reported by hasidic narrators—the dybbuk's clairvoyance, the mark on the small toe, the crack in the window—act as empirical reinforcement for the hypothesis. It may seem that the rebbe's helping function in this instance is based on an unwarranted acceptance of an unsophisticated hypothesis. However, any anthropologist, in dealing with those myths that are active in our society today, could point out that we too naively accept certain phenomena and yet manage to produce empirical results.

Demons were real inhabitants of the universe of those who lived in the shtetl. They often took the form of incubi or succubi, plaguing innocent people. Here again the essentially moral nature of the hasidic universe comes to the fore, and the rebbe attacks the problem from a moral standpoint. He is primarily interested in three questions: Has the person in distress broken his relationship with the succubus (or incubus), and is he henceforth protected from its incursions? Is the succubus properly banished, and has the person begun his reparative work? Finally, how is one to recapture the investment of the subject in the succubus?

Since the children begotten with the succubus constitute tangible evidence of the sin's effects, one of the expectations of the penitent and of the rebbe is that these children will be destroyed. This means that deep penitential catharsis is accompanied by supernatural intervention. The demon children die and the traces of sin are removed. The result is that the hasid is absolved of his sin.

The measures that the shtetl rebbe utilized, or that apparently came as a result of supernatural intervention, seem to have been very cruel. The night before an infant's circumcision was said to be a time of great danger, and a watch was to be kept over the child in order to protect him from demonic invasion. In the case of a changeling, a child believed to have been snatched away by demons and replaced by a demon child, the rebbe counseled that the parents beat the demon infant mercilessly so that the real child might be returned to them. One infant (who later became a rebbe) was said to have been returned to his rightful parents by this method. It is clear that no quarter was given to demons. If we consider the matter in psychopathological terms, we can understand why cruel, oppressive entities, arising from other realms of consciousness, were attacked with drastic measures.

Hysteria

It was said of one rebbe that "He healed the halt, the lame, and the blind: he gave back speech to the mute." Many hasidim today speak this way of their own rebbe, as have devotees down through the ages. The holy man is the healer of many diseases. Those diseases that manifest themselves in the impairment of sensory-motor control, and that are generated by psychogenic causes, have been called hysteria. Another definition of hysteria is the following:

> An illness resulting from emotional conflict and generally characterized by impulsiveness, attention seeking and the use of mental mechanisms of conversion and dissociation, classically manifested by dramatic physical symptoms involving the voluntary muscles or the organs of special senses.[66]

The rebbe was called upon to minister to many ills that were essentially hysterical manifestations. Many a rebbe was called upon to assist a woman in labor. A "word" from the rebbe, or an amulet, might facilitate the delivery. So it was with the lame and the blind. In one instance a man's sight was restored and then taken from him again, in order to illustrate that the rebbe had the power to heal him, but he did not deserve it.

It is important to note that, had a rebbe been known to cure only hysterics and not patients with "real" diseases, even the hysteric would not have been helped by the rebbe's fiat alone. The hysteric is what he is in order to escape the burden of his guilt or conflict. If the rebbe is to alleviate his symptoms, and in some sense relieve his guilt, he must not give the show away. The hasid must be able to come to the rebbe in the confidence that the rebbe will give his illness as much credibility as any other. Only in this way will the hysteric feel that he can be helped and cured rather than unmasked and shamed.

Sometimes the rebbe will demand a certain sacrifice on the part of the hasid or on the part of a close relative before he will agree to effect the cure. The father of a deaf and dumb boy was asked to promise that he would no longer shave. Because of the strong social sanctions involved, this represented a real sacrifice on the father's part. Only after the father had accepted the rebbe's condition did the rebbe effect the cure.

We have no way of knowing what percentage of those who came to the rebbe with physical ills were actually hysterics. However, the psychodynamics that would permit a classical hysteric to be healed by the rebbe's fiat are clear. Since the conflict that the hysteric faces brings about the establishment of defenses to ward off the pain of inner tension, and since the patient knows of the rebbe's power to heal physical ills, the rebbe can help the patient by accepting his symptoms as real, and yet banishing them without shaming the patient who was well served by the disease. The residual tendency to take on these or other symptoms after they have been banished is negated by the patient's new status as "one who has been healed." His craving for attention has been satisfied, and his need to be blocked has served him as long as it was necessary; but it is no longer necessary, now that the needs that brought on the conflict have already been met. From this point of view, there is no reason why the patient should not respond to the rebbe's ministrations. At worst, he can, from time to time, return for more healing and attention. However, a patient who repeatedly exhibits the same symptoms will no longer have a good story to tell. Along with other factors, this tends to inhibit a "relapse." Again, it can be argued that, from the description of deaf and dumb healings, we can see that the patient was able to hear the rebbe's initial admonitions to reply to his urging. "A rebbe once said in a mute one's presence, 'Drown him, shock him, wake his nerves,' and this alone healed him."[67] A believing hasid would reply that the rebbe first healed the patient's hearing and then helped his speech. It is obvious that the rebbe himself did not act as if he were treating hysteria, but rather as if he were treating a real illness.

Depression

R. Nahman's counsel to his hasidim, "For heaven's sake, do not despair," is simple and to the point. Yet in the shtetl, sadness and melancholia were far from rare. It was the appearance of joy that was difficult to explain. Powerlessness, inadequacy, and hopelessness easily become chronic and pathological. Living for a long time with conditions that, if they were to occur suddenly, would bring on grief (a realistic and proper emotional reaction), will eventually cause one's depressed mental state to become chronic. Action outlets for frustrations in the shtetl were few, and where demand did not exceed supply, even the sense of business aggressiveness could not offer relief. Many aspects of shtetl life, from a lack of sensory gratification and an absence of possible action outlets, to a constant sense of inadequacy before man and God, created the atmosphere that led Hasidism to give so much attention to the acquisition of joy.

The Besht is quoted as saying:

> This is a great rule in the service of the Creator: Guard yourself from sadness every possible way. Weeping is very bad. A person must serve in joy, but if the weeping is occasioned by joy, it is very good. Sadness is a great frustrator of divine service. It is much better to serve His Blessed Name with joy and without austere means, for they cause sadness.[68]

There are many more statements of this nature in hasidic literature. "Nowhere is joy commanded; yet that which joy can bring, no commandment can bring."[69] Because of Hasidism's preoccupation with joy, rebbes were concerned when hasidim suffering from great depression and sadness were brought before them. Yet there is little material available dealing with somatically conditioned depressions, and one cannot find any cases of identifiable schizophrenia in hasidic literature. When depression or sadness occurred, it was subsumed under nonpathological categories.

Hasidism distinguishes between *atzvut* and *m'rirut*, sadness and bitterness. *Atzvut* was seen as occasioned by the same misapplied inertia that characterized what was considered the "evil aspect of the element of earth." *M'rirut* was seen as the bitterness resulting from grief over a reality which, when faced, tended to move one to do something about it. Both are similar in their lethargic manifestation. R. Zussia distinguished between *atzvut* and *m'rirut* by pointing out that a person in *atzvut* complains about what the world owes him, whereas the person in *m'rirut* makes demands upon himself. Usually *atzvut* is accompanied by dullness of heart and mind. In *m'rirut* mind and heart are keen. "*Atzvut* itself is not a sin, but to what state it can bring one, no sin can."[70] In this sense, *atzvut* is always a moral condition, and its treatment is pursued by moral exhortation. It is an issue of means rather than of ends, and therefore is not generally handled by miraculous intervention. In fact, if the rebbe felt that it was necessary for the hasid to work out his sadness on his own, he would offer him no help.

The two basic methods that the rebbe uses in dealing with a hasid's depression are negative and positive feedback. Often a combination of both is used. If the rebbe can alter the hasid's frame of mind so that he can anticipate his gratifications from spiritual sources, or if the rebbe can institute such regressions as allow for physical gratification in a licit and hasidic manner, he may do so; at the same time, he will reinforce the withdrawal of libido and gusto from other areas of life. To relax the regimen of discipline and to expect that this will lead to a fuller level of happiness and more meaningful fulfillment would only result in disappointment. The rebbe is committed to helping his hasid overcome this problem.

We will now look at positive feedback in order to highlight a method that some rebbes used more consciously than others. This method arises from Habad's theory of *bitushim*. *Bitush* refers to a shattering of the animal soul or libido, accompanied by an increase in frustration to the point where the hasid is driven to an inner bankruptcy, which breaks the dullness of a more chronic depression to make it piercingly acute. This leads to an identity crisis that is resolved by further mortification of the desires of the animal soul. Because the hasid can no longer remain in identification with his animal soul, he abandons it and identifies with either the rational or the divine soul. Symbolically, the animal soul represents Egypt. Its destruction as a subject, and the identification of the self with the other soul, symbolizes the Exodus from Egypt. The Exodus itself is only a prelude to the Theophany of Sinai, in which the divine soul says "*Na'aseh v'nishma*" (We shall do and we shall obey), and the animal soul is buried under the mountain. The poison of the serpent's taint is obliterated while the dew of Torah resurrects the divine soul.

This scheme, based on a homiletic allegorization of the biblical account, is very real in Hasidism. The hasid has lived through the liturgical seasons via the Torah thoughts taught by the rebbe. He reenacts these seasons annually, and their symbolism is fully alive to him. It is a dimension that has become for the hasid the life-space in which he lives and moves. If the scheme were merely a verbal representation, the hasid would be unable to derive any benefit from the yehidut. This is why Hasidism insists on Hasidut first, yehidut next. In this way, the hasid reaffirms the mythic life as taught by the rebbe. To be worthy of the Exodus, the hasid must sacrifice the lamb, the animal soul, and paint the lintel and the doorpost with its blood. The claim of the animal soul that it is the firstborn only leads to its death. The firstborn of Egypt must die.

How is this death accomplished? The rebbe may temporarily increase the hasid's discipline in terms of fasting and solitude. However, he often acts according to the dictum "Why punish the poor—the stomach. Tax the rich—the eyes, the ears, and the imagination—instead."[71] Or, "Batter the shell from within. Call the animal soul by all the vile names it deserves: 'You are wicked, evil, abominable and vile.'"[72] All the frustration is now aimed at the jailer who keeps the prince imprisoned. The body, the snake's skin, must yield. Bitterness must bring the frustration to the arena of feeling. Weeping must be brought on. Not the weeping of form, which pleads, and which, after it has its wish, can be shut off; but an uncontrollable weeping, focusing on "how bad and bitter it is to have abandoned God."[73] Instead of feelings of distance from God—still a sign of life—there is only dullness. "Am I only a cut-off limb?" The cry, "Help, Father!" becomes a wordless scream. Like the shofar blast on Rosh Hashanah, first comes a long wail, then a broken weeping, and finally a shattered whimpering. (To the esoteric, the mixing of seasons does not matter. The aim of the shofar and of the Exodus is the same.) Only after utter despair comes joy— life! The weeping over distance and separation is no longer the weeping of the animal soul. Now the divine soul, the prince, weeps with longing and yearning to return to the Father. The weeping that characterized the inescapability of death has now become the weeping of a flight to life.

Not every hasid is strong enough to weather such a crisis; but palliatives are of no real help. As long as the hasid can manage it, no one can spare him his ordeal. *Agōnia*, the pain of struggle, has yielded its benefit. It has annihilated *pathein*, the pain of depression. The inner mortification is the begetter of the rebirth. The intensification of the process in which the rebbe, through positive feedback, increases the depression, is the surest and quickest way through it. Palliatives and premature reassurance can only create situations reinforcing the hasid's tendency to test the intensity and frequency of the reassurance; consequently, this keeps him in the depressive bind.

Scrupulosity and Compulsion

Hasidim afflicted with a sense of perpetual anxiety over their fulfillment of religious obligations, thinking that after they had done all that they could do, their acts still lacked completion, have often come to the rebbe for guidance. The rebbe does not accept their set of mind.

Among Habad hasidim there is a story current about a hasid who, at a rabbinic convention, caused his colleagues a great deal of puzzlement when, as they preened themselves on how scrupulous their religious observance was, each one trying to outdo the other, he announced his scrupulous abstinence from yellow cucumbers. When his colleagues were unable to find any reference to substantiate this custom, they pressed him for the reason—whereupon he solemnly announced that he abstained from yellow cucumbers because they tasted bitter, thus rebuking his colleagues for a scrupulosity that was sick with pride.

Hasidim who have sought the rebbe's help for reasons of scrupulosity have usually been in for a shock. As R. Nahum of Stephanesht once said: "Scrupulosity is a cloak made of pride, lined with anger, and sewn with melancholia."[74]

Most hasidim who come to the rebbe with problems of scrupulosity merely seek the rebbe's approval. By denying this satisfaction, the rebbe has been able to open the hasid to other, more positive directions. To reinforce scrupulosity would make the hasid even more compulsive.

ETZOT DEALING WITH LIVELIHOOD

Vocations

The Rebbe's Presuppositions

When a hasid comes to ask the rebbe about what he should do to earn his livelihood, he is not trying to find out about his aptitude or interest. While the hasid may not always be aware of his calling as a human being and as a Jew, the rebbe, in his counseling, must help him discover his vocation in terms of the sparks of holiness sunken in this world. It is the hasid's task to redeem these sparks. In order to fulfill this mission, it may be necessary for the hasid to be involved in an occupation for which he has neither aptitude nor interest; yet it is part of his life task. Here too we have a dimension in which the rebbe acts differently from all other helpers. He could not do so unless he considered himself to have information of another kind. The hasid, in his implicit trust, could not carry out the duty the rebbe assigns to him unless he believed that the rebbe knows something that others do not. The hasid knows that when a particular task is completed, another may then be assigned. Therefore, if a task is unpleasant, the best means for the hasid to be rid of it is to complete it successfully.

ERRANT SOULS

> Every Jew has his mission. To fulfill it is the purpose of his soul's
> descent. When the *yetzer hara* wishes to dissuade him from his work,
> knowing full well that he will not be obeyed if he tells the soul not to
> serve God at all, the *yetzer hara* consents to the work for God, but he
> seduces the soul to do the work that belongs to another.[75]

The hasid who is doing another's work instead of his own is an errant
soul. In one of his tales, R. Nahman of Bratzlav points to the tragedy of a
child who was exchanged for another, the tragedy of the errant soul. "The
prince and the pauper" is a theme mentioned in his teachings as well as his
tales.

The hasid who is intended to lead an active life, but who is leading
the life of a contemplative, is considered an errant soul. Similarly, the
contemplative who is pursuing the active life is not fulfilling his life task.
In each case, the rebbe must steer the hasid toward his proper vocation.
R. Nahman taught that the change from one's central life task to a task
that is not one's own is tantamount to "the rigors of Egypt," and these
rigors lead to an embittered life. The man who is asked to donate to
charity and who pleads that his task is not to engage in acts of charity but
to study Torah, is embittering his own life, as is the yeshivah student who
claims that he must work for the greater good of others at a time when he
should be studying. In fact, the person who escapes his own life task will
find that—although in the beginning he invests unusual energies into the
work that is not his own—his ardor soon cools. A blocking occurs and the
hasid can no longer function in either his own task or his assumed one.

Exchanges in vocation create problems not only in this world but
also in the next. R. Zussia's oft-quoted question, "But what will I say,
God, when you ask me why was I not what *Zussia* could have been?"
applies here. The person whose life task was taken from him will summon
his competitor to trial. A new set of reincarnations may have to be
endured.

LIFE TASKS

"A soul may wait for a millennium to descend to earth, and then live a
whole lifetime for the one moment when he will be able to do another a
favor."[76] So R. Joseph Isaac Schneersohn reported in the name of the
Besht. Yet, even when the rebbe counsels one who has such a brief life
task—as the Besht did the man who had denied his friend from a previous
incarnation the alms he sought in this one—he treats the soul of this hasid

not as the means or tool for another's benefit, but rather as a soul that will achieve its own end and purpose through that unique act. When the Besht traveled for miles to light a great gaon's pipe or to light the stove for another, he saw such actions as an end in the service of God.

Generally, however, life tasks are seen in a larger context. The relation of the person to his peer group, family, friends, and neighbors, and to his own hopes and dreams and potential, are all taken into consideration, as are the constitution and origin of both body and soul.

Even if the hasid has completed his life task, the rebbe can help him by giving him a new direction. Otherwise the hasid faces destitution. But, "A wise man does not have to wait for his next incarnation; he can begin it in this life."[77] When the hasid changes his vocation, he changes his *mazal* (fortune) and his source of energy inflow, and increases their abundance.

When the vocation and the ethical demands of the Torah are not in harmony, the rebbe still counsels according to what he sees as the hasid's life task.

> R. Israel, the Magid of Kozhinitz, once told a hasid that his task was to become a thief, a master burglar. The hasid did not understand the counsel, but he had no choice but to comply. Only later, when the hasid had achieved the purpose of his life through his vocation as a thief, did he understand. After making restitution, he settled down to a life of honest wealth.[78]

Sometimes even poverty may be desirable as a means of helping a hasid's progress. Some rebbes have discouraged their hasidim from amassing greater wealth. Such counsel as "The greater the businessman, the smaller the Jew,"[79] and "Go back and face your poverty in God's service," has often been given by the rebbe.[80] Yet the life of the mendicant in God's service was obviously not suited to all. Some are meant to serve God with their affluence. The wealthy were meant to "serve God in other ways than faith and trust."[81] The essential thing was not whether one was rich or poor, but where the emphasis lay. The chief concern should not be with the acquisition of wealth.

Often the rebbe's vocational counsel dealt not so much with the choice of vocation as with the manner in which this vocation was best pursued.

> A man who was an entertainer at weddings came to complain to R. Pinhas of Koretz about his lack of an adequate livelihood. The rebbe's advice was: "Keep yourself from telling jokes when you are

not entertaining for money, and you will find that you will make a better living." He explained this as follows: "It is written that a person's income is budgeted from Rosh Hashanah to Rosh Hashanah. It doesn't say that his food is budgeted, but that his enjoyment is budgeted. Since you derive so much enjoyment from the jokes you tell, you cut off your own income."[82]

Sacerdotal Vocations

In the hasidic world, the chief sacerdotal vocation is that of the rebbe. Next in line in the sacerdotal hierarchy are the *mashpiy'a* and the (communal) ordained rabbi. In addition to the vocations of rebbe, *mashpiy'a*, and rabbi, there are several other sacerdotal vocations. These are discussed in the following pages.

THE SHOHET (RITUAL SLAUGHTERER)

The shohet's vocation is one that has carried with it a great deal of responsibility. The ritual slaughterer is responsible for ensuring that all the meat the Jews eat is kosher and unblemished. He is responsible for killing the animal in a kosher and humane manner, in strict accordance with the Law. The shohet's vocation has been considered so important that, in cases where one had to choose between being a ritual slaughterer and being a rabbi, particularly if there was only one hasid available, the hasid chose the former. In addition, whenever a community was divided between hasidim and mitnagdim, if the hasid elected to become a ritual slaughterer, he acted as an insurance policy for his fellow hasidim. With regard to legal decisions, the hasid felt that he could rely on the mitnaged. Therefore, the hasid could accept a mitnaged in the position of communal rabbi. However, where the everyday piety of the shohet was concerned, both rebbe and hasidim preferred to be served by the hasid.

There are several reasons given for this preference. Hasidic lore is rife with stories of anti-hasidic ritual slaughterers who were secretly sinners and could not be trusted to feed the Jews of the shtetl unblemished kosher food. In addition to this, Hasidism had made some important innovations in the special knife used in slaughtering animals to be used as meat. The knife that the mitnagdim used was primitive in comparison to the hollow-ground knife introduced by Hasidism. The new knife was sharper and thus could be relied upon to kill the animal in a more humane manner, in keeping with the spirit of the Law.

It is obvious that the vocation of shohet cannot be compared to that of a secular butcher. Shtetl Jews held the shohet to be a very pious and religious man. His personal halakhic life was expected to be exemplary in order to make him worthy of his priestly vocation. His daily life was an example to all in the community. Each day he would dip in the miqveh. His prayers were the epitome of fervor. "The shohet," said R. Joseph Isaac Schneersohn, "is the heart of the community." (The rabbi was the head.) The ritual slaughterer was also involved in public education, often teaching the daily lessons between the evening services. In short, he was to be, as the *Shulhan Arukh* demands, "more pious than the many."

The rebbe would often counsel a young man whom he considered reliable to become a shohet. When the rebbe counseled one man in this manner, the young man jokingly retorted: "Rebbe, why should others eat my flesh? Better that I eat someone else's!" The rebbe warned him that he would soon lose his dowry and then would be forced to become a ritual slaughterer. True to the rebbe's word, the man lost his dowry and became a shohet.[83] Another young man replied, when he was counseled to become a shohet, "Rebbe, I am afraid of such great responsibility." The rebbe retorted: "So, what would you have me do—appoint one who is not afraid?"[84]

When a delegation of householders came to complain to R. Shalom Dovber of Lubavitch, "Rebbe, our shohet is too timid. He is afraid even of the animals," the rebbe replied: "Perhaps you are mistaken about the origin and the aim of his fear? I don't know if he is afraid of the animal. I do know that he fears Him who created the animal."[85]

In counseling a hasid to become a ritual slaughterer, the rebbe kept in mind whether or not the hasid had an inner drive for murder. If so, the rebbe would channel it in the direction of a purposeful vocation. One prospect whom the rebbe counseled to become a shohet began to cry: "Am I really a murderer?" The rebbe replied calmly, "Yes. Would you not rather serve God with this urge than fulfill your bent in sinful and harmful ways?"[86] To another, a rebbe said: "In your last life you were a murderer. Now you must atone for it by killing in cold blood for the love of Israel so that your meat will be without blemish."[87] Still another rebbe said: "You are a spark of the soul of King Saul. He did not kill when told to do so, and now you must atone for this."[88] A shohet who later became a rebbe claimed that the animals came to him for a *tiqun*. Since they wished to attain the next level, the human level, it was necessary for them first to die. His master accepted this, but pleaded with him to help those human beings who needed a *tiqun*, and so he became a rebbe.[89]

Although rebbes encouraged those whom they felt to be suited to the vocation, they were still very selective in choosing a shohet. To one who was too tender-hearted, a rebbe was heard to say: "Before you will be able to kill the calf, it will be a bull. Don't become a shohet."[90] He would often caution a young man who was considering the vocation, asking him if he thought himself worthy of it. One rebbe used a drastic method to test a postulant's vocation. He took the hasid with him to "see" a man who stood on the roof of a house and cut his own throat. The man bled to death and then rose again and repeated the act. The rebbe then turned to the postulant: "This is what happens to one who should not be a shohet, but who becomes one."[91]

Sometimes a rebbe found it necessary to remove a shohet from his vocation.[92] The rebbe might also be involved in various disputes between the community and the ritual slaughterer. His task was to settle the conflict. If it was discovered that the slaughterer was at fault, the rebbe would take measures to remedy the situation. In severe instances, it was necessary for the rebbe to forbid a shohet to pratice his vocation. However, in these cases, the rebbe was responsible for finding the shohet another means of livelihood.[93]

THE CANTOR AND THE MASTER OF PRAYER

The *hazan* (cantor) who conducted services with the help of *m'shor'rim* (singers) was generally not favored by hasidim. "A *hazan* is a fool," R. Pinhas of Koretz was fond of saying. "He is so close to the gates of repentance, but does not enter; for the gates of song and *t'shuvah* are adjacent."

Very few rebbes showed any understanding of the cantor's work. They felt that the purpose of prayer was surrender to God and that the cantor's vocation, which called attention to his own very prominent part in the service, made such surrender extremely difficult. It was for this reason that R. Nathan of Nemirov was amazed when his master, R. Nahman, counseled a cantor who had been invited to pray at the Bratz-laver synagogue, to do so in the style of the *hazan* rather than the style of the *ba'al t'filah* (master of prayer). However, R. Nahman admonished the cantor not to assume his usual weeping tone on the Sabbath, since on the Sabbath one should be joyful.[94] In general, hasidim were used to the simple, fervent, musically unadorned style of the *ba'al t'filah*. However, R. David of Tolna was also known for his fondness for artistic cantorials.

The Besht was the only rebbe who trained a cantor—Mordecai of Zasslav—to conduct services. Other rebbes who tolerated cantors would not allow them to conduct services. The Besht himself also conducted his own services, establishing a precedent. By conducting their own services, rebbes were able to dispense with the priestly vocation of cantor. Or, in some cases, they allowed their hasidim to conduct services. In spite of this, there were times when a rebbe saw fit to bless a hasid with a pleasant voice and counsel him to become a *hazan*. This they did in the service of the hasid's life task. The cantors of the Ruzhiner dynasty were honored wherever there were Ruzhiner hasidim, as were the cantors of the Tolna Rebbe. Yossele Rosenblatt, the famous cantor of the 1930s, was said to have been blessed by the Tiferet Shlomo of Radomsk. The late Luba-vitcher Rebbe had one of his students, the late Cantor Shmuel Kantrowitz, assist at public functions. However, he would never allow a cantor to lead services.

The *ba'al t'filah*, who has been generally favored over cantors in hasidic circles, is known for a style of prayer that is more of a spontaneous outpouring than the controlled and prepared style of the cantor. R. Joshua of Belz once asked a child to sing at a *m'laveh malkeh*—the ushering out of the Sabbath, or the accompanying of the Sabbath Queen—and, as he rejoiced over the voice and fervor of the child's song, he asked him to promise that he would never sing any secular songs. The child promised and became famous in hasidic circles as a *ba'al t'filah*. His name was R. Itshele Krakowitzer, and he composed many melodies for the courts of Galician hasidic rebbes.[95]

In general, it seems that while most rebbes have not favored the cantorial vocation, they are not averse to counseling a hasid to pursue it when they feel this to be his particular life task. The life task is the all-important determinant of vocation.

TEACHER

The vocation of *m'lamed* (teacher) has always been part and parcel of many a rebbe's grooming for rebbehood. The Besht, the Magid, and many others after them spent their hidden and preparative years in the task of teaching. Often a rebbe would call upon a young man and ask him to teach his own children. So it happened that R. Shneur Zalman called a young man and said to him:

> Let us assist each other in the mitzvot we must fulfill. You must fulfill the command to feed wife and children. I must fulfill the command to teach my children diligently. You take on my task and I shall take on yours.[96]

A teacher is required not only to transfer information and skills to a student but also to help shape his attitudes. R. Shalom Dovber, in his "Treatise on Education and Guidance," sets forth a structure for the *m'lamed* to follow in the process of shaping a young pupil's attitudes.

Even with regard to the teaching vocation, the attitudes of rebbes have varied. Some rebbes feel it an honor to be a teacher, while others, like R. Nahman, have not wished to counsel young men to undertake the task. A teacher, in this case, was paid only twice a year, and therefore divine providence manifested itself to him less frequently than to someone engaged in business. For this reason, R. Nahman felt that it was more helpful to counsel one to engage in business, where the mysteries of divine providence were far more in evidence.

Lower on the hierarchy than the *m'lamed* is the *b'helfer* (the helper), also known as the "schoolbus" because he often shepherded the children to school. He was also likely to be the lesson repeater. The Besht served in this capacity, but there is little evidence of rebbes advising their hasidim to become teacher's assistants. It is part of the rebbe's duty to help his hasidim ascend on the socioeconomic scale. Whenever a rebbe has favored poverty among his hasidim, he has advocated either mendicancy or a small business run by the hasid's wife, through which she could eke out a small living while her husband devoted himself to the contemplative life.

THE STORYTELLER OR MAGID

The itinerant preacher, the magid, was generally a phenomenon of the nonhasidic world, where there were such greats as Jacob Krantz (known as the Dubner Magid). Yet the early hasidic masters were also often called by the name of *magid*. R. Dovber of Mezhirech, R. Shneur Zalman, R. Abraham of Trisk—all were known by this title. In the early time of hasidic propaganda, many disciples, at their rebbe's request, assumed the role of magid for a certain time, during which they traveled incognito in order to teach the doctrines of Hasidism in a role that was easily accessible to them and needed little explanation to the public.

We know of at least one man whom the Besht advised to become a storyteller and who specialized in telling stories of the Besht. One day this magid came to a town where a man offered to pay him a gold coin for every story. The magid miraculously forgot all his stories until a story came to him whose ending he did not know. This story turned out to be the story of the man's life, and when he told the story to the man, the man knew that he had been forgiven for his sins.[97]

There have been many hasidim who wrote books telling of the lives of their favorite rebbes. These books received approbations from the rebbes themselves or from their descendants or disciples. The books took the form of biographies, or better, hagiographies, and were replete with stories of the rebbes involved. When R. Isaac of Homel asked R. Israel of Ruzhin why he gave a better and speedier approbation to the author of such a biography than he did to the author of a weighty talmudic work, the Ruzhiner replied: "The author of the talmudic work writes only his own *hidushim* (new insights). The other writes about God's *hidushim*, as it is written: 'He renews each day the act of creation.'"[98]

THE SCRIBE

Another sacerdotal vocation is that of the scribe, whose task it is to write and repair Torah scrolls, phylacteries, and mezuzot. For the scribe, it is not merely the mechanical work of writing and repairing the holy parchments that is important, but rather the special holiness with which he binds the Divine Name to the script. Frequent immersions in the miqveh are the rule of the scribe's life. Only a truly pious and observant Jew is worthy of the vocation. Particular intentions must be held in mind when certain passages are written.

The scribe also writes *gitin*, bills of divorce, and here too he must keep in mind the persons for whom the bill is being written and the purpose of the divorce. This was part of the halakhic demand on the scribe. Hasidism feels that it is essential for the scribe to be consciously aware of both person and purpose in writing sacred documents. Thus, while writing the document, the scribe will bear in mind the door of the house that is to bear the mezuzah or the person who is to wear the phylacteries, and this intentionality should enhance the efficacy of the mitzvah. In the case of a Torah scroll donated for a specific purpose, such as one written in memory of a childless woman who has no one to say Kaddish for her, the scribe is to keep her soul in mind when writing the scroll.

The scribe's vocation has often been even more honored than that of the shohet.

There are other vocations that border on both the sacerdotal hierarchy and the business world. These involve business concerns specializing in religious articles. Rebbes have often aligned themselves with the producers of prayer shawls (*talitot*), the importers of holiday citrons (*etrogim*), the bakers of Passover *sh'murah* (specially guarded matzoh), and, more recently, with those handling kosher meat and catering.

Business Vocations

THE PROBLEMS OF THE MERCHANT

According to R. Ber of Radoshitz, the tzaddik is called upon more often to help the hasid manage his world and to serve as the focus for the miraculous manifestations of God's providence, than to help specifically with spiritual work. This becomes more tangible in business than in any other area of life. Even where both rebbe and hasidim frown on the manifestation of *moftim* wrought by the rebbe on the mundane level, they still talk of them whenever it suits their purpose.

There are various reasons given to account for the rebbe's degree of involvement in the business world. First, the rebbe's natural love for his fellow Jew means that he wishes for the well-being of the Jew, and that his vision opens him to the means by which he can best bring this about. Since all benefits to the hasid accrue through the rebbe, the rebbe must search for a natural sequence of benefits for the hasid. Second, only the rebbe can see the world with sufficient detachment to render his vision accurate and undistorted. Third, according to R. Nahman, the tzaddik is the banker through whom all exchanges must be transacted. He can advise in business because he is the master of all conversions from one state of energy to another. Fourth, and most important, the gift of discernment in matters of business has been given to the rebbe in order that he might lead the hasid from the level of economic help, which even the lowest-level hasid realizes he needs, to other, more exalted levels that he is not yet ready to see.

> Thus R. Joseph Isaac Schneersohn wrote to a man who was accustomed to consulting him in matters of business and following the rebbe's counsel to his own gain. This time the rebbe demanded that the hasid initiate some level of observance among his children and outlined the strategy that the hasid was to follow. However, the man was unwilling to accept the rebbe's counsel. On hearing this, the rebbe rebuked him, saying: "In matters of business, which are not my concern, you accept my competence; yet in matters that are my own specialty and competence, you do not!"[99]

The rebbe seldom speaks as an expert in market trends. Generally, he advises the hasid to buy the first merchandise offered for sale. Often, the rebbe does not even tell the hasid where he will get the money to pay for his purchase. All he does is initiate a causal chain. When the causal chain proves successful, the success story is told and retold among hasidim. Since these are the only reports we receive, we have no way of ascertaining any instances where the chain may not have been brought to a successful conclusion.

> One rebbe advised a hasid to buy a lottery ticket, and when the hasid did not win, the rebbe entered seclusion, sulking that heaven had

280   *Spiritual Intimacy: A Study of Counseling in Hasidism*

ignored him. Another, more experienced rebbe came to rebuke him, saying, "Don't tell heaven the means by which the hasid is to be helped. Heaven may have better ways." Thus rebuked, the rebbe resumed his practice and no longer indicated the precise means for gain.[100]

Neither rebbe nor hasid views the rebbe's practice of offering business counsel as anything unethical. This is due to the belief that a particular providence is in operation. In the words of a hasidic song paraphrasing the psalm in Hallel, "What He will, He does; and [to] whom He will, He gives." Still, the rebbe is responsible not only for seeking the hasid's highest benefit, but also for reminding him of his ethical obligations to his customers and business associates. One rebbe even asked a poor merchant to pray for his competitors. This way the lot of his competitors might be improved, while at the same time the hasid might accumulate merit by praying for his rivals instead of praying only for himself.

Often the rebbe's counsel in matters of business is nothing more than a bit of psychological advice. The following story serves as an illustration:

> There was once an innkeeper who sold schnapps to the Gentiles in order to make his living. However, a Gentile opened another bar across the road from the innkeeper, selling a quart of schnapps for one kopek cheaper than his Jewish competitor. Since the Jew was selling a quart of schnapps for five kopeks, and the Gentile for four, all the Gentiles began to buy from the Gentile innkeeper. The Jew was distressed at the loss of business, and traveled to the Lubavitcher Rebbe to ask his advice. The Rebbe counseled him to set out two barrels of schnapps, one marked "four kopeks per quart—like across the street," and the other "better quality—five kopeks per quart." All the people came to buy the "better quality" schnapps, though the quality was actually the same as the "cheaper quality" schnapps, and the hasid recovered his trade.[101]

> Another hasid, a tailor, sewed a garment for the wife of the *poritz*, who claimed that the garment was too tight. When the tailor who had labored over the garment came and wept before the rebbe, the rebbe advised the tailor to rip the seams in the presence of the woman, and then resew them again. This he did, and the woman was satisfied.[102]

In the previous chapter we told of the rebbe's solution to the problem of the hasid who was crowded in his small home. There are many other instances in which the rebbe's counsel amounted to psychological trickery. As is the case with other therapists, this is a perfectly legitimate part of the rebbe's arsenal.

In business, as in other matters, the rebbe may be asked to serve as the arbiter in a dispute between one Jew and another, or between a Jew and a non-Jew. The rebbe's duty is to ensure the fair treatment of both parties. Sometimes a rebbe will find it necessary to advise two prospective partners in a conflicting manner. He may advise one of the partners to seek the partnership, while advising the other not to become a partner. When asked to explain his advice, he will simply reply that he advised each one according to his need.[103]

THE PROBLEM OF DEALING WITH THE *PORITZ*

In Eastern Europe, from the sixteenth century to 1850, the country squire, a non-Jew, was the symbol of authority problems for the Jew. He belonged to the class of wealthy landowners, the landed gentry. The squire made great demands on his Jew, whom he regarded as being in a special category—not quite a serf, yet not a free man. The Jew was often called "Moshke," regardless of his real name. Many stories relate how these rival *pritzim* preened themselves on their Moshkes' loyalty and wisdom. However, the Moshke was not so much the wise one as was the rebbe who stood behind him with his counsel.

There seems to be no consistent pattern that rebbes utilized to guide their hasidim's relationships with the squire. Sometimes the rebbe counseled a hasid to play the role of a *nebakh*, a poor nitwit, in order to avoid persecution. At other times the rebbe would counsel a hasid to assume a more aggressive and proud role. It is impossible to generalize except to say that the rebbe treated each case and occasion as a unique constellation, and counseled accordingly.

As was the case with many of his counsels, the rebbe's assistance in dealing with the squire often assumed a miraculous nature.

> One of the hasidim of R. Shneur Zalman came to him for help in getting the *poritz* to extend his lease. The *poritz* had another prospective tenant who was anxious to raise the rent for the establishment and thus force the hasid to vacate. The hasid, however, when he came to R. Shneur Zalman, could not supply the name of the man who wished to raise the rent. Since there was a Jew who was in the favor of the *poritz*, the hasid felt that this Jew might intercede with the *poritz* on his behalf, and consequently he asked the rebbe for a letter to this Jew. The rebbe wrote the letter, but instead of addressing it "correctly," he wrote only the Jew's first name, along with a different last

name and a different address. When the hasid wanted to return to the rebbe to have him correct the seeming error, the *gabbai* would not permit it, and instructed the hasid to go to the person to whom the letter was addressed. The hasid followed the *gabbai*'s instructions and found that there was indeed such a man, and the man was instrumental in helping him extend his lease. Only later did the hasid discover that the person to whom he had asked the rebbe to address the letter was in reality the one who had attempted to rent the establishment away from him in order to help one of his own relatives.[104]

It is apparent that hasidim interpreted what seemed to be a mere slip of the rebbe's pen as a conscious miracle.

Rebbes themselves would often cite heroic acts of faith on the part of the *arendar* (lessee), the Jew who was subject to the squire's authority by virtue of being his tenant. One such story tells of an *arendar* who had no idea where he would receive the money he needed to pay the *poritz*; yet even when the due date arrived, he remained unruffled, trusting in God. His help came only a few steps from the *poritz*'s domicile when a man came along and gave the *arendar* an order for merchandise, issuing a down payment sufficient to pay the rent.

When no help was available to the hasid, the rebbe might have to ransom the *arendar* in order to save him from incarceration. One approach was to tell a group of hasidim a story that illustrated how God rewarded heroic generosity. The rebbe would then offer the hasidim a share in the great mitzvah of ransoming the captive.

At times the hasid had to face the problem of a competitive bid for the rent of his establishment. Rebbes were very strict in their treatment of those who infringed on the rights of Jews who rented property from the *poritz*. One rebbe openly attacked unfair competitors and threatened them with dire consequences if they disregarded his injunction. By treating the offenders in this manner, the rebbe strengthened the existing *taqanot* (arrangements) and upheld the *hazaqah* (hereditary right of the incumbent).

THE REBBE AS AGENT

The rebbe takes for granted the fact that his hasidim know him in the role of agent or *sirsur*.[105] He has often used the image of the agent as a teaching model. "Moshe was a good agent: he knew that at least once one has to bring the customer and the seller to a meeting together. This meeting was Mount Sinai."[106]

Since the rebbe is often in possession of information with regard to supply and demand, he can inform a needy hasid of the place of both demand and supply, thus giving him the opportunity to act as a *maekler* or agent. In this role, the hasid could earn enough money to pursue his studies afterward with some ease.

Matchmaking also belongs in the category of agency. The rebbe has often helped both the *shadkhan* (matchmaker) and the parents of the bride and groom. Sometimes he tells the parents whom to approach as a suitable match for their son or daughter. The parents can then send the matchmaker to make the approach. Or, the rebbe might simply tell the parents the name of the matchmaker and allow the matter to proceed from there.

In an earlier part of this work, we dealt with the rebbe's agency in mediating between heaven and earth. Here it is sufficient to mention the rebbe's role as intercessor insofar as it relates to the hasid's livelihood. For example, hasidim might sometimes ask their rebbe to bring about a change in climate. The farmer might ask the rebbe for a few weeks of rain. One who was in the lumber business might ask for snow to slide the logs into the river, and might ask later for the best river conditions in order to float the lumber to port. However, if a traveler were to ask the rebbe to ensure fair weather for his journey, when the farmer might require rain, the rebbe would not intercede on behalf of the traveler. In fact, the folk belief would have it that whenever rebbes themselves traveled, it must always rain. When it rained full force, people would say that R. Zussia and R. Elimelekh must surely be traveling.

The rebbe's work as agent and intercessor has been celebrated in folk humor. Such humorous anecdotes, however, always contain a more serious message.

> A hasid who was in the lumber business came to the rebbe to ask that he intercede with heaven on his behalf in order that he might have the snow necessary to slide his logs into the river. The rebbe agreed to intercede, but demanded of the hasid 333 rubles, which he then contributed to charity. The hasid returned to the rebbe the next year, crestfallen. Instead of snow there had been incessant rain. The rebbe asked the hasid if he had sought the help of another rebbe, and the hasid admitted that he had. The rebbe then inquired of him how much he had given to the other rebbe. The answer was "ten rubles." The rebbe explained to the hasid that he had brought his own misfortune upon himself. 333, he explained, is the numerical value of SHeLeG—snow; but the numerical value of 343 is GeSHeM—rain."[107]

This ironic tale contains a dual message. First of all, the rebbe disapproved of the hasid's consulting another rebbe. His decision to do so showed that he lacked faith in his own rebbe, producing a rift in the rebbe–hasid relationship. Perhaps it was the hasid's own lack of faith that precipitated his misfortune. The deeper message, which is interwoven with the first, is that the rebbe's intercession with heaven on the hasid's behalf is a grave matter. In asking for the rebbe's help and intervention, the hasid must be fully aware of the seriousness of his request and of the consequences he will face if he treats the matter too lightly, trying each rebbe in order to discover which one could give him, as it were, the better deal. Implicit in the hasid's request for the rebbe's help is the understanding that the rebbe can truly intercede on his behalf. If the hasid believes this, there will be no need for him to travel from one rebbe to another. If he chooses to act foolishly, then he must face the repercussions of his own folly. Typical of most hasidic stories, this story can be read on a number of levels, and on each level it assumes a new meaning. One need never think that, having once understood a hasidic story, one understands it once and for all. It is the hasid's eternal joy to learn that the story always awaits rediscovery, bearing within it the seeds of many new insights.

The Craftsman

Although the craftsman or artisan had many problems in common with his fellow hasidim, some of his problems were unique to those of his vocation. There are few anecdotes that relate how a rebbe counseled his hasid with regard to the way he was to pursue his craft. Perhaps such counsel was too mundane to be treated in the anecdote. However, we do know that some rebbes helped hasidim plan labor-saving devices or directed them to people who knew about these devices. We also know that rebbes offered counsel regarding the ethics with which one pursued a particular craft or trade. For example, the leftovers of leather, cloth, and fur were generally appropriated by the workman. In the classic story by Peretz, *Berl the Tailor*, however, we see that R. Levi Yitzhaq of Berditchev did not share Berl's attitude with regard to the leftover skins that Berl kept for himself. Similarly, it was considered unethical for the builder to keep those building materials that remained after his task had been completed.

Problems Dealing with the Government

The Eastern European Jew was bewildered by a government he could not understand. For the Jew it was impossible to believe that the same government that sanctioned pogroms and persecution was also the guarantor of law and order. The Jew who saw a brass button knew only one thing: If the official would "take," he was a good official; if he was incorruptible, he was also untrustworthy. If the official could be bought, he could at least be relied upon to be human. The Russian-czarist official was, by his meager salary and the load of bureaucracy, condemned to "take." This was no joke for the Jew who, often taking on the last name of Gold or Silver, was required to pay in kind.

Military Service

The military was not the profession of the nineteenth-century Eastern European Jew. "By thy sword thou shalt live" was the heritage of Esau. To defend a country in which one was manifestly in exile was not worth a single drop of Jewish blood, unless there were other values involved. Rebbes were glad to collaborate with their hasidim in avoiding conscription. A hasid might petition the rebbe in the following manner: "Rebbe, my son has to go for his physical tomorrow. Please pray that he be found unfit." The rebbe might then bless the son with the formula "Be well and healthy; but in their eyes may you appear sick." However, sometimes a hasid who wished to avoid conscription might be instructed by the rebbe to "Go and serve. You are well and healthy and it will not harm you. Later, you will survive because of this training." R. Yitzhaq Meir of Kopishentz instructed one hasid in this way. True to the rebbe's word, the hasid's army training and knowledge of terrain became an instrument of survival when he fought with the partisans during World War II. One hasid was told by a rebbe: "May you be saved from *goyishe* hands." When the hasid came to consult the rebbe's son, the latter said: "I see no reason for you to appear at the physical. Run away and cross the border." However, the hasid, who had made arrangements for the doctor to be bribed, insisted on appearing, hoping to settle the matter. He was not successful, was accepted for service, and had to flee prior to the induction.

While rebbes did not often counsel self-mutilation, some hasidim cut their trigger fingers off, and it was generally a mark of distinction to have a hernia. Occasionally, a draught prescribed by the rebbe would induce a temporary condition resembling a chronic disease.

Sometimes the rebbe counseled a change of name or the secret adoption of a person by a couple who had lost a son owing to natural causes. If the real son had been exempted from service, it was assumed that the adopted one could live on his exemption and in his name.

Once a hasid was inducted, the rebbe would receive him on furlough, sometimes even prior to his term of service, and give him a cameo or make a spiritual rendezvous with him for occasions of temptation and danger. R. Menahem Mendl Schneersohn I of Lubavitch delivered an address to soldiers that has since been reprinted and become a famous tract, the *Sh'ma Yisrael*. Many a soldier present at its delivery claimed that the words helped them over difficulties. Rabbi Israel Meir Hakohen wrote the compendium *Mahaneh Yisrael* (Camp of Israel) to help the soldier with special problems arising in the course of military duty. R. Hakohen issued the famous decision: "You may eat nonkosher meat; but you may not gnaw at the bones." Some rebbes even offered chaplaincy services to the soldiers. (This was not a government post but an impromptu gesture, often without the knowledge of the army authorities.)

This concern for the soldier is active to this day and was dramatically demonstrated when R. Menahem Mendl Schneerson II sent a delegate to Greenland to conduct High Holy Day services for Jewish servicemen. He also sent food for the meal prior to the fast, and rubber shoes for Yom Kippur. More recently, this same concern was manifested when Lubavitch made countless pairs of phylacteries available to Israeli soldiers.

From Taxes and Passports to the Pogrom and Self-Defense

In the area of taxes and passports, there was little practical advice that the early rebbe could give his hasid. The taxes had to be paid, and the passports had to be issued by the government. Yet, in any case where the hasid feared complications, he would appear at a yehidut to ask the rebbe's blessing. Whenever there was something to suggest, the rebbe would do so. Generally, however, it was a matter of making a favorable impression on the official, and the hasid was more confident after receiving the rebbe's blessing. The hasid himself believed that the rebbe drew down a "thread of grace" in order to help him.

In the matter of the pogrom and self-defense, the rebbe worked in an unseen world. He had to contend with the "Prince of the Nation" and with that nation's "guardian angel." All subsequent events were the result of the rebbe's ability or inability to prevail over the latter. Some rebbes participated in, or even instituted, petitionary delegations to the government in the matter of pogroms. R. Shmuel of Lubavitch even dared to tell the Czarist Russian Minister of the Interior that he would inform foreign Jewish capitalists of the government's refusal to honor his protest against its official support of pogroms. Enraged, the minister ordered him arrested; but the rebbe did not give an inch, and when the government saw that its foreign capital and image would suffer, it squelched the pogroms.

The Rebbe's Attitude toward Emigration

There was a dual attitude among nineteenth-century Eastern European rebbes with regard to emigration. Many rebbes yearned to go to the Holy Land, and a number of them did go. At least one rebbe resigned his post, leaving a son in charge, and went to live in the Holy Land. In spite of this yearning, however, there were obviously many rebbes who felt that their duty bade them to remain in the Diaspora, and few rebbes counseled their hasidim to journey to the Holy Land.

When R. Wolf Kitzes felt a desire to journey to the Holy Land, he first planned to seek the counsel of the Besht. However, before going to the rebbe, he went to the miqveh. As he immersed, he opened his eyes and beheld a vision of the Holy Temple. Entering into the sanctuary, he proceeded to the holy of holies, and there he saw an empty space. Upon asking where the ark and the tablets were, he received the reply: "In Mezhibuzh with the Besht." This story was often told as an answer to those who wished to "ascend" to the Holy Land. In fact, many of the Karliner hasidim who immigrated to the Holy Land came back from time to time, to consult their rebbes in the Diaspora. It was also the custom to travel from the Holy Land to seek a rebbe.

Few hasidim came to seek the rebbe's counsel about proposed emigration to America. Instead, they announced their plans and came to ask the rebbe's blessing. With the blessing the rebbe would pledge the hasid to observance and loyalty to his faith. Very seldom did a rebbe actually advise emigration to America. More often, such emigration was denounced with words like these: "America, the depth of evil. The streets are *trefah* [unfit]. The Sabbath is disregarded and profaned." "When the Torah was given on this hemisphere, it was dark in America!"

In general, therefore, emigration was not encouraged: "Better a dry morsel of bread in the company of the rebbe, than the fanciest repast far from the rebbe." Even today, many a hasid is willing to contend with difficult conditions in New York, the place of his rebbe's domicile, rather than seek a more comfortable and lucrative position elsewhere. Rebbes themselves favor keeping hasidim close by rather than urging them to settle elsewhere.

ETZOT DEALING WITH MARRIAGE AND CHILDREN

In a world where marriages are made in heaven, and where forty days before the formation of a fetus, his or her marriage partner is decreed, it is necessary for parents of a prospective bride or bridegroom to consult the rebbe about an appropriate *shidukh* (match). From the time of the Besht, the rebbe served as a *shadkhan* (matchmaker). It was the custom for the father of the bride or groom to come to the rebbe and inquire about the suitability of a particular match. At such times the Hebrew name of the prospective partner, as well as that of his or her mother, were mentioned. Once again, the process that hasidim believe occurs at every yehidut occurs here. The rebbe is able to see clairvoyantly the prospective partner and, on this basis, to judge his or her suitability. There is an anecdote about the Zyditchoyver Rebbe's being queried by the parents of a groom as to the suitability of a bride they had chosen for their son. He answered that it was not fitting that he look at her at that moment, as she was combing her hair. Characteristically, we never learn what happened later, since the story was told primarily to celebrate the rebbe's clairvoyant powers.

Today, when many young hasidim do not come from hasidic families, inquiries concerning an appropriate match may not come from the father, but from the bride or groom.

The foregoing is merely a brief recapitulation of what has been said earlier in this book, in our discussion of specific questions that the married hasid may bring to his rebbe at the yehidut.

Sex: The Ascetic versus the Mystical View

In order to understand the nature of the hasid's marital problems, particularly those that deal with the sexual aspect of marriage, it is necessary to look at Hasidism's basic attitude toward sex.

In the Zohar, we find a bifurcation of the kabbalistic view of sex. On the one hand, woman and death are equated; on the other hand, one who lacks both a "consort of the higher level" and a "consort of the lower level" is considered impoverished. The consort of the higher level is called the Mother, and the consort of the lower level is called the Spouse, the wife. The Divine Name—YHVH—has two H's, each H standing for a woman. There are two types of union. The supernal union is the union of Wisdom and Understanding: this union is the union of the two lovers who never separate, the union of mother and father. The lower union is also the union of two lovers, but these lovers are not mother and father. In the time of exile, their union is disturbed because the Divine Presence cannot become purified: she is always in *nidah*, the state of impurity. There is nothing that can interfere, however, with the union of father and mother.

The kabbalist and the hasid take a very positive attitude toward sex, provided that sex is harmonized at the right time with the conjunction of the Holy One and the Shekhinah. On the Sabbath, the hasid is permitted to see himself in the supernal image. Just as pleasure in the form of eating, which must be atoned for during the week, and even on a holiday, is perfectly permissible on the Sabbath, so too is the union of husband and wife. On the Sabbath the righteous person eats for the satisfaction of his soul: on the Sabbath husband and wife, as King and Matrona, celebrate a blissful and ecstatic union.

It is obvious that the latitude given to the layman, that he may "order his table as he likes it, and upset it too," is not granted to the hasid. Sexual union outside of the Sabbath and the night of the monthly immersion is to be shunned. If the hasid feels constrained to inquire of the rebbe whether he may have sexual relations with his wife during the week, if she makes all the chaste advances permitted to her, the rebbe will probably permit the question to stand in the ambiguity of "One may"; but the hasid knows that, in Hasidism, whatever is permitted ought not to be done unless it constitutes a mitzvah. Another maxim instructs as follows: "Those mitzvot from which the body derives pleasure are not to be sought in frequency." Since it is stated in the *Tanya* that even permitted pleasures, when sought for their own sake, come under the category of temporary evils, and as such are punishable by the "beating in the grave,"[108] a hasid must seek atonement for such pleasures.

In sum, there is an ambivalence about permitted sex, to which the hasidic custom of miqveh, immersion for males after intercourse and prior to prayer and study, adds its own weight. It would be a mistake to see the divergence between the mystical and the ascetical views as one that makes for two distinctly different points of view. Both views usually inhabit and create the ambivalence in one and the same person. In fact, it is the self-denial of the ascetic that provides the great impact of ecstatic release for the mystic.

This dual attitude manifests itself in another way. The Talmud describes those who manage to "contain themselves upon the belly" and postpone their climax until after the climax of the wife in order to beget male children. Solomon Maimon describes the hasidic milieu at the court of the great Magid, where a young man was beaten for having sired a daughter, a sign that he did not contain himself. Yet, at the same time, statements such as the following are made by rebbes: "I like someone who completes his mitzvah as quickly as possible." This ambivalence is noted in the Talmud, where a man is instructed not to spend much time in love play and talk, but then observes his own master engaged in precisely such play.[109] When the man brings this to his master's attention, the master explains that when it is necessary for a man to bring the mind of his wife into union with his mind, love play and talk in His Presence are not only permitted but essential. The Zohar, too, makes a statement in favor of the naked immediacy of husband and wife, and the need for their coincidence.

Relationships between the Sexes in the Familial Setting

Among hasidim there is a current saying based on the sentence: "And unto him shall be thy desire, and he shall rule over thee."[110] This statement has been interpreted in the following way: If her desire is greater than yours, then you will rule over her—but in the case of a henpecked husband, the reverse holds true. While rebbes, in their teachings, often celebrate the holiness of the union between husband and wife, and paint verbal images of its idyllic beauty, hasidim have often related stories like the following:

> A hasid once went to the *bet hamidrash*, and there he met a Kotsker hasid who remained in the *bet hamidrash* on Passover night, and, after studying the Talmud for the whole day, settled down with his matzohs for a quick seder. A friend of his, who inquired of him why he did not see fit to go home and celebrate the seder with his family, received the reply: "What! You call that a seder—to sit with your shrew?"[111]

Often the attitude of a husband toward his wife (and other female members of the family) was regionally determined.

> When R. Jacob Isaac [Horowitz] of Lublin came to visit R. Barukh of Mezhibuzh, he found the latter's family seated at the table, among them his marriageable daughters. R. Jacob Isaac was upset by their presence, since, in his own home, the women were separated from the men during the Sabbath meal, especially at the home of a rebbe. In order to avoid the temptation of looking at the daughters, R. Jacob Isaac suggested to R. Barukh that it would be better if they were not present; but R. Barukh, who followed the Russian custom and not the Polish one, insisted that his family remain with him, and rebuked the Lubliner, saying: "It is written, 'Remove my eyes from seeing vanity,' and not 'Remove the vain from the seeing of my eyes.'" R. Jacob Isaac then turned his chair away from the daughters. Later, it was necessary for one of the daughters to leave the table, since she felt her menstruation coming on. R. Barukh, who was aware of the Lubliner's magical effects, rebuked the Lubliner with "Have you come to disturb my Sabbath?"[112]

These stories are far from isolated instances. The whole problem of the proper relationship between the sexes is of great concern to the hasid even in the legitimate interaction between husband and wife. The virtues of the relaxed and peaceful family life, and the love between husband and wife, may have been celebrated by the rebbe, but among hasidim and even among rebbes themselves they have been often the exception rather than the rule. During the year of mourning his mother, the present Lubavitcher Rebbe spent every Sabbath, between the hours of 1:30 and 4:30 in the afternoon, with his hasidim. When a delegate of the women's group came to see the rebbe and pointed out how his action was disrupting his marital harmony, the rebbe did not take kindly to the reproach.

In short, the relationship betwen husband and wife in the hasidic milieu has often been far from idyllic. What was celebrated in the teachings and the literature is likely to be adhered to more on the esoteric level than on the earthly one. Even the rebbe, who often extols family life, in particular the relationship between husband and wife, might set a poor model for his hasid to follow in terms of his own marital relationship. The rebbe may be more available to his hasidim than to his wife and family; the great love relationship has often been that between rebbe and hasid. Yet, in spite of all this, the following story is told of the Ba'al Shem Tov, Hasidism's founder:

> The Ba'al Shem Tov believed that, like Elijah, he would rise up to Heaven in a storm. When his wife died, he said: "I thought that a storm would sweep me up to Heaven like Elijah. But now that I am only half a body, this is no longer possible.[113]

It is obvious that, even in the area of the marital relationship, the contradiction persists. Sometimes a rebbe has so valued the wisdom of his wife or daughter (as was the case with R. Shalom of Belzer and his daughter) that he actually sent hasidim to her for counsel or *s'gulot*. Yet at other times a rebbe has considered the least of his hasidim more important than a member of his family.

Sexual Relationship with an Illicit Heterosexual Partner

In the matter of illicit sexual contact, the relative weight of a sin and the *t'shuvah* necessary to make reparation depend to a large extent on the degree of forbiddenness associated with the act committed. The most grievous offense is one in which a hasid becomes involved in a sexual relationship with a married woman. In the case of mutual consent, this offense was punishable by death. Offenses against blood relatives—that is, incest—were also punishable by death. The least offense involves contact of a male with an unmarried female who is not menstruating and who has gone to a miqveh to cleanse herself after her seven clean days. Nevertheless, even this is a serious offense and requires *t'shuvah*.

No matter how serious each of these offenses is on the halakhic scale, it could not compare on the social scale with the offense of a man who married or set up house with a gentile woman and who begot children with her. This has been considered the very worst transgression. The extremely severe sanction against it is partly due to the kabbalistic view, according to which the life force of a Jew remains "captive" by the issue of his marriage and their progeny. In general, wherever issue is involved, both the penitent and the rebbe have considered the offense to be of far greater weight. Among the sins incapable of repair, therefore, is the sin committed by one "who brings forth *mamzerim* [bastards] into the world"; for, as long as these children remain alive, his life is anchored in them and their issue.

In counseling the penitent and in giving him an etzah to help him make reparations for his sin, there are several considerations that the rebbe must keep in mind. He must consider the halakhic breach, the breach on the kabbalistic scale, the social situation, the abiding attraction of the illicit partner, and the degree to which the penitent has dissociated himself from her. In addition to these factors, the rebbe must bear in mind the innocent partners who have become caught up in the situation through no overt fault of their own—the spouse of the one who has committed the offense, or the *mamzer* children who are unable, by law, to marry others of the Jewish faith.

In the matter of sexual sin, as with other types of transgressions, rebbes have differed widely both in their attitude toward a particular sin and in their prescription for its reparation. There are at least two hasidic stories concerning strong disagreements between two hasidic masters about the proper penance to prescribe for a particular sin. In one case the disagreement resulted in the division of the camps of the Bratzlaver and the Shpoller Zeyde; in the other case, the result was a division between the camps of the Strelisker and the Premishlaner. The unifying element, however, is the level to which the rebbe hopes to raise the hasid. If the rebbe does not aim to raise the hasid to high levels of knowledge, being, and service, but wants only to raise him to the level where he can once again be an effective agent in Halakhah, then the rebbe will be satisfied when he feels assured that the hasid has undergone deep remorse, and with it, has forsaken the sin completely so that it will not be repeated. Beyond that, there is no need in such a case for great ascetic exertion. If, however, the rebbe feels that the penitent has deep and holy aspirations, and that these aspirations are to be encouraged and raised, then the penance he prescribes will be more severe, and, in prescribing the penance, he will attempt to raise the hasid to the next level.

Sexual Relationship with a Homosexual Partner

Once it is understood that, in the hasidic milieu, boy does not meet girl unless matrimony between them has been arranged, it is clear that, by and large, the problem of heterosexual sexuality does not loom very large. When and where it does occur, it represents a drastic deviation from the general group behavior. The normative social setting of Hasidism, established and reinforced by the hasidic rebbe, discourages mixed social gatherings: dancing and even going for walks are considered improper behavior prior to engagement.

In contrast to the strong injunctions against heterosexual contact is the attitude toward close personal contact between male hasidim. Close contact of males has always been part and parcel of the cultural milieu. Males visit the miqveh together, undress in a side room, and then go to immerse themselves in the nude. Men kiss and hug one another in greeting after long absences; they drink and dance together, and they bathe together. These customs, still very much extant today, might strike the outsider as encouraging serious homosexual problems. However, although the tenor of social relationships is more homosexual than heterosexual, this acts to discourage rather than encourage overt homosexuality. The biblical prohibition against masculine homosexuality is accompanied by the sanction of death; but the deterrent is not so much the fear of penalty or the recognition of the gravity of the offense, as the fact that there is an acceptable social outlet for homosexual tendencies.

Masturbation

If heterosexual and homosexual deviation are rare, such is not the case with masturbation. Here, the person who has never masturbated is by far the exception. The average hasid has stood in need of counseling for the "sins of his youth."

The available literature does not indicate how rebbes have counseled hasidim who have difficulty ceasing the habit of masturbation, since the rebbe generally deals with hasidim who come to him after they discontinue the sinful practice and stand in need of counsel for reparation. There is little preoccupation in the hasidic system with the etiology of sexual sin: this is considered closed business. The chief preoccupation of both rebbe and hasid is the neutralization of the sinful and evil effects of sin.

There are special prayers in the liturgy that deal with the problem of masturbation; and here prescriptions range from eighty-four fast days for each masturbatory ejaculation, to immersion in a cold miqveh and the recital of ten chapters of the Psalms. In general, however, most prescriptions are derived from the pre-hasidic Kabbalah, and handed down by the rebbe to his hasid almost verbatim.

Counsel for masturbation has often extended even to methods of avoiding nocturnal emissions. Such counsels range from dietary prescriptions to prescriptions for prayer or for the location of one's shoes, or a warning not to share esoteric knowledge with the undeserving.

Although not punishable now by human agency, masturbation has, among hasidim, been connected with the death penalty.

Barrenness and Children

To be barren is to be dead. To have nobody to recite the Kaddish after one dies is to lack even the assurance of ultimately being released from eternal torment after death. Who can help the barren? Did not Sarah conceive by miraculous divine intervention, and did not the Shunamite woman conceive when Elisha promised her offspring? For the hasid, there is only one who can help, and that is the rebbe. Thus, hasidim travel to the rebbe to receive his blessing and his counsel. His blessing alone is not considered to be enough. Rebbes compare the blessing to the watering of the plant—but first the seed must be sown. To obtain the "seed" for planting requires an etzah from the rebbe.

The etzot that the rebbe prescribes in order to overcome barrenness are all of the *s'gulah* variety. The rebbe does not broach the issue of biological fertility with the hasid, and there is no question of medical prescription. The rebbe may, however, ask the hasid whether he abides by the talmudic prescription to eat fish, which increases semen, and garlic, which causes greater stimulation. Questions concerning the regularity of the wife's period, or any intimate questions concerning such matters as the timing of the husband's ejaculation, are usually not raised in the yehidut, though there are some exceptions. For example, the counsel to take cold-water baths every morning for sixty days has been offered as a means of retarding ejaculatio praecox; and various suggestions, such as the drinking of rain water, have been offered as aphrodisiacs. R. Naftali of

Ropshitz suggested that, for irregular menstruation, the husband keep his wife in mind when saying the words "They shall not change their appointed times" during the ceremony for the sanctification of the new moon. For this same concern, R. Elimelekh suggested that the husband study the section *Nashim* (Women) in the Mishnah.

Thus, rather than deal with the biological determinants of sterility or infertility, the rebbe concerns himself with the magical–religious determinants.

Hospitality

Perhaps the chief counsel offered for barrenness has been the mitzvah of hospitality. The rebbe has often pointed out to hasidim the exemplary hospitality of Abraham and of the Shunamite woman, which resulted in their being blessed with children. The great test of the Besht's father was also held up as an example—how Elijah came to test him to see how well he fulfilled the commandment of hospitality.

Hospitality is the first *s'gulah* for barrenness, since it is by the performance of this mitzvah that one demonstrates to God that he is capable of taking care of another of His children. In this sense, children do not "belong" to their parents, but rather are temporarily entrusted to them.

Shalom Bayit (*Marital Harmony*)

In order to ensure that a wife would conceive, the rebbe might suggest various measures to bring husband and wife into the proper kind of harmony. At times, the couple's inability to have children is related to a lack of peace (*shalom bayit*) in the household. Yet at other times the very opposite might be the case, and it might be necessary for the rebbe to urge a couple not to strive for too much harmony. At times, even a divorce and subsequent harmonious remarriage was counseled in order that the woman might conceive. For example, when a childless couple came to R. Barukh of Mezhibuzh after ten years of barrenness, he suggested that they be divorced, and he himself supervised the administration of the divorce. After the divorce, he called the couple back again and said: "Now get married again. This time I will supervise the wedding and you will have children." R. Barukh then explained the reason for this maneuver in a manner that sheds light on the spiritual interpretation of the significance of the marriage ceremony. He explained that, at the time of their wedding, the couple had not undergone the proper ritual in which the bride

surrounds the groom seven times under the canopy. Since man is basically
polygamous, it is necessary that the bride surround her groom seven times
in order that she be like seven wives unto him. Because the couple had
omitted this ritual at their wedding, the husband was not completely
bound to his wife, and female succubi had adhered to him, robbing his
semen of potency. Now that the divorce and remarriage had been effected,
R. Barukh was able to promise the couple children.

    Here, it is obvious that we are touching on devices that are close to
the magical, or, in other words, close to the psychology of the unconscious. The efficacy of these devices has become legendary and has
brought more and more hasidim to the rebbe to seek solutions to their
own particular problems.

Other S'gulot

    Since the problem of barrenness, and particularly that of begetting
male children, is so serious in the hasidic milieu, there are numerous
s'gulot prescribed to deal with this. In order to give the reader an idea of
the range of counsels offered, we list the following etzot, most of which
are taken from the *Sefer Hahayim* (also called the *S'gulot Yisrael*) written by
Shabbatai Lipshitz of Orshiva. The book was published privately in
Brooklyn by Isaiah Karpen, grandson of the author.

S'GULOT FOR BARRENNESS

> Be very careful in adding the additional time before and after the
>   Sabbath.
> Study Torah before intercourse.
> The woman should go to the miqveh after the Sabbath.
> According to R. Pinhas of Koretz, joy is a means whereby pregnancy
>   can be assured, for Sarah "laughed." So we find in the Torah. And
>   in the Prophets we find, "Sing, oh barren one!" And again in the
>   Psalms, a woman becomes a mother of children because she is
>   joyful.
> Mandrakes aid conception.
> To give charity aids in conception.
> To study Halakhah and to be able to act as a decisor in questions of
>   Law helps in begetting.
> Recite the *ma'amadot* (the breviary).
> Ascetic practices and the practice of humility help.
> Husband and wife must not curse one another.
> Unfair competition inhibits begetting.

Backbiting and slander inhibit begetting.

Thoughts of fornication inhibit begetting.

At times a woman cannot conceive because she is full of pride.

Recite psalms before the rising of the Morning Star.

Pray with exertion.

One should be careful in observing the commandment to build the *sukkah.*

Fasting helps.

Pronounce, prior to intercourse, the sentence, "And on your new moons. . . ."

S'GULOT TO ENSURE MALE OFFSPRING

The Midrash in *Emor* says that to one who buys books and lends them to others, God will grant male children.

For the woman to have holy thoughts at the time of intercourse helps beget sons who will be tzaddikim.

To say Havdalah (at the parting of the Sabbath) over wine helps.

To give charity on the night of a woman's return from the miqveh helps.

OTHER S'GULOT REGARDING CHILDREN

If you have beautiful children, give them nicknames that point to ugliness in order to protect them from the "evil eye."

One who has no children or whose children die, should write a Sefer Torah.

One can prevent a child from dying in his youth if the mother will, after intercourse, take some of the semen mixed with her own fluid and feed it to the child.

To light extra candles and to practice hospitality on the Sabbath helps to ensure offspring.

There have been times when a rebbe either could not or would not help a childless couple. Utilizing his clairvoyance, a rebbe might point out to his hasid that the children he would beget would not walk in the way of Torah. The hasid might still insist that he wanted children, but the rebbe would attempt to dissuade him and would not offer his blessing.

At other times, the rebbe would not agree to bless a hasid with children until the hasid fulfilled some very demanding conditions. This might involve some special achievement or an ordeal of great exertion and expense. If the rebbe could not find, in the storehouse of souls, a soul ready to become the guest of the couple desiring children, he would have to bring down a "new" soul. New souls, *n'shamot hadashot*, usually require some very special and arduous conditions in order to effect their entry into the world. The imprisonment of the father or the death of the mother might even be required.

In exacting such severe conditions, the rebbe is not establishing a precedent. On the contrary, he is following the biblical model. In the Bible we read concerning the wife of Manoah, the father of Samuel:

> And the angel of the Lord appeared unto the woman, and said unto her, Behold now, thou art barren, and bearest not: but thou shalt conceive, and bear a son. Now therefore beware, I pray thee, and drink not wine nor strong drink, and eat not any unclean thing: For, lo, thou shalt conceive, and bear a son; and no razor shall come on his head: for the child shall be a Nazirite unto God from the womb: and he shall begin to deliver Israel out of the hand of the Philistines (Judges 13:2–5).

Thus, the great prophet or tzaddik, the mighty man, became a model that the rebbe utilized in establishing the conditions surrounding birth, particularly the birth of one who was destined to greatness. The Ba'al Shem Tov promised R. Barukh, R. Shneur Zalman's father, that a child would be born to him, and this child would give two lights to the world—the light of the manifest part of Torah, and the light of the hidden Torah. However, he exacted the promise from R. Barukh that the child be brought to him at the age of three for his first haircut. The birth of Israel of Kozhinitz was accompanied by the condition that the child be named after the Ba'al Shem Tov.

One hasid who asked the Ruzhiner Rebbe for his blessing in order that he might have children, received the reply: "After 1840, there are only ugly souls left for assignment. Accept your fate, and don't ask for one of these."[114] Still, parental merit can operate in such a way as to bring down a good soul. It is for this reason that much of the rebbe's counsel is geared toward raising the level of parental merit.

It is obvious that rebbes consider their work in helping the childless as a very special task. Yet the very specialness of the task means that certain conditions must be required of the parents in order for them to merit children. These conditions often tested the parents' desire to have children as well as their ability to raise them in the manner of the Torah. The *s'gulot* for barrenness were offered more for their magical, religious, and agentic value than for their intrinsic value. If the rebbe felt that a couple did not merit children, or that their children would not grow up to be good Jews, he would not offer them a *s'gulah* and would withhold his blessing. Sometimes the rebbe would demand a token gift from a hasid; but to a hasid who told the rebbe he had no money to give to charity, the rebbe replied: "Give faith, just as Abraham had faith, and God reckoned it as charity."[115]

Difficult Delivery

In the case of difficult delivery, the rebbe was approached for intercession and for a *s'gulah* that would assist the mother to complete the birth. Sometimes a rebbe would make suggestions to his hasid regarding the procedures the hasid's wife should follow during pregnancy in order to facilitate birth. R. Elimelekh suggested that during pregnancy, every Saturday night, women should eat something for the sake of the *M'laveh Malkah* (the departing of the Sabbath Queen) and should declare that they do this for the sake of the *M'laveh Malkah*.

> Hershel Ostropoler, the court fool of R. Barukh of Mezhibuzh, once took his master's place when the latter was absent. A woman came to seek the rebbe's counsel, complaining of her daughter's difficult childbirth. As a *s'gulah*, Hershel gave the woman a penny and in-structed her to place the penny close to the vagina of her daughter.
> Several days later, the woman returned to thank the rebbe for the miraculous money. In the meantime, R. Barukh had returned, but the woman did not know the difference between one and the other. In hearing of the miraculous *s'gulah*, R. Barukh sensed Hershel's work and called him before him, asking: "What made you think that a penny would help?" Hershel replied: "Very simple. Show a Jew a penny and he jumps out of his skin!"[116]

We have here a story in which humor borders on the miraculous and the unconscious. Perhaps a more accurate explanation of the *s'gulah*'s efficacy is that once a woman is assured of her own and her baby's survival through the rebbe's visible token, she is able to relax and cooperate with the rhythmic movements of birth, and thus facilitate the delivery.

Charity is a *s'gulah* often recommended in cases of difficult delivery.

> A young man who went to his rebbe for yehidut was greeted warmly, and the interview proceeded in a warm and friendly manner. How-ever, when the young man reported that his wife was pregnant, the rebbe's manner and attitude changed immediately. Assuming a more serious mien, he impressed upon the hasid the importance of giving

charity. After this, the young man carried with him a small *pushke*, a charity box, and would from time to time deposit money in it to be given to charity. The time came for the women to deliver the child, and the hasid was waiting in the waiting room when he was informed that his wife was having serious difficulties because the child was in the breech position. The hasid took out his *pushke* and deposited some money in it, shaking the box vigorously. A few minutes later, he was informed that the child had suddenly changed position and had been easily delivered head first. The hasid concluded that this miracle was the direct result of the rebbe's counsel.[117]

Still another counsel offered to offset difficult delivery is a graveside vigil. The husband of the woman in difficult labor is instructed to pray by the graveside of some person by whose merit his wife may be redeemed from her suffering.

Infant Mortality

In order that "[hasidim] not exert [themselves] in emptiness, nor give birth to tumult," it was often necessary for rebbes to offer *s'gulot* for infant mortality in the earlier days of Hasidism. Because childbed antisepsis was yet unheard of, and virus and respiratory diseases took a large toll, infant mortality was high. Following the model of the Shunamite woman who placed her moribund son immediately into Elisha's bed and sought the prophet's help to revive him (2 Kings 4:34–35), hasidim sought the help of the rebbe. A child of a hasid was a child that the rebbe had promised to sustain in life; this was particularly so in cases of difficult delivery where the rebbe had interceded on behalf of the mother at the time of birth. If the child was then stricken ill, the mother would come herself or would send her husband to seek the rebbe's help.

Sometimes a mother who had borne a child, or was about to bear one, and whose previous children had died, would come for a *s'gulah*. In one such case, the parents were instructed to call their child by the name Alter and no other name. One father came to ask the rebbe's help, complaining that all his children had died in infancy. The Yiddish phrase that he used, literally translated, means that his children did not "hold on." Since the hasid was a clean-shaven young man, the rebbe advised him to let his beard grow so that his children would have something to "hold onto." He followed the rebbe's instructions, and all the children born to him after that time remained alive.

In the Ukraine there was a custom of "selling children." At the request of the rebbe, a child would be "bought" by a friend or relative, who would give some money to the parents. The parents would then add money of their own, give the sum to charity, and make out a deed claiming that their child had been sold for the stated consideration. The idea of such an exchange was to foil the angel of death, a ploy akin to changing the child's name at a time of mortal crisis.

Raising Children

Hasidim have sought their rebbe's help with all phases of the upbringing of their children, particularly those phases dealing with a religious initiation into a particular stage of Jewish life. The counsel sought and given runs the gamut: the weaning of a child, the name he should be given, who should serve as *mohel* (circumcisor), the cutting of the child's hair (at three years of age), the child's initiation into the observance of laws and customs, his initiation into study, and the teacher to be employed—all these and many more have been concerns of rebbe and hasid.

Children who are believed to have a special destiny in their lives receive particular attention from the rebbe, and their parents bring any special problems or concerns to the rebbe. Sometimes the parents of such a child might bring him before the rebbe at the time of his circumcision, in the hope that his attendance and assistance at the circumcision ceremony could ensure the child's chastity. Trusting in the promise of R. Nahman, "Any child brought to me before the age of seven will not sin before his wedding," the parents bring their child before the rebbe. The rebbe and the godfather act as sponsor and guarantor of the child's moral life. It is for this same reason that the first lock of a child's hair would often be cut by the rebbe. Some very special children have even been taught their Hebrew alphabet by the rebbe.

Parents who notice their children straying from the path of Torah and mitzvot—becoming lax in the observance of the commandments, trapped by the lure of the "Enlightenment" or by the attraction of another religious system—experience extreme anxiety. More disturbing is a child who became enamored of Christianity and seeks to convert, or who became interested and involved in a hasidic group other than the one to which his father belonged. In either case, the grave tensions that result cause the parents to urgently seek the rebbe's counsel and blessing. The rebellious son might himself be brought before the rebbe, who would seek to reason with him directly. Or, the rebbe might offer various counsels to the parents so that they might act as his deputies. Sometimes the rebbe has felt that the parents need to be rebuked for following a lifestyle that serves as a model for their child's deviation.

The Abandoned

Cases of abandoned wives have been numerous, especially in the past. These unfortunate women came to the rebbe in the hope that he would help them find their missing mates. Their plight was far greater than that of the man whose wife had forsaken him. He could obtain a decree signed by one hundred rabbis that would set the Ban of Rabbenu Gershom (against polygamy) aside; but it was impossible for a woman to obtain a divorce without the consent of her husband. For this reason, the rebbe's task was largely to reassure her and to indicate to her where she might find her husband. In most cases of abandonment, the couple did not become reconciled once the husband was found, but he could be moved to release his wife from the marriage contract.

Etzot given in cases of abandonment were usually vague rather than specific. Rather than describing the specific place where a husband might be found, the rebbe would send the woman to the general vicinity, sometimes telling her only the town to which she was to travel, and assure her that there she would find her husband. The manner in which she discovered her husband was celebrated by hasidim as evidence of the rebbe's miraculous powers. The rebbe himself would most likely deny the miraculous nature of his vision and dress it in some common-sense guise.

Some rebbes did not wish to accept cases of abandonment at the yehidut, since there was little opportunity for significant interaction or for imparting Torah—the primary task being the restoration of the legal freedom to marry. The Tzemah Tzedeq of Lubavitch did not wish to receive women for yehidut until his wife once declared to him that the reason for her enduring illness was her husband's refusal to help those women who sought his assistance. From that time on, he received women for yehidut.

THE BLESSING

Power, Place, and Function

"The tzaddik decrees and God fulfills."[118] The decree is given with the blessing, and no interview is complete without it. It is the stamp of fulfillment given by the rebbe. Like the final prayer of Yom Kippur, the blessing is the time of the seal. God and nature are committed to follow the rebbe's expressed wish. By granting the blessing, the rebbe recharges the energy source within himself: he needs, therefore, to grant the blessing before he can counsel and bless the next hasid.

For all the power of the blessing in influencing heaven, in recharging the rebbe's energy source, and in reassuring the hasid, its most crucial value still lies in the fact that it serves to ratify the covenant between rebbe and hasid and reinforce the latter's relationship with his fellow hasidim and with those persons involved in the etzah and blessing. It is obvious, therefore, that the power of the blessing is not absolute; it requires the hasid's collaboration. The hasid's implicit decision to abide by the rebbe's etzah is the sowing of the seed: the blessing is the watering of the plant. The hasid must, with the help of the rebbe, create the vessel in which the seed can take hold.

> A blessing needs something to take hold of. For example, the blessing of rain requires a ploughed and seeded field; but if the field is not ploughed and seeded, no use will come of it, no matter how much rain falls.[119]

The place of the blessing in the yehidut process is appropriate. The blessing could not come before the closing of the yehidut; it is the final seal. Just as a handshake finalizes a completed business deal, so the blessing finalizes the yehidut. The hasid himself need only say "Amen" to the rebbe's blessing. He need not even hear it fully. "God has heard the blessing," and this is what counts.

Once the hasid has received the parting blessing, it is obvious that the yehidut is finished. It is considered bad form for the hasid to introduce any new material at this point. The rebbe himself will not introduce new material. To indicate to the hasid that he is dismissed, the rebbe may turn to the open book in front of him. The rebbe will seldom accompany the hasid to the door. When he does so, it is a sign of his great esteem for the hasid.

The rebbe follows the yehidut with an intercessory prayer for the hasid, after which he clears his mind and "divests" himself of the hasid in order to prepare himself for the next yehidut.

The Ways and Means of Blessings

In most cases, the blessings follow the formulae of the liturgical devices for intercession. However, each rebbe uses a different formula.

Some rebbes have preferred long and detailed formulae that pull together the "teaching word" and the etzah. Some rebbes have recited the formula while holding the hasid's hand; others place their hands on the hasid's head. Some pronounce the blessing without any physical contact.

Neither rebbe nor hasid wishes to trifle with the blessing, which is perhaps the most solemn moment of the yehidut. Some rebbes rise to their feet when they bestow the blessing. Knowing how the hasid hangs on every word of the blessing, they enunciate it clearly. Other rebbes slur over the words. The late Lubavitcher Rebbe had a speech impediment, and hasidim had to strain their ears to hear his blessing. Rebbes who purposely slurred the blessing may have sought to reinforce the hasid's simple faith in God by heightening the mystery surrounding the blessing. Or perhaps the hasid lacked the information to understand the intent of the blessing—information about the future, which the rebbe has already foreseen.

Some rebbes were noted for giving what sounded like curses, but which later proved to be blessings. They explained this tactic as a ruse against Satan, who would have blocked a straightforward blessing but would not seek to block what seemed to be a curse.

The Zanzer Rebbe (R. Hayim Halberstamm) was noted for slapping some of his hasidim at the time of the blessing. The word was out that if a hasid was slapped by him on the face, he was already helped. One man, who had hoped to be blessed with children, instinctively ducked the slap; and when he realized what he had done, he pleaded with the rebbe to slap him again, but it was too late.

R. Zussia was known to bless children with the formula "May you be as healthy as a *goy*." Once again, the formula was explained as a ruse against Satan. Since Satan protected the Gentiles, he could not block such a blessing.

Hasidim do not always wait politely for the rebbe to bless them. When the rebbe does not see how he can promise a hasid the requested boon—heaven seemed to offer no such blessing—the hasid often presses the rebbe very hard. The hasid might ask the rebbe to promise that he will not cease trying, and might make a statement such as: "I shall not leave this room, rebbe, unless you promise and bless." Such insistence on the part of the hasid is not considered improper because the rebbe, in his relationship with God, has set the example. The hasid mimics the rebbe's persistent tactics. The rebbe, in responding favorably to such treatment, makes the hasid's stubbornness a point in his prayers: "See, Lord, how they insist. And why? Because they want to serve You better. Do they not deserve to be helped?"

When the rebbe has felt certain that there exists no possible opening for help, he would not succumb to the hasid's pleas. The hasid is forced to surrender to his lot. Some hasidim have refused to accept their lot and sought the help of other rebbes. At times this has helped. What one rebbe could not do, another might be able to.

Another way of forcing the blessing was to come upon the rebbe unawares. Asking for one thing, the hasid also sought another.

> A woman sent her mute son with a note to the Tzemah Tzedeq, asking that he help her find her husband. The Tzemah Tzedeq asked the boy a question and, when he did not answer, commanded him to speak. The boy began to speak, and the rebbe told him to tell his mother to go to a particular town for the fair, and there she would find her husband. When the woman's son came out and told her what the rebbe had said, she fainted for joy. When the hasidim told the Tzemah Tzedeq how he had helped the woman not only by finding her husband, but also by healing her son, he quipped: "Why doesn't anyone tell me these things?"[120]

When indirection is so richly rewarded, it becomes a gambit to be used again. The rebbe himself uses such gambits to secure for his hasidim the blessings they need. This is how R. Pinhas of Koretz was able to sue for sustenance when he could not promise health; and having received sustenance, was able to work for health. When hasidim use these same tactics on the rebbe, he rejoices that they have learned well from him.

After the Yehidut

After having received the blessing from the rebbe, the hasid seeks some secluded place where he will be able to rethink the yehidut in order to fasten it securely in his thought and memory. Other hasidim will wish him "*gut gepoyelt*" (lit., "well achieved"), or as was the case in the early ministry of R. Shneur Zalman, involve him in a post-yehidut dance—the yehidut *mahol*. For the hasid, the stress of the yehidut is now behind him. In the ease of the dance, he may reach a celebrative ecstasy and pour out his thanks to God for having vouchsafed him such counsel and given him the merit to be with the rebbe. So important is the yehidut to the hasid— and this applies particularly to the first yehidut—that "many hasidim have counted the day on which they came to Lubavitch as their spiritual birthday."[121]

When groups of hasidim are about to leave the town of the rebbe's domicile, the rebbe at times comes to see them off. The hasidim may then sing a *nigun* (hasidic melody) expressing their sadness at leaving the rebbe, and their desire, God willing, to meet again. When traveling along the road home, hasidim have often met one another and spent an extra day en route, recounting what had been seen and heard at the rebbe's court.

If the rebbe had come for yehidut to a town away from his regular domicile, which was common in earlier times, hasidim would accompany him at his leavetaking, singing melodies that expressed their sorrow at his departure. When the rebbe was ready to travel on at greater speed, he stopped the carriage, and, with another parting blessing, took leave of his hasidim. The covenant was thus sealed and renewed.

Rebbe and hasid remain bound to one another after the yehidut. At appropriate moments, the rebbe will think of the hasid, and if the hasid is sensitive, he will feel this at home. The yehidut has not terminated the relationship, but has reinforced it.

Both rebbe and hasid leave the yehidut with an understanding. This understanding is not always explicit. However, if the hasid's understanding differs greatly from that of the rebbe, the yehidut has not been satisfactory. By definition, the yehidut demands that there exist a clear understanding. Yet at the same time the rebbe knows that the hasid's understanding will not be identical to his: still, he hopes that it will not be too divergent.

The obligations that the rebbe has undertaken cover a wide range, from promising that "he who touches my doorknob will not die without *t'shuvah*," to making sure that the hasid actually receives the promised blessing. The rebbe's surveillance of the hasid, the promise to be with him in various crises and to keep in touch with him by means of telepathy—these are all implicit. The hasid knows that, at appropriate times, the rebbe will reread the kvittel and intercede on his behalf.

The hasid's understanding is that he will implement the rebbe's etzah, that he will maintain his association with other hasidim, that he will work with his *mashpiy'a*, that he will participate at farbrengens and other hasidic gatherings, that he will undertake the financial obligations in keeping with his position (the monthly retainer to the rebbe, and other approved charities), and that he will keep in touch with the rebbe by mail in order to report on his progress.

Most often rebbe and hasid will not plan the next yehidut. In part the yehidut is sought as a result of a unique crisis moment, and neither rebbe nor hasid wishes to anticipate a crisis. The hasid may discuss his next visit with the rebbe—a particular Sabbath or holiday—so that the rebbe's concern for him will prevent the appointment from being canceled by the vicissitudes of life. The rebbe will rarely indicate a time when he wishes to see the hasid again, except in the case of a disciple or trainee.

In blessing the hasid, the rebbe has commended him to God's care; the hasid, in turn, has wished that the rebbe be strong and well and has expressed his hope to find him again in health and joy.

Chapter 8

Retrospect and Prospect

Many distinguished contemporary representatives of Jewish religion and thought have proclaimed enthusiastically the renaissance of Hasidism. Such proclamations are human, useful and edifying, . . . but not altogether reliable. . . . As a religio-historical phenomenon, the Beshtian Hasidism, located in a specific time–space moment, interests us enough to observe and research it. Much in it is condemned to die. Much in it is foreign to Orthodox Judaism and cannot become united with it. But something of its teaching will remain relevant without being gilded or diluted to a vague interreligious idealism. It will serve as a yeast to give health to the dough of its mother religion.

T. Ysander (*Studien zum Bestschen Hasidismus*)

And what is individual redemption? That everyone shall destroy the evil in himself. At that time there will be the will in every man to leave evil and destroy it from his heart—and this is the "lower awakening." God, blessed be His name, will help that there shall also be a "higher awakening," and all people will destroy the evil in their hearts and there will be individual redemption and later on there will be a general redemption, Amen. No man should say that we are unable to do such a great thing. Every one has his own part, and how great his capacity is he will not know until he makes an effort with all his might.

M. Buber (*The Origin and Meaning of Hasidism*)

RETROSPECT

In Hasidism, rebbe and hasid have been united in a relationship that surpasses the demands of any ordinary helper–helped relationship. The love they experience is nurtured by a "myth" system whose range is the entire cosmos. In addition to the moral–ethical aspect of their relationship, there is a "romance" of tremendous aesthetic proportions.

The rebbe believes that he was returned to earth not for his own needs, but for those of his hasidim. To hasidim, the small chamber in which the yehidut is conducted has been called the "Upper Paradise." There they have been able, with the rebbe's help, to return to their place of origin and resume the original dream and task that had brought about their present incarnation. It is there that the rebbe reminds them of their life task and helps them order their lives in harmony with it. No other consultation room is so laden with significance.

The rebbe, in receiving the hasid in his yehidut room, is more than the mediator between God and man. He himself acts in the supernal image, and in this role receives the hasid. The Torah "word" that the rebbe speaks to his hasid is on the same plane as the ten words of Creation, the ten words of Revelation, and the single word of Redemption. It is a presaging of the last word ever to be spoken in the cosmos.[1] These moments of meaning, all coinciding and pinpointing in the "now" of the yehidut, are the transformation points in the hasid's life myth—the transformation of t'shuvah, the eternal renewal.

The yehidut is a drama of immense import and significance, although neither tragedy nor comedy; for even if the hasid's birth was occasioned by tragedy, his faith in the ultimately positive resolution of his life precluded a sense of despair. Thus the yehidut hovers between tragedy

311

and comedy—no longer tragedy, not yet comedy, but always drama. This drama partakes of the same momentousness as the High Holy Days, Passover, and even Purim (when the actors are neither villains nor heroes, neither to be cursed nor to be blessed, but merely to be applauded for the way in which they maintain the suspense).

The rebbe, as rebbe, has the power to act as producer and director of the drama. "God does not need a world, but tzaddikim like to play at leading, and He, loving them, creates a world."[2] But the rebbe too needs his hasidim. Together they constitute a troupe of God's entertainers. God is all alone, and "There is no Other to tell Him a parable and to be His friend."[3]

As the drama unfolds, we see that it is of a moral nature. The rebbe is cast as the hero, and as such he needs the villain—Satan, the *yetzer hara* (evil inclination)—as well as the victim who is to be the battleground for the forces of good and evil—the hasid. The rebbe is moved to help the hasid because he is filled with compassion not only for God but also for his fellow actors. Thus, the drama assumes a twofold meaning. Not only does the rebbe come to play his own part, but the drama is given movement and meaning by the rebbe's act of rescue while onstage.

The yehidut then is the stage and the Audience is none other than God. Some scenes are played out in the world, but the real transformations occur in the privacy of the yehidut chamber. Since the rebbe knows that the actors—his hasidim—are also sparks of God, he has the additional joy of helping Him by helping them. Knowing that he is also part of God, he does this great service but gives the credit to God who, in His subjectivity, provides the "I-amness" that enables the rebbe to feel himself as rebbe. In this sense, then, the rebbe is in the supernal image, and each man who needs his help stands in the supernal thought of Adam Qadmon.

The constant union of the Shekhinah and the Holy One, blessed be He, is celebrated by rebbe and hasid and is reenacted by their Torah and mitzvot. Just as husband and wife, as lovers, provide a sympathetic means for this union, so do rebbe and hasid. In both cases, it is the myth of *mashpiy'a* and *m'qabel*—male and female, giver and receiver—that is reenacted. The upper waters strive toward the lower waters, and the lower waters toward the upper ones. The lower waters know that they cannot reach the upper waters; yet they keep on striving, and this pleases God who is on the mighty waters.[4] The union of rebbe and hasid is not sexual but mythic, and the tryst is the yehidut.

The drama that rebbe and hasid reenact is not merely a pastime: it has social significance. In a world where there has often been so little myth in operation, where life can be harsh and its demands stringent, rebbe and hasid have played out their roles, and the harmonics showed themselves in the manner in which hasidim handled the tasks and relationships of their everyday life. The yehidut encounter has provided them with a mythic structure that results in the hallowing of life. The divine Audience and the rebbe, who acted as the stage prompter, kept the hasid *sub specie aeternitatis*. The hasid knew that he was not alone. "Behold the Lord is positioned over him and He checks his innards and reins."[5]

PROSPECT

Since the advent of Hasidism almost two hundred years ago, the rebbe has continued to serve as helper. Hasidim come to him with only life as the limit of their problems. His method of helping assumes many forms. He may help by changing the hasid's external or internal environment, or only by changing the hasid's attitude toward his environment and his problem.

During the last two hundred years, many things have changed for the Jew. The "Enlightenment" swept through the shtetl. Upheaval after upheaval occurred in the politics of Eastern Europe. Each new government represented a new menace. Eastern European Jewry has been almost wiped out; Polish Jewry, for example, has been left with only an infinitesimal remnant of its original three million. Jews in Israel, surrounded by hostile neighbors, live in constant danger of extinction; and Jews in the United States and Canada fear that, through assimilation and the low birth rate, they might vanish entirely.

Social conditions have moved from relative stability to an unprecedented mobility. Is there anyone today who began and ended a normal lifespan in the same house? Communications are global and instantaneous; human life has extended not only in the direction of life-easing innovations but also in the direction of death-dealing technology that is no less global and instantaneous. At no time in human history have people lived under such pressures, and at such a high degree of socialization and delay. At the same time, regression from these pressures has never been so readily available. The availability of serviceable, if not always acceptable modes of regression has increased our life-loving instincts, while at the same time paving the way for the crime and violence that are the scourge of the very cities that have given people their greatest power and dominion over nature.

The Survival of Hasidism

In spite of all of society's pronounced and dynamic changes, Hasidism has survived, and the rebbe and his hasidim in these huge megalopolises still celebrate their holy days in a manner that disciples of the Besht would easily recognize. Still, there have been changes in the methods and practices of Hasidism. Whereas the Besht traveled by means of "the Name of the Jumping Road," his grandchildren today are likely to travel by jet. On weekdays, when there is a hasidic celebration, communication is by means of public address systems that would have seemed miraculous to the rebbe's ancestors. Most hasidim today hold jobs that guarantee them a steady income and a standard of living that even the Ruzhiner rebbes in Europe did not enjoy.

Modern medical science has made great strides and has produced its own miracles, no less striking then those of the rebbe. All varieties of helpers are available today with skills that have placed the rebbe's miracles in a shadow. These helpers are being paid either by the client or by social service budgets that stagger the imagination. For all the prestige of the modern helping professions, however, the helper today is not as devoted to his client as the rebbe has always been to his hasid. But the work of the modern-day rebbe has been curtailed to a large degree. Devoting himself primarily to liturgical functions, the rebbe is on the one hand closer to his ideal of the spiritual guide than he is to being the proverbial "veterinarian"; but, on the other hand, he is also more incidental.

Today, many hasidic dynasties seem to have reached a biological end, and during the past seventy-five years there have been fewer and fewer nondynastic disciples who actually became rebbes. In the absence of intensive rebbe-to-be training, the outlook for the future is bleak. Will there be anyone who is qualified to serve as a rebbe?

The answer to this question is twofold. Regarded from the negative point of view, it is obvious that, if we continue to define the institution of rebbe in the same manner in which it was defined in the past, it will not be long before we can find no one to fill the position. A more positive and futuristic outlook necessitates the redefining of the institution.

At the outset, we must make clear the fact that no hasidic rebbe of today is looking for a redefinition of his role. Nor will any of the rebbes who exist today wish to consult us for counsel as to how he and his institution can best survive. The rebbe is not consciously empirical in his functioning and will not look to empirical ways and means in order to survive. Retaining his own world-view, he will do the best he can to survive in the contemporary world and to ensure the survival of his institution after his demise. There is no way, therefore, in which we can apply our findings so that they will have relevance for the actual hasidic rebbe of the future. The rebbes themselves, and those who succeed them, are the only ones who can determine their future. Our interest is in the "new rebbe" who will emerge in the future.

The "rebbe" of the future may not be a rebbe at all in the original sense of the term; yet he qualifies as a rebbe by virtue of the fact that many of the tasks and functions he performs were originally performed by the rebbe. The contemporary congregational rabbi acts like a rebbe in many aspects of his work; however, there is still much he can learn from the rebbe in order to better meet his own needs and those of his congregants. In short, the rebbe of the future is the Jewish religious helper who operates, as does the hasidic rebbe, within the realm of the myth and assumptive systems that constitute a believer's faith.

Hasidic rebbes themselves will probably survive, operating largely on the basis of nostalgia, for some time yet. They will have to keep to the larger cities in order to ensure a large enough following; but they will not likely take on the music, language, or thought symbols of the dominant culture in which they find themselves, for this would work toward their assimilation rather than their survival. Mutant rebbes may arise who will have undergone the training and discipline of a particular hasidic system, but who will have broken away in order to pursue their own path. In the process, they will have gathered followers about them who are searching for a new and relevant translation of the old values. Such rebbes will probably be more consciously empirical, and will utilize Western liturgical and symbolic modes. They too will make use of nostalgia; but it will be Messianic and projected into the future.

What the Modern Congregational Rabbi
Can Learn from the Rebbe

Myth and Assumptive Systems

Today's suburban congregational rabbi is more like the rebbe than he is like the rav. He is more concerned with presiding at liturgical celebrations and with counseling congregants than with ruling on points of law. Like the rebbe, his counsel centers around a specifically Jewish set of values. Like the rebbe, his task is both to help his congregants integrate his assumptive structure, and to help them function within the appropriate mythic structure. In order to equip him properly for this task, the rabbi's training must include the study of pastoral psychology.

In the modern counterpart of the yehidut, the rabbi can learn much from the rebbe with regard to myth making. Congregants may come to a rabbi laden with guilt feelings because they are not sure if what they believe is in line with what a good Jew ought to believe. No matter how often they have heard that Judaism is a religion that allows for a broad range of beliefs and belief systems, they have always heard it from a rabbi and therefore are convinced that rabbinic sanction for their own beliefs is necessary. Having been nurtured in a Christian environment in which "faith" and "creed" play an important role, and having accepted many of the coordinates of "modern" thought, congregants often find they cannot maintain the creed that they think they ought to maintain. When they come to the rabbi, they claim that they no longer know what to believe.

The rabbi's response may be far from speaking to this need of his congregant. He may consider the task of helping the congregant work through an entire thought structure too burdensome, and may be eager to impart his own compromise as the only really relevant and viable one. Or, what is worse, the rabbi may treat his congregant's own problem as an opportunity for intimacy, confiding how he himself suffers from lack of clear belief.

We have no wish to state categorically the procedure a rabbi must follow in helping his congregants. However, one thing is clear: he must listen. He must, like the rebbe, divest himself of any other concerns that may be clouding his mind, in order to be fully present to congregants and their problems. Only when he has truly listened to a congregant, so that he understands his or her need, is he in a position to help. This may seem like a simple counsel; yet the art of "listening" with all his faculties, and absorbing all the cues that the congregant brings to the counseling session, is too seldom practiced by the rabbi. In this, he must again learn from the rebbe. And like the rebbe, he must ask himself about the life tasks of his congregant before offering any counsel. Then, like R. Mosheh of Kobrin, he may help his congregant to say: "Would that I believed." The rabbi who advises such congregants to reject belief—when the very concern that brought them to the rabbi was their need to *adhere* to a creed by which they could pattern their lives—denies their basic need. To advise congregants to hold on to the creed when they cannot is equally cruel. But to say *Halevai she'ani ma'amin*—"Would that I believed," preserves the congregant's values. At the same time, it keeps the goals within that individual's range of yearning. Neither complete frustration nor full relaxation of all tensions makes for life. Life moves within frames of forward-moving tensions that have built-in opportunities for decompression. Yet it is in the nature of these opportunities that they are not altogether effective: the ideal is to place the congregant in a position of manageable responsibility, allowing for a reasonable amount of play between the "is" and the "ought."

But even this is not enough. The rebbe teaches a system of thought that relates to life in a dynamic and ongoing way. Relevancy is a two-edged sword. When it is so precise that it becomes reductive, it is like an epitaph: it can come only at the end, and can never permit ongoing life. The growing edge of life defies precision. Like the anlage cells, it is capable of all kinds of adaptation. Adaptation is usually the antithesis of specialization and precision. The value of imprecision is contrary to the value of precise relevancy. In helping his congregants build a viable thought structure, the rabbi must do more than help them make the operative statement: "Would that I believed." He must help them make their present system permeable.

When a system can yield to dilation and still maintain some semblance of its earlier form, it is no longer a philosophy: it is a myth. The original structure of a myth, being dynamic, changes and accommodates itself to the flow of events. Thus, when R. Shneur Zalman discusses the verse, "Teach the lad according to his way: even when he grows old he shall not depart from it,"[6] he is saying that a person's "own way" can grow along with his or her own rises and falls, and thus each of life's stations can be managed without relinquishing one's way. If, in order to serve God better, and in order to be fully oneself in this service, a person needs to think deistically—this is good. When that person is ready to think theistically, this is also good. In his own "yehidut," the modern rabbi cannot afford to be theologically consistent. If he were consistent, it would be at his congregants' expense. The working hypothesis that all people have a theology of their own that arises from the root of the soul and the position it holds in God's service, is not bad theology. On the contrary, it is good pastoral psychology. If he can trust himself and dilate his own thought system enough, the rabbi can help his congregant map his or her myths. In doing so, he must take care not to reduce the myth to a laissez-faire relativism or nihilism, or to stress a fascistic one-creed-for-all; by avoiding this he can design with his congregant a structure that allows for further growth and movement, retaining some tensions while, at the same time, relating the congregant to *klal Yiśrael* and tradition.

It is unlikely that the congregant's creedal concern, however real and basic it may be, is his or her sole concern or reason for coming to the rabbi for help. Like the Kotsker Rebbe, the rabbi can and should ask: "And what about your umbilicus?" In other words, "In which way is your myth problem, your creedal formulation, relevant to your life?" He may be wise to pose this question even before dealing with the creedal concern. The creedal crisis may reflect a crisis in life, and in designing a viable myth, the rabbi should know in which way the creed will bear upon his congregant's life problems. He may have to point out to his congregant that there is only one level of consistency to which he or she is responsible, and this is the working hypothesis necessary for one's personal life task. All other levels can best be dealt with after the problem has been solved and the rabbi returns to the level of "pure" myth making.

Still another dimension the rabbi must keep in mind concerns the liturgical action outlets that the myth affords to his congregant. The myth must be viable enough to allow for ethics, mitzvot, synagogue involvement, and prayer. A myth-theology that robs congregants of synagogue involvement cannot be good, since it also robs the rabbi of contact with them. (It may be that the rabbi will see that a congregant should renounce his or her synagogue affiliation in order to work out certain other problems, but this is an ad hoc move and need not negate later possibilities for return to the synagogue.)

In order to keep our parallel open and productive, we wish to make it clear that a rebbe never tells his hasid to renounce observance of the commandments, or, for example, to become a mitnaged. These are not viable possibilities. The rebbe may, on occasion, suggest that greater emphasis be given to one or another aspect of a situation, but the premise for the rebbe–hasid relationship remains the hasidic affiliation and the mitzvah observance required of the hasid.

At this point the constructs "terminable" and "interminable" are useful. In order to offer help with specifics, the ad hoc terminable arrangement has to be protected. However, in order for the terminable arrangement to remain effective, the ground in which the helper acts must be interminable; in other words, the rabbi accepts the client's future needs. In this way, the theology or myth does not have to be designed for all time, but only for the present and the near future. Should clients need help in redesigning their myth, they must be assured by the rabbi that this is a normal product of growth and does not represent fickleness on anyone's part. If this understanding is implicit from the start, the client will feel free to return to the rabbi for future counsel. Would that the rabbi himself were taught his theology in the same manner. It would be reflected in his preaching and counseling, and in his own openness toward future growth.

The Rabbi as Spiritual Director

In the past, when Hasidism was at its peak, the rebbe was able to refer to eschatology as a model for the spiritual "way." The hasid was helped by knowing this model and placing himself on the ascending scale. In expecting certain upsets and pains in the process of purgation, he had a system under which he could subsume his pain and discomfort. He could always credit it to the experience of purgatory. Not so the present-day aspirant. He does not expect any upsets, any anguish or pain. Thinking that he is on the way to self-improvement, he expects that each step of the way will lead to the amelioration of his problems. This is not so.

> So great a change, so fundamental a transformation, is marked by several critical stages, which are not infrequently accompanied by various nervous, emotional, and mental troubles. These may present to the objective clinical observation of the therapist the same symptoms as those due to more usual causes, but they have in reality quite another significance and function, and need very different treatment. . . .
>
> We might, for the sake of clarity, tabulate four critical stages:
> 1. Crises preceding the spiritual awakening.
> 2. Crises caused by the spiritual awakening.
> 3. Reactions to the spiritual awakening.
> 4. Phases of the process of transmutation.[7]

These categories of psychosynthesis are useful to the modern congregational rabbi in his role as spiritual director, in that they afford him a simple frame of reference within which to deal with the crises his congregant experiences in the process of spiritual growth. If the rabbi is equipped for his role as spiritual director of his congregants, he will not be taken by surprise when a member of his synagogue comes to him in the throes of a spiritual crisis. He will be able to help with reassurance and guidance. Although he may not have as clear an eschatological model as the rebbe before him, the rabbi will still be able to counsel his congregant, being careful to steer clear of the psychopathological models that are also myths, and that may serve only to confound both rabbi and congregant when the crises of spiritual growth occur.

Once we accept the *structure* of psychosynthesis, the safest *method* of interaction for the modern rabbi and client is that of Carl Rogers. The client-centered, nondirective approach safeguards the integrity of the client and keeps the rabbi from forcing his own preconceptions on the client. Even if rabbi and client share a belief structure with many similarities, the rabbi will still best achieve his end by employing nondirective techniques in the counseling session.

If the rabbi is both counselor and teacher to a particular client, he will find that the product of his teaching will make its appearance in the counseling session. In order to help the client work through his or her problem, the rabbi will have to help the client determine which part of the teaching is immediately involved.

The Necessary Qualifications

The modern rabbi must realize that more important than the so-called "professional" qualifications is the fact that the helper must be "a serious student of, or better still, the experienced traveler along the way to self-realization."[8] If the rabbi is conversant with hasidic literature and has, in a serious self-referring way, studied it and worked with the texts and method, and if he has also enjoyed the personal help and counsel of a trainer or spiritual director, he will be in a much better position to help others. It is hoped that he will have experienced the way in which time and steady effort manage to control the curves of experience. Having learned the process of his own ups and downs, he will, in the words of R. Nahman, be "an expert in Halakhah—one proficient in the forward surge and the backward draw."[9]

The Transference of Techniques and Resources

It is obvious from the very uniqueness of the rebbe–hasid relationship that not all the techniques and resources employed by the rebbe in counseling his hasid are available to the modern rabbi who is counseling his congregant. Even if they were, their use would not always be desirable: in fact, they might prove detrimental rather than beneficial to today's congregant.

The rebbe has always operated within a conceptual framework rooted in a sacral view of the world. The Jewish myth formed its center. This myth was refined by the Kabbalah and had taken on cosmic proportions. The myth called for Messianic measures, which could succeed only in small groups committed to common values.

The hasidic universe of discourse is roughly a three-storey universe. This world, the battleground of the cosmos, is the lowest storey. The higher worlds of *asiyah, yetzirah,* and *briy'ah* form the next storey, the level of spiritual worlds. The third storey consists of the Atzilic and trans-Atzilic worlds, which are divine emanations.

The rebbe, as God's agent (*maekler*), serves as the channel of connections between the worlds. It is the hasidic doctrine of the fallen sparks that gives life its purpose, and the rebbe, who in himself unites the all for God, helps himself by helping his charges. The way in which he leads his hasidim is the way in which he personally walks, and as he leads them to God, he himself moves closer to Him.

The world-view of our time is not oriented in this way. The cosmos is one, and all that takes place in it is natural. Each person has a world-view dealing with his or her own myths. Often persons find themselves in conflict because of their inability to make their myth specific enough to yield life and action directives. Other persons are afflicted with well-thought-out myths that are mutually exclusive. Unlike the rebbe of the past, the modern rabbi cannot count on having his congregants incorporate his own world-view. For them to do so might prove disastrous, as it is not likely that the rabbi's world-view will be either as stable, or as productive of life and action directives, as was that of his hasidic predecessor. The rabbi, in counseling his clients, must be more functional and problem-centered. Unlike the hasidic rebbe, the modern rabbi must counsel a Jew who is the product of the implosion of several cultures. In the past, the hasid's spiritual life-view was his total life-view: his world-view was *the* world view. Today, the modern rabbi must counsel Jews whose lives are becoming increasingly compartmentalized, and indeed his own life is unavoidably so. Many of the functional problems of contemporary Jews must be solved by bridging the gaps among the several cultures that implode on him at once. This is the task of the rabbi, as it will increasingly become the task of the surviving hasidic rebbes.

The vast changes in the world-view of the contemporary Jew have created a palpable impact on the techniques and resources that the rebbe utilized in the past; however, many of the rebbe's techniques remain not only applicable but highly valuable to both rebbe and rabbi in the present.

During the course of this work, we have emphasized the fact that the rebbe's investment and empathy, his involvement with his hasid, has been an essential part of the yehidut process. Only by investing himself in his hasid, by fully empathizing with the hasid and his problem, is the rebbe able to discover the true nature of the hasid's problem and to find within the hasid himself the answer to that problem. This is basic to the yehidut process and it might well be basic to the session in which the rabbi counsels a client. Only if the rabbi can empathize with his client and place himself, in his imagination, in the client's shoes and in the fullness of the client's being, will he be able to understand in depth what the client's problem is all about. And only after he has gained this understanding should he venture a counsel, knowing that his counsel is truly directed at the client's real problem.

The counseling process itself is dynamic; yet so much of counseling, if it is to be successful, must involve *dynamic receptiveness*. For the rabbi to be effective in his role as counselor, he must do more than merely "give advice." In fact, the advice itself is useless if it does not come, like the rebbe's etzah, as the culmination of a process, the keynote of which is dynamic receptiveness. In order to counsel successfully, the rabbi must learn from the rebbe the ability to divest himself of all concerns extraneous to the concern at hand, and to prepare himself, through prayer and meditation, for his congregant.

This quality of dynamic receptiveness, coupled with the ability to discern and interpret all the cues that the client provides during the session, are as indispensable to the modern rabbi as they are to the rebbe. Just as the rebbe utilized the kvittel, the pidyon nefesh, the hasid's manner of dress, his body stance, his verbal and other habits, as well as his knowledge of the setting of the hasid's life, so must the rabbi utilize all the available arsenal of cues in order to best serve his congregants and help them perform better in their service to God.

It becomes evident that the rabbi's role as counselor and spiritual director is a serious responsibility. If the rebbe of the past, in spite of his disciplined training and his "gifts of the spirit," was made vulnerable by his investment in his hasid, how much more vulnerable the modern rabbi, who lacks the training and the "supernatural" gifts? Still, there is no way out of this vulnerability if the rabbi wishes to perform that task to which he has dedicated himself. He must take the risk in order to be true to his calling and in order to answer the need of the client who seeks his help. But, like the rebbe, he can protect himself from overinvestment and, like the rebbe, can seek the help of God, through prayer and meditation, if he has trouble disengaging himself. But he cannot avoid the cost of involving himself with his clients and their problems. The client may come to the rabbi with a problem that masks the real issue. A client may do this consciously or unconsciously. In any case, it is the rabbi's task to treat not the superficial problem, but the real one. Like the rebbe, he must seek the root and source of the client's difficulty, and attack it on that level in order to effect a cure.

Even though the art of empathy is one that the rabbi should cultivate in order to be more effective in his counseling, the rabbi should not delude himself by thinking that he can manage his empathy as effectively as the rebbe. The average rabbi will have great difficulty managing such problems as countertransference and divestment. He does not have the *t'shuvah* resources of the rebbe. By doing *t'shuvah* for and with his hasid, the rebbe managed to take care of his countertransferences by raising them to God in the act of repentance. By completing his countertransference, the rebbe was able to identify with the hasid, and in this identification, he managed to rid himself of the negative aspects of countertransference. The analyst, like the rebbe, has to manage countertransference in his own way. Unlike the rebbe or the analyst, however, the modern rabbi may not be equipped to deal with countertransference, having neither the penitential resources nor the experience of didactic analysis at his disposal. His counseling will be most effective, therefore, if he follows a nondirective path until he becomes more knowledgeable and effective in the realm of empathy. Through use of nondirective techniques, the rabbi will make himself receptive to the workings of empathy, and once he has better understood the process of empathy and its application, he will be in a position to utilize it in his own counsel.

Another technique utilized by the rebbe, and from which the rabbi can learn, is the reinforcement of motivation and shoring up of defenses. The congregant's coping mechanisms ought not to be ripped away but reinforced, if only temporarily, and rendered more effective. Only when the rabbi has undertaken the responsibility of shoring up his congregant's defenses, should he attempt to substitute a new and more effective method of problem solving and defense for an old and no longer useful one. Obviously the rabbi will not employ the shock techniques of the rebbe. No modern rabbi holds such authority over his congregant. If he feels he does, then he would do well to examine how he managed to become so powerful a person in his congregant's life. In the contemporary Jewish congregational setting, this is not the normal case, and for this reason a rabbi should be suspicious of any excessive authority he might have in a congregant's life.

The Etzah

The etzot of the early rebbe dealt with all aspects of life: the rebbe was believed to have the answer to all of life's problems. He was believed to possess an arsenal of *s'gulot*, and his prescriptions varied according to his own and his hasid's belief system and his skill in prescribing and administering them. The more illogical the *s'gulah* seemed, the more the hasid believed in and relied on its miraculous power. Not so the modern congregant. He knows something of the workings of nature, and his expectations are cause-and-effect linked, according to natural law. In prescribing his etzah the rebbe could invoke traditional methods, ignoring the cause and effect of science. The hasid expected the miraculous, although the rebbe often denied the miraculous nature of his *s'gulah*. In dealing with childlessness, for example, the rebbe could ignore biological factors and rely on the magical agentic workings of the *s'gulah*. The modern rabbi is in no position to do this. Where he himself would consult a physician, he cannot ask his congregant to do less. The congregational rabbi is not qualified to prescribe for many of the problems that the rebbe, in the past, was able to resolve. In such cases, it is essential that he recognize his own limitations and refer congregants to the one who can best help them. It is probable that if the institution of rebbe is to survive, the rebbe himself will have to work more cooperatively with specialists in all fields and resort more often to referral. His clients will no longer have the same world-view, and their faith in his illogical *s'gulot* will not be as strong as that of their predecessors. The rabbi must be able to distinguish between pathological forms of dysfunction and those that are occasioned by spiritual awakenings: the one necessitates referral, while the other he himself should be qualified to deal with.

In order to understand the difference in the stances that the rebbe and the rabbi must take toward counseling and prescribing etzot, it is essential to bear in mind the difference in their roles as authority figures. In the past, the rebbe was in a position of immense authority, and his counsel reflected this. He could afford to make a statement at the yehidut and expect that it could not be questioned. The hasid who came to him for help believed in the rebbe's miraculous powers, which were much celebrated in hasidic lore and at farbrengens and gatherings of hasidim. The hasid was not interested in how the rebbe did what he did. The rebbe's absence from the synagogue was only a sign that he was in heaven. (A Lithuanian hasid, who tended to doubt the foregoing statement, one day "shadowed" his rebbe; and when he discovered that the rebbe was engaged in an errand of mercy, the Lithuanian hasid was glad to echo the belief of the others. When they said "The rebbe is in heaven," he added, "if not higher." Knowing what the rebbe had done, he expanded his mythic response to include the unsophisticated "He is in heaven." In his own experience of the facts, he was able to say: "if not higher.")[10]

Modern congregants are not in this mood. Their posture toward the rabbi is based on their knowledge that the rabbi is a man like everyone else, who would not have been engaged by his congregation had he shown miraculous proclivities: he would not have been trusted. Curiously, the congregant's trust in the rabbi depends on those factors that are in direct opposition to those that inspired the hasid's trust in his rebbe. Prizing in his rabbi such traits as personal warmth, effective preaching, and accessibility, the congregant wants him to be a "regular fellow." It is for this reason that the rabbi has much less leeway in his use of authority than did the rebbe. In his counseling, he must negotiate each move in the problem-solving sequence on the basis of mutual understanding. The congregant's trust will depend on his or her ability to see the validity of the rabbi's suggested move. Congregants will be much more receptive to change if they can see clearly why the rabbi suggests a particular course of action. The covenantal bond of rebbe and hasid, which created the sustained motivation to follow the rebbe's counsel, is not available to the present-day rabbi and client.

THE CONTEMPORARY STATUS
OF THE RABBINICAL COUNSELOR

At one time, Freud wanted to appropriate for himself the place of religion in the helping field; but, although his contributions have been great, they have not supplanted the need for pastoral counselors. On the contrary, because of Freud, pastoral psychology has become informed and professionalized, and has been introduced into clinical training and practice. In fact, so much is expected of modern pastoral psychology that its area of competence has become staked out for referral from medical sources. Medical psychotherapists have found that some of their patients can be better helped by the pastoral psychologist. Recognizing this fact, and noting the special nature of stresses in assumptive systems, Jerome Frank makes the following statement:

> Resolution of culturally induced stresses lies beyond the psychiatrist's powers. The best he can do is improve the patient's ability to deal with them; their correction lies in the hands of political, social, and religious leaders. . . .
>
> It may be hoped eventually that the situationally distressed or morally perturbed will come to seek sources of help other than psychiatrists, who then will be free to devote themselves to the treatment of the severely mentally ill, for which their medical training uniquely qualifies them.[11]

Referral is therefore a reciprocal matter. When the pastoral psychologist—in our case, the congregational rabbi—is aware that the problem of one of his congregants can best be handled by a specialist in a particular field, it is his task to refer the congregant to that person. Similarly, when the medical psychotherapist becomes aware that a patient suffers from stresses that are culturally induced, and not from a psychopathological illness, the therapist will refer the patient to a pastoral psychologist.

Because of this trend, it is encouraging to see that pastoral psychology is being intensively taught at various seminaries and graduate schools. It is hoped that rabbis will emerge who will make use of some of the methods and resources of the hasidic rebbe. In this way, the rabbi's office will become the yehidut room of the congregation. If this occurs, the hasidic yehidut will have made its contribution to the future of the American rabbinate, as will the institution that trained the rabbi and made the discipline of human relations available to him.

תושלב״ע

Notes

CHAPTER 1

[1]HaBaD, acronym for Hokhmah, Binah, and Da'at; see Glossary.

[2]The word *kameye*, derived from cameo, refers to a parchment amulet on which a sacred formula is inscribed; we prefer to spell it "cameo" in the text.

[3]Master of the Good Name; see Biographical Index.

[4]Preface to Shneur Zalman Baruchovitch, *Tanya*.

[5]S. Zalmanov, *Sefer Hatamim*, vol. 1, p. 9.

[6]J. I. Schneersohn, *HaYom Yom*, p. 101.

[7]Frontispiece to B. Mintz, *Shivhey HaBesht*.

[8]I. Rapoport, *Divrey David*, p. 59.

[9]Malachi 2:7.

[10]Leviticus 13.

[11]Deuteronomy 17:19.

[12]See Bakan's use of the term in *The Duality of Human Existence*, p. 15.

[13]Deuteronomy 28.

[14]*Brakhot* 34.

[15]Isaiah 28:29 and *Avot* 6.

[16]*Avot* 6.

[17]*Hagigah* 14b.

[18]Yerushalmi, *Brakhot* 9.

[19]*Hagigah* 3.

[20]P. E. Johnson, *Psychology of Pastoral Care*.

[21]Rigor (*gevurah*) and grace (*hesed*) are not only names of divine attributes but also functional terms.

327

[22]See J. Frank, *Persuasion and Healing*.

[23]Y. K. K. Rokotz, *Siah Sarfey Qodesh*, vol. 3, p. 130.

CHAPTER 2

[1]Relevant readings for this chapter are: (a) S. Dubnow, *Geschichte fun Hassidism*, and *Memoirs of the Lubavitcher Rebbe*; (b) S. Dresner, *The Zaddik*; (c) Foreword and Introduction to Jiri Langer, *Nine Gates to the Chassidic Mysteries*; also by the same author under his official name and title, Georg Langer, M.D., *Liebesmystik der Kabbalah*, the chapter "Der Chassidismus," where the formative period of a young Belzer hasid is described; and concerning the psychopathology and therapies of the Middle Ages, which in the shtetl continued up to the eighteenth century, see (d) the first five chapters of G. Zilboorg, *A History of Medical Psychology*.

[2]Some derive this word from the Hebrew root *prz*, to burst, shatter— meaning one who breaks all covenants and promises. However *purets* is an early Slavic word, equivalent to lord, that in later usage degenerated into slang, meaning "big shot." The Hebrew most probably represents a folk etymology based on personal experiences the users of the word had with the *poritz*. See also T. Ysander, *Studien zum Bestschen Hasidismus*, pp. 44–48.

[3]A. J. Heschel, *The Earth is the Lord's*, pp. 43–45.

[4]E. Steinman, *Be'er HaHasidut*, vol. 10, p. 47.

[5]See references.

[6]K. Shapira, *Hovat HaTalmidim*, chap. 1, and *Hakhsharat Ha'Avrekhim*, chap. 12.

[7]I. B. Singer, *Gimpel the Fool and Other Stories*.

[8]S. Zalmanov, *HaTamim*, vol. 2, p. 28.

[9]Heard in the name of R. Aaron of Karlin.

[10]E. Steinman, *Be'er HaHasidut*, vol. 7, p. 186.

[11]Baruchovitch, Schneur Zalman (of Liadi), *Tanya*, chaps. 26–30.

[12]Anonymous, *Nahal Nove'a*, p. 41; J. I. Schneersohn, *Liqutey Diburim*, p. 282.

[13]Hasidic reading of *Habakkuk* 2:4.

[14]*Nahal Nove'a*, p. 42; A. Kahane, *Sefer HaHasidut*, p. 149; Steinman, *Be'er HaHasidut*, vol. 9, p. 341; I. Shub, *Seder Yesod Ha'Avodah*, p. 9; Ysander, *Studien zum Beshtschen Hasidismus*, p. 107.

[15]I. Shub, *Seder Yesod Ha'Avodah*, p. 9.

[16]Naftali of Ropshitz, *Ohel Naftali*, p. 32.

[17]In *Pshiskhe un Kotzk*, M. Unger reports the following conversation between the Kotsker and Rabbi Yitzhaq Meir Alter of Ger:

"There is no exit," the Kotsker said with a broken voice. "Both of us aim toward the same point, I and Mendl of Lubavitch. The difference is only that we began with the heart and they with the mind."

"Pshysskha began with the point of the heart, Habad began with the issue of the mind. It drew us upward toward the mind and it drew him downward toward the heart. Now we have both met. Each one of us dug deeply for his way and so we met. Two different ways that we have come and now both of us do not know how to go further. . . ."

"It is easier for him, Mendl of Lubavitch, he goes toward the heart and the heart has no ground. But how far can one go with one's poor mind?"

[18]A. Heschel, *Reb Mendel of Kotsk.*

[19]J. I. Schneersohn, *Liqutey Diburim*, p. 282.

[20]Heard at a farbrengen.

[21]Heard at a farbrengen.

[22]Heard at a farbrengen.

[23]S. D. Schneersohn, *Torat Shalom*, p. 19.

[24]Gershom Scholem, quoted in S. Dresner, *The Zaddik.*

[25]This section is of importance to the reader because it deals with the assumptive structure of the rebbe and the hasid. Jerome Frank in his *Persuasion and Healing* sees many forms of mental illness and healing connected with the assumptive structure of an individual and his culture. George Kelly in his *Psychology of Personal Constructs* makes the same point when he writes that a "person's processes are psychologically channelised by the ways in which he anticipates events." The cognitive element in the management of the mind is more important than an unsophisticated reading of the Freudian view would have it. R. B. Laing and T. Szasz, each in ways significant to his own system, make use of the assumptive structure of a patient. So do Osmond and El-Meligi who, in order to facilitate the clinical work, have designed an *Experiential World Inventory* (1966) so that the clinician may have access to the assumptive structure of the patient.

Frank shows how religious healing depends on the assumptive structure of the healer and the patient. In this sense we have hoped to make the hasidic assumptive structure available to the reader for greater insight.

For documentation for this section, see vol. 1 of Lachover and Tishby's *Mishnat HaZohar* (Jerusalem: Mossad Bialik, 1957); vol. 2 of Tishby's *Mishnat HaZohar*, published 1962; Cordovero's *Tomer Devorah*; Luria's (Vital's) *Etz Hayim*; and R. Schneur Zalman's *Torah Or* and *Liqutey Torah*. This last volume in its latest edition has excellent indexes and footnotes. All I have done here is summarize and organize this material. Our task here is not to expound the world-view of the hasid per se; our task is to bring to bear the influence of this world-view on counseling and the yehidut. We shall have done what we set out to do if the readers can orient themselves sufficiently in the world-view to understand how, why, and where it enters into the hasid–rebbe relationship. In some cases, however, where an idea is mentioned and is not generally found in the literature, I feel responsible for documentation and offer it.

See especially the sixth lecture in G. Scholem's *Major Trends in Jewish Mysticism* (New York, Schocken Publishing House, 1941).

[26]Heard from the present Lubavitcher Rebbe in a talk given to Hillel directors.

[27]I. Berger, *Eser Zahzahot*, p. 23.

[28]M. Buber, *Tales of the Hasidim: Later Masters*, p. 269.

[29]Heard at a farbrengen; see J. Kaidaner, *Sipurim Noraim*, p. 47, and K. Shapira, *Esh Qodesh*, p. 11 of the biography.

[30]M. M. Schneerson, *HaYom Yom*, p. 40.

[31]*Brakhot* 12b.

[32]M. Buber, *Tales of the Hasidim: Early Masters*, p. 66.

[33]*Brakhot* 7b.

[34]*Zohar*, vol. 1, 217b.

[35]R. Nahman, *Nahal Nove'a*, p. 42.

[36]E. Steinman, *Mishnat Habad*, vol. 1, p. 62.

[37]Preface to *Tanya*.

[38]M. Buber, *Tales of the Hasidim: Early Masters*, p. 313.

[39]Notes for a lecture by J. I. Schneersohn, *Quntres* 79, *Shavuot*.

[40]Isaiah 63:9.

[41]I. Rapoport, *Divrey David*, p. 6.

[42]S. Zalmanov, *Sefer HaTamim*, vol. 1, p. 12.

[43]Heard.

[44]*Tanya*, chap. 2.

[45]A. Kahane, *Sefer HaHasidut*, p. 66.

[46]R. A. Roth, *Sefer Shomer Emunim*, p. 244.

CHAPTER 3

[1]See Unger's *Hasidus Un Lebn*, S.V. "R. Meirl Premishlaner"; see also *Nahal Nove'a*, p. 266 and compare with Louis Newman and Samuel Spitz, *The Hasidic Anthology*, p. 274.

[2]M. M. Schneerson, *HaYom Yom*, p. 41.

[3]Rashi on Genesis 33:18.

[4]Preface to M. C. Luzzatto, *Mesilat Yesharim*.

[5]*Zohar Vayikra*, p. 81.

[6]See *Kerem Yisrael* and I. Safrin, *Megilat Setarim*, p. 8.

[7]M. Unger, *Hasidus un Lebn*, p. 186.

[8]Based on *Hagigah* 2a, *Hulin* 110a.

[9]Heard at a farbrengen.

[10]*Nedarim* 64b.

[11]C. Bloch, *Aus Miriam's Brunnen*, p. 74; H. M. Perlow, *Liqutey Sipurim*, p. 61.

[12]J. Kaidaner, *Sipurim Noraim*, p. 55.

[13]E. Brandwein, *Degel Mahaneh Yehudah*, p. 55.

[14]R. Kahan, *Shmu'ot Vesipurim*, p. 34.

[15]J. Kaidaner, *Sipurim Noraim*, p. 30.

[16]Ibid., p. 48.

[17]Belz, *Sefer HaHasidut*, vol. 2, p. 252.

[18]J. Kaidaner, *Sipurim Noraim*, p. 47; Y. Rokotz, *Siah Sarfey Qodesh*, p. 49.

[19]I. Rapoport, *Divrey David*, p. 43, A. Kahane, *Shmu'ot Vesipurim*, p. 22.

[20]Preface to Dov Baer Schneori, *Poqeah Ivrim*.

[21]A. Kahane, *Sefer HaHasidut*, pp. 225, 234; M. H. Kleinman, *Or Yesharim*, p. 4.

[22]A. Kahane, *Sefer HaHasidut*, pp. 37, 47; I. Berger, *Eser Orot*, p. 131; Y. Rokotz, *Siah Sarfey Qodesh*, vol. 2, p. 10; R. U. Bronfenbrenner, *Or Olam*, p. 191; *Nahal Nove'a*, p. 107; Belz, *Sefer HaHasidut*, pp. 275, 291.

[23]J. I. Schneersohn, *Liqutey Diburim*, p. 282.

[24]Levi Yitzhaq of Berditchev was a threat to Satan, who permitted his soul to descend only if Levi Yitzhaq would serve as communal rabbi. Thus his influence to change lives would be diminished. See Kalisch, Zvi Elimelech of Muncazc, *Toldot R. Levi Yitzhaq*, in *Qedushat Levi*, p. 150b.

[25]*Brakhot* 34b.

[26]M. Unger, *Hasidus un Lebn*.

[27]J. I. Schneersohn, *Liqutey Diburim*, p. 282.

[28]*Hagigah*, 13a.

[29]A. Kahane, *Sefer HaHasidut*, pp. 36, 83; E. Steinman, *Be'er HaHasidut*, vol. 10, p. 144ff.

[30]Heard.

[31]Deuteronomy 18:15.

[32]Deuteronomy 13:2.

[33]A. Kahane, *Sefer HaHasidut*, p. 63.

[34]Ibid., p. 83.

[35]*Seder HaDorot HaHadash*, p. 2; A. Kahane, *Sefer HaHasidut*, p. 83.

[36]"They peek into the *Etz Hayim* and think they can fly around Heaven," R. U. Bronfenbrenner, *Imrey Qodesh*, p. 207.

[37]I. B. Radoshitz, *Niflaot Hasaba*, p. 16.

[38]H. M. Hielman, *Sefer Beyt Rabi*, p. 6.

[39]*Liqutey Sipurim*, p. 42.

[40]E. Steinman, *Be'er HaHasidut*, vol. 9, p. 288.

[41]Anonymous, *Nahal Nove'a*, p. 228.

[42]I. Rapoport, *Divrey David*, p. 6.

[43]E. Steinman, *Be'er HaHasidut*, vol. 9, p. 299.

[44]E. Steinman, *Be'er HaHasidut: Mishnat Habad*, vol. 2, p. 176.

[45]Y. Rokotz, *Siah Sarfey Qodesh*, p. 57.

[46]E. Steinman, *Be'er HaHasidut*, vol. 10, p. 203.

[47]C. Bloch, *Aus Miriam's Brunnen*, p. 74.

[48]Belz, *Sefer HaHasidut*, vol. 2, p. 252.

[49]Anonymous, *Nahal Nove'a*, p. 68; Steinman, *Be'er HaHasidut*, vol. 10, p. 203; *Siah Sarfey Qodesh*, vol. 2, p. 20.

[50]G. Scholem, *Major Trends in Jewish Mysticism*, p. 349; M. Kleinman, *Or Yesharim*, p. 41.

[51]Deuteronomy 18:15.

[52]Exodus 33:19.

[53]Hosea 14:5.

[54]2 Chronicles 33.

[55]2 Kings 5.

[56]D. Friedman, *Magid Devarav LeYa'aqov*, p. 6.

[57]E. Steinman, *Be'er HaHasidut*, vol. 9, p. 289.

[58]*Tanya*, Igrot no. 27.

[59]Zohar quoted in *Tanya*, p. 292.

[60]M. Kleinman, *Or Yesharim*, p. 46.

[61]J. I. Schneersohn, *Liqutey Diburim*, vol. 4, p. 1510; A. Roth, *Sefer Uvda d'Aharon*, p. 62.

[62]H. Greenberg (*The Inner Eye*, p. 67) thinks, perhaps unfairly, that they are parasites.

[63]M. Buber, *Tales of the Hasidim: Early Masters*, p. 100.

[64]See preface to D. Schneori, *Poqeah Ivrim*.

[65]D. Schneori, *Tract on Ecstasy*, Preface.

[66]Based on Exodus 18:21.

[67]*Rosh Hashanah* 28b.

[68]*Tanya*, chap. 2.

[69]*Zohar Vayiqra*, p. 53; *Liqutey Torah*, vol. 3, p. 2d.

[70]Heard.

[71]*Avot* 1:12.

[72]Preface to D. Schneori, *Poqeah Ivrim*.

[73]Based on Esther 2:12; this usage is recorded in *HaTamim*, vol. 1, p. 75.

CHAPTER 4

[1]Besides the intended pun—that the rebbe-to-be is married to a young woman from another rebbe's family—the training is at once more formal and stylized than professional training and, on the other hand, less academic and professional than is usual in the helping professions. Given that a rebbe-to-be is the scion of a dynasty, he is groomed like a crown prince to the crown, and instead of royal chamberlains there are special hasidim who will either, on the appointment of the previous rebbe or by consent of the other hasidim (if the previous rebbe is dead), groom the rebbe-to-be in the ways of the court. R. Berele, the present Belzer Rebbe, is a case in point. His uncle, the late R. Arele, died. His own children were killed by the Nazis. His brother, R. Mordecai of Bilgoray, left a little son, whose mother was unwilling at first to have the Belzer hasidim groom her child. Yet at their insistence she relented. The child was groomed by a special cadre of Belzer hasidim and was later married to the granddaughter of the Vizhnitzer Rebbe of B'nai B'raq. His grandfather-in-law trained him in the special skills of a rebbe, while the elders of Belz groomed him in the special ancestral Belzer forms.

Old Belzer hasidim who have since encountered the new Belzer consider the grooming to have been successful.

[2]A. Roth, *Sefer Uvda d'Aharon*, p. 24.

[3]E. Steinman, *Be'er HaHasidut*, vol. 3, p. 50.

[4]M. Buber, *Tales of the Hasidim: Later Masters*, p. 276.

[5]Leviticus 6:2. (The letter *mem* is written in smaller size according to the *Massorah*.)

[6]See G. Heard, *Five Ages of Man*, p. 42.

[7]*Avot* 4:1.

[8]A. Roth, *Sefer Uvda d'Aharon*, p. 20.

[9]Ibid.

[10]*Zettel Qatan*, taken from *Sefer No'am Elimelekh* by R. Elimelekh of Lizhensk.

[11]H. Hielman, *Beyt Rabi*, p. 112.

[12]Heard; R. Shneur Zalman said: "My brother records my teachings as I *say* them, my son as I *mean* them, and my grandson as I say them *and* as I mean them."

[13]J. I. Schneersohn, *Liqutey Diburim*, p. 154.

[14]Ibid.

[15]Ibid.

[16]*Qhilah* and *edah* (congregation) are both feminine words.

[17]One of the activities banned by Rabbenu Gershom (known as the Light of the Exile) was the reading of people's mail. In order to impress a person carrying a letter with the urgency to keep the contents of a letter unread, the writer of the letter would mark the envelope B"HADRA"G, to indicate that it was private and personal (*BeHerem D'Rabbenu Gershom*). By sealing the book with such a mark and adding that the ban will not be removed in the next world, R. Shneur Zalman wanted to ensure that no one would read the book.

[18]Heard at a farbrengen.

[19]M. Buber, *Legend of the Besht*; S. Zalmanov, *HaTamim*, vol. 1, Letters; A. Kahane, *Sefer HaHasidim*, p. 29; B. Mintz, *Shivhey HaBesht*, p. 44.

[20]Hayim Yosef David Azulai, *Avodat HaQodesh*.

[21]The present Lubavitcher Rebbe during the shiv'ah for his father-in-law, the late Rabbi Joseph Isaac Schneersohn.

[22]R. Katz, *Empathy*, p. 66.

[23]M. Buber, *Tales of the Hasidim: Early Masters*, p. 107.

[24]A. Roth, *Sefer Uvda d'Aharon*, p. 21.

[25]Preface to Schneori, *Poqeah Ivrim*.

[26]E. Steinman, *Sefer Be'er HaHasidut*, vol. 9, p. 211.

[27]Ezekiel Rothenberg and Moses Shanefeld, *HaRabi Mikotsk V'shiyshiym Giborim, Saviv Lo*, p. 375.

[28]*Nahal Nove'a*, p. 42.

[29]Heard at a farbrengen.

[30]M. Buber, *Tales of the Hasidim: Later Masters*, p. 87.

[31]M. Buber, *For the Sake of Heaven*, p. 37.

[32]*Liqutey Sipurim*, p. 80.

[33]This is how he interpreted the portion of the *Brikh Shmeyh* prayer, *l'mehevey ana pqida* (the overseer, *paqid*) *b'goy zadiqaya*.

[34]A. Kahane, *Sefer HaHasidut*, p. 319.

[35]E. Steinman, *Be'er HaHasidut*, vol. 9, p. 317.

[36]Ibid., p. 101.

[37]Ibid., p. 289.

[38]Anonymous, *Nahal Nove'a*, p. 38.

[39]Ibid., p. 37.

[40]E. Steinman, *Be'er HaHasidut*, vol. 9, p. 346.

[41]Heard at a farbrengen.

[42]Heard at a farbrengen.

[43]*Tanya*, p. 30.

[44]One of the rebbes of the Vurker dynasty left Poland to go to the Holy Land and left his son in charge.

[45]Y. K. K. Rokotz, *Siah Sarfey Qodesh*, p. 131.

[46]Ibid., p. 58.

[47]R. Nahman of Bratzlav, *Liqutey Tinyana*, p. 20.

[48]I. Berger, *Eser Zahzahot*, p. 112.

[49]The Lentchner in Mordecai of Lekhovitz, *Torat Avot*, p. 34.

[50]Anonymous, *Nahal Nove'a*, p. 32.

[51]M. Buber, *For the Sake of Heaven*, p. 64.

[52]I. Rapoport, *Divrey David*, p. 55.

[53]I. Berger, *Eser Zahzahot*, p. 108.

[54]S. Zalmanov, *HaTamim*, Letters, no. 152.

[55]J. I. Schneersohn, *Liqutey Diburim*.

[56]Ibid., p. 4.

[57]H. Hesse, *Siddhartha*, at the conclusion of the book.

[58]See "A Letter about Faith" in A. J. Heschel, *God in Search of Man*.

[59]*Ibid*.

[60]J. I. Schneersohn, *R'shimah* in *Liqut 79*.

[61]A. Kahane, *Sefer HaHasidut*, p. 334.

[62]I. Berger, *Eser Orot*, p. 43.

[63]*Imrey Qodesh*, p. 64.

[64]M. Kleinman, *Or Yesharim*, p. 96.

[65]Ibid., p. 27.

[66]E. Steinman, *Be'er HaHasidut* vol. 9, p. 334.

[67]*Nahal Nove'a*, p. 101.

[68]Ibid., p. 43.

[69]U. Bronfenbrenner, *Or Olam*, p. 202.

[70]Ibid., p. 190.

[71]A. Roth, *Sefer Uvda d'Aharon*, p. 27.

[72]*Or Yesharim*, p. 164.

[73]Y. Rokotz, *Siah Sarfey Qodesh*, p. 29.

[74]M. Unger, *Besht*, p. 369.

[75]A. Kahane, *Sefer HaHasidut*, p. 114.

[76]*Tzadiq—yesod* is the sixth *s'firah* and therefore rebbes were often called to read the sixth portion. To call another in his presence to his *aliyah* was to ordain him.

[77]Belz, *Sefer HaHasidut*, vol. 2, p. 268.

[78]Y. Rokotz, *Siah Sarfey Qodesh*, p. 30.

[79]R. Nahman of Bratzlav, *Liqutey Tinyana*, p. 20.

[80]E. Steinman, *Be'er HaHasidut: Mishnat Habad*, vol. 1, p. 263.

[81]R. Kahan, *Shmu'ot Vesipurim*, p. 124.

[82]Heard.

[83]E. Steinman, *Be'er HaHasidut*, vol. 9, p. 309.

[84]Ibid.

CHAPTER 5

[1]In writing this chapter we have been strongly aware of E. Goffman's *Encounters* and R. L. Katz's *Empathy*. Steinman has gathered some material under the heading *Yehidut* in vol. 2 of *Mishnat Habad*, p. 167.

[2]M. M. Schneerson, *HaYom Yom*, p. 86.

[3]Heard from a *mashpiy'a* ((Rabbi Israel Jacobson).

[4]In all likelihood the term *yehidut* began to be used in Lyozhna. Among the *taqanot* (*Igrot Ba'al HaTanya*, p. 58) there were some in relation to entering for a private interview (see p. 60, op. cit.) and the word *yehidut* is used. The same term is also used in the introduction to the *Tanya*.

[5]A. Kahane, *Shmu'ot Vesipurim*, p. 89; Anonymous, *Nahal Nove'a*, p. 40.

[6]*Tanya*, p. 2.

[7]S. Baruchovitz, *Liqutey Torah*, vol. 3, p. 3c.

[8]E. Steinman, *Sefer Be'er HaHasidut, Mishnat Habad*, vol. 2, p. 85.

[9]A. Kahane, *Sefer HaHasidut*, p. 148.

[10]E. Steinman, *Sefer Be'er HaHasidut, Mishnat Habad*, vol. 1, p. 65.

[11]Ibid.

[12]E. Steinman, *Sefer Be'er HaHasidut*, vol. 9, p. 298.

[13]J. I. Schneersohn, *Liqutey Diburim*, p. 85.

[14]Ibid.

[15]From the Slavic *spraviat* (to celebrate) and *pravitch* (to govern, direct, steer and correct).

[16]Bentchen, a contraction from the Latin *benedicere*.

[17]See G. Hager, *Hemdah Genuzah*, p. 15 for the Besht's own kvittel.

[18]Based on the psalmist's "I am thy servant, the son of thy maid."

As R. Nahman says: "When praying it is good to deal with that which is certain, and the father is an act of faith but the mother is certain." Thus, while the body is reckoned after the father, the soul is reckoned after the mother.

[19]See A. Kahane, *Shmu'ot Vesipurim*, p. 72 for a sample of a kvittel. It is

rather difficult to trace the origin of the kvittel. We conjecture that little notes and petitions were stuffed into the walls of holy places and left at graves in the Holy Land. Originally the pilgrim-tzaddik on his way to the Holy Land would take such kvittlekh along on his journey. Hasidim would thus consider their rebbes as holy places too, as the following tale recounts:

R. Wolf Kitzes wanted to go to the Holy Land. As he went to dip in the miqveh, he found himself in Jerusalem. He dipped again, and he found himself in the *bet hamidrash*. He dipped once more and found himself in the Holy of Holies and looked for the ark, and he saw that it was not there. So, he asked the prophet Elijah: "Where is the ark and where are the *luhot*, the tablets of law?" Elijah replied: "They are in Mezhibuzh, where the Besht lives."

According to Unger (*Hasidus un Lebn*, p. 133), the Ba'al Shem Tov had not yet begun the custom of taking kvittlekh and ransom money from his hasidim. Unger quotes the *Devarim Arevim*, chap. 4: "He never took a pidyon, a ransom or a kvittel from anyone, but the congregation gave him a certain amount from their account. However, even when hasidim came to the Ba'al Shem Tov they would remind him of their name and their mother's name."

[20]I. Rapoport, *Divrey David*, p. 42.

[21]Ibid.

[22]Ibid., p. 64.

[23]E. Steinman, *Be'er HaHasidut*, vol. 9, p. 341.

[24]I. Shub, *Yesod Ha'Avodah*, p. 9.

[25]Numbers 3:47.

[26]C. Bloch, *Aus Miriam's Brunnen*, p. 164.

[27]Belz, *Sefer HaHasidut*, vol. 2, p. 292.

[28]Heard; cf. Belz, *Sefer HaHasidut*, vol. 2, p. 292.

[29]F. Schneersohn, *Hayim Grawitzer*, p. 201.

[30]Y. Rokotz, *Siah Sarfey Qodesh*, p. 74; E. Steinman, *Be'er HaHasidut*, vol. 10, pp. 68 and 97.

[31]Belz, *Sefer HaHasidut*, vol. 2, p. 234.

[32]Ibid., p. 259; compare with I. M. Padua, *Or HaNer*, p. 23.

[33]A. Kahane, *Shmu'ot Vesipurim*, p. 57.

[34]When the Zyditchover came to the Lubliner, he read his kvittel and said: "Your initials make ABYA [the four worlds Azilut, Briy'ah, Yezirah, and Assiyah], you will be a rebbe." Or when this writer came to the Bobover, he said: "Meshullam Zalman Hakohen makes Mazeh. Mazeh ben Mazeh" [an allusion to a *Kohen* who sprinkles blood on the altar; see *Brakhot* 28a].

[35]Heard.

[36]Belz, *Sefer HaHasidut*, vol. 2, p. 252.

[37]M. Unger, *Rabbi Israel: Ba'al Shem Tov*, p. 369.

[38]*Vayiqra Rabbah*, p. 13.

[39]Ibid., p. 66.

[40]Genesis 2:7.

[41]*Tanhuma, Beshalah*, p. 9.

[42]S. Zalmanov, *HaTamim*, vol. 7, p. 28.

[43]S. Baruchovitch, *Liqutey Torah*, vol. 3, p. 1a.

[44]P. Shapiro of Koretz, *Midrash Pinhas*, p. 6.

[45]Heard from the Bobover in the Apter's name: "I wish my hasidim came to me in their weekday clothes; all dressed in their Sabbath finery, how can I help them where they hurt?"

[46]*Bereshit Rabbah*, p. 53.

[47]Heard.

[48]Heard.

[49]J. I. Schneersohn, "Quntres Klaley HaHinukh VehaHadrakhah," in *Quntres Hay Elul*, p. 62.

[50]Heard.

[51]J. I. Schneersohn, op. cit., p. 63.

[52]Ibid., p. 64.

[53]See story quoted on p. 136.

[54]S. Schneersohn, *Quntres Uma'ayan, MiBeyt HaShem*, p. 62.

[55]Heard.

[56]Genesis 8:21.

[57]Ecclesiastes 4:13.

[58]Discussed in *Tanya*, chap. 12.

[59]*Tanya*, chap. 5.

[60]S. Z. Baruchovitch, *Hilkhot Talmud Torah*.

[61]S. Baruchovitch, *Liqutey Torah*, vol. 3, p. 37d.

[62]*Tanya*, chap. 5; *Liqutey Torah*, vol. 3, p. 48d.

[63]*Tanya*, chap. 8.

[64]Heard from Rabbi M. Schwartzman.

[65]*Berakhot* 7a.

[66]*Tanya*, chap. 40.

[67]J. I. Schneersohn, *Liqutey Diburim*, p. 1434.

[68]M. M. Schneerson, *HaYom Yom*, p. 5.

[69]S. Baruchovitch, *Liqutey Torah*, vol. 5, p. 13b.

[70]J. I. Schneersohn, *Liqutey Diburim*, p. 59.

[71]J. I. Schneersohn, *Principles of Education and Guidance*, chap. 4.

[72]*Berakhot* 61a.

[73]Heard from Rabbi M. Schwartzman.

[74]Pinhas Shapiro of Koretz, *Midrash Pinhas*, p. 10.

[75]L. Newman and S. Spitz, *Hasidic Anthology*, p. 327.

[76]Ibid., p. 335.

[77]Psalm 34:9.

[78]S. Baruchovitch, *Liqutey Torah*, vol. 3, p. 79a.

[79]Ibid., vol. 4, p. 34c.

[80]S. Baruchovitch, *Liqutey Sipurim*, p. 45.

[81]Besht, in a letter printed as an appendix to *Toldot*.

[82]M. Buber, *Tales of the Hasidim: Early Masters*, p. 269.

[83]S. B. Schneersohn, *Quntres Hat'filah*, chap. 4.

[84]*Tanya*, chap. 14.

[85]S. Baruchovitch, *Sipurey Ha'Ari*, p. 44.

[86]Heard from Rabbi M. Schwartzman.

[87]Heard at a farbrengen.

[88]Heard at a farbrengen.

[89]*Avodah Zarah*, 19a.

[90]J. I. Schneersohn, *Education and Guidance*, chap. 10.

CHAPTER 6

[1]From the High Holiday Service.

[2]S. D. Schneersohn, *Quntres Uma'ayan, MiBeyt HaShem*, chap. 2.

[3]J. I. Schneersohn, *Klaley HaHinukh VehaHadrakhah*, vol. 1.

[4]*Tanya*, chap. 46.

[5]Ze'ev Volf of Zhitomir, *Or HaMeir*, "The Sons of My Mother," and R. Nahman's tale of the snuffbox as told by Peretz in *Hasidic Tales*.

[6]S. D. Schneersohn, *Torat Shalom: Sefer HaSihot*, p. 5.

[7]See A. Hayman, *Otzar Divrey HaHakhamim Upithgameyhem*, p. 524, for a discussion of the origin of this phrase.

[8]Mordecai of Lehovitz et al., *Torat Avot*, p. 240.

[9]*Tanya*, chap. 2.

[10]M. Kleinman, *Or Yesharim*, p. 5.

[11]Berger, I. "Eser Qedoshot," in *Sefer Zekhut Yisrael*, p. 19.

[12]Belz, *Sefer HaHasidut*, vol. 2, p. 252.

[13]M. Buber, *Tales of the Hasidim: Early Masters*, p. 221.

[14]Ibid., p. 75.

[15]*Torat Avot*, p. 241.

[16]*Tanya*, preface to Part II.

[17]Heard at farbrengen; see also E. Steinman, *Be'er HaHasidut: Besht*, p. 186.

[18]S. Y. Agnon, "L'ahar Has'udah," in *Lifnim Min HaHomah*, p. 263.

[19]V. E. Frankl, *The Doctor and the Soul*, p. 105.

[20]Nathan of Nemirov, ed., *Meshivat Nefesh*, p. 75.

[21]Mishnah commentary to *Sanhedrin* 10.

[22]*Avot* 2:4.

[23]J. I. Schneersohn, "*Quntres* Im Ru'ach HaMoshel."

[24]Menahem Mendl Schneerson II, *Sefer Toldot Maharash*, p. 20.

[25]Compare Berger, *Eser Zahzahot*, p. 86.

[26]See the biography at the end of Shapira, *Esh Qodesh*, p. 11.

[27]R. Katz, *Empathy*, p. 41.

[28]Ibid., p. 45.

[29]Ibid.

[30]*Shemot Rabbah* 1:13.

[31]J. I. Schneersohn, "Im Ru'ach Hamoshel," quoted on p. 283.

[32]Compare Buber's *Tales of the Hasidim: Later Masters*, p. 283; heard as quoted here. (Menahem Mendl of Kotsk in *Amud HaEmeth* quotes it like Buber.)

[33]B. Parnas, *Sipurey Ha'Ari*, p. 19; discussed also in *Sihot Haran* by R. Nahman, p. 150.

[34]Belz, *Sefer HaHasidut*, vol. 2, p. 211.

[35]I. Berger, *Eser Zahzahot*, p. 90.

[36]*Sihot Haran*, p. 149.

[37]*Igrot Ba'al HaTanya*, p. 59.

[38]R. Katz, *Empathy*, p. 44.

[39]M. M. Schneerson, *HaYom Yom*, p. 32.

[40]R. Katz, *Empathy*, p. 161.

[41]Ibid., p. 162.

[42]Ibid., p. 43.

[43]*Sihot Haran*, p. 141.

[44]M. Buber, *Tales of the Hasidim: Later Masters*, p. 111.

[45]Ibid., p. 112.

[46]*Sihot Haran*, p. 141.

[47]R. Katz, *Empathy*, p. 146; cf. J. I. Schneersohn, *Quntres Klaley HaHinukh VehaHadrakhah*, chaps. 3–5, and 15.

[48]Heard. Cf. J. I. Schneersohn, *HaYom Yom*, p. 23.

[49]Elijah DiVidas, *Reshit Hokhmah* in *Sha'ar HaQdushah*, chap. 17, often quoted at farbrengens.

[50]*Bereshit Rabbah*, p. 45.

[51]"Zettel Qatan" at end of *No'am Elimelekh*.

[52]G. W. Allport, *Personality: A Psychological Interpretation*, p. 27.

[53]When this writer wept after his first interview with the late Rebbe J. I. Schneersohn of Lubavitch, the *gabbai* said: "You did so because the spark approaching the luminary weeps." This phrase often is used in this connection.

[54]J. I. Schneersohn, "In Thy Great Mercy" (a pamphlet printed in Brooklyn, 1940); also D. Schneori, *Sefer Derekh Hayim*, chaps. 7–9.

[55]Heard at a farbrengen. S. Y. Zevin, *Sipurey Hasidim* (Tel Aviv: Abraham Zioni, 1960, p. 290) tells it of R. Uri and the Neshkhizer.

[56]Heard at a farbrengen.

[57]H. Weiner, "*Exercise in Hasidism*," *Midstream* (April 1967).

[58]M. Buber, *Tales of the Hasidim: Later Masters*, p. 196.

[59]*Sidur T'hilat HaShem*, p. 671.

[60]Excerpt from a letter of J. I. Schneersohn.

[61]Y. Rokotz, *Siah Sarfey Qodesh*, p. 68.

[62]This hasid was my late grandfather.

[63]Heard from the subject.

[64]Compare with M. Buber, *Tales of Rabbi Nahman*, p. 35.

[65]M. Buber, *Origin and Meaning of Hasidism*, p. 228.

[66]R. Nahman, *Liqutey Sihot*, p. 851.
[67]Zevin, *Sipurey Hasidim*, p. 438.
[68]Heard.
[69]M. Buber, *Tales of the Hasidim: Early Masters*, p. 255.
[70]Ibid., p. 256.
[71]J. I. Schneersohn, *Quntres Klaley HaHinukh VehaHadrakhah*, chap. 14.
[72]S. Zalmanov, *HaTamim*, vol. 3, p. 9.
[73]Heard from M. Unger; cf. Buber's *Later Masters*, p. 293.
[74]M. Unger, *Hasidus Un Lebn*, p. 77; cf. Parnas, *Sipurey Ha'Ari*, p. 62.
[75]"Boneh Yerushalayim" in *Nefesh Hash'fela*.
[76]Genesis *Rabbah* 8.
[77]*Sihot Haran*, p. 112.
[78]Translation of letter to this writer.
[79]Heard.
[80]*Eruvin* 22a.
[81]See sections dealing with dreams in Moses Hayim Ephraim of Sdilkov, *Degel Mahaneh Ephraim*; Steinman, *Be'er HaHasidut: Bratzlav*; R. Zadoq HaKohen of Lublin, *R'sisey Laylah*; and R. Israel Besht (Habad), p. 158.

CHAPTER 7

[1]R. Nahman of Bratzlav, *Liqutey Maharan*, p. 65.
[2]See R. Kahan, *Shmu'ot VeSipurim*, pp. 55, 133; and H. Perlow, *Liqutey Sipurim*, p. 245.
[3]Pinhas of Koretz, *Midrash Pinhas*, p. 3b (no. 11).
[4]I. B. Singer, "A Piece of Advice," in *Spinoza of Market Street*, p. 122.
[5]D. M. Rabinowitz, *Tiferet Avot*, p. 165.
[6]Told of R. Barukh of Mezhibuzh.
[7]Told in the name of R. Groenen Estherman of Zhebin, a *mashpiy'a* in Lubavitch (circa 1900) who reported R. Shalom Dovber's opinion to his students. See also Belz, *Sefer HaHasidut*, vol. 2., p. 342.
[8]See also R. Kahan, *Shmu'ot VeSipurim*, p. 79.
[9]J. Kaidaner, *Sipurim Noraim*, pp. 29, 53, 54.
[10]Psalm 106:2.
[11]R. Pinhas Shapira, *Nofet Zufim*, p. 42; and Pinhas of Koretz, *Midrash Pinhas*, p. 10 (the same author).
[12]*Nahal Nove'a*, p. 73.
[13]Zohar, *Shemot*, 15b.
[14]J. Kaidaner, *Sipurim Noraim*, p. 22, based on Sanhedrin 42b.
[15]Pinhas of Koretz, *Midrash Pinhas*, p. 14b.
[16]Y. Rokotz, *Siah Sarfey Qodesh*, p. 42.
[17]S. Zalmanov, *HaTamim*, Letter no. 246.
[18]S. Y. Agnon, *Ad Henah*, p. 343.

[19]The chaplain at the Mayo Clinic at that time was the writer's brother, Rabbi Joseph Hayim Schachter.

[20]*Nahal Nove'a*, p. 78.

[21]M. Kleinman, *Or Yesharim*, p. 92.

[22]E. Steinman, *Be'er HaHasidut: Galicia*, p. 267.

[23]*Psychology of Religion*, Basic Books.

[24]Y. Rokotz, *Siah Sarfey Qodesh*, p. 42.

[25]M. Buber, *Tales of Rabbi Nahman*, p. 31.

[26]E. Brandwein, *Degel Mahane Yehudah*, p. 18.

[27]Psalm 119; Belz, *Sefer HaHasidut*, vol. 1, p. 240.

[28]A. S. B. Michelzohn, *Dover Shalom*, p. 14.

[29]Shabbatai of Orshiva, *Segulot Yisrael*.

[30]*Avot* 5, *Or Haner*, p. 22.

[31]I. Berger, *Eser Orot* 9, p. 97.

[32]Shabbatai of Orshiva, *Segulot Yisrael*, p. 104.

[33]R. Kahan, *Shmu'ot Vesipurim*, p. 57.

[34]*Hemdah Genuzah*, p. 14.

[35]S. Zalmanov, *HaTamim*, p. 144.

[36]J. I. Schneersohn, *Liqutey Diburim*, p. 503.

[37]Heard from M. Unger; see also *Niflaot Hasaba*, p. 31.

[38]Leviticus 26:16.

[39]A. Kahane, *Sefer HaHasidut*, p. 31.

[40]Belz, *Sefer HaHasidut*, pp. 289, 293.

[41]*Nahal Nove'a*, p. 96.

[42]Ibid., p. 51.

[43]E. Steinman, *Be'er HaHasidut: Galicia*, p. 198.

[44]M. Unger, *Hasidus Un Lebn*, p. 186.

[45]A. Kahane, *Sefer HaHasidut*, p. 38.

[46]J. Kaidaner, *Sipurim Noraim*, p. 28.

[47]Heard at a farbrengen.

[48]A. Kahane, *Sefer HaHasidut*, p. 274.

[49]*Segulot Yisrael*, p. 103b.

[50]E. Steinman, *Be'er HaHasidut: Galicia*, p. 299.

[51]See B. Mintz, *Sefer HaHistalqut*; J. Kaidaner, *Sipurim Noraim*, p. 37; A. Kahane, *Sefer HaHasidut*, p. 68.

[52]Anonymous, *Emunat Tzadiqim*, p. 32.

[53]M. Kleinman, *Or Yesharim*, p. 9.

[54]Belz, *Sefer HaHasidut*, vol. 2, p. 257.

[55]*Nahal Nove'a*, p. 56.

[56]Ibid., p. 99.

[57]Heard.

[58]A. Kahane, *Sefer HaHasidut*, p. 43.

[59]Y. Rokotz, *Siah Sarfey Qodesh*, ch. 2, p. 10.

[60]*Nahal Nove'a*, p. 107.

[61]Ibid., p. 34.

[62]See R. Kahan, *Shmu'ot VeSipurim*, p. 34.

[63]S. B. Schneersohn, *Quntres Heyhalzu*.

[64]A. Hoffer and H. Osmond, *How to Live with a Schizophrenic*.

[65]*Zohar Vayiqra*, p. 37, and *Nahal Nove'a*, p. 228.

[66]*American Psychiatric Glossary*, p. 21.

[67]Y. Rokotz, *Siah Sarfey Qodesh*, p. 36.

[68]*Tzava'at Harivash* (Anonymous).

[69]Aaron of Karlin, *Beyt Aharon*, aphorisms at the end of the book.

[70]Ibid.

[71]R. Kahan, *Shmu'ot VeSipurim*, p. 182; E. Steinman, *Be'er HaHasidut: Rishonim Aharonim*, p. 57.

[72]*Tanya*, chap. 29.

[73]D. B. Schneori, *Derekh Hayim*, chaps. 6–8.

[74]E. Steinman, *Be'er HaHasidut: Galicia*, p. 302.

[75]M. M. Schneerson II, *Liqutey Sihot*, p. 850.

[76]M. M. Schneerson II, *HaYom Yom*, p. 51.

[77]Heard from R. Menahem Mendl Schneerson II.

[78]Heard.

[79]J. L. Peretz, "Four Generations, Four Wills," taken from S. Liptzin's *Peretz*.

[80]*Nahal Nove'a*, p. 232.

[81]Ibid., pp. 60, 226.

[82]Shabbatai of Orshiva, *Segulot Yisrael*, p. 88.

[83]This happened to this writer's grandfather.

[84]Heard at a farbrengen from R. Yohanan Gordon, a hasidic shohet.

[85]See reference 84.

[86]See reference 84.

[87]See reference 84.

[88]See reference 84.

[89]R. Uri Bronfenbrenner of Strelisk, *Or Olam*, p. 186.

[90]D. M. Rabinowitz, *Tiferet Avot*, p. 175.

[91]Anonymous, *Emunat Tzadiqim*, p. 31.

[92]A. Kahane, *Sefer HaHasidut*, p. 66; *Nahal Nove'a*, p. 103.

[93]A. Kahane, *Sefer HaHasidut*, p. 65.

[94]E. Steinman, *Be'er HaHasidut: Bratzlav*, p. 353.

[95]Told to this writer by his father, a grandson of R. Itzele Krakovitzer; see also M. Kleinman, *Or Yesharim*, p. 156.

[96]E. Steinman, *Be'er HaHasidut: Mishnat Habad*, vol. 2, p. 174.

[97]M. Buber, *Legends of the Ba'al Shem Tov*, p. 107.

[98]Heard from J. I. Schneersohn.

[99]E. Steinman, *Be'er HaHasidut: Mishnat Habad*, vol. 2, p. 355.

[100]Told of the Strettiner.

[101]Heard.

[102]M. Kleinman, *Or Yesharim*, p. 147.

[103]Belz, *Sefer HaHasidut*, vol. 2, p. 210.

[104]Heard.

[105]Z. Kalish in the biography appended to *Qedhusat Levi*: "I am an agent between Israel and God, their heavenly father. I trade Israel's merit for blessing and influx. . . . God said to me, 'Levi Yitzhaq! This will be your agent's fee. I give you children, health, and sustenance. You give it to whomever you wish and take it from whomever you wish.' Turning to the man who refused to obey him, he said, 'Levi Yitzhak will do what he has to do to see that the Torah is upheld'" (p. 150a, Muncacz edition).

[106]Heard from J. I. Schneersohn.

[107]Heard.

[108]*Tanya*, chap. 7.

[109]*Hagigah* 5b.

[110]Genesis 3:16.

[111]Heard from Rabbi M. Schwartzman.

[112]Heard.

[113]M. Buber, *Tales of the Hasidim: Early Masters*, p. 82.

[114]E. Steinman, *Be'er HaHasidut: Galicia*, p. 292.

[115]*Nahal Nove'a*, p. 58.

[116]Heard; see also *Hershele Ostropoler*, p. 35 (anonymous).

[117]Heard from the subject.

[118]Based on *Moed Qatan* 16a.

[119]M. M. Schneerson, *HaYom Yom*, p. 33.

[120]Heard.

[121]*HaYom Yom*, p. 24.

CHAPTER 8

[1]The word of redemption, "*Salahti*—I have forgiven" (Numbers 14:20); and the last word, "*Ehad*" (Zechariah 14:40) from the sentence "On that day the Lord shall be One and His Name shall be One."

[2]Shlomo Luzker, *Magid Devarav LeYa'aqov*, p. 4.

[3]Hasidic paraphrase of a verse in the hymn *Adon Olam*.

[4]Heard in the name of the Kotsker Rebbe.

[5]*Tanya*, chap. 41.

[6]*Tanya*, Introduction to Part II.

[7]R. Assagioli, *Psychosynthesis*, p. 40.

[8]R. Assagioli, "Self-Realization and Psychological Disturbances," a P.S.F. pamphlet.

[9]N. Sternhartz, *Meshivat Nefesh*, No. 1.

[10]See Y. L. Peretz's story, "If Not Higher?!"

[11]J. Frank, *Persuasion and Healing*, pp. 223 and 232.

Glossary

Accedia (Latin)
A state of mind characterized by indifference or even repugnance toward religious exercises, a repugnance not of conviction, but resembling ennui. It was reckoned as one of the Seven Deadly Sins.

Adam Qadmon (Hebrew)   אדם קדמון
Primeval man; man in God's conception; also pre-Atzilic level of divine emanations.

Agónia (Greek)
The pain of struggle.

Ahavat HaShem (Yitbarakh) (Hebrew)   אהבת השם (יתברך)
Literally, love of the Name (of God).

Ahavat Yisrael (Hebrew)   אהבת ישראל
Love of Israel, love of fellow Jews.

Aliyat Han'shamah (Hebrew)   עלית הנשמה
Ascent of the soul.

Am Ha'aretz (Hebrew)   עם הארץ
Literally, a person of the land; figuratively, peasant, ignoramus, boor.

Amidah (Hebrew)   עמידה
Prayer in Jewish liturgy, the "Eighteen Benedictions" recited three times daily; on Sabbaths and Festivals the Amidah has seven benedictions; literally, the standing.

345

Amud (Hebrew)   עמוד
Prayer desk.

Ana B'koah (Hebrew)   אנא בכח
Pneumatic prayer of the kabbalistic liturgy; composed of eight sentences and often said on its own for the benefit of another person to
protect him from distress.

Aqitzah (Hebrew)   עקיצה
Sting.

Areingeyen (Yiddish)   אריינגייען
Literally, to enter; colloquially, to visit the rebbe.

Arendor (Slavic)
Lessee.

Asiyah (Hebrew)   עשיה
The world of action according to kabbalistic teachings; the lowest world
just below *Yetzirah*.

Avodah (Hebrew)   עבודה
Service.

Atzilut (Hebrew)   אצילות
Emanation. In kabbalistic cosmogony, the archetypal world.

Atzmi (Hebrew)   עצמי
Absolute, bone-like.

Atzvut (Hebrew)   עצבות
Sadness.

Ba'al Habayit (Hebrew)   בעל הבית
Literally, house owner. A full-fledged member of the community.

Ba'al Mofet (Hebrew)   בעל מופת
Master of the miraculous sign.

Ba'al M'qubal (Hebrew)   בעל מקובל
Kabbalist.

Ba'al T'filah (Hebrew)   בעל תפילה
Literally, master of prayer. Conductor of prayers during a public worship; a reader of the religious worship.

Ba'al T'shuvah (Hebrew) בעל תשובה
Literally, a penitent. A person who has undergone a conversion experience.

Baqi (Hebrew) בקי
The well-oriented one; the one who has studied much and remembers much.

B'arikhut (Hebrew) באריכות
Literally, at length. The hasidic way of denoting meditative solitary prayer.

Bentchen Zikh (Yiddish) בענטשן זיך
Literally, to bless oneself. To go to the rebbe.

Bet Hamidrash (Hebrew) בית המדרש
House of study. Place for religious services and study. Synagogue.

Beynoni (Hebrew) בינוני
The man in between (the Tzaddik and the Rasha).

B'helfer (Yiddish) באהעלפער
Literally, helper. Assistant to the *m'lamed*, usually in charge of small children.

Birkhat Hapridah (Hebrew) ברכת הפרידה
The parting blessing bestowed by the rebbe on a hasid leaving the town where he was visiting the rebbe.

Birur (Hebrew) בירור
Literally, sorting. The process of separating good from evil.

Bitushim (Hebrew) ביטושים
Literally, choppings; figuratively, rebukes; administered by oneself or by others.

Biyehidut (Hebrew) ביחידות
In the privacy of the rebbe's chamber.

Brakhah (Hebrew) ברכה
Blessing.

Briy'ah (Hebrew) בריאה
According to the Hebrew Kabbalah, the world of creation, produced from the world of Adam Qadmon, the heavenly man. Also called Briatic World.

B'yahid (Hebrew)   ביחיד
Alone.

Daven (Yiddish)   דאווען
To pray, worship, live the liturgy. Etymology uncertain. Popular ety-
mology derives it from דבר, speak; דובב, lip movements; דאבינון, from
our fathers. My current view is that it derives from *divinum* (Latin),
"the divine [service]." As German Jews used to say, "going *oren*" from
orate (Latin, "to pray").

Derlangen a kvittel (Yiddish)   דערלאנגן א קוויטל
Literally, to hand a note. To visit the rebbe.

D'rushim (Hebrew): see **Ma'amarim**   דרושים

Dybbuk (Hebrew)   דיבוק
Possessing spirit.

Ejaculatio praecox (Latin)
Premature orgasm of the male.

Elterer Hasid (Yiddish)   עלטערער חסיד
Older hasid.

Emunat Tzadiqim (Hebrew)   אמונת צדיקים
Literally, faith in the tzaddikim.

Eshet Hayil (Hebrew)   אשת חיל
A woman of valor.

Etrog (Hebrew)   אתרוג
Citron employed during the Tabernacles holidays.

Eymata (Aramaic)   אימתא
Awe, trembling.

Eynikl (Yiddish)   אייניקל
Grandson.

Eyn Sof (Hebrew)   אין סוף
The Infinite [One]. The Godhead.

Etzah (Hebrew, plural **Etzot**)   עצה
Council or advice; direction to be followed, solution to a problem.

Farbrengen (Yiddish)   פארברענגן
A session of hasidic fellowship, at times presided over by the rebbe.

Fonya Ganev (Yiddish) פֿאָניע גנב
Pejorative for Russian establishment; Russian thief.

Gabbai (Hebrew) גבאי
Overseer, secretary.

Gan Eden (Hebrew) גן עדן
Paradise.

Gaon (Hebrew, plural **Geonim**) גאון
Genius; title given to an exceptionally brilliant talmudist.

Gartel (Yiddish) גארטל
Prayer sash worn to separate higher from lower aspects. Also, to gird
one's loins to "prepare to meet the Lord."

Gevir (Hebrew) גביר
Literally, the mighty; figuratively, rich man, man with authority.

Gilgulim (Hebrew) גלגולים
Reincarnations.

Gitin (Hebrew) גיטין
A tractate of the Talmud dealing with divorce procedure. Plural of
"get," which means a Jewish religious writ of divorce.

Goyim (Hebrew) גוים
Literally, nations, ethnics. Non-Jews.

Goyishe (Yiddish) גוישע
Pertaining to or of goyim; non-Jewish.

Guf (Hebrew) גוף
Body.

Gufa d'Malka (Aramaic) גופא דמלכא
Body of the King.

Gut gepoyelt (Yiddish) גוט געפועלט
Well-achieved.

Guter Yid (Yiddish) גוטער ייד
Good Jew; designating a rebbe.

Ha'ala'at Hamidot (Hebrew) העלאת המדות
Literally, the raising up of the emotions; figuratively, the practice
wherein the devotee overcomes temptation by pursuing a stimulus to its
sublimest source in the Divine.

Habad (Hebrew)   חב״ד
Abbreviation of Hokmah, (wisdom), Binah (understanding), and Da'at (knowledge). Hasidism's intellectual movement.

Ha'olam (Hebrew)   העולם
Literally, the world; in Yiddish, the crowd.

Hakhnasat Orhim (Hebrew)   הכנסת אורחים
Hospitality.

Halakhah (Hebrew)   הלכה
The way, the law; literally, the "way to walk"; figuratively, Jewish law.

Halel (Hebrew)   הלל
Psalms; introduced and closed by a blessing; recited on feast days.

Halitzah (Hebrew)   חליצה
Freeing of childless widow from her brother-in-law's levirate connection.

Hanahot (Hebrew)   הנחות
Literally, setting down; figuratively, a rebbe's notes of his own discourse.

Harbatzat Torah (Hebrew)   הרבצת תורה
Literally, to spread Torah; establish schools of Torah.

Harif (Hebrew)   חריף
Literally, a sharp one; figuratively, incisive thinker.

Haroset (Hebrew)   חרוסת
Mixture of nuts, raisins, and apples; signifying mortar used by Jews in Egypt. Used on seder nights of Passover.

Hasagat G'vul (Hebrew)   הסגת גבול
Literally, the moving of boundaries; figuratively, interference in somebody else's business.

Hasid (Hebrew)   חסיד
Follower; a member of the hasidic movement; for our purposes, one who seeks the rebbe's counsel in the yehidut.

Hasidic
Of or pertaining to Hasidism or hasidim.

Hasidisher Ba'al Habayit (Yiddish)   חסידישער בעל הבית
Hasidic head of the household.

Hasidisher Bocher (Yiddish)   חסידישער בחור
A young lad who is a member of a hasidic community.

Hasidisher Yid (Yiddish)   חסידישער ייד
A hasidic Jew.

Hasidism
A religious movement founded by Israel Ba'al Shem Tov in the seventeenth century.

Hasidut (Hebrew)   חסידות
The teachings of Hasidism.

Hayah (Hebrew)   חיה
In kabbalistic terminology, the second highest state of the soul.

Hazan (Hebrew)   חזן
Cantor.

Hazaqah (Hebrew)   חזקה
Legal term for holdings, possession.

Ha'elem (Hebrew)   העלם
That which is hidden.

Heqdesh (Hebrew)   הקדש
Literally, that which is dedicated to a sacred purpose; figuratively, city hospice for paupers.

Hevrah Qadisha (Hebrew)   חברה קדישא
Literally, holy society; figuratively, an organization that takes care of all the necessary rituals in preparation for burial.

Hibut Haqever (Hebrew)   חיבוט הקבר
Literally, "the beating of the grave"; a punishment of purgation in the afterlife.

Hidushim (Hebrew)   חידושים
Novellae; new interpretations or insights in Torah study.

Hirhurey d'yoma (Aramaic)   הרהורי דיומא
Thoughts, imaginations of the day.

Hithalqut (Hebrew)   התחלקות
Literally, sundering; figuratively, that which sees no possibility of harmonizing; alienation.

Hitkal'lut (Hebrew)   התכללות
Literally, the blending; figuratively, merging, harmonizing of all things; integration.

Hitlabshut (Hebrew)   התלבשות
Investment.

Hitpa'alut (Hebrew)   התפעלות
Ecstasy.

Hitqashrut (Hebrew)   התקשרות
Literally, self-binding; figuratively, commitment to a rebbe.

Hiyunah (Hebrew)   חיונאה
To derive one's livelihood.

Hitzon (Hebrew)   חיצון
Literally, exterior one; figuratively, emotionally shallow person.

Hokhmah (Hebrew)   חכמה
Wisdom.

Hush Hatziyur (Hebrew)   חוש הציור
Imaginative ability.

Incubus (Latin)
A term generally applied to designate a demon; astral form of a dead person or of a sorcerer, which has sexual intercourse with a mortal woman.

Itkafia (Aramaic)   אתקפיא
Literally, self-forcing; aesthetic discipline.

Kaddish (Hebrew)   קדיש
The mourner's prayer after the death of a close relative, usually after the death of a parent; the son who recites the prayers after the death of his parent.

Kaf haqela (Hebrew)   כף הקלע
The "catapult"—a purgative punishment of the afterlife.

Kapoteh (Yiddish)   קאפּאָטע
A long-sleeved gown, fastened by a sash, worn by hasidim on Sabbaths and Festivals.

Kashrut (Hebrew)   כשרות
Laws that define what is ritually fit and prepared.

Kavanah (Hebrew)   כונה
Intention.

Khalat (probably Tatar)
Damask coat worn at the table.

Khosen (Hebrew)   חתן
Bridegroom.

Kittel (Yiddish)   קיטל
White shroud one wears on the Day of Atonement, which is also the
shroud in which one wraps the dead.

K'lal Yisrael (Hebrew)   כלל ישראל
Literally, the all of Israel; figuratively, the entire Jewish people.

Kriy'at Sh'ma Sh'al Hamitah (Hebrew)   קריאת שמע שעל המטה
The reading of the Sh'ma at the bedside, the night prayer.

K'tav Hitqashrut (Hebrew)   כתב התקשרות
A group kvittel given to a rebbe-to-be announcing that the undersigned
wish to be led by him.

Kvittel (Yiddish)   קוויטל
Short note; slip; figuratively, a written request presented to the hasidic
leader.

Lahash (Hebrew)   לחש
Literally, whisper; figuratively, a formula whispered into the ear of a
sick person.

Lamdan (Hebrew)   למדן
Scholar of the Torah.

Landsleit (Yiddish)   לאנצלייט (לאנדסלייט)
Members of a landsmanschaft.

Landsmanschaft (Yiddish)   לאנצמאנשאפט (לאנדסמאנשאפט)
Immigrant organization of people who come from the same point of
origin in Europe.

Lehishah (Hebrew)   לחישה
Whisper.

Lekakh (Yiddish)   לעקאך
From German *lebkuchen*; honey and spice cake.

L'vush (Hebrew)   לבוש
Garment.

Ma'amadot (Hebrew)   מעמדות
Literally, stands; referred to service periods in the Temple; figuratively,
periodic retainer fees to rebbe.

Ma'amarim (Hebrew)　　　　　　　　　　מאמרים
Oral discourses.

Ma'asiyot (Hebrew, plural of **Ma'asseh**)　　מעשיות
Stories.

Maekler (German)
Business agent.

Mamzerim (Hebrew, plural of **Mamzer**)　　ממזרים
Bastards.

Mashpiy'a (Hebrew, plural **Mashpiy'im**)　　משפיע
Guide, tutor, or spiritual director.

Maskil (Hebrew)　　　　　　　　　　משכיל
Literally, the enlightened one; figuratively, erudite; follower of the
Haskalah. In hasidic terminology, an intellectual whose contemplative
endeavor turns to significance instead of service.

Mazal (Hebrew)　　　　　　　　　　מזל
Luck.

Medameh (Hebrew)　　　　　　　　　מדמה
Imaginative quality.

Meshuga (Hebrew)　　　　　　　　　משוגע
Mentally disturbed.

Minyan (Hebrew)　　　　　　　　　מנין
Quorum of ten men for public religious worship.

Miqveh (Hebrew)　　　　　　　　　מקוה
Ritual immersion pool for purification; ritual bath.

Mitnaged (Hebrew, plural **Mitnagdim**)　　מתנגד
Literally, opponent; figuratively, anti-hasid, name for the opponents of
the hasidic movement.

Mitzvah (Hebrew)　　　　　　　　　מצוה
Precept; divine commandment; good deed; merit.

M'lamed (Hebrew)　　　　　　　　　מלמד
A Hebrew teacher.

M'laveh Malkah (Hebrew)　　　　　מלוה מלכה
Literally, escorting the queen; figuratively, the last festive meal at the
exit of the Sabbath.

Mofet (Hebrew, plural **Moftim**) מופת
Literally, sign, miracle; figuratively, a miracle performed by the rebbe in the service of his pastoral work.

Mokhiah (Hebrew) מוכיח
Chastiser, admonisher.

Moreh derekh (Hebrew) מורה דרך
Teacher of the way.

M'rirut (Hebrew) מרירות
Bitterness.

M'shor'im (Hebrew) משוררים
Choristers.

M'sirat Nefesh (Hebrew) מסירת נפש
Self-sacrifice; literally, giving of one's soul.

Mussar (Hebrew) מוסר
Movement in Judaism devoted to the improvement of one's service to God via moral exhortation.

Na'al (Hebrew) נעל
Shoe.

Nebakh (Yiddish) נעבאך
Poor, pitiful; miserable one.

Nefesh (Hebrew) נפש
The lowest soul level; functional part of the soul.

Nidah (Hebrew) נדה
Period of menstrual impurity; a woman in the state of menstrual impurity.

Nigun (Hebrew, plural **Nigunim**) נגון
Melody; "a tune flowing in search of its own unattainable end" (Heschel).

N'ilah (Hebrew) נעילה
Special prayer in Jewish liturgy recited at the conclusion of the Day of Atonement.

Nistar (Hebrew) נסתר
Hidden tzaddik.

N'shamah (Hebrew) נשמה
The kabbalistic name of the divine soul in man; third highest level, intellective part of soul.

N'shamah K'lalit (Hebrew) נשמה כללית
General soul.

N'shamot Hadashot (Hebrew) נשמות חדשות
New souls.

N'shikhah (Hebrew) נשיכה
A bite.

Oved (Hebrew) עובד
Literally, servant; figuratively, hasidic devotee whose contemplative endeavors turn to service as opposed to significance.

Parnas (Hebrew) פרנס
One of the twelve members of the board who lead the community, an alderman.

Passover Sh'murah (Hebrew) שמורה
Special matzot called Matzot Sh'murah, "guarded Matzot"; these are baked from flour milled from wheat that has been carefully watched from the time of reaping.

Pathein (Greek)
To feel the pain of depression.

Pidyon (Hebrew) פדיון
Ransom.

Pidyon Nefesh (Hebrew) פדיון נפש
Literally, soul ransom; sum of money given to the rebbe at the yehidut.

Pilpul(ic) (Hebrew) פלפול
Sharp intellectual discernment; casuistic argument, hairsplitting.

P'nimi (Hebrew) פנימי
Inner-directed person.

P'nimiyut HaTorah (Hebrew) פנימיות התורה
Innermost part of the Torah; the way in which hasidim refer to the teachings of Hasidism.

Poritz (uncertain; possibly Slavic) פריץ
Non-Jewish country squire; landowner; a member of the landed gentry.

Posqim (Hebrew)   פוסקים
  Codifiers; authoritative decisors in Halakhah.

Poyeln bam rebbn (Yiddish)   פועל׳ן ביים רבי׳ן
  Literally, to exact from the rebbe; figuratively, to visit the rebbe.

Pravven zich (Yiddish and Slavic)   פראווען זיך
  Literally, to celebrate onself; figuratively, to go to the rebbe.

P'shat (Hebrew)   פשט
  Simple meaning of the Torah.

Pushke (Slavic)   פושקע
  Charity or alms box.

Qever Rahel (Hebrew)   קבר רחל
  Rachel's tomb.

Qidush HaShem (Hebrew)   קדוש השם
  The sanctification of His Name; often refers to martyrdom.

Q'lipah (Hebrew)   קליפה
  Kabbalistic term for the "world of shells"; synonym for evil.

Q'piydah (Hebrew)   קפידה
  Wrathful contempt.

Quntresim (Hebrew)   קונטריסים
  Sacred tracts.

Rav (Hebrew)   רב
  Rabbi. Was used to designate a city's chief rabbi.

Rebbe (Hebrew)   רבי
  The spiritual leader of a hasidic sect; religious leader of a hasidic
  community.

Reckel (Yiddish)   רעקל
  Jacket.

Remazim (Hebrew)   רמזים
  Hints.

Rosh B'nai Yisrael (Hebrew)   ראש בני ישראל
  Literally, the head of the sons of Israel; the acronym spells rebbe in
  Hebrew.

Roshey Alafim (Hebrew)   ראשי אלפים
The head of thousands.

Rosh Yeshivah (Hebrew)   ראש ישיבה
Head of the seminary; specifically a teacher of Talmud and the manifest
part of the Torah.

R'shaim (Hebrew)   רשעים
Evildoers.

R'shut Hayahid (Hebrew)   רשות היחיד
World of inner domain of the Single One.

Ruah (Hebrew)   רוח
In kabbalistic terminology, the divine soul in man; second emotive part
of the soul.

Ruah Haqodesh (Hebrew)   רוח הקדש
The Holy Spirit.

Sefardit (or Sephardi) (Hebrew)   ספרדית
Pertaining to Sephardim or Oriental Jews.

Sela (Hebrew)   סלע
Ancient Hebrew measure of money or weight; equivalent to 2 shekels,
or 4 dinars.

S'gulah (Hebrew)   סגולה
A charm, such as an amulet, that a rebbe gives a hasid, especially
charged with healing, guarding, or enriching powers.

Shadkhan (Hebrew)   שדכן
Professional or semiprofessional marriage broker; matchmaker.

Shait'l (Yiddish)   שייטל
Wig worn by Orthodox Jewish married women.

Shalom Bayit (Hebrew)   שלום בית
Literally, peace of the house; figuratively, domestic harmony.

Sharayim (Yiddish)   שריים
Food favors from the rebbe to the hasid; leftovers from the rebbe's meal
distributed to or taken by his followers.

Shekhinah (Hebrew)   שכינה
Presence of God, of the Divine Mind, among mortals.

Shemot (Hebrew)   שמות
Names.

Sheva Brakhot (Hebrew)   שבע ברכות
The seven nuptial blessings.

Sheynfrumkeit (Yiddish)   שיינפרומקייט
Popular piety.

Shidukh (Hebrew)   שדוך
Match, marriage.

Shir HaShirim (Hebrew)   שיר השירים
Literally, Song of Songs.

Shishi (Hebrew)   ששי
Literally, sixth; figuratively, the sixth portion at the Sabbath Torah
reading, reserved for the tzaddik.

Sh'lemut (Hebrew)   שלמות
Perfection, completion.

Sh'lihey d'Rabanan (Aramaic)   שליחי דרבנן
See **Shudar**.

Sh'lihey d'Rahmana (Aramaic)   שליחי דרחמנא
See **Shudar**.

Shmussen (Yiddish)   שמועסן (שמועות׳ן)
Informal conversation conducted by the rebbe.

Shofar (Hebrew)   שופר
Ram's horn blown on Rosh Hashanah as part of the ritual.

Shohet (Hebrew)   שוחט
Ritual slaughterer.

Shoteh (Hebrew)   שוטה
Feeble-minded person.

Shtetl (Yiddish)   שטעטל
Small town; village.

Shtibel (Yiddish)   שטיבל
Literally, little room; figuratively, hasidic conventicle.

Shtreiml (probably old High German)   שטריימל
Festive fur hat worn on Shabbat by most rebbes and some hasidim.

Shudar (Acronym of Aramaic) שוד״ר
Sh'lihey d'Rabanan or Sh'lihey d'Rahmana; emissary of the rebbe for funds or for causes supported by the rebbe.

Shul (Yiddish) שול
House of worship; synagogue.

Shulhan Arukh (Hebrew) שולחן ערוך
Literally, the set table; figuratively, title of the most popular compendium of rabbinical law, by R. Joseph Caro.

Sihot (Hebrew) שיחות
See **Shmussen**.

Simhah (Hebrew) שמחה
Joy; a joyous occasion.

Sirsur (Hebrew) סרסור
Agent, middleman.

Slai'm (Hebrew) סלעים
Plural of **Sela**.

Succubus (Latin)
A demon; the astral body of a dead person or of a witch, which takes the form of a woman and has sexual intercourse with a mortal man.

Sukkah (Hebrew) סוכה
Temporary hut constructed for the Festival of Booths.

Talitot (Hebrew) טליתות
Fringed prayer shawls. (Yiddish, **Taleysim**.)

Tamim (Hebrew) תמים
Official designation of one who studied at Tomchei Temimim, the Lubavitcher Yeshivah.

Timtum Hamo'ah Vehelev (Hebrew) טמטום המוח והלב
Blocking of the brain and heart; similar to accedia.

T'filin (Hebrew) תפלין
Phylacteries.

Tiqun (Hebrew) תקון
Literally, ordering, repairing; a counsel on how to make reparation and restitution.

Tish (Yiddish)   טיש
Literally, table; figuratively, table of the rebbe.

Tohu (Hebrew)   תהו
Chaos.

T'shuvah (Hebrew)   תשובה
Repentance; sometimes penance.

Tzaddik (Hebrew)   צדיק
Literally, the just one; figuratively, term for a saintly, righteous person; charismatic leader; particularly employed for the hasidic leader, the rebbe.

Tzava'ah (Hebrew)   צוואה
Command, will, testament.

Tzorkhey Gavohah (**Hefzey Shamayim**) (Hebrew)   צרכי גבוה
Needs of the Sublime One; desired acts by Heaven; spiritual endeavors.

Tzorkhey Haguf (Hebrew)   צרכי הגוף
Bodily needs.

Yehidah (Hebrew)   יחידה
In kabbalistic terminology, the highest state of the soul.

Yehidut (Hebrew)   יחידות
Literally, one-ing; figuratively, a hasid's private encounter with his rebbe.

Yeridat Han'shamah (Hebrew)   ירידת הנשמה
Descent of the soul, incarnation.

Yetzer Hara (Hebrew)   יצר הרע
The evil inclination.

Yetzer Hatov (Hebrew)   יצר הטוב
The good inclination.

Yetzirah (Hebrew)   יצירה
According to kabbalistic teachings, the world of angels, formed from emanations of the Briyah; also called Yetziratic World. Yetzirah is also the title of the most occult of kabbalistic books, *Sefr Hayetzirah*.

Ye'ush (Hebrew)   יאוש
Despair.

Yihud (Hebrew)   יחוד
Unification.

Yoshev (Hebrew)   יושב
A hasid who studies at the rebbe's yeshivah.

Yoshev Ohel (Hebrew)   יושב אוהל
Literally, tent dweller; figuratively, a contemplative, supported by others.

Yungerman (Yiddish)   יונגערמאן
Recently married young man.

References

Aaron ben Moshe. *Sefer Ma'avar Yavoq*. Vilna: Rom Publishers, 1883.

Aaron of Karlin. *Beyt Aharon*, ed. Israel Perlow. New York: Karlin Stolin Publishing Committee, 1875.

Abeli, A., ed. "Darkhey Yesharim." In *Yalqut Kitvey Qodesh*, pp. 240–264. Jerusalem: Ha-Ma'amin Publishing Co., 1962.

Agnon, S. Y. *Ad Henah*. in *Edo Ve'Eynam*. Jerusalem: Schocken Publishing House Ltd., 1955.

———. "L'Ahar HaSeudah." In *Lifnim Min HaHomah*, pp. 291–298. Jerusalem: Schocken Publishing House Ltd., 1975.

Alfasi, I. *Sefer HaAdmorim*. Tel Aviv: Ariel Publishing Co., 1961.

Allport, W. *Pattern and Growth in Personality*. New York: Holt, Rinehart and Winston, 1961.

———. *Personality: A Psychological Interpretation*. New York: Henry Holt & Co., 1937.

Anonymous. *Even Shlomoh*. Vilna: P. Matz, 1911.

———. *Hershele Ostropoler*. New York: Hebrew Publishing Co., 1927.

———. *Leshon Hasidim (The Teachings of the Besht Alphabetized)*. Offset. Lemberg, 1876. Tel Aviv: Yeshivat Lelov.

———. *Ma'aseh MiGimel Ahim*. Vilna: Tzvi Hirsch Matz, 1925.

———. *Ma'aseh Tzadiqim*. Jerusalem: P. D. Weberman, 1962.

———. *Ma'asiyot Tzadiqim*. Warsaw: Lewin-Epstein Bros. & Co., 1924.

———. *Nahal Nove'a*. Jerusalem: Yovel Publishers, 1961.

———. *Pe'er MiQedoshim*. Jerusalem: Lewin-Epstein Bros. & Co., 1951.

———. *Seder HaDorot HaHadash*. No publication data available.

———. *Sefer Emunat Tzadiqim*. B'nai B'raq: no further data available.

———. *Sefer Razin Qadishin*. Jerusalem: Lewis-Epstein Bros. & Co., no date available.

———. *Toldot Rabi Yehudah HaHasid*. Poland: A. Sontag, 1928.

———. *Tzava'at HaRivash*. Lemberg: II. M. Stand, 1864.

Apter Rav, Abraham Joshua Heschel of Apt. *Sefer Ohev Yisrael*. Zhitomir: Meshullam Zussia of Zinakov, 1863.

Assagioli, R. *Psychosynthesis: A Manual of Principles and Techniques*. New York: Hobbs, Dorman & Co. Inc., 1965.

Azaria, M. of Fano. *Gilguley Neshamot*. Lemberg: A. J. Madfes, 1865.

Azulai, H. Y. D. *Sefer Avodat HaQodesh*. Warsaw: N. D. Zisberg, 1874.

———. *Sefer Shem HaGedolim*. Tel-Aviv: Dov Ganzburg, 1960.

Bakan, D. *Disease, Pain and Sacrifice: Toward a Psychology of Suffering*. Chicago: The University of Chicago Press, 1968.

———. *The Duality of Human Existence*. Chicago: Rand, McNally & Co., 1966.

Baruchovitch, Shneur Zalman (of Liadi). *Hilkhot Talmud Torah*. New York: Kehot Publication Society, 1962.

———. *Liqutey Torah*. New York: Kehot Publication Society, 1965.

———. *Liqutey Amarim: Tanya*. New York: Kehot Publication Society, 1958.

———. *Ma'amarey Admor HaZaqen*. 3 vols. New York: Kehot Publication Society, 1964.

———. *Seder Tefilot Mikhol HaShanah*. Also known as *Sidur HaRav*. New York: Kehot Publication Society, 1965.

———. *Torah Or*. New York: Kehot Publication Society, 1954.

Barukh of Mezhibuzh. *Buziyna d'N'hora*. New York: Yeshiva Ohr Mordecai, 1956.

Belz. *Sefer HaHasidut* (Mi Torat Belz). 2 vols., ed. Israel Klopholtz. Jerusalem: Belzer Institute, 1965.

Ben Yehezqel, *Sefer HaMa'asiyot*. 6 vols. Tel Aviv: Dvir Company, 1961.

Berger, I. *Eser Atarot*. In *Sefer Zekhut Yisrael*. Jerusalem: Jerusalem Hebrew Book Store, 1954. (An offset printing of the 1906 edition.)

———. *Eser Orot*. In *Sefer Zekhut Yisrael*. Jerusalem: Jerusalem Hebrew Book Store, 1954. (An offset printing of the 1906 edition.)

———. *Eser Qedoshot*. In *Sefer Zekhut Yisrael*. Jerusalem: Jerusalem Hebrew Book Store, 1954. (An offset printing of the 1906 edition.)

———. *Eser Zahzahot*. In *Sefer Zekhut Yisrael*. Jerusalem: Jerusalem Hebrew Book Store, 1954. (An offset printing of the 1906 edition.)

Bernat, A. N. *Gedulat Rabeynu Yisrael Besht*. Jerusalem: Bernat, 1959.

Berne, E. *Games People Play: The Psychology of Human Relationships*. New York: Grove Press Inc. 1964.

Bikel, Dr. S. *Yidden Davenen*. No publication data available.

Birnbaum, S. *Life and Sayings of the Ba'al Shem Tov*. New York: Hebrew Publishing Co., 1933.

Bloch, C. *Aus Miriam's Brunnen*. Darmstadt: Joseph Meltzer Verlag, 1966.

Boisen, A. T. *The Exploration of the Inner World: Study of Mental Disorder and Religious Experience*. New York: Willett, Clark & Co., 1936.

Brandwein, E. *Degel Mahaneh Yehudah*. Jerusalem: 1957.

Brandwein, E., Kaidaner, J., and Nathan Nota of Kalbiel. *Shaiy Levar Mitzvah*. Contains *Degel Mahaneh Yehudah*, *Sefer Buzina Qadisha*, and *Sipurim Noraim*. Jerusalem: Mordecai David ben Malkha Zwi, 1957.

Bronfenbrenner, Uri (of Strelisk). *Imrey Qodesh*. In *Yalqut Kitvey Qodesh*, pp. 203–220. Jerusalem: HaMa'amin Publishing Co., 1962.

———. *Or Olam*. In *Yalqut Kitvey Qodesh*., pp. 175–203. Jerusalem: HaMa'amin Publishing Co., 1962.

———. *Yalqut Kitvey Qodesh*. Contains *Nofet Zufim*, *Buzina d'N'hora*, *Imrey Qodesh*, and *Sefer Darkhey Yesharim*.

Buber, M. *For the Sake of Heaven*. Philadelphia: The Jewish Publication Society of America, 1964.

———. *Hasidism and Modern Man*, ed. and trans. Maurice S. Friedman. Book II: "My Way to Hasidism." New York: Horizon Press, 1958.

———. *The Legend of the Ba'al Shem*, trans. Maurice S. Friedman. New York: Harper and Bros. London: East and West Library, 1955.

———. *Tales of Angels, Spirits and Demons*. New York: Hawk's Well Press, 1958.

———. *Tales of the Hasidim*. 2 vols. New York: Schocken Books Inc., 1948.

———. *Tales of Rabbi Nahman*. New York: Horizon Press, 1956.

Bunim, S. *Sefer Simhat Yisrael*. Warsaw: A. J. Kleinman, 1910.

Chadwick, O. *Western Asceticism*. Philadelphia: Westminster Press, 1958.

Committee on Public Information. *A Psychiatric Glossary*. Washington: American Psychiatric Association, 1957.

Cabot, R. C., and Dicks, R. L. *The Art of Ministering to the Sick*. New York: MacMillan Co., 1936.

Derbaremdiker, Rabbi Levi Isaac of Berditchev. *HaZekhirot*. In *Igeret HaQodesh*, pp. 32–44. Warsaw: Naphtali Herz Herzog, 1879.

———. *Sefer Qedushat Levi*. Warsaw: Razumovsky, 1902.

Dicks, R. L. *Pastoral Work and Personal Counseling*. New York: MacMillan and Co., 1944.

Doniger, S., ed. *Religion and Human Behavior*. New York: Association Press, 1954.

Dresner, S. H. *Prayer, Humility and Compassion*. Philadelphia: Jewish Publication Society of America, 1957.

———. *The Zaddik: The Doctrine of the Zaddik According to the Writings of Rabbi Yaakov Yosef of Polnoye*. New York: Aberlard-Schuman, 1960.

Dubnow, S. *Geschichte fun Hassidism*. 3 vols. Berlin: Judische Verlag, 1931.

Duchman, Z. *Liqut L'Shema Ozen*. Brooklyn: Balshan, 1963.

R. Elimelekh of Lizhensk. *Hanehagat Adam*. In *Sefer No'am Elimelekh*. New York: Israel Ze'ev, 1956.

———. *Zettel Qatan*. In *Sefer No'am Elimelekh*. New York: Israel Ze'ev, 1956.

English, O. S., and Pearson, G. H. J. *Emotional Problems of Living: Avoiding the Neurotic Pattern*. New York: W. W. Norton & Co. Inc., 1945.

Erikson, Erik H. *Childhood and Society*. New York: W. W. Norton Co. Inc., 1950.

———. *Insight and Responsibility*. New York: W. W. Norton & Co. Inc., 1964.

Eshliak, L., ed. *Sihot Hayim*. Warsaw: further publication data unavailable.

Eysenck, H. J. *Uses and Abuses of Psychology*. London: Penguin Books, 1953.

Flew, A. *Body, Mind and Death*. New York: MacMillan Co., 1964.

Frank, J. D. *Persuasion and Healing: A Comparative Study of Psychotherapy*. Baltimore: Johns Hopkins Press, 1961.

Frankl, J. A. *Sefer Menorah HaTehorah*. Pshemishl: Amkraut und Freindt, 1911.

Frankl, V. E. *The Doctor and the Soul: An Introduction to Logotherapy*. New York: Alfred A. Knopf, 1955.

Freud, S. *Studies in Para-Psychology*. New York: Collier Books, 1963.

Friedlander, M. J. *Batey Avot*. Jerusalem: published by author, 1965.

Friedman, D. *Magid Devarav L'Ya'aqov*, ed. Abraham of Lutsk. Satumaru: Abraham Barish, 1905.

Fromm, E. *The Art of Loving*. New York: Bantam Books Inc., 1956.

———. *The Forgotten Language: An Introduction to the Understanding of Dreams, Fairy Tales and Myths*. New York: Grove Press Books, 1951.

———. *The Heart of Man: Its Genius for Good and Evil*. New York: Harper and Row Publishers, 1964.

———. *You Shall Be as Gods: A Radical Interpretation of the Old Testament and Its Tradition*. New York: Holt, Rinehart & Winston, 1966.

Frumkin, A. *Qahal Hasidim*. New York: Star Hebrew Books.

Galdston, I. *Ministry and Medicine in Human Relations*. New York: International Universities Press Inc., 1955.

Geshuri, M. S. *Enziqlopediyah Shel HaHasidut: HaNigun VehaRiyqud BaHasidut*. 2 vols. Tel Aviv: Nezah Publishing Co., 1956 and 1959.

Glitzenstein, A. C. *The Arrest and Liberation of Rabbi Shneur Zalman of Liadi*, trans. Jacob Immanuel Schochet. Brooklyn: Kehot Publication Society, 1964.

Glitzenstein, A. C., ed. *Or HaHasidut*. Kfar Habad, Israel: Kehot Publication Society, 1965.

Goffman, E. *Encounters*. Indianapolis: The Bobbs-Merrill Co. Inc., 1961.

———. *The Presentation of Self in Everyday Life*. New York: Doubleday & Co. Inc., 1959.

Goldbrunner, J. *Cure of Mind and Cure of Soul: Depth Psychology and Pastoral Care*. Indiana: University of Notre Dame Press, 1962.

Goldstein, M. *Mas'ot Yerushalayim*. New York: Talmidey VeHasidey Munkatch, 1931.

Greenberg, E., and Howe, I., eds. *A Treasury of Yiddish Stories*. No publication data available.

Greenberg, H. *The Inner Eye*. No publication data available.

Hager, G. *Hemdah Genuzah*. Photo offset. Briegeleisen Publishers. Further publication data unavailable.

HaLevi, J. I. *Divrey Emet al HaTorah*. New York: Rabbi Pincus E. Spiegel, 1946.

HaLevi, Y. Z. *Shem HaGdolim HeHadash*. New York: Rabbi Jeno Klein, 1948.

Hall, C. S., and Gardner, L. *Theories of Personality*. New York: John Wiley and Sons Inc., 1962.

Harms and Schreiber. *Handbook of Counseling Techniques*. New York: MacMillan, 1963.

Hayman, A. *Ozar Divrey HaHakhamim uPitgameyhem*. Tel Aviv: Dvir Publication Society, 1955.

Heard, G. *The Five Ages of Man: The Psychology of Human History*. New York: The Julian Press Inc., 1963.

———. *Training for a Life of Growth*. Santa Monica, California: The Wayfarer Press, 1959.

Herrigel, E. *Zen and the Art of Archery*, trans. R. F. C. Hull. New York: Pantheon Books, 1953.

Heschel, A. J. *The Earth is the Lord's/The Sabbath*. Philadelphia: Jewish Publication Society, 1963.

———. *God in Search of Man*. Philadelphia: The Jewish Publication Society of America, 1955.

———. *Man's Quest for God*. New York: Charles Scribner & Sons, 1954.

———. "Reb Mendel of Kotsk." In *HaDoar* 38 (28 Iyar, 5719).

Hesse, H. *Siddhartha*, trans. Hilda Rosner. New York: New Directions Publishing Corp., 1957.

Hielman, D. Z., ed. *Igrot Ba'al HaTanya u-Venay Doro*. Jerusalem: Mesoroh Publishing Co., 1953.

Hielman, H. M. *Sefer Beyt Rabi*. Tel Aviv: Sito Offset of Berditchev, 1903.

Hiltner, S. *Educative Approach in Pastoral Counseling*. New York: Abingdon-Cokesbury Press, 1959.

Hoffer, A., and Osmond, H. *How to Live with a Schizophrenic*. London: Johnson Publications, 1966.

Horodezky, S. A. *HaHasidut VehaHasidim* 4 vols. Tel Aviv: Dvir Co. Ltd., 1963.

———. *Leaders of Hassidism*. London: Hasefer Agency for Literature, 1928.

Hutschnecker, A. *The Will to Live*. New York: Garden City, 1951.

Huxley, A. *The Devils of Loudun*. New York: Harper and Row Publishers, 1952.

———. *The Perennial Philosophy*. London: Fontana Books, 1946.

Ibn Paquda, B. *Sefer Hovat HaLevavot*, trans. Judah Ibn Tibbon. Tel Aviv: Moriyah Publishing Co., 1960.

Jacob Joseph of Polnoye, ed. *Keter Shem Tov*. Lemberg: A. J. Madfes, 1865.

———. *Toldot Ya'aqov Yosef*. Warsaw: Amkraut und Freindt, 1909.

Jacobs, L. *Seekers of Unity*. New York: Basic Books Inc., 1966.

Jacobsohn, H., von Franz, M. L., and Hurwitz, S. *Zeitlose Dokumente Der Seele*. Zurich: Rascher et Cie, 1952.

James, W. *The Varieties of Religious Experience: A Study in Human Nature*. New York: Random House, 1902.

Johnson, P. E. *Personality and Religion*. New York: Abingdon Press, 1957.

———. *Psychology of Pastoral Care*. New York: Abingdon-Cokesbury Press, 1953.

———. *Psychology of Religion*. New York: Abingdon-Cokesbury Press, n.d.

Joseph of Nemirov. *Sefer Viquha Rabah*. Warsaw: Y. Klieman, 1913.

Kagan, I. M. (the Hafetz Hayim). *Sefer Nidhey Yisrael*. New York: Torath Hafetz Hayim Publications, 1951.

Kahan, R. *Shmu'ot VeSipurim*. Israel: Village of Habad, 1964.

Kahane, A. *Sefer HaHasidut*. Warsaw: Die Welt Publications, 1922.

Kaidaner, J. *Sipurim Noraim*. In *Shaiy LeVar Mitzvah*. Jerusalem, 1957.

Kamelhar, J. A. *Dor De'ah*. Poland: Israel Kamelhar, 1933.

Kaplan, A. H. "Social Work Therapy and Psychiatric Psychotherapy." In *Archives of General Psychiatry*, November 1963.

Katz, R. L. *Empathy: Its Nature and Uses*. London: Collier-MacMillan Ltd., 1963.

Kelly, G. A. *The Psychology of Personal Constructs*. 2 vols. New York: W. W. Norton & Co. Inc., 1955.

Kiev, A. *Magic, Faith and Healing: Studies in Primitive Psychiatry Today*. London: The Free Press of Glencoe, Collier-MacMillan Ltd., 1964.

Kleinman, M. H., ed. *Or Yesharim*. Jerusalem: Private publication by anonymous Slonimer Hasid, 1958.

———. *Sefer Mazkeret Shem HaGedolim*. No publication data available.

Kramer, R. *Sefer HaKhamey Yisrael Besht*. New York: Agudath HaHassidim, Kolel Habad, 1924.

Kranzler, G. *Williamsburg: A Jewish Community in Transition*. New York: Philipp Feldheim Inc., 1961.

Kronbach, A. *Reform Movements in Judaism*. No publication data available.

Laing, R. D. *The Divided Self: An Existential Study in Sanity and Madness*. Baltimore: Penguin Books Ltd., 1960.

———. *The Self and Others: Further Studies in Sanity and Madness*. No publication data available.

Langer, G. *Liebesmystik der Kabbala*. Munich: Otto Wilhelm, 1956.

Langer, J. *Nine Gates to the Chassidic Mysteries*. New York: David McKay Co. Inc., 1961.

Levine, M. *Psychotherapy in Medical Practice*. New York: The MacMillan Co., 1943.

Liebman, J. *Peace of Mind*. New York: Simon and Schuster, 1946.

———. *Psychiatry and Religion*. Boston: The Beacon Press, 1948.

Link, H. C. *The Rediscovery of Man*. New York: The MacMillan Co., 1938.

———. *The Return to Religion*. New York: The MacMillan Co., 1936.

Lipshitz, Shabbatai of Orshiva. *Sefer Hahayim* (also called *S'gulot Yisrael*). Brooklyn: published privately by Isaiah Karpen, grandson of the author. No date available.

Luzzatto, M. C. *Mesilat Yesharim*. Philadelphia: The Jewish Publication Society of America, 1948.

Maimon, S. *Solomon Maimon: Autobiography*. New York: Schocken Books Inc., 1947.

Maimonides, M. *Shemoneh Praqim*. In *Perush HaMishnah LehaRambam*. No publishing data available.

Malik, H. I. *Sefer Sipurim Nifla'im*. Offset of Satmar print, no publication data available.

Menahem Mendl of Kotsk. *Amud HaEmet*. Tel Aviv: Pe'er Publishing Co., no date available.

Meshulam Feibush of Zbarazh. *Sefer Derekh Emet*. Jerusalem: Rabbi Herskovitz, no date available.

Michelzohn, A. Simcha Bunam. *Dover Shalom*. Pshemishel: Amkraut und Freindt, 1910.

————, ed. *Oholey Tzadiqim*. Includes *Ohel Elimelekh*, *Ateret Menahem*, *Ohel Naftali*, *Ohel Avraham*, *Menorah HaTehorah*, and *Ateret Tiferet*. New York: E. Grossman Publishing House, no date available.

Mintz, B. *Sefer HaHistalqut*. Tel Aviv: Ketubim Publishers, 1930.

————, ed. *Shivhey HaBesht*. Tel Aviv: Talpioth Publishers, 1961.

Mordecai Joseph of Izhbitz. *Mey HaShiloah*. Jerusalem: Hasiday Radzin of Israel, 1956.

Mordecai of Lechowitz et al. *Torat Avot*. Jerusalem: Yeshivat Beth Abraham of Jerusalem, 1961.

Moses Hayim Ephraim of Sdilkov. *Sefer Degel Mahaneh Efrayim*. New York: Rabbi Joel Be'er, 1947.

Moustakas, C. E. *The Self: Explorations in Personal Growth*. New York: Harper and Bros. Publishers, 1956.

Mowrer, O. H. *The Crisis in Psychiatry and Religion*. New York: D. van Nostrand Co. Inc., 1961.

R. Nahman of Bratzlav. *Liqutey Etzot*. Jerusalem: Hassidim Bratzlav, 1957.

————. *Liqutey Maharan*. New York: Rabbi Eliezer Shlomo Bresler, 1966.

————. *Liqutey Tinyana*. New York: Rabbi Eliezer Shlomo Bresler, 1966.

————. *Sipurey Ma'asiyot*, ed. Nathan Sternhartz. New York: Chevra Hassidei Bratzlav, 1948.

Nathan of Nemirov, ed. *Meshivat Nefesh*. Jerusalem: Hassidei Bratzlav, 1960.

Nathan Nota of Kalbiel. *Sefer Buzinah Qadisha*. Jerusalem: Mordecai David ben Malkha Zvi, 1957.

Newman, L. I., and Spitz, S. *The Hasidic Anthology: Tales and Teachings of the Hasidim*. New York: Schocken Books, 1963.

Nikhilananda, Swami, trans. *Gospel of Ramakrishna*. New York: Ramakrishna-Vivikananda Center, 1958.

Oppenheim, D. *Hanhagot Adam*. Munkatch: M. Herskovits, 1895.

Ortner, N. *Dvar Hen*. Tel Aviv: Lipa Freedman and B. Ortner Publishing Houses, 1963.

Ouspensky, P. D. *The Fourth Way*. New York: Alfred A. Knopf, 1957.

Padua, I. M. *Or HaNer*. Offset of Pietrikov ed., no publication data available.

Parhi, J. S. *Oseh Phele*. Jerusalem: Ezra Yaffe, 1955.

Parnas, B. *Qehal Hasidim VeShivhey Besht*. New York: Star Books, 1928.

———. *Sipurey HaAriy VeShivhey R. Hayim Vital*. New York: Star Hebrew Book Co., no date available.

Peretz, I. L. "Fir Doyres Fir Zavoes." In *Geqliybene Dertzaylungen*. Winnipeg: Fun Kval, 1942.

———. *HaSidut*. Tel Aviv: Dvir Co. Ltd., 1952.

Perlow, H. M. *Liqutey Sipurim*. Israel: Kefar Habad, 1966.

Poll, S. *The Hasidic Community of Williamsburg*. New York: The Free Press of Glencoe Inc., 1962.

Rabinovitch, Z. *Lithuanian Hasidim*. Jerusalem: Bialik, 1961.

Rabinowitz, D. M. *Tiferet Avot*. Hagiographies of R. Shlomo Leib of Lentchno, R. Joshua Ostrowa, and R. Jacob Isaac of Biala. Jerusalem, 1961.

Radoshitz, I. B. *(Sefer) Niflaot HaSaba (Qadiysha)*. Tel Aviv: Israel American Offset. Photo offset of Pietrikov ed., 1929.

Rapoport, I., ed. *Sefer Divrey David*. Tshortkov: Israel Rapoport, 1904.

Reik, T. *Listening with the Third Ear: The Inner Experience of a Psychoanalyst*. New York: Farrar, Straus and Co., 1954.

———. *The Secret Self: Psychoanalytic Experiences in Life and Literature*. New York: Farrar, Straus and Co., 1952.

Revel, E. Z. *Simhah al pi Derekh HaHasidut*. New York: Balshon Publishers, 1953.

Rofe, H. *The Path of Subud*. Dharma Press, 1959.

Rogers, C. R. *Client-Centered Therapy: Its Current Practice, Implications and Theory*. New York: Houghton Mifflin Co., 1951.

Rokotz, Y. K. (ed.). *Sefer Siah Sarfey Qodesh*. Brooklyn: Jerusalem Hebrew Book Store, n.d.

———. *Tiferet HaYehudi*. Warsaw: A. S. Kleiman, no date available.

Roth, R. Aaron. *Igrot Shomrey Emunim*. Jerusalem: Hevrath Shomrey Emunim, 1942.

———. *Sefer Shomer Emunim*. Jerusalem: Yeshivat Shomrey Emunim, 1964.

———. *Sefer Uvda d'Aharon*. Jerusalem: Horeb Publishers, 1948.

Rothenberg, E., and Shanefeld, M., eds. *HaRabi MiKotsk V'Shishim Giborim Saviv Lo*, 2 vols. Tel Aviv: Netzach Publishers, 1959.

Safran, A. *Die Kabbala*. Munich: Francke Publishers, 1966.

Safrin, Isaac of Komarno. *Megilat Setarim*. Jerusalem: Mosad Harav Kook, 1944.

Schachter, Z. M. Two facets of Judaism. *Tradition* 3: 191–210, Spring 1961.

Schneersohn, F. *Hayim Grawitzer*. Tel Aviv: Abraham Zioni, 1956.

Schneersohn, J. I. *Liqutey Diburim*. 4 vols. Brooklyn: Kehot Publication Society, 1957.

———. *Kuntres 79*. Brooklyn: Kehot Publication Society, 1950.

———. *Kuntres Bikur Chicago*. Brooklyn: Kehot Publication Society, 1955.

———. *Lubavitcher Rebbe's Memoirs*. Brooklyn: Kehot Publication Society, 1960.

———. "Quntres Im Ru'ach HaMoshel." In *Sefer HaMaamorim Quntreisim HaMoshel*. Brooklyn: Kehot Publication Society, 1962.

———. *Quntres Klaley HaHinukh VehaHadrakhah, Kuntres Hay Elul*. Brooklyn: Kehot Publication Society, 1955.

Schneerson, M. M. I. *Shema Yisrael*. No publication data available.

Schneersohn, S. D. *On Learning Chassidus*. Brooklyn: Kehot Publication Society, 1959.

———. *Quntres Heyhalzu*. Brooklyn: Kehot Publication Society, 1956.

———. *Quntres Uma'ayan, MiBeyt HaShem*. Brooklyn: Kehot Publication Society, 1958.

———. *Torat Shalom: Sefer HaSihot.* Brooklyn: Ozar Hachasidim Lubavitch, 1946.

Schneerson, M. M. II, ed. *Sefer HaToldot Maharash.* Brooklyn: Ozar Hachasidim-Lubavitch, 1947.

———. *HaYom Yom.* Brooklyn: Kehot Publication Society, 1956.

Schneori, D. B. *Poqeah Ivrim.* New York: Agudat Chasidei Habad, 1940.

———. *Tract on Ecstasy,* trans. Louis Jacobs. London: Vallentine Mitchell in association with The Society for the Study of Jewish Thought, 1963.

———. *Sefer Derekh Hayim.* Brooklyn: Kehot Publication Society, 1947.

———. *Sefer Quntres HaHitpa'alut.* Photo offset, 1935. No publication data available.

Schnitzer, J. L. *The Story of the Ba'al Shem,* trans. Samuel Rosenblatt, ed. Abraham Brustein. New York: Pardes Publishing House Inc., 1946.

Schnitzer, Y. *New Horizons for the Synagogue.* New York: Bloch Publishing Co., 1956.

Schochet, Y. I. *Rabbi Israel Ba'al Shem Tov.* Toronto: Lieberman's Publishing House, 1961.

Scholem, G. *Jewish Gnosticism, Merkabah Mysticism and Talmudic Tradition.* New York: The Jewish Theological Seminary of America, 1960.

———. *Major Trends in Jewish Mysticism.* New York: Schocken Publishing House, 1941.

———. *On the Kabbalah and Its Symbolism.* New York: Schocken Books Inc., 1965.

———. *Von der Mystischen Gestalt der Gottheit.* Zurich: Rhein-Verlag, 1962.

Schwartz, G. *Sefer Be'erot HaMayim.* London: Hachinuch. Date unavailable.

Schwartzman, M. *HaMaor HaGadol.* Israel: Netzach Publishers, 1966.

———. *V'Eyleh Toledot HaRishon MiGer.* Jerusalem: Nahaliel Publishing Co., 1958.

———. *Esh HaTamid.* Tel Aviv: Niv Publishing Co., 1962.

Shabbatai of Orshiva. *Sefer Segulot Yisrael.* Offset of 1895 ed. Brooklyn: S. Karpen.

Shapira, Kalonymus. (R. Kalmish of Piasetzno). *Esh Qodesh.* Tel Aviv: Va'ad Chasidei Piasezno, 1960.

————. *Hakhsharat Ha'Avrekhim.* No publication data available.

————. *Hovat HaTalmidim.* Published in Israel. No further data available.

Shapira, Z. E. *Agra d'Pirqa.* Tel Aviv: E. Y. Kalish, 1942.

Shapiro, R. Pinchas ben Abraham (of Koretz). *Norfet Zufim.* In *Yalqut Kitvey Qodresh.* Jerusalem: HaMa'amin Publishing Co., 1962.

————. *Sefer Midrash Pinhas.* Jerusalem: Yom-Tov Zipa Weiss Publishers, 1953.

Shemen, N. *Das Gezang fun Hassidut.* 2 vols. Buenos Aires: Centre-Farband for Polish Jews in Argentina, 1959.

Shmuel of Shinavi. *Tana d'Vay Eliyahu: Ramatayim Zofim.* Jerusalem: Lewin-Epstein Bros. & Co. Ltd., 1954.

Shtern, A. *Sefer Hutim Ham'shulashim.* Montreal: Abraham Shtern, 1953.

Shub, Isaiah of Odessa. *Seder Yesod Ha'Avodah.* Warsaw: Dov Baer Schuhman, 1889.

Singer, I. B. *Gimpel the Fool and Other Stories,* trans. Saul Bellow et al. New York: Noonday Press, 1963.

————. *The Spinoza of Market Street.* New York: Avon Book Division, The Hearst Corp., 1958.

Slater, T. *A Manual of Moral Theology.* Cincinnati: Benziger, 1924.

Soddy, K., ed. *Identity, Mental Health and Value Systems.* Chicago: Quadrangle Books, 1961.

Sofer, Z. E. *Sefer HaHayim HaNiqra S'gulot Yisrael.* Brooklyn: S. Karpen. Date unavailable.

Steinman, E. *Sefer Be'er HaHasidut.* Tel Aviv: Knesseth Publishing Co. Date unavailable.

Stern, K. *The Third Revolution: A Study of Psychiatry and Religion.* New York: Doubleday and Co. Inc., 1954.

Sternhartz, N. *Sihot HaRan.* In *Shivhey HaRan.* Jerusalem: Hevrat Hassidei Bratzlav. Date unavailable.

————. *Y'mey Maharnat.* B'nai B'raq: Keren Hadpasa Publishers, 1956.

Szasz, T. *The Myth of Mental Illness.* New York: Dell Publishing Co. Inc., 1961.

Teitelbaum, M. *HaRav Miladiy uMifleget Habad.* Warsaw: Toshiya, 1913.

Torm, M. R. *Ilna Dnaya*. Tel Aviv: Lyon Publishing Co. Date unavailable.

Unger, M. *Die Hassidishe Velt*. New York: Hassiduth Publishers, 1955.

———. *Hasidus un Lebn*. New York: Publisher unknown, 1946.

———. *Hasidus un Yom-Tov*. New York: Hassiduth Publishers, 1963.

———. *Pshiskhe un Kotzk*. Buenos Aires: Farband for Polish Jews in Argentina, 1949.

———. *Rabbi Israel: Ba'al Shem Tov*. New York: Hassiduth Publishers, 1963.

———. *Sefer Qedoshim*. New York: Shulsinger Bros. Inc., 1967.

Vital, H. *Sefer HaGilgulim*. Vilna: Abraham Katzenellenbogen, 1885.

———. *Sefer Sha'arey HaQedushah*. Warsaw: Reb Pesah Lebensohn, 1876.

Vivekananda, Swami. *Raja Yoga*. New York: Ramakrishna-Vivekananda Centre, 1955.

White, R. W. *Lives in Progress: A Study of the Natural Growth of Personality*. New York: The Dryden Press, 1952.

Ysander, T. *Studien zum Bestschen Hasidismus*. Uppsala: Lundequistska Bokhandeln, 1933.

Zadoq Hakohen (of Lublin). *Resisey Laylah*. New York: Menachem Mendel Ager (of Lublin), 1953.

———. *Sefer Tzidqat Hatzadiq*. Tel Aviv: Pe'er Publishing Co., 1902.

Zalmanov, S., ed. *Sefer HaNigunim*. New York: Nichoach Publishers, 1957.

———. *Qovez HaTamim*. 8 vols. Warsaw: Igud Talmidei T'mimim, 1936.

Zaritsky, D. *Ozar Mishlay Hasidim*. 4 vols. Tel Aviv: Abrahami Zioni Publishing Co., 1957–1960.

Zborowski, M., and Herzog, E. *Life is with People: The Culture of the Shtetl*. New York: Schocken Books Inc., 1952.

Ze'ev Volf of Zhitomir. *Sefer Or HaMeir*. New York: Ziv Publishing Co., 1954.

Zeilingold, A., ed. *M'orot HaG'dolim*. Warsaw: Further publication data unavailable.

Zilboorg, G. (in collaboration with G. W. Henry). *A History of Medical Psychology*. New York: W. W. Norton & Co. Inc., 1941.

Zimer, U. *Rabbi Israel Ba'al Shem Tov*. New York: Kehot Publication Society, 1960.

Zitrin, M., ed. *Shivhey Tzadiqim*. Warsaw: Further publication data unavailable.

Biographical Index

Aaron ben Yaaqov of Karlin (Perlow) (b. 1733, d. 19th of Nisan, 1772). Known as Aaron the First, Aaron the Great, Aaron Karliner. Son of Rabbi Yaaqov.

Aaron of Karlin (b. 1801, d. Sivan, 1872 in Malinov). Known as Aaron the Second. Son of Asher of Stolin; author of *Beyt Aharon*.

Aaron of Karlin (the Third) (killed by the Nazis in 1942). Son of Rabbi Israel of Stolin.

Aaron, son of Mordecai of Chernobil (b. 1787, d. 8th of Kislev, 1872). Famous for his miracle working.

Aaron Starosselye (b. 1766, d. 1828). Was Rabbi Aaron ben Moses HaLevi Horovitz of Starosselje. Author of *Shaarey HaYihud VehaEmunah, Shaarey Avodah, Avodat HaLevi*.

Abraham ben Dovber Friedman (b. 1740, d. 12th of Kislev, 1777, in Tastov). Known as the Angel. Author of *Hessed L'Avraham*.

Abraham Joshua Heschel of Apt (b. 1755, d. 5th of Nisan, 1825). Called the Apter Rav, and the Ohev Yisrael. Author of *Sefer Ohev Yisrael*.

Abraham of Trisk (b. 1806, d. 2nd of Tamuz, 1889). Son of Mordecai of Chernobil; author of *Magen Avraham*.

Adam Ba'al Shem. Was third in line in a series of four Ba'al Shems. They were, in chronological order:

Elijah Ba'al Shem of Worms
Joel Ba'al Shem of Zamoshch
Adam Ba'al Shem of Ropshitz
Israel Ba'al Shem, the Besht

Adile (d. circa 1790), the daughter of the Besht and wife of Rabbi Yehiel Ha'ashkenazi; the Besht considered her one of his students.

Ahiyah Hashiloni, a prophet of ancient Israel during the latter days of Solomon and the first days of Jeroboam ben Nevat. He was the teacher of Elijah the Prophet, and according to legend, he was the spiritual guide of the Ba'al Shem.

Ahron ben Yisakhar Dov Roqeah of Belz (b. 1880 in Belz, d. 21st of Av, 1957, in Israel). The late Belzer Rebbe.

Akavyah ben Mahalalel (circa 200 B.C.E. and 10 C.E.). A pre-Tannaitic scholar of the Mishnah.

Akiva, Rabbi (main period of prominence 120–140 C.E.). Was a third-generation Tanna of the Mishna.

Al-Sheikh, Moshe ben Hayim. Lived in Safed in the sixteenth century. Belonged to the Safed circle and was a great homileticist; author of *Torat Moshe*.

Arele Roth, of Satmer, Bergsas, and Jerusalem (b. 1894 in Ungvar, d. 1956). Had hasidim in Satmer, Jerusalem, Bergsas, and Pest; author of *Shomer Emunim* and others.

Bahiya ibn Paquda (b. first half of 11th century); author of *Hovat Halevovot*.

Baruchovitch, Shneur Zalman of Liadi (b. 18th of Elul, 1745, in Liozhno; d. 24th of Tevet, 1813, in Hadiz); known as "Elder Rebbe"; author of *Tanya, Sidur HaRav, Torah Or, Liqutey Torah*, and *Ma'amarey Admor HaZaqen*.

Barukh of Mezhibuzh (b. 1758, d. 18th of Kislev, 1812); author of *Imrot Tehorot, Buzina diNehora*.

Barukh Mordecai of Babroysk (d. 14th of Elul, 1857). Was a rebbe for 40 years in Babroysk; affiliated with Habad.

Ber of Radoshitz (b. 1765, d. 18th of Sivan, 1843). Also known as Rabbi Issacher Ber of Radoshitz, son of R. Isaac, the Radoshitzer.

Berele Rogeach (b. 1949), who is the current Belzer Rav.

Berishil of Krakow Known also as Harzblut (Ba'al T'shuvah). (See Unger, *Hassidus un Lebn*, p. 203.)

Besht (b. 18th of Elul, 1698, in Okup; d. Shavuot, 1766, in Mezhibuzh). The Ba'al Shem Tov—Israel ben Eliezer Talismacher.

David (b. 1822, d. 19th of Adar, 1874). Son of the Holy Master of Dinov; author of *Zemah David*.

David Biederman of Lelov (b. 1746, d. 7th of Shevat, 1813). Called the Lelover Rebbe; author of *Ahavat Yisrael, Migdal David, Qodesh Hilulim*.

David Moshe of Chortkov (b. Shavuot, 1827, d. Hoshanah Rabbah, 1904). Son of Rabbi Yisrael of Ruzhin. Known as the Magid of Chortkov and Chortkover Rebbe; author of *Divrey David*.

David of Tolna (b. 1808, d. 10th of Iyar, 1889). Son of Mordecai of Chernobil. Was known as Tolna Rebbe and had thousands of followers; author of *Birkhat David, Magen David, Qohelet David*.

Dovber ben Avraham Friedman (b. 1704 in Lucatch, d. 19th of Kislev, 1772, in Anipoly); known as the Great Magid and the Magid of Mezhirech; author of *Magid Dvarav L'Ya'aqov*.

Dovber ben Shneur Zalman Schneori of Lubavitch (b. 9th of Kislev, 1774, in Liozhno, d. 9th of Kislev, 1828, in Niezhin). Known as the "Middle" Rebbe; author of *Imrey Binah, Quntres HaHitpa'alut, Poqeah Ivrim*.

Eleazar (d. 28th of Tamuz, 1806). Son of Elimelekh of Lizhensk, he was a famous tzaddik in his generation, renowned for his *moftim*.

Eleazar ben Durdaia (a contemporary of Rabbi Judah The Prince). For his repentance at the end of his life, he merited happiness in the hereafter despite having spent his life in licentiousness.

Eleazar ben Yehuda of Garmaiyza (Worms) (b. circa 1176 in Mayence, d. 1238 in Mayence). Also known as Eleazar Roqeah; was the author of *Roqeah*.

Eliezer of Dzhikov (d. 3rd of Heshvan, 1861). Was the Rebbe of Dzhikov, and son of Rabbi Naftali of Ropshitz.

Elijah (d. 1729). Son of Shlomoh Abraham HaKohen of Izmir; author of *Shevet Musar* and thirty other books.

Elijah ben Moses de Vidas (sixteenth century). Was a kabbalist at Safed; a pupil of Moses Cordovero; the author of *Reshit Hokhmah*.

Elimelekh ben Elazar Wagschal of Lizhensk (b. 1717, d. 21st of Adar, 1786). Author of *No'am Elimelekh*, *Hanhagat Adam*, *Zettel Qatan*.

Gershom, Rabbenu (b. 960 C.E. in Metz, d. 1040 C.E. in Mainz). Called Gershom ben Yehudah; also known as "Maor Hagolah" and "Ba'al Hata-qanot." Spread Torah in France and Germany.

Gershon Kittover, a contemporary of the Besht—the Ba'al Shem Tov— as well as his brother-in-law.

Hanina ben Dosa (period of prominence, 80–120 C.E.). Was a second-generation Tanna of the Mishna.

Hayim Abraham (d. 1848); son of Shneur Zalman of Liadi.

Hayim ben Yitzhaq of Volozhin (b. 7th of Sivan in Vilna, 1749; d. 14th of Sivan in Vilna, 1821). Was also known as Hayim of Volozhin. Established the famous Volozhin Yeshivah, was a prolific writer and a disciple of the Gaon of Vilna.

Hayim of Chernowitz, son of Shlomo. Disciple of Dovber the Magid of Mezhirech. Author of books forming the basic texts of Hassidut: *Eretz HaHayim*, *Be'er Mayim Hayim*, *Sha'ar HaTefilah*.

Hayim Halberstamm of Zanz (b. 1793, d. 25th of Nisan, 1876). Son of Arieh Leib Halberstamm. Was believed by some to be the greatest rebbe of his generation; was looked to for leadership by many famous rebbes of the time. Author of *Divrey Hayim*.

Hershele Ostropoler, the court fool of Rabbi Barukh of Mezhibuzh.

Isaac of Homel (b. 1780, d. 1857). R. Yitzhaq Isaac HaLevi Epstein of Homel. Was author of *Hanah Ariel*.

Isaac Judah Yehiel ben Alexander Sender Safrin of Komarno (b. 25th of Shevat, 1806, d. 10th of Iyar, 1874). Author of *Asiyrit Ha'eyfah*, *Czar HaHayim*, *Heykhal HaBrakhah*, *Zohar Hay*, *Netiv Mizvotekha*, *Ma'aseh Ereg*, *Atzey Eden*, *Notzar Hesed*, *Paley Zaken*.

Israel ben Barukh of Vishnitz (b. 1860, d. 2nd of Sivan, 1936). Buried in B'nai B'raq; renowned for his courtesy and kindliness when receiving people.

Israel ben Shalom Shakna Friedman of Ruzhin (Sadigora) (b. 3rd of Tishri, 1797, d. 3rd of Heshvan, 1851). Author of *Irin Qadishin*.

Israel of Kozhinitz (b. 1736, d. 14th of Tishri, 1814). Also known as Israel ben Shabbetai and the Magid of Kozhinitz. One of the founders of Hassidut in Poland; author of *Geulat Yisrael, Gevurat Yisrael, Beyt Yisrael, Magid Meysharim, Agudat Yisrael, Or Yisrael, Nezer Yisrael, Ner Yisrael*.

Israel, Rabbi (b. 5th of Iyar, 1854, d. 13th of Kislev, 1934). Son of the Magid of Chortkov (R. David Moses of Chortkov); author of *Tiferet Yisrael*.

Itshele Krakowitzer (d. circa 1870). Contemporary of Rabbi Joshua of Belz, and his disciple.

Jacob Joseph of Polnoye (d. 1788). First writer of Hasidut; author of *Toldot Ya'aqov Yosef, Zofnat Pa'neyah, Ben Porat Yosef, K'tonet Pasim*.

Jacob Joseph Isaac Horowitz (b. 1745, d. 9th of Av, 1815). Also known as the Seer of Lublin and the Lubliner. Almost all the great rebbes in Polish Jewry of his day were his followers; his books are key sources on Hasidut. Author of *Zot Zikaron, Zikaron Zot, Torat Emet*.

Jacob Shimshon of Spitovka (d. 3rd of Sivan, 1821, in Tiberias). Disputed with the opponents of Hasidism.

Joseph Isaac Ben Shalom Dovber Schneersohn of Lubavitch (b. 12th of Tamuz, 1880, in Lubavitch; d. 10th of Shvat, 1950, in Brooklyn). Author of *Ma'amarim*.

Joshua Dov of Belz (b. 1825, d. 23rd of Shvat, 1894). Son of Rabbi Shalom of Belz.

Judah the Pious of Ratisbon (b. circa 12th century in Shapira, Germany; d. month of Adar, 1217). Established a large yeshivah in Regensburg.

Kagan, Rabbi Henry Enoch (b. Sharpsburg, Pa., Nov. 28, 1907).

Kalonymus Kalmish (Shapira) of Piasetzno (b. 15th of Iyar, 1889; killed by the Nazis on 4th of Heshvan, 1943). Became a rebbe at the age of 19 and thousands flocked to him. Author of *Hovat Hatalmidim, Hovat Ha'avraikhim, Bnei Mahshavah Tovah*.

Kantrowitz, Shmuel (d. circa 1950). Was a disciple of Jacob Joseph of Lubavitch.

Kletzker, Benjamin (d. circa 1828). Was a disciple of Shneur Zalman of Liadi.

Krantz, Jacob (b. 1740 in Vilna, d. 17th of Tevet, 1804, in Zamotsh). Dubner Magid; author of *Ohel Ya'aqov*, *Kol Ya'aqov*, and several others.

Landau, Ezekiel ben Judah (b. Oct. 8, 1713, in Opatow; d. April 29, 1793, in Prague). Author of many well-known responsa.

Lao Tzu (probably lived in 4th century B.C.E.). Was the founder of Taoism.

Leib of Shpolla (b. 1725, d. Tishri 1812). Son of R. Barukh the Shpoller Zeyde. Was famous as a miracle worker.

Leib Sures (b. 17th of Tamuz, 1730, d. 4th of Adar Sheni, 1790). A great exemplar of Hasidut; occupied himself often with freeing captives and feeding hidden righteous men. His life has become the subject of wonderful legends.

Levi Yitzhaq ben Meir (b. 1740, d. 25th of Tishri, 1810). Called the Berdichever, and Derbaremdiker of Berdichev; was the author of *Q'dushath Levi*. Known for his love of Israel, his concern for its welfare in his prayers, and his effectiveness in the performance of precepts.

Luria, Isaac (b. 1534 in Jerusalem, d. 5th of Av, 1572, in Safed). Also called Isaac ben Shlomo Ashkenazi. Was founder of a new approach to the wisdom of Kabbalah.

Maimon, Solomon (b. 1753 in Eastern Poland, d. 1800 in Germany). Known as Solomon ben Joshua.

Maimonides (b. 14th of Nisan, 1135; d. 2nd of Tevet, 1206, in Fostat, Egypt). Moses the son of Maimon the Sephardi; known as the Rambam. Author of *Yad Hazaqah*, *Moreh Nevukhim*, *Sefer Hamitzvot*, and *Peyrush Hamishnah*.

Meir Baal Ha-nes (period of prominence 140–165 C.E.). A Tanna of the fourth generation of Tannaim; disciple of Rabbi Akiva and Elisha ben Avuyah. Famous for a special prayer said in his name by givers of charity.

Meirl ben Ahron Leib (b. 1787, d. 1st of Sivan, 1858). From Premishlan; known as the Premishlaner.

Menahem Mendl of Kotsk (b. 1787 in Goray, d. 22nd of Shvat, 1859). The Kotsker, son of Reb Judah Leybush. Known for his sharpness in learning, and his perceptiveness with regard to people.

Menahem Mendl II ben Levi Yitzhaq Schneerson (b. 11th of Nisan, 1902, shlita). Is the present Lubavitcher Rebbe.

Menahem Mendl I ben Shalom Shakhna Schneersohn of Lubavitch (b. 1789, d. 13th of Nisan, 1826). Known as the Tzemah Tzedeq. Author of *Tzemah Tzedeq* and other works.

Menahem Mendel of Vitebsk (d. 2nd of Iyar, 1788). The son of R. Moshe.

Menahem Mendel Torm of Rymanov (d. 19th of Iyar, 1814). The author of *Menahem Ziyon, Divrey Menahem, Ateret Menahem.*

Menahem Nahum ben Zvi Twersky of Chernobil (b. 1730, d. 11th of Heshvan, 1798). Author of *Maor Eynayim, Yismah Lev.*

Merton, Thomas (b. 1915, d. 1968). American Trappist monk.

Meshulam Zussia ben Elazar of Anipoly (d. 2nd of Shvat, 1800).

Meyer ibn Gabbai (b. 1480). Also known as Meyer ben Yehezqel Gabbai. Important writer on Kabbalah; author of *Avodat Haqodesh, To'elet Ya'aqov,* and others.

Mordecai ben Menahem Nahum Twersky of Chernobil (b. 1770, d. 20th of Iyar, 1837). Known as the Chernobiler. Was author of *Liqutey Torah.*

Mordecai of Bilgoray (b. 1902, d. 24th of Heshvan 1950). Was the son of Rabbi Yisacher Dov of Belz.

Mordecai Joseph of Izhbitz (b. 1801, d. 1st of Tevet, 1854). Known as the Izhbitzer. Was the son of Rabbi Jacob.

Mordecai of Lehowitz (b. 1742, d. 13th of Shvat, 1810). Was known as the Lehowitzer.

Mordecai of Zasslav (18th century Poland). Also known as the Hazan of Zasslav. Was a pupil of the Ba'al Shem Tov.

Moshe Leib of Sassov (b. 1745, d. 4th of Shvat, 1807).

Mosheh ben Yehiel Ashkenazi of Sdilkow (b. 1748, d. 17th of Iyar, 1800). Wrote *Degel Mahane Ephraim.*

Mosheh Cordovero (b. 1522 in Safed, d. 1570 in Safed). Was a famous kabbalist; author of, inter alia, a long commentary on the Zohar.

Mosheh of Sambar (d. 6th of Iyar, 1840). Was the son of Rabbi Yitzhaq Isaac of Safran. Wrote *Tephilah LeMosheh.*

Mosheh Polier of Kobrin (b. 1784, d. 29th of Nisan, 1858). Was also known as the Kobriner.

Mosheh Teitelbaum of Uykel (Usheli) (b. 1759 in Premishle, d. 28th of Tamuz, 1841). Son of Rabbi Zvi. Wrote *Heyshiv Mosheh, Yismah Mosheh,* and other works.

Mosheh Zvi of Savran (d. 27th of Tevet, 1838). Also known as Master of Savran. Was son of Shimon Shlomoh. Wrote *Liqutey Shoshanim.*

Naftali Zvi Horwitz (b. Shavuot 1760, d. 11th of Iyar, 1827). From Ropshitz. Author of *Zera Qodesh, Ayalah Shluhah.*

Nahman ben Simhah (b. 1st of Nisan, 1772, d. 18th of Tishri, 1810, in Uman). From Bratzlav. Author of *Liqutey Maharan, Sefer Hama'asiyot, Sefer Hamidot.*

Nahum, grandson of R. Shneur Zalman. Was the son of Dovber of Lubavitch, the "Middle" Rebbe.

Nahum of Grodna; see (in References) Unger, *Hasidus un Lebn.*

Nahum of Stephanesht (d. 14th of Kislev, 1869). Was also known as the Stephaneshter. The son of Rabbi Israel of Ruzhin.

Nathan of Nemirov (b. 1780 in Nemirov, d. in 1845). A great disciple of Nahman of Bratslav, and recorder and transmitter of his teachings.

Noah of Lechowitz (b. 1774, d. 8th of Tishri, 1833). Was known as the Lechowitzer. The son of Reb Mordecai.

Nota (d. 1st of Shvat, 1812). From Chelm. The author of *Neta Sha'a-shuim.*

Onias (lived in 1st century B.C.E.). Known as Hony Hame'agel (the circle drawer). Teacher and miracle worker. Was an Essene, tradition declaring him to be a descendant of Moses.

Onkelos (1st century C.E.). Called the Proselyte. Translated the Pentateuch (the first 5 books of Moses) from Hebrew into Aramaic.

Pak-Subud (b. June 22, 1901). Known as Muhammed Subuh. Was head of the Subud Movement, probably a (Sufi) technique for surrendering to God.

Pesah Molastovker. Was a disciple of Rabbi Shneur Zalman of Liadi.

Pinhas ben Abraham Abba Shapira of Koretz (b. 1728, d. 10th of Elul, 1791). Known as the Koretzer. Author of *Midrash Pinhas.*

Pinhas ben Yair (period of prominence 165–200 C.E.). Fifth-generation Tanna of the Mishnah.

Pinhas Halevi Horowitz (b. 1760, date of death unknown). Of Frankfurt-am-Main. Brother of Shmelke of Nicholsburg; author of *Ba'al Hafla'ah*.

Piotrikover Rebbe, Dr. Bernard of Piotrikov; see in References Unger, *Hasidus un Lebn*.

Qaro, Joseph (b. in Toledo, 1488; d. in Safed, 13th of Nisan, 1575). Author of *Shulhan Arukh* and many other books and commentaries.

Raphael of Bershad (d. 1816). The greatest pupil of R. Pinhas of Koretz.

Rashbatz, Shmuel Bezalel (b. 1829, d. 14th of Sivan, 1905). Was the private tutor (*mashpiy'a*) of two Lubavitcher rebbes, Shalom Dovber and Joseph Isaac; was himself a disciple of Menahem Mendl I of Lubavitch.

Rashi (b. Troyes, France, in 1040; d. 29th of Tamuz, 1105). Name is an acronym of R. Shlomoh Yitzhaqi. The most famous commentator on T'nach and Talmud.

Riccanati, Menachem ben Binyamin (lived in Italy, end of 13th century, beginning of 14th). Renowned for kabbalistic commentary on Pentateuch; also wrote commentaries on prayers and precepts (mitzvot).

Rosenblatt, Yossele (b. May 9, 1882 in Byelaya Tzerkov, Russian Ukraine; d. circa 1933 in Jerusalem). Was a famous cantor; began career as a child prodigy.

Salanter, Israel (b. in Zagar, 6th of Heshvan, 1810; d. in Koenigsburg, Prussia, 25th of Shvat, 1883).

Schneersohn, Dr. Fishl (d. circa 1952, Tel Aviv). Novelist, psychiatrist. Wrote about play elements and dream elements in children; author of *Hayim Grawitzer*.

Shalom ben Elazar Roqeah (b. 1779 in Brody, d. 27th of Elul, 1855, in Belz). The Belzer Rav.

Shalom Dovber ben Shmuel Schneersohn (b. 20th of Heshvan, 1861; d. 2nd of Nisan, 1920, in Rostov). Of Lubavitch. Author of *Quntres Hatefilah* and other works.

Shalom of Kaminka (d. 2nd of Heshvan, 1852). Shalom Halevi Rosenfeld of Kaminka, son of Jacob Joseph of Rava. Great pupil of Shalom of Belz; good friend of Hayim of Zanz.

Shapiro, Nathan of Krakow (b. 1575, d. 1633). Author of *Sefer M'galeh Amuqot*.

Shimshon of Ostropol. The Rabbi of Podolya, killed during the massacres of 1648. Author of *Din Yadin, Liqutey Shoshanim*, and numerous other works.

Shlomoh II ben Benzion Halberstamm of Bobov. Shlita; present Bobover Rebbe.

Shlomoh ben Meir Nathan Halberstamm of Bobov (b. 1847, d. 1st of Tamuz, 1906).

Shlomoh HaKohen Rabinowitz of Radomsk (b. 1803, d. last day of Adar, 1866). Known as the Tiferet Shlomoh of Radomsk. Son of Dov Zion of Valshazvah; author of *Tiferet Shlomoh*.

Shlomoh Halevi Gottlieb of Karlin (b. 1738 in Tulchin, d. 22nd of Tamuz, 1792). Author of *Shema Shlomoh* and *Beyt Aharon*.

Shlomoh Leib (d. 13th of Nisan, 1842). Known as the Lentshner. Son of Barukh of Lentshna. Was famous for his charity.

Shlomoh Shapira of Munkatch (b. 7th day of Hannukah, 1832; d. 21st of Sivan, 1893). Son of R. Eliezer. Author of *Shem Shlomoh*.

Shmuel (b. 2nd of Iyar, 1834, in Lubavitch; d. 13th of Tishri, 1833, in Lubavitch). Known as the Maharash. Son of Menahem Mendl Schneersohn of Lubavitch; author of *Liqutey Torat Shmuel*.

Shmuel Gurarie. A disciple of R. Shalom Dovber of Lubavitch.

Shmuel Shmelke Halevi Horowitz (d. 1st of Adar, 1778). Of Nicholsburg.

Sholem of Probisch (b. 1766, d. 13th of Tishri, 1803). Was the father of the Ruzhiner, and son of Abraham the Angel.

Simhah Bunim of Pshysskha (b. 1767, d. 12th of Elul, 1827). Known as R. Przysucha. Author of *Qol Simhah*.

Simpson, Eli (b. circa 1900). Secretary of the late Lubavitcher Rebbe, Joseph Isaac.

Thurman, Dr. Howard (contemporary). University Minister at Large of Boston University.

Underhill, Evelyn (b. 1875, d. 1941). British poet, novelist, writer on mysticism.

Uri of Strelisk (b. in Yanov; d. 1826). Known as the Seraph and the Strelisker. Son of R. Pinhas; author of *Imrey Qodesh*.

Uspenskii, Peter Demianowitch (b. 1878 in Moscow; d. 1947 in Virginia Waters, Surrey, England). (Alternate spelling: Ouspensky.) Author of *Tertium Organum* and other works.

Viazshiner, Barukh (contemporary of the Besht). Hero of the *Memoirs* of the Lubavitcher Rebbe.

Vilner Gaon (b. Seliz, 15th of Nisan, 1720; d. Vilna, 19th of Tishri, 1797). Elijah ben Solomon Zalman; a genius who wrote over 50 books on the Bible, Talmud, Hebrew grammar, and Kabbalah. A leading opponent of Hasidism.

Vital, Hayim (b. Safed, 1543; d. Damascus, 1st of Iyar, 1620). Famous disciple of Isaac Luria; author of *Sha'arey HaQedushah, Sefer HaGilgulim*.

Vizhnitzer Rebbe (b. 1888). Hayim Meyer Hager of B'nai B'raq. Son of Israel of Vizhnitz.

Volper. Anonymous disciple of the Great Magid. A colleague of R. Shneur Zalman of Liadi.

Von Hügel, Friedrich (b. Florence, 1852; d. 1925). Famous professor of mysticism and religion; the teacher of Evelyn Underhill.

Wolf Kitzes. R. Ze'ev Kitzes. Disciple of the Besht.

Wolf of Zbarazh (d. 1800). Son of Yehiel Mikhael of Zlochov.

Wolf Strikover (b. 1806, d. 11th of Elul, 1891). R. Ze'ev Wolf of Strikov. Son of Abraham Landau of Tshekhanov.

Ya'aqov of Boyan (killed by the Nazis in Stiry). Known as the Boyaner Rebbe. Son of Rabbi Isaac.

Yehiel Mikhael of Zlochov (b. 1721, d. 25th of Elul, 1786). Known as the Zlotchover. Son of Isaac of Drohobitch. Was a disciple of the Besht.

Yehoshua ben Shalom Roqeah (b. 1825, d. 23rd of Shvat, 1894). Of Belz.

Yehudah Zvi of Stretyn (d. 1844). Known as the Strettiner Rebbe; disciple of R. Uri of Strelisk.

Yehudi, Ya'aqov Isaac of Pshysskha (b. 1766, d. 19th of Tishri, 1814). Known as "Hayehudi Haqadosh." Son of Asher of Pshedborz. Was a great pupil of the Seer of Lublin.

Yekutiel Yehudah of Sziget (b. 1808, d. 6th of Elul, 1883). Known as the Szigeter. Son of R. Eliezer Nissan of Drohobitch.

Yekutiel Yehudah Halberstam (b. 1905). Of Klausenburg. Shlita, present Klausenburger Rav.

Yeshaya of Dynawitz (d. 22nd of Iyar, 1794). Famous for his hasidic music.

Yisrael Meir Hakohen (d. 24th of Elul, 1933). Known as Hafetz Hayim; author of *Mishnah B'rurah*.

Yissakhar Dov ben Yehoshua Roqeah (b. 1854, d. 22nd of Heshvan, 1927).

Yitzhaq Isaac of Kalov (b. 1744, d. 7th of Adar II, 1821). Known as the Kalover Rebbe. Son of Moshe Yehezkel Taub.

Yitzhaq Meir Alter of Ger (b. 1799, d. 23rd of Adar, 1866). Son of R. David Israel Rothenberg of Ger. Was author of *Sefer Hazekhut*.

Yitzhaq Meir of Kopishentz (b. 21st of Kislev, 1865, d. 2nd of Tishri, 1932). Known as the Kopishenitzer. Son of Abraham Joshua Heshel of Mezhibuzh.

Yitzhaq of Drohobitch. Father of Yehiel Mikhael of Zlochov.

Yitzhaq of Squira (b. 1812, d. 17th of Nisan, 1885). Known as the Squerer. Son of Mordecai of Chernobil.

Yitzhaq of Vurky (b. 1779, d. last day of Passover, 1848). Known as the Vurker. Son of R. Shimon Kalish. Was noted for his communal work.

Yoel Teitelbaum of Satmar (b. 1881, d. 1983). Was the son of Yomtov Lipa of Sziget; the late Satmarer Rebbe.

Yohai, Shimon Bar (period of prominence, 140–165 C.E.). Tanna of the Fourth Generation; tradition ascribes to him the authorship of the Zohar, the most important book of Jewish mysticism.

Yomtov Lipa. Was the Szigeter Rebbe, father of Yoel Teitelbaum of Satmar.

Yosef of Byeshenkovitch. Disciple of Shneur Zalman of Liadi.

Zalman Aaron (b. 1859). Brother of Shalom Dovber of Lubavitch.

Zalushiner Rebbe (b. 1788, d. 1868). Otherwise known as Dr. David Bernard.

Subject Index

ABOUT THE AUTHOR

Zalman Schachter-Shalomi was ordained as a Lubavitch-trained rabbi and has counseled men and women for more than 35 years. He received his master's degree in psychology from Boston University and a doctorate from Hebrew Union College.

Rabbi Schachter-Shalomi is currently President of P'nai Or Religious Fellowship and Professor Emeritus of Religion in Psychology of Religion and Jewish Mysticism at Temple University, Philadelphia, Pennsylvania. He has published more than 150 articles and translations, and his books include *Fragments of a Future Scroll* and *The First Step: A Guide for the New Jewish Spirit*. Rabbi Schachter-Shalomi designs and conducts seminars on spiritual eldering, and he is currently preparing a book on this subject.